Criminological Skills and Research for Beginners

Criminological Skills and Research for Beginners, Third Edition, is a comprehensive and engaging guide to research methods in Criminology, and the skills required for academic success. Written primarily for undergraduate students and novice researchers, this book has been designed as a lively and accessible guide to planning, conducting and reporting research in the subject. It emphasises practical skills required in studying Criminology, the importance of criminological research, and places-related methodology firmly in the context of students' broader study of the discipline, before moving on to provide a detailed guide to the actual processes of research that students can return to at each stage of their study, all the way through to their dissertation.

This book presents:

- an examination of the theoretical, political and ethical debates in criminological research;
- a complete guide to planning criminological research, assisting student researchers in identifying their research questions, choosing their research methods and critiquing the available literature;
- guidance on the practicalities and processes of collecting data;
- contemporary examples and case studies;
- a discussion of the process of analysing data and writing up research.

New to the third edition is a brand new chapter on using online and social media data sources. This edition also includes new coverage of mixed-methods approaches, preparing a research proposal, a spotlight on researcher well-being and guidance on writing reflective essays.

Including an extensive glossary and online support material with extra examples, exercises and videos to further develop students' understanding, this book is essential reading for any undergraduate on a Criminological Research Methods or Research Skills course, or for anyone in need of practical guidance on any or all of the various stages involved in conducting thorough and effective criminological research.

Laura Caulfield is Professor and Chair of the Institute for Community Research and Development at the University of Wolverhampton, UK.

Jane Hill was the Programme Director for the Criminology BA at Birmingham City University, UK, before her retirement in 2012.

"This book is a one stop shop for being able to grow and succeed at university! It is a fantastic resource written and presented in a friendly and accessible way to support undergraduate students to develop their criminological and research skills. The book is broken down into bite-sized chunks, and filled with practical tips, activities and tools that empower students to personalise their learning approach to achieve the best grades possible."

David Patton, Associate Professor in Criminology, University of Derby, UK

"This third edition offers students both transferrable academic skills as well as specialist knowledge of criminological research and how to put skills into action.
The book covers the whole of the research journey and provides contemporary reflections on mixed methods and the use of social media, which is highly relevant to students. There is strength in the coverage of how to analyse a range of research data and make sense of this in a way that can be articulated for assignments and non-academic audiences."

Teela Sanders, Professor in Criminology, University of Leicester, UK

"This is a well thought-out study skills companion for all those engaging with Criminology and wider Social Science subjects. It is written in a clear and accessible way, with each chapter offering valuable knowledge and support that assists with development of the Criminological self. A highly recommended book."

Tina G. Patel, Senior Lecturer in Criminology, University of Salford, UK

"*Criminological Skills and Research for Beginners* is an accessible yet theoretically sophisticated guide to the research and study skills students need. It is a text that captures the imagination with real-life examples and reassures students taking those first (and subsequent) steps in conducting criminological research. The new chapters in this third edition on conducting online research and writing reflective essays are a welcome addition to the topics covered in previous editions. This continues to be an essential text for my research students."

Eleanor Peters, Senior Lecturer in Criminology, Edge Hill University, UK

"This book is an essential read for all criminology students! The new edition covers common issues that students struggle with like referencing and revision but also offers important sections on researcher well-being, and skills that will be useful beyond university, for example preparing a research proposal and research drawing on mixed method approaches. Key research skills including negotiating ethics, collecting and analysing data and writing up research projects are outlined in an easy to understand and accessible format. Students are encouraged to pause and reflect on their practice throughout. *Criminological Skills and Research for Beginners* is an invaluable tool to get you through your degree. Highly Recommended!"

Mary Laing, Lecturer in Sociology, University of York, UK

"*Criminological Skills and Research for Beginners 3rd Ed* is bolstered by the inclusion of discussion of researcher well-being, in particular. This topic is important, but all too often overlooked in research texts. Similarly, the new guidance on reflective essays is welcome and will be of great assistance to our students."

Alice Gerlach, Lecturer in Criminology, Oxford Brookes University, UK

"This small book packs a punch. It is insightful, comprehensive and as such is a valuable resource and reference book for any student of criminology. This updated third edition is timely, including further material on doing research online and writing reflective pieces of work, ensuring that it remains relevant for students – and should be at the top of any reading list."

Victoria Bell, Senior Lecturer in Sociology, Teesside University, UK

Criminological Skills and Research for Beginners

A Student's Guide

Third Edition

Laura Caulfield
and Jane Hill

LONDON AND NEW YORK

Designed cover image: © Getty Images | melitas

Third edition published 2025
by Routledge
4 Park Square, Milton Park, Abingdon, Oxon, OX14 4RN

and by Routledge
605 Third Avenue, New York, NY 10158

Routledge is an imprint of the Taylor & Francis Group, an informa business

© 2025 Laura Caulfield and Jane Hill

The right of Laura Caulfield and Jane Hill to be identified as authors of this work has been asserted in accordance with sections 77 and 78 of the Copyright, Designs and Patents Act 1988.

All rights reserved. No part of this book may be reprinted or reproduced or utilised in any form or by any electronic, mechanical, or other means, now known or hereafter invented, including photocopying and recording, or in any information storage or retrieval system, without permission in writing from the publishers.

Trademark notice: Product or corporate names may be trademarks or registered trademarks, and are used only for identification and explanation without intent to infringe.

First edition published by Routledge 2014
Second edition published by Routledge 2018

British Library Cataloguing-in-Publication Data
A catalogue record for this book is available from the British Library

Library of Congress Cataloging-in-Publication Data
Names: Caulfield, Laura, 1981- author. | Hill, Jane, 1954- author.
Title: Criminological skills and research for beginners : a student's guide / Laura Caulfield and Jane Hill.
Description: Third edition. | Abingdon, Oxon ; New York, NY : Routledge, 2025. | Includes bibliographical references and index. |
Identifiers: LCCN 2024038288 (print) | LCCN 2024038289 (ebook) | ISBN 9781032645636 (hardback) | ISBN 9781032645629 (paperback) | ISBN 9781032645698 (ebook)
Subjects: LCSH: Criminology--Research. | Criminology--Methodology.
Classification: LCC HV6024.5 .C38 2025 (print) | LCC HV6024.5 (ebook) | DDC 364.072--dc23/eng/20241209
LC record available at https://lccn.loc.gov/2024038288
LC ebook record available at https://lccn.loc.gov/2024038289

ISBN: 978-1-032-64563-6 (hbk)
ISBN: 978-1-032-64562-9 (pbk)
ISBN: 978-1-032-64569-8 (ebk)

DOI: 10.4324/9781032645698

Typeset in Akzidenz Grotesk & Eurostile
by Deanta Global Publishing Services, Chennai, India

Access the Support Material: www.routledge.com/9781032645629

For Aaliyah and Jessica who bring me such joy
For Tim, who keeps me smiling no matter what

With thanks to the following colleagues and students for their support with this third edition:

Sophie Badger, Emma Burgess, Sian Caulfield, Sophie Cole, Alexandra Demertzidou, Jenna Essex, Amy Fenn, Dr Kyros Hadjisergis, Amy Jones, Dr Paula McLean, Cara Perry, Dr Mary-Rose Puttick, Lily Read, Dr Karlie Stonard, Nicola Taylor-Brown, Dr Caroline Wesson, Ashleigh Whitwell.

CONTENTS

List of figures		ix
List of tables		x
List of boxes		xi
Visual tour (How to use this book)		xiv

PART I
Study skills for criminology students — 1

Chapter 1	Writing skills and essay writing	3
Chapter 2	Referencing	15
Chapter 3	Revision skills and examination techniques	28
Chapter 4	Presentation skills	36

PART II
The importance of criminological research — 49

Chapter 5	The context of criminological research: power, knowledge, politics and values	51
Chapter 6	The significance of criminological research: understanding the philosophical roots of our claims to know about crime in society	67
Chapter 7	The ethics of criminological research	87

PART III
Getting going with criminological research — 109

Chapter 8	Planning: where do research ideas come from? How do we 'fine-tune' them?	111

Chapter 9	Critiquing the literature and the process of writing your formal review	128
Chapter 10	Theories, methods and their relationships to theories of knowledge	140
Chapter 11	Preparing for the practical challenges of 'real-world' crime research	164

PART IV
Doing criminological research: data collection — 187

Chapter 12	Qualitative approaches to research	189
Chapter 13	Questionnaires and surveys	222
Chapter 14	Using documentary and secondary data sources	248
Chapter 15	Using online and social media data sources in criminological research	263

PART V
Doing criminological research: analysis and writing up — 279

Chapter 16	Analysing the data: quantitative analysis	281
Chapter 17	Analysing the data: qualitative analysis	313
Chapter 18	Analysing the data: documents, texts and other data	335
Chapter 19	Writing up criminological research	352

Glossary — 379
Index — 385

FIGURES

4.1	(a) Example visual aid;	
	(b) Example visual aid	41
4.2	Example visual aid	42
4.3	Example visual aid	43
4.4	Example visual aid	44
4.5	Example visual aid	44
7.1	Ethics continuum	95
8.1	Interrogating your literature sources: policy documents	118
8.2	Interrogating your literature sources: academic texts	121
10.1	The dimensions of criminological research frameworks	143
10.2	The subjective/objective continuum	144
12.1	Researcher roles in observation studies	203
12.2	Simpson's eight frame storyboard	216
16.1	Standard deviation	286
17.1	An example of thematic mapping showing themes and sub-themes	325
19.1	(a) Example contents page from a qualitative dissertation;	
	(b) Example contents page from a quantitative dissertation	355
19.2	A traditional report structure	356
19.3	Structuring your literature review	358

TABLES

2.1	Checklist of what to include for the most common information sources	23
3.1	Sample timetable	30
7.1	Upholding ethical principles	89
9.1	How to keep records of your reading	131
11.1	Participant recruitment strategies	175
11.2	Research in action: a summary of the research process in a men's prison in England	182
12.1	Data gathering via interviews and focus groups	196
12.2	Data gathering via observation	208
12.3	Example structure for an arts-based focus group	215
13.1	Advantages and disadvantages of questionnaires and surveys	227
13.2	Advantages and disadvantages of closed and open-ended questions	230
14.1	Broad-ranging texts	251
15.1	Online data sources	265
16.1	Common types of study and statistical analyses	290

BOXES

1.1	Common essay 'commands'	4
3.1	Key revision points	31
4.1	Assessment example	39
4.2	Our top ten presenting tips	45
5.1	Student activity: politics and research	54
5.2	Learning from experience	58
5.3	Identifying value positions	60
5.4	Official knowledge about crime: key questions	61
6.1	What are the characteristics of a 'good' piece of research?	68
6.2	Key terms explained	70
6.3	Half a story?	73
6.4	Using research to influence policy	76
6.5	Key terms explained: *epistemology* and *ontology*	76
6.6	Student activity: can men carry out pro-feminist research?	80
6.7	Becoming a reflexive researcher	81
6.8	Assessing your understanding	82
6.9	What have we left out?	82
7.1	Learning from the past: real ethical dilemmas	91
7.2	Learning from recent experiences: consequences of breaking ethics approvals	92
7.3	Student activity: informed consent	96
7.4	Student activity: covert, invisible, non-participatory observation (Pollock, 2009)	97
7.5	Researching drug markets: considering confidentiality, anonymity and participation	99
7.6	Can covert observational research be carried out ethically?	101
8.1	Breaking down concepts	114
8.2	Specifying concepts and identifying variables	117
8.3	Developing your research ideas	121
8.4	Research proposal format	124
9.1	Critical reading	130
9.2	Student activity	135
10.1	Early theories of crime and punishment	147

10.2	Classicist ideas in use today	147
10.3	Were biological positivists able to avoid the use of values in their research into crime?	150
10.4	The study of suicide	150
10.5	Living up to and challenging labels	154
10.6	The assumptions of the labelling perspective	154
10.7	Researching the crimes of the powerful	156
10.8	Corporate denial: the power of organisations	156
10.9	Policing the crisis	157
10.10	Using a mixed methods critical approach to research in order to influence policy	159
11.1	Key term explained: offender assessment system	170
11.2	Research in action: piloting research with people who have been in prison	171
11.3	The 'call-in system' explained	177
11.4	Critical activity	183
12.1	Student activity: when should I use in-depth interviewing methods?	191
12.2	Power and the interview process	194
12.3	A semi-structured interview schedule	197
12.4	Student activity: critical qualitative research	200
12.5	Observation and theories of knowledge	204
12.6	Biographical congruence	209
13.1	Types of random samples	228
13.2	Spot the deliberate mistakes	235
14.1	Student activity (O'Leary, 2021)	259
14.2	Analysing secondary data	259
14.3	Student activity: 'the prison crisis'	260
15.1	Student activity	269
16.1	Perception of intimate partner violence: dependent and independent variables	284
16.2	Research example	291
16.3	Research example	294
16.4	Reporting statistical tests	302
16.5	Research example	303
17.1	Transcribing interviews	316
17.2	Braun and Clarke's phases	322
17.3	Describing a thematic analysis in a method section of a research report	323
17.4	Coding activity	328
17.5	Getting started with NVivo	331
18.1	Suggestions for a qualitative content analysis coding manual	340
18.2	What to do when you have developed your initial codes	342
18.3	Jupp and Norris' discourse analytic research agenda	345
18.4	Activity	346

18.5	Getting started with NVivo	349
19.1	Our top three tips for successfully writing up criminological research	354
19.2	Beginning your literature review by stating the extent of the problem or issue under investigation	359
19.3	Relating the findings to the existing literature	363
19.4	Example conclusions	364
19.5	Example titles: domestic violence	366
19.6	Example titles: female prison staff	366
19.7	Writing abstracts	367
19.8	Reflecting on my own positionality: insider-outsider	372

VISUAL TOUR
(HOW TO USE THIS BOOK)

TEXTBOOK FEATURES

Listed below are the various pedagogical features that may be found both in the margins and within the main text, with visual examples of the boxes to look out for, and descriptions of what you can expect them to contain.

Goals of this chapter

Each chapter begins with a list of the key areas in which you can expect to gain knowledge through reading the chapter and completing its accompanying online resources.

Overview

Following the goals of the chapter, an overview is provided which summarises the key issues that will be covered in the chapter.

Boxed features

Boxed features appear throughout the text containing helpful extra material for students, such as definitions of key terms, real-life examples, case studies, exercises, activities, discussion questions and useful tips.

> **BOX 1.1 COMMON ESSAY 'COMMANDS'**
>
> Compare and contrast ... You are being asked to examine the similarities and differences between specific sources or theoretical positions.
>
> Critically evaluate ... You are being asked to judge an idea, theory or argument. In order to do this you must look at other sources and make an effort to comment on how these sources may be better or worse than the one being evaluated. You will need to weigh up the strengths and weaknesses of each (this is what is meant by being critical – it is not the same as criticising) in order to demonstrate to the reader how you have made your judgements (yes, you can make

Key learning points

Here the fundamental concepts covered by the chapter are listed, highlighting both best-practice research methods and potential pitfalls.

> **KEY LEARNING POINTS**
>
> • When assessing the research of others and planning your own research, you must be able to interrogate 'common sense'. In particular you should be able to identify the ways in which 'common sense' is constructed in media reporting about crime, as this often forms part of the contextual backdrop to policy research.
>
> • You need to learn how to judge the strength of evidence that is presented to the public. When a crime has been committed there is often a sense of moral outrage that is frequently fuelled by the media. Politicians will want to be seen to be responding to such outrage and they are quite likely to support harsh and inappropriate responses to crime in such circumstances, such as some

VISUAL TOUR (HOW TO USE THIS BOOK)   xv

Pause to think

Take a moment to 'read between the lines': consider the wider implications of the concepts, examples or themes discussed in the chapter.

Conclusion

Each chapter ends with the main conclusions that may be drawn from the concepts discussed in the chapter.

Glossary

Key terms that are highlighted in bold within the text may be found in the comprehensive glossary at the end of the book.

LINKS TO SUPPORT MATERIAL FEATURES

Whenever you see one of the boxed features below in the margins of the book containing the 'Support Material' logo, look for the related supplementary material for that chapter in the support material. The related material will have the same title that appears in the box ('Getting started with referencing' in the first example below).

For students

For instructors

PART I

Study skills for criminology students

Chapter 1

Writing skills and essay writing

GOALS OF THIS CHAPTER

At the end of this chapter you will:

1. have the tools to enable you to write clearly;
2. be able to unpick essay questions in order to produce clear arguments in relation to those questions;
3. be able to plan and structure your essay;
4. have the editing skills to improve your early drafts.

Writing in an academic setting can be a fear-provoking activity. In this chapter we hope to reduce such fears but also to reduce the complacency that is sometimes exhibited when students – who have after all made the grade to get a place at university – first begin a course. During your degree you will be expected to carry out assignments that require different styles of writing, but we are beginning with essay writing as this is something with which most students are familiar, although about which they are not necessarily confident.

We are well aware that 'life' can get in the way of a good essay. It may be for some that university life is providing new and exciting social opportunities, a time for fun and freedom, but students are increasingly balancing work and family commitments with their studies. For these reasons it is important to be as organised as possible. The more skills you are able to develop early on in your studies, the easier it will become to complete assignments to the standard required. We want you to have time for fun, family and friends but also we hope to equip you with the skills you will need to maximise your chances of doing well and of enjoying the process of writing. Producing a well-constructed piece of writing, and gaining good marks for it, can be a highly rewarding activity.

PREPARING TO WRITE

First, some basics: when you begin a course, your first week may seem overwhelming. You will be given many course materials, all of which will provide you with essential and further reading lists, essay and other assignment details as well as deadlines. We

DOI: 10.4324/9781032645698-2

believe that one of the most important things you should do in your first week is to make a note of the dates on which your assignments are due (put the dates in your phone and set reminders). There are usually penalties for work that is handed in late so, no matter how good you are at writing, missing a date could be catastrophic to your overall grade. The next thing you should do is to have a good look at the course materials. It is unusual to have no choice about an assignment, so read through the essay questions carefully and choose topics that 'light your fire'.

> **TIP**
>
> Don't forget to check the word length. Writing succinctly is also a skill you will need to practise in order to ensure that you do not lose marks.

> **BOX 1.1   COMMON ESSAY 'COMMANDS'**
>
> | | |
> |---|---|
> | Compare and contrast … | You are being asked to examine the similarities and differences between specific sources or theoretical positions. |
> | Critically evaluate … | You are being asked to judge an idea, theory or argument. In order to do this you must look at other sources and make an effort to comment on how these sources may be better or worse than the one being evaluated. You will need to weigh up the strengths and weaknesses of each (this is what is meant by being critical – it is not the same as criticising) in order to demonstrate to the reader how you have made your judgements (yes, you can make judgements but you must back them up). |
> | Discuss … | After examining the evidence develop an argument. |
> | Examine … | Consider an idea, theory or argument in depth. Try to probe the assumptions behind the subject of your discussion and make comments that allow your reader to understand what you have deduced from your examination. |
> | Illustrate … | Many questions will include this term which should signal that you must provide examples that will enable you to explain and clarify a point. |
> | Review … | Suggests an in-depth assessment and critical analysis. |

What is the question asking you to do?

Before you begin to write you must ensure that you are clear about what the question is asking you to do. You must also have done enough reading to enable you to answer the question in a logical and coherent fashion. One of the most common reasons for poor grades is the failure to provide a direct answer to the question. It is quite common for students to display a lot of knowledge about a topic without displaying the ability to analyse the sources they have used. Such descriptive writing does not demonstrate to the reader that the sources referred to in the essay have been understood. (We call this the 'vomit' approach to writing because everything a student can find on a given topic is spewed out with no thought given to the task of answering the question that has been set.)

What does the question entail?

All questions entail certain assumptions that you will need to unravel. Questions may use general terms that you may need to define for yourselves. For example, consider the following question:

Critically discuss	**the view that illegal drug use**	**is a major cause of violent crimes**
The **PEE** approach: make **P**oints; provide **E**vidence; **E**xplain your points by discussing the evidence. Ask yourself: 'How convincing are my points?' Can you rebut an opposing view?	What is the key term here? You are being asked to discuss the issue of illegal drug use but you will need to break down the concept of illegal drug use in order to define the terms of your answer.	The key terms here are major cause and violent crimes. The assumption behind the question is that there is a significant relationship between the independent variable (drug use) and the dependent variable (violent crime).

Once you have broken down the question you will need to decide where to go from there. Do you agree with the assumption behind the question? From what you have learned on your course so far, can you say why you agree or disagree? Does the question, in your opinion, disguise a more important issue? For example, you may have read something about the violence in the United States during the period in which the use of alcohol (now a legal drug) was prohibited, which leads you to think that maybe it is not necessarily the use of drugs that is the problem. Alternatively, you may have some knowledge about the numbers of violent crimes that appear to be related to excessive (legal) use of alcohol, which makes you think that there may be an excessive focus on illegal drug use in society. Note that as a criminology student you will need to be aware of the different ways in which statistics on crime are produced. When an author quotes crime figures you will need to think about the source of those figures and how far they can tell us the 'truth' about crime (see Chapter 6). In order to formulate your (at this stage, disparate) ideas into a coherent argument your next step in the process of preparation is to consult your reading list.

Reading 'smart'

Being familiar with relevant literature is the key to doing well in your assignments but you have to be smart! Reading takes a long time, so you must try to ensure that what you read is going to help you complete your task. The first thing to look for is a hint from your tutor about the texts that will help you to answer the questions they have set. This may sound obvious but we know from experience that some students ignore the detailed guidance with which they are usually provided, so we will state the obvious: START WITH THE TEXTS IDENTIFIED AS *ESSENTIAL*. Your tutors are familiar with the literature already, so they are saving you a lot of time. You should also read a relevant general chapter in a textbook, as this will give you an overview of the key debates and the different theoretical perspectives on the topic under discussion. If the essential reading list is quite short you need to find some other sources. A general rule of thumb for an essay early on in your studies is 15 to 20 sources. As you get better at sifting through the literature you should manage to reference more texts. However, reading smart means developing strategies that enable you to identify the key sections in a book. Often you will not need to read the whole book, as it won't all be relevant to the question you are working on. You will find a précis on the back cover of books which will help you to ascertain its relevance to your study. You might also look at the introduction and conclusion and also scan the index, all of which will provide quick ways of assessing the usefulness of a text to your task. Similarly, when you are searching for articles from refereed journals they will always include an abstract that will provide a succinct outline of the study. Furthermore, authors will always cite other academic texts, so look at their citations as an indication of where else to look. This will save you hours of searching.

TIP

The internet is a wonderful source of information but you must be discerning. You need to ensure that the sources you cite are reputable; at worst you could be accessing sites that are operated by hate groups (Siegel, 2020) so take care. Here are some tips to help you be discerning: Look for the author's name – if there isn't one be very cautious; if there is have you heard of them? If not, look that person up to find out what else they have written. Can you discern the agenda of the author? For example, are there assumptions about gender or ethnicity that you find worrying or offensive? Can you find out the reason the internet site exists and how long it has existed? Also, when was it last updated? Does the author mention other writers that you have heard of and provide evidence to back up what is being said? During the early stages of academic study we suggest that you might want to consult internet sources in order to get a flavour of a topic area but if you find it hard to judge the quality of a source avoid citing them in your assignments.

If you are struggling to work out whether a source is reputable or not, be safe and stick with books and journal articles that appear in searches through your university library website. Caution on interpreting government reports and statistics is reiterated at several points within this book (for example, see Chapter 5).

Smart readers read critically. We have seen many essays over the years of the 'patchwork quilt' variety, by which we mean essays characterised by a string of (sometimes interesting) ideas, theories and quotations that are not linked by a 'common thread'. Reading critically is the key to writing more coherently. It requires you to think about what authors are saying; how they justify what is being said; the strength of the evidence provided by the authors; whether they are saying something that you have seen refuted or substantiated in another text. You will need to make careful notes about each source you have used, ensuring that you have a complete record of the reference as it will appear in your reference list/bibliography and a record of the page numbers by each idea or quotation (for further information on this see Chapter 2). This is important and you will lose marks if you do not heed this advice.

Once you have amassed all this information you should ask yourself: 'How can I synthesise it in order to construct an argument in relation to the question?' It is a good idea to colour code your notes so that you can group together authors with similar viewpoints. As you go through this process you should try to formulate an overarching view in relation to the question. Remember that you *are* entitled to have a particular viewpoint but that viewpoint has to be backed up with evidence. You cannot ignore alternative viewpoints but you can try to show why some are more convincing than others. At this point you are ready to produce an essay plan.

BEGINNING TO WRITE

We talked earlier about how to unravel a question. The example we have chosen, like many within the discipline of criminology, is not entirely straightforward, so the question requires you to demonstrate that you are aware of its contentious elements. There are many ways in which you could answer this question, so we are just going to give you an idea of the key ingredients of a good essay so that you can use this guidance to help with any question.

By the time you begin to write you should have an idea of your overall argument in relation to the question. Jot down a sentence or two that sums up your overall argument and keep this in mind as you plan each point in relation to the question. For example:

> The view that illegal drug use causes violent crime is problematic for a variety of reasons. There is a need for criminologists to examine when, where, and in what

circumstances violence and drug use (legal or illegal) coincide in order to obtain deeper understanding of the relationship between illegal drug use and crime.

You should be thinking all the while about how this summary might help you to address the question and to construct your argument.

Next, list the points you wish to make based on your reading.

PEE (as opposed to vomit)

This is how you might address the question posed earlier in this chapter ('Critically discuss the view that illegal drug use is a major cause of violent crimes'):

- POINT 1. Research on drug use over a number of years has consistently revealed a relationship with violent crime.

    KEY EVIDENCE: Goldstein (1985) Tripartite taxonomy (many authors continue to use and expand this taxonomy – reference them too).

    EXPLAIN: Three types of drug-related violence: psychopharmacological, economic-compulsive, systemic violence (associated with illegal markets and 'turf wars').

    Add any other references (there are many to choose from) that support Goldstein's taxonomy. Say how they support Goldstein's propositions (e.g. Steele, 2016, provides evidence from a qualitative study in which participants admit that they steal to pay for drugs – economic-compulsive).

- POINT 2. It is important to note that correlation differs from causation and that we may not always know the direction of the variables. PROVIDE AN EXAMPLE/S.

    EVIDENCE: Hammersley et al., 1989; Pudney, 2003; D'Amico et al., 2008; Hales et al., 2009.

    EXPLAIN: Drug use might promote crime but it may be that criminal careers may lead to more drug use and/or drug use could increase confidence to commit a crime. It may also be the case that there are other important variables, such as social environment. Parker and Auerhahn (1998) found a great deal of evidence that the social environment is a much more powerful contributor to the outcome of violent behaviour than are pharmacological factors associated with the drugs they considered. (Might the term 'cause' be a problem?)

- POINT 3. Illegal drug use is not the only problem. Violence associated with alcohol use is well documented and is increasing among the young.

    EVIDENCE: Alcohol stimulates or augments a great deal of criminal behaviour, almost certainly more than the street drugs combined (MacCoun, Kilmer and Reuter, 2001; Parker, 1996). It is commonly assumed that illegal drug use creates psychopharmacological violence (as opposed to economic-compulsive or systemic) but much research suggests this is rare and attributable mostly to alcohol rather than to illegal drugs (Goldstein, 1985; Fagan, 1990; Parker and Auerhahn, 1998; White and Gorman, 2000).

EXPLAIN: This is significant because the discourses linking illegal drug use to violent crimes are misleading (this is not the same as saying illegal drug use is not linked to crime).

- POINT 4. Most drug users are not otherwise criminally active and those who commit violent crimes are not all drug users. However, serious problem drug use does seem to be associated with violent crime.

    EVIDENCE: Bryan, Del Bono and Pudney (2013) found no evidence at all of any drug-induced crime committed by people who use cannabis alone. While drug problems are associated with some types of crime, particularly lower level acquisitive crimes, in general they make up a relatively small proportion of all offences (UKDPC, 2012). We need, therefore, to keep the debate about the link between drugs and crime in perspective. Some researchers (e.g. Wright and Klee, 2001) looked at specific types of drug use – amphetamine users were more likely to be involved in all three types of violence in Goldstein's taxonomy.

    EXPLAIN: This contradicts perceptions shown by many of the general public in a survey carried out by the Advisory Council on the Misuse of Drugs (2008); it suggests media amplification and increases stigmatisation of users who may become more involved in crime. This also suggests that it is important to disaggregate the different types of drug use when talking about the relationship between illegal drugs and violence.

- POINT 5. There is a need to understand the different drug markets and the impact of policing these markets.

    EVIDENCE: Reuter, 1989; Riley, 1998; Eck and McGuire, 2000; MacCoun et al., 2001; Hallsworth and Silverstone, 2009; Pitts (2021); Whittaker et al. (2018); Havard et al. (2021).

    EXPLAIN: Some markets have few incidences of violence while others are very violent and recruit vulnerable young 'employees' who are supplied with guns. Risks to vulnerable young people; impact of enforcement of different communities and the displacement of violent crimes.

Structuring your essay

Once you have made a plan you will need to organise your essay into three main parts: Introduction (5 to 10%), Main body (80 to 85%) and Conclusion (10 to 15%).

TIP

Do not write your introduction until you are happy with the main body and conclusion. It is much easier to write this at the end when you have fine-tuned your argument.

Writing the main body of your essay

The main body of your essay should consist of a series of paragraphs. As the plan above indicates, these paragraphs should begin with the point you wish to make. Once you have made a point you need to provide evidence and explain the significance of this evidence. If you don't have any evidence, LEAVE IT OUT. You will need to analyse this evidence; that is, take it apart and discuss how it helps support your point (see the plan above) and why it is significant. You will not get good marks if you just describe what you know. It is very important that your paragraphs are linked in some way. You have an overall argument to make but it will have different elements that need to be pulled together (think of it as weaving a thread all through your essay). As you write, following your plan, you may discover that in order to weave such a thread it makes more sense to change the order of the points you wish to make. In the plan above it may be that it makes more sense to swap points 3 and 4 around, for example. At the end of each paragraph try to spell out why this point contributes to your overall argument. So, for example, at the end of the first paragraph you could say something like:

> While the research evidence does demonstrate some consistency of findings over time and space, it does not necessarily demonstrate that it makes sense to speak of a causal relationship between illegal drug use and violent crime.

This will provide a neat link into the next paragraph, which begins with the point that correlations are not the same as causes. Note that this is a new but related subject; you do not need to reiterate what you said in the last paragraph. Remember: you should be trying to reveal how your thoughts are developing from one paragraph to the next. Repeat this process for every point that you make and you shouldn't go far wrong.

Writing your conclusion

The purpose of a conclusion is to bring all your points together. You don't repeat them in the same way; rather you say them in a succinct and, if possible, more interesting way. Try to think about the implications of what you have argued for future research on this aspect of crime. It is always useful to look at journal article conclusions as these will give you a good idea of how to pull all the points together. In the case of the above example you would write something like this:

> While there is clear evidence of a relationship between illegal drug use and violent crime, the idea that illegal drug use causes violent crime is misleading for a host of reasons ... [proceed to list the significance of each of your points: e.g. a focus on illegal drugs serves to mystify the violence associated with the use of alcohol, which in turn suggests that political imperatives may be intervening].

When you have completed your synthesis of the main points, end with a statement that spells out the implications of your argument:

> In the future, in order for criminologists to gain a more nuanced understanding of the relationship between illegal drug use and violent crime, they will need to focus upon the changing contexts in which violent crimes are committed as well as upon the different types of drugs in use at any given period.

Note: *Never, never, never introduce a new topic in your conclusion.*

Writing your introduction

We believe that all good introductions are best left to the end. Your introduction should put your 'stamp' on the essay and it is your chance to define the terms of your answer to the question. There is more than one way to write an introduction but there are some key elements that should always be included:

- An outline of the main subject of your essay: what is your central argument in relation to the question?
- A quick resumé of the key points.
- An indication of how you will conclude.

Here is an example:

> Since Goldstein (1985) first developed his tripartite conceptual framework of the drugs/violence nexus there has been much evidence to suggest that there is a relationship between drug use and violent crime [insert your references here]. However, the view that illegal drug use causes violent crime is problematic for a variety of reasons, not least because most studies in this area do not leave out alcohol, a legal drug. The claim is contentious not only because of the methodological difficulties involved in identifying causal relationships when studying the social realm, but also because many illegal drug users are not otherwise involved in criminal behaviour. Furthermore, the term 'illegal drugs' is too vague and the failure to differentiate between different types of drugs gives the impression that all illegal drug use is equally likely to cause violence. The focus upon illegal drug use also serves to mystify the association between alcohol use and violence, gives the false impression that legal drug use does not lead to violence, and legitimises policy responses that fail to deal with problem drug use in society and that may also increase the potential for violence to occur. These issues will provide the focus of discussion through which it will be argued that there is a need for criminologists to examine when, where and in what circumstances violence and drug use (legal or illegal) coincide in order to obtain a more nuanced understanding of the relationship between illegal drug use and crime.

If you wish, you may simply outline what you are going to do in an orderly fashion – First, this essay will examine … next it will … – but such introductions are less interesting to read. In any event you should always try to begin with a general statement that leads your reader straight into the topic you are discussing. The main thing is that you provide a 'map' of where your essay is going and how it ends up.

The above outline does rather over-simplify the process of planning your essay. In reality you are likely to make several drafts before you are happy with the structure of your essay. This is normal; academics do this too.

Proof-reading and editing your essay

We cannot stress too much the importance of proof-reading and editing. This process can really make the difference of a grade, so it is worth the effort. In our experience, when students first start to write they very rarely proof-read and edit their work. Academics always proof-read and edit – several times. It's a good idea to leave the proof-reading until the day after you have completed the essay (although this can be difficult if you have left it until the last minute and your essay is due in the next day) because your head will be clearer and you will be more likely to spot your mistakes. In general, editing will involve the following:

1. Run a spell and grammar check and make the appropriate changes.
2. Don't rely on the spell and grammar check – read your essay out loud as this will help you to spot words that you didn't intend to use but which are words nevertheless. For example, after running a spell check the previous sentence was not highlighted as a problem, but in fact the word 'intent' had been typed instead of 'intend'. The error was only picked up by proof-reading.
3. If you can read your essay to a friend they will be likely to pick up on things that you have missed. If you don't want to do this, at least read it out loud to yourself; it really does help.
4. Make sure that you have not neglected to acknowledge a quotation or idea that is not your own. You do not want to be accused of plagiarism.
5. Make sure that your referencing is consistent (see Chapter 2).

Some general points to remember

- You will need to write more than one draft in order to produce your best work.
- All of your essay should be written in your own words (unless you are using an author's idea, or a direct quote, in which case you must reference it) and in the clearest way possible.
- Avoid colloquial expressions.
- Avoid using the first person unless your tutor has advised otherwise.
- Stick to one idea per sentence where possible.
- Do not refer to authors by their first names (we have seen this many times – refer to Chapter 2 for more guidance on citations and references).
- Do not use headings in an essay unless your tutor says you may. (Note: It is usual to use headings in reports.)

REFERENCES

Advisory Council on the Misuse of Drugs (2008) *Cannabis: Classification and Public Health*, London: Home Office.

Bryan, M., Del Bono, E. and Pudney, S. (2013) 'Drug Related Crime', Institute for Social and Economic Research, No.2013-08. University of Essex online report.

D'Amico, E.J., Edelen, M.O., Miles, J.N.V. and Morral, A.R. (2008) 'The Longitudinal Association between Substance Use and Delinquency among High-risk Youth', *Drug and Alcohol Dependence*, 93: 85–92.

Eck, J. and McGuire, E. (2000) 'Have Changes in Policing Reduced Violent Crime? An Assessment of the Evidence', in A. Blumstein and J. Wallman (eds) *The Crime Drop in America*, New York: Cambridge University Press, pp. 207–265.

Fagan, J. (1990) 'Intoxication and Aggression', in M. Tonry and J.Q. Wilson (eds) *Drugs and Crime, vol. 13 of Crime and Justice: A Review of Research*, Chicago, IL: University of Chicago Press, pp. 241–320.

Goldstein, P. (1985) 'The Drug/Violence Nexus: A Tripartite Conceptual Framework', *Journal of Drug Issues*, 14: 493–506.

Hales, J., Nevill, C., Pudney, S.E. and Tipping, S. (2009) *Longitudinal Analysis of the Offending Crime and Justice Survey 2003–6*, London: Home Office: Online Research Report 19.

Hallsworth, S. and Silverstone, D. (2009) '"That's Life Innit": A British Perspective on Guns, Crime and Social Order', *Criminology and Community Justice*, 9(3): 359–377.

Hammersley, R., Forsyth, A., Morrison, V. and Davies, J.B. (1989) 'The Relationship between Crime and Opioid Use', *British Journal of Addiction*, 84: 1029–1043.

Havard, T., Densley, J., Whittaker, A. and Wills, J. (2021). 'Street Gangs and Coercive Control: The Gendered Exploitation of Young Women and Girls in County Lines', *Criminology & Criminal Justice*. https://doi.org/10.1177/17488958211051513

MacCoun, R., Kilmer, B. and Reuter, P. (2001) 'Research on Drugs–Crime Linkages: The Next Generation', *National Institute of Justice, Special Edition*, July: 65–90.

Parker, H. (1996) 'Young Adult Offenders, Alcohol and Criminological Cul-de-sacs', *The British Journal of Criminology*, 36(2): 282–298.

Parker, R. and Auerhahn, K. (1998) 'Alcohol, Drugs, and Violence', *Annual Review of Sociology*, 24: 291–311.

Pitts, J. (2021). *County Lines.* [Online]. Her Majesty's Inspectorate of Probation. Last Updated: January 2021. Available at: https://www.justiceinspectorates.gov.uk/hmiprobation/wp-content/uploads/sites/5/2021/01/Academic-Insights-county-lines-.pdf

Pudney, S.E. (2003) 'The Road to Ruin? Sequences of Initiation to Drugs and Crime in Britain', *Economic Journal*, 113: C182–C198.

Reuter, P. (1989) 'An Economist Looks at the Carnage', *Washington Post*, 26 March.

Riley, K.J. (1998) 'Homicide and Drugs: A Tale of Six Cities', *Homicide Studies*, 2: 176–205.

Siegel A.A. (2020). 'Online Hate Speech', in N. Persily and J.A. Tucker (eds) *Social Media and Democracy*. SSRC Anxieties of Democracy. Cambridge University Press, pp. 56–88.

Steele, R. (2016) 'How Offenders Make Decisions: Evidence of Rationality', *British Journal of Community Justice*, 13(3): 7–20.

UK Drug Policy Commission (UKDPC) (2012) *A Fresh Approach to Drugs*, London: UKDPC.

White, H.R. and Gorman, D.M. (2000) 'Dynamics of the Drug–Crime Relationship', in *Crime and Justice 2000, Vol. 1: The Nature of Crime: Continuity and Change*, Washington, DC: U.S. Department of Justice, National Institute of Justice, NCJ 182408, pp. 151–218.

Whittaker, A.J., Cheston, L., Tyrell, T., Higgins, M.M., Felix-Baptiste, C. and Harvard, T. (2018). *From Postcodes to Profits: How Gangs Have Changed in Waltham Forest*, London: London South Bank University. https://doi.org/10.18744/PUB.002234

Wright, S. and Klee, H. (2001) 'Violent Crime, Aggression and Amphetamine: What Are the Implications for Drug Treatment Services?', *Drugs, Education, Prevention and Policy*, 8(1): 73–90.

Chapter 2

Referencing

GOALS OF THIS CHAPTER

At the end of reading this chapter and by completing the online resources that accompany it, you will:

1. understand the purpose and importance of appropriate referencing;
2. know how to use the Harvard referencing system;
3. understand how to cite and reference a variety of sources;
4. appreciate that different referencing systems exist.

INTRODUCTION

As we discussed in Chapter 1 on writing skills and essay writing, you will be expected to carry out a variety of assignments during the course of your degree. One of the new skills you need to perfect as part of the writing process is how to reference your work correctly. Ensuring you provide accurate references for the research studies and other sources you discuss in your assignments is essential to demonstrate to the reader (in this case your tutor or lecturer) what sources you have accessed, how well you understand the relevant literature, how you have used the work of others to develop arguments in your writing, and how clearly you are able to differentiate your own work and ideas from those whose work you have read. This allows your reader to judge the reliability of your sources (refer back to the section in Chapter 1 on internet sources for more on this). Accurate referencing also helps you avoid inadvertent plagiarism. You must ensure you reference all the sources you use when producing a piece of work.

Most Criminology and other Social Sciences courses will require you to use the Harvard referencing system. However, you should always check what is required. For example, if you are taking a Law or Psychology module, you may well be required to use a different form of referencing. You will probably find that your own university or university library has a guide to the different types of referencing that you can access. However, below you can find a link to guidance on referencing from the University of Wolverhampton (www.wlv.ac.uk/lib/skills-for-learning/referencing).

DOI: 10.4324/9781032645698-3

The Harvard referencing system is an author–date system where the author's/authors' surname(s) and year of publication are included in in-text citations and reference lists/bibliographies (more on this below). There are other, similar, author–date systems such as APA and the Chicago author–date referencing systems. It is important to use the exact system required on your course, even though the differences between these systems might seem small.

Task: Look up the different types of referencing systems (via your university library website or the link above) and note the different conventions for each type of resource.

KEY TERM EXPLAINED: PLAGIARISM

> Plagiarism is the act of taking someone else's work and passing it off as your own. This includes incorporating either unattributed direct quotation(s) or substantial paraphrasing from the work of another/others/or yourself. It is important to cite all sources whose work has been drawn on and reference them fully in accordance with the required referencing standard used in each subject area.
>
> (University of Wolverhampton, 2022)

Plagiarism is a significant offence and it is taken very seriously in universities. We usually think of plagiarism as deliberately trying to pass someone else's work off as your own. However, it is all too easy to inadvertently plagiarise through inaccurate or poor referencing. Inadvertent plagiarism is not an excuse. Plagiarism offences are often addressed via an academic misconduct committee and can result in exclusion from your degree course.

If you are unsure whether something you have written might constitute plagiarism, make an appointment with the learning support/study skills team at your university.

REFERENCE LIST VS BIBLIOGRAPHY

You may hear people talking about reference lists and bibliographies but be unsure about the difference. Indeed, it is not unusual to hear these terms used interchangeably.

This chapter has talked about citations and references. A reference list is a list of all the sources you have cited in your work. If your work includes citations from every source you have read, then you only need to provide a reference list.

If you have read other sources but not cited them in your writing, then you could list them as a separate bibliography.

If not noted in the module handbook, or assessment guidance, it is worth checking with your tutor or lecturer whether they prefer a reference list and/or a bibliography.

PLACEMENT AND ORDER OF REFERENCES

In the Harvard referencing system, citations are presented within the body of an essay or article (called in-text citations), and the full reference is provided in a list at the end in your reference list or bibliography. If you are including any appendices in a report or dissertation, these come after the reference list. We will go into more detail about this later.

Task: Look at the reference list at the end of this chapter, paying attention to the order in which references are presented. Note that the references are listed in alphabetical order.

TIP: KEEPING TRACK OF YOUR REFERENCES

From the minute you begin to do your background reading you should keep track of your references. Set up a file on your computer and make sure that you always record what you have read using the Harvard system. Many universities now have packages such as Endnote and help is often provided in university libraries.

REFERENCING IN YOUR TEXT (OR IN-TEXT CITATIONS)

When you refer to someone's work in your writing (whether by quoting them or summarising their work) you need to acknowledge the source. We call this an 'in-text citation'. Look at this example, taken from Chapter 6 of this book:

> Alizai's (2023) consideration of Islamophobia provides a good example of work where the values of the writer are clearly identified.

The full reference for the in-text citation provided above may be found in the reference list for Chapter 6. This is what it looks like:

> Alizai, H. (2023) 'European Approaches to Stopping Islamophobia are Inadequate: Lessons for Canadians Combating Anti-Muslim Racism and Hatred', *Journal of Hate Studies*, 18(1): 63–79.

Here is another example, this time from Chapter 7:

> Since 'ethics is concerned with the attempt to formulate codes and principles of moral behaviour' (May, 2001: 59), it is bound to be underpinned by values about what is good or bad conduct in research.

Direct quotes must be placed in quotation marks. Note that the page number (59) is given in the in-text citation because a quote is provided. You should also include page numbers when you paraphrase a point or an idea, and if you include tables, diagrams, etc.

The full reference for the in-text citation provided above may be found in the reference list for Chapter 7. This is what it looks like:

> May, T. (2001) *Social Research: Issues, Methods and Process*, Buckingham: Open University Press.

The next example is from a journal article written by Tallent, Phillips and Coren (2022: 1):

> in England and Wales, it is estimated that half of all crime is committed by those who have previously offended (Ministry of Justice, 2015). In Ireland in 2010, 45% of people in the criminal justice system (CJS) reoffended within 3 years (Central Statistics Office, 2016).

References for the citations provided in the text above then appear at the end of the article:

> Central Statistics Office. (2016) *Prison Recidivism 2010 Cohort*. Cork: Central Statistics Office. Available at https://www.cso.ie/en/releasesandpublications/er/prir/prisonrecidivism2010cohort
>
> Ministry of Justice. (2015) *Policy Paper–2010 to Government Policy: Reoffending and Rehabilitation*. London: Ministry of Justice. Available at https://www.gov.uk/government/publications/2010-to-2015-government-policy-reoffending-and-rehabilitation/2010-to-2015-government-policy-reoffending-and-rehabilitation

Note that the references are listed in alphabetical order. Note that where multiple references are listed by the same author(s), these are listed with the earliest work first.

Some published items are written by multiple authors. Rather than write all the names in full every time you cite them in your text, you write an abbreviated form. For example:

One author	(Hill, 2024)	… Hill (2024) argues that …
Two authors	(Hill and Harris, 2024)	… according to Hill and Harris (2024) …
Three or more authors (the first time you cite their work)	(Hill, Harris and Caulfield, 2024)	… research by Hill, Harris and Caulfield (2024) showed that …
Three or more authors (subsequent times you cite their work)	(Hill et al., 2024)	Hill et al. (2024) found that …

All author names should be provided in the reference list.

HOW TO REFERENCE DIFFERENT TYPES OF SOURCES

Books

Author(s) (year of publication) *Title of Book*, Place of publication: Publisher.

Example (single author)

Giddens, A. (1979) *Central Problems in Social Theory*, London: Macmillan.

Note that if there is more than one edition of a book, you should state which edition it is (except for the first edition). For example:

Jewkes, Y. (2011) *Crime and the Media*, second edition, London: Sage.

Examples (two or more authors)

Gray, D. and Kinnear, P. (2011) *IBM SPSS Statistics 19 Made Simple*, London: Psychology Press.

Example (edited books)

An edited book is a collection of chapters written by different authors, put together by an editor(s).

Garner, A. and Caulfield, L.S. (eds) (2024) *Arts in Criminal Justice and Corrections: International Perspectives on Methods, Journeys, and Challenges*, London: Routledge.

Example (chapter in an edited book)

> Cohen, M. (2024) 'Collaboration as a Tool for Transformative Justice', in M. Gardner and L.S. Caulfield (eds) *Arts in Criminal Justice and Corrections: International Perspectives on Methods, Journeys, and Challenges*, London: Routledge.

Note that in the above example, the initials of the editors come before their surnames.

Journal articles

> Author(s) (year of publication) 'Title of Article', *Title of Journal*, Volume number (Issue number): Page numbers of whole article.

Example

> Ellis, S. and Bowen, E. (2017) 'Factors Associated with Desistance from Violence in Prison: An Exploratory Study', *Psychology, Crime, and Law*, 23(6): 601–619.

Note that some journals may not include a volume or issue number. If this is the case, don't worry. If a month or season is noted (e.g. February or winter), provide that information instead.

Reports

> Author(s) (year of publication) *Title of Report*, Place of publication: Publishing organisation.

Example (authored report)

> Hitchcock, A., Holmes, R. and Sundorph, E. (2017) *Bobbies on the Net: A Police Workforce for the Digital Age*, London: Reform.

Example (report authored by an organisation)

> Ministry of Justice. (2010) *Breaking the Cycle: Effective Punishment, Rehabilitation and Sentencing of Offenders*, London: Ministry of Justice.

Example (report accessed online)

>HMI Probation. (2016) *Desistance and Young People: An Inspection by HM Inspectorate of Probation* (online). Available at www.justiceinspectorates.gov.uk/hmiprobation/inspections/desistance-and-young-people/ (accessed 1 September 2017).

Newspaper articles

>Author(s) (year of publication) 'Title of Article', *Newspaper Name*, Day and month published, page numbers(s).

Example (printed newspaper article)

>Moody, O. (2014) 'Man "Read Wilde Poem after Stabbing Lover"', *The Times*, 26 February, p. 15.

Example (online newspaper article)

>Knowles, M. (2023) 'Officers on High Alert after Met Police Security Break', *Daily Express* (online), 28 August. Available at https://www.express.co.uk/news/uk/1806688/Met-police-security-breach (accessed 11 October 2023).

Note that some newspaper articles don't include a named author. Where that is the case, provide the name of the newspaper instead.

Dissertations and theses

>Author (year of publication) *Title of Thesis*, Qualification, Awarding institution.

Example (in print)

>Hill, J. (1999) *The Discourse of Inter-agency Co-operation: Towards Critical Understanding of the Theory and Practice of Child Protection Work*, PhD thesis, University of Keele.

Example (electronic)

>Caulfield, L.S. (2012) *Life Histories of Women Who Offend: A Study of Women in English Prisons* (online), PhD thesis, Loughborough University. Available at https://dspace.lboro.ac.uk/dspace-jspui/handle/2134/10178 (accessed 1 June 2024).

Web pages

>Author (year of publication) *Title of Webpage.* Available at [full web address] (accessed date).

Example (web page with a named author)

>Dehnavi, O. (2023) *Social Prescribing in the Criminal Justice System – Building the Evidence Base.* Available at https://www.clinks.org/community/blog-posts/social-prescribing-criminal-justice-system-building-evidence-base (accessed 10 October 2023).

Example (web page authored by an organisation)

>Clinks. (2022) *Navigating the Criminal Justice System.* Available at https://www.clinks.org/publication/navigating-criminal-justice-system#:~:text=The%20criminal%20justice%20system%20in%20England%20and%20Wales%20can%20be,organised%20and%20how%20it%20work (accessed 10 October 2023).

If a website has no obvious author, use the site's full URL. However, be wary. If you cannot identify the author or organisation responsible for the website, you should question whether this is a suitable source for academic work. If a date isn't on the web page, write (no date). If there is a date range (e.g. Clinks, 1993–2023) then use the most recent date given.

A note on citing lecture and seminar materials

It is worth noting that not all lecturers will be happy for you to cite lecture materials, preferring you to access original sources. In this way you are better able to demonstrate that you have really engaged with the research literature.

If your lecturer is happy for you to cite lecture notes or slides, you should do so as follows:

>Lecturer Name (Year) Details of item (e.g. lecture title). *Module Code: Module Title* (date accessed).

Example

> Caulfield, L. (2023) Lecture 6: Offender Profiling. *PS5008: Criminological and Investigative Psychology* (online). Available at http://canvas.wlv.ac.uk/ (accessed 17 January 2024).

You can find guidance on referencing other sources (e.g. images, videos, emails) via www.wlv.ac.uk/lib/skills-for-learning/referencing/

Table 2.1 Checklist of what to include for the most common information sources

	Author	Year	Title of article	Title of publication	Issue	Place	Publisher	Edition	Page number(s)	URL	Date accessed
Book	Y	Y		Y		Y	Y	Y			
Chapter	Y	Y	Y	Y		Y	Y	Y	Y		
Journal article	Y	Y	Y	Y	Y				Y		
E-Journal article	Y	Y	Y	Y	Y				Y	Y	Y
Internet site	Y	Y	Y	Y						Y	Y
Newspaper article	Y	Y	Y	Y	Y				Y		

Adapted from Pears and Shields (2022).

> **TIP**
>
> A common mistake among beginners to research is to place journal article titles in italics. An easy way to remember which part of a journal reference should be italicised is to remind yourself that the different articles in a journal are like book chapters. The title of the journal itself – like a book title – should be in italics. Therefore the article title should be in inverted commas.

SOME GENERAL RULES

We talked about the following rules earlier in this chapter:

- Page numbers must be provided in the in-text citation when a quote is used. You should also include page numbers when you paraphrase a point or an idea, and if you include tables, diagrams, etc.
- References are listed in alphabetical order. If there are multiple references by the same author(s) in different years, place the earliest one first.

- When there are three or more authors for a piece of work, rather than write all the names in full every time you cite them in your text, you write an abbreviated form (et al.), referencing all authors only at the first mention.

There are a number of other general rules to follow when using the Harvard referencing system. The following guidance is adapted from the University of Wolverhampton Harvard Referencing Guide.

The author has published two or more items during the same year

If two or more documents are by the exact same author(s) in the same year, add lower-case letters after the year (a, b, c, etc.) to distinguish between them in your text and in your reference list. The first of the sources you mention in your essay would be a, the next b and so on.

For example:

Howitt, D. and Cramer, D. (2014a) *Introduction to SPSS in Psychology*, eighth edition, Harlow: Pearson.

Howitt, D. and Cramer, D. (2014b) *Introduction to Statistics in Psychology*, sixth edition, Harlow: Pearson.

Howitt, D. and Cramer, D. (2014c) *Introduction to Research Methods in Psychology*, fourth edition, Harlow: Prentice Hall.

Organisation as author

If there is only an organisation's name on an item and no named individuals, use the organisation as the author.

Example: University of Wolverhampton (2024) ...

Note: some organisations are also known by an abbreviation; for example, the Ministry of Justice (MoJ). Give the full name the first time you use the organisation in your text and then use the abbreviation for the citation and any later mentions.

Example: Information from the Ministry of Justice (MoJ, 2022) suggests ...

Multiple sources for the same point

You can group together sources that talk about the same point by listing them within the same in-text citation. Use semicolons to separate each item. List by year with earliest first and use a semicolon to separate each citation.

Example: A number of studies (Smith, 2018; Jones, 2019; Brown, 2021; Williams et al., 2023; Thomas and Lewis, 2024) provide evidence that ...

Secondary referencing (authors quoting other authors)

Sometimes you may want to reference an author who is quoting another information source that you haven't seen. You should try to find the original source, but if that is not possible you need to make it clear that you have not seen the original source yourself.

Within your text, you cite the original author, followed by the author of the secondary source.

Examples

> 'It will not require violence to succeed, and it cannot be successfully resisted by violence' (Reich, 1971, in Singer, 1997: 90).

> Reich (1971, in Singer, 1997: 90) stated that 'it will not require violence to succeed, and it cannot be successfully resisted by violence'.

In your reference list at the end of your essay, you list the book or article you actually read:

> Singer, P. (1997) *How Are We to Live?*, Oxford: Oxford University Press.

Author/date missing

Ideally you should only reference sources where the author and date information is clearly available. However, there may be times where this information is missing. In such instances, make sure that the source would still be considered reliable enough to use in an academic assignment.

If there isn't an author (named individual or organisation) given, use the title (in italics) for your citation and at the start of your main reference. For example:

> (*Oxford English Dictionary*, 1989).

> *Oxford English Dictionary* (1989) second edition, Oxford: Clarendon Press.

Website Student activity

Getting started with referencing

If no date of publication can be identified, use (no date) for the citation and in your main reference.

For example:

> (Sandwell and West Birmingham NHS Trust, no date)

> Sandwell and West Birmingham NHS Trust. (no date) *Privacy and Dignity*. Available at https://www.swbh.nhs.uk/patients-visitors/statutory-information -for-patients/privacy-and-dignity (accessed 13 October 2023).

Website Instructor exercise

Referencing

Reference list entries

Each citation in your text leads the reader to the full information about the item in your reference list. Each item in your reference list should only appear once, regardless of how many in-text citations you have for that item.

Your list should be completed in alphabetical order by author surname regardless of the information source. Look again at the reference list at the end of this chapter for an example of a completed reference list.

REFERENCES

Caulfield, L.S. (2012) *Life Histories of Women Who Offend: A Study of Women in English Prisons* (online), PhD thesis, Loughborough University. Available at https://dspace.lboro.ac.uk/dspace-jspui/handle/2134/10178 (accessed 1 September 2017).

Caulfield, L. (2023) Lecture 6: Offender Profiling. PS5008: Criminological and Investigative Psychology (online). Available at http://canvas.wlv.ac.uk/ (accessed 17 January 2024).

Central Statistics Office. (2016) *Prison Recidivism 2010 Cohort.* Available at https://www.cso.ie/en/releasesandpublications/er/prir/prisonrecidivism2010cohort

Clinks (2022) Navigating Guide to the Criminal Justice System. Available at https://www.clinks.org/publication/navigating-criminal-justice-system#:~:text=The%20criminal%20justice%20system%20in%20England%20and%20Wales%20can%20be,organised%20and%20how%20it%20works

Cohen, M. (2024) 'Collaboration as a Tool for Transformative Justice', in A. Gardner and L.S. Caulfield (eds) *Arts in Criminal Justice and Corrections: International Perspectives on Methods, Journeys, and Challenges*, London: Routledge.

Dehnavi, O. (2023) *Social Prescribing in the Criminal Justice System – Building the Evidence Base.* Available at https://www.clinks.org/community/blog-posts/social-prescribing-criminal-justice-system-building-evidence-base (accessed 10 October 2023).

Ellis, S. and Bowen, E. (2017) 'Factors Associated with Desistance from Violence in Prison: An Exploratory Study', *Psychology, Crime, and Law*, 23(6): 601–619.

Gardner, M. and Caulfield, L. S. (2024) *Arts in Criminal Justice and Corrections: International perspectives on methods, journeys, and challenges*, London: Routledge.

Giddens, A. (1979) *Central Problems in Social Theory*, London: Macmillan.

Gray, D. and Kinnear, P. (2011) *IBM SPSS Statistics 19 Made Simple*, London: Psychology Press.

Hill, J. (1999) *The Discourse of Inter-agency Co-operation: Towards Critical Understanding of the Theory and Practice of Child Protection Work*, PhD thesis, University of Keele.

Hitchcock, A., Holmes, R. and Sundorph, E. (2017) *Bobbies on the Net: A Police Workforce for the Digital Age*, London: Reform.

HMI Probation (2016) *Desistance and Young People: An Inspection by HM Inspectorate of Probation* (online). Available at www.justiceinspectorates.gov.uk/hmiprobation/inspections/desistance-and-young-people/ (accessed 1 September 2017).

Howitt, D. and Cramer, D. (2014a) *Introduction to SPSS in Psychology*, sixth edition, Harlow: Pearson.

Howitt, D. and Cramer, D. (2014b) *Introduction to Statistics in Psychology*, sixth edition, Harlow: Pearson.

Howitt, D. and Cramer, D. (2014c) *Introduction to Research Methods in Psychology*, fourth edition, Harlow: Prentice Hall.

Jewkes, Y. (2011) *Crime and the Media*, second edition, London: Sage.

Knowles, M. (2023) 'Officers on High Alert after Met Police Security Break', *Daily Express* (online), 28 August. Available at https://www.express.co.uk/news/uk/1806688/Met-police-security-breach (accessed 11 October 2023).

May, T. (2001) *Social Research: Issues, Methods and Process*, Buckingham: Open University Press.

Ministry of Justice. (2010) *Breaking the Cycle: Effective Punishment, Rehabilitation and Sentencing of Offenders*, London: Ministry of Justice.

Ministry of Justice. (2015) *Policy Paper – 2010 to Government Policy: Reoffending and Rehabilitation*. Available at https://www.gov.uk/government/publications/2010-to-2015-government-policy-reoffending-and-rehabilitation/2010-to-2015-government-policy-reoffending-and-rehabilitation

Moody, O. (2014) 'Man "Read Wilde Poem after Stabbing Lover"', *The Times*, 26 February, p. 15.

Moran, D., Jewkes, Y., Blount-Hill, K.-L. and St John, V. (eds) (2022) The Palgrave Handbook of Prison Design, London: Palgrave Macmillan. https://doi.org/10.1007/978-3-031-11972-9.

Oxford English Dictionary (1989) second edition, Oxford: Clarendon Press.

Pears, R. and Shields, G. (2022) *Cite Them Right: The Essential Referencing Guide*, twelfth edition, Basingstoke: Palgrave Macmillan.

Sandwell and West Birmingham NHS Trust. (no date) *Privacy and Dignity*. Available at https://www.swbh.nhs.uk/patients-visitors/statutory-information-for-patients/privacy-and-dignity/ (accessed 13 October 2023).

Singer, P. (1997) *How Are We to Live?*, Oxford: Oxford University Press.

Tallent, J., Phillips, J. and Coren, E. (2022) 'PROTOCOL: Arts-based Interventions for Offenders in Secure Criminal Justice Settings to Improve Rehabilitation Outcomes: An Evidence and Gap Map'. *Campbell Systematic Reviews* 18(3).

The Swedish National Council for Crime Prevention (Brå). (2017) *Reintegration Assistance After Prison: Follow-Up on the Prison and Probation Service's Work with Special Reintegration Assistance Measures*. Available at https://bra.se/bra-in-english/home/publications/archive/publications/2018-02-06-reintegration-assistance-after-prison.html

University of Wolverhampton. (no date). *Referencing* (online). University of Wolverhampton. Available at https://www.wlv.ac.uk/lib/skills-for-learning/referencing/

University of Wolverhampton (2022) *Turnitin – Detecting Plagiarism?* Available at www.wlv.ac.uk/about-us/internal-departments/the-college-of-learning-and-teaching-colt/learning-and-teaching-technologies/turnitin-detecting-plagiarism/ (accessed 11 January 2024).

Chapter 3

Revision skills and examination techniques

GOALS OF THIS CHAPTER

At the end of this chapter you will:

1 have strategies that will improve your revision skills;
2 know how to write essays under exam conditions;
3 have strategies that will help you reduce exam stress and nerves.

Examinations are usually one of the most stress-provoking activities that students encounter. In our experience some students are so afraid of examinations that they will avoid even some of the most popular modules on their course if they see that part of the assessment is an examination. The anxiety attached to examinations often stems from experiences at school and students will then carry those bad experiences with them into adulthood. One of us was very fearful of examinations at school but as a result of being taught good examination techniques (and of choosing a degree course that was inspiring) the fear morphed into enjoyment in the university setting. Once you learn the right techniques it really is possible to do well so long as you have chosen a degree subject in which you have a genuine interest.

DEVELOPING MORE EFFECTIVE REVISION STRATEGIES

Many people fool themselves that they are working hard at revising for examinations but in fact they often do not work productively. The key reasons for this are lack of organisation and failure to take regular breaks. However, another reason revision can be a problem for some students is because they have not attended sufficient lectures, seminars and tutorials to get a handle on their subjects and then they dash around at the last minute reading up on subjects they have skipped. This means that their preparation for examinations cannot be truly called revision; rather it would be better named 'do-it-yourself last-minute self-tutoring'. So, the first step towards good examination results is attendance at all your classes. By the time you have had a lecture, tutorial and/or seminar on a topic the information should be entering your long-term memory, which will aid the process of pre-exam revision. Thus the very first step towards effective revision is regular attendance in lectures and seminar

DOI: 10.4324/9781032645698-4

discussions. It is important to make good notes that you will understand and be able to read later. When you do your reading in preparation for classes make notes as you read. Don't copy chunks from the books or articles but rather make meaningful notes and critical comments (see Chapter 1 on writing an essay). Think as you read. Don't forget to keep a note of your references so that you can learn who said what. If you can get into the habit of reading through your notes each week, you will discover that not only is much of the knowledge you gain in each module transferable but also that your powers of recall will be improving noticeably. You will need to decide how to condense your notes. If you are a visual person you may find it easier to remember your notes if you convert them into a diagram, chart or mind map.[1] You can colour code key ideas as this may also help you visualise your notes once in an exam.

> **TIP**
>
> Use mnemonics: these are aide-memoires which use the initial letters of a word in order to trigger key concepts. For example, PEE stands for **P**oint, **E**vidence, **E**xplain, which is a useful mnemonic to help you remember what you should be doing in each paragraph of an essay.

You should start some serious revision about five weeks before an exam. Before beginning your revisions, there are a number of initial, important steps:

1. It is important that you get a copy of your exam timetable as soon as possible to enable you to plan the order of your revision.
2. It is also important to obtain past papers (often held by the University library) so that you can practise making essay plans.
3. Next, make yourself a revision timetable (see Table 3.1 and/or online resources[2]), and set out your revision schedule. Remember that it is really important to take regular, short breaks as these improve concentration. Often students will shut themselves in a room for hours on end pretending to themselves and the world that they are working hard when in fact they are on their mobile phones, thinking about cake or just falling asleep. So, be smart and start as you mean to go on. Intersperse short spells of concentration with a bike ride, a walk, a coffee with a friend – anything to clear your head – then be disciplined and get back to work for another spell. This is far more likely to work than sitting at a desk for hours on end.

This sample timetable is very full and we would expect this type of intensive revision during a two-week run-up to your exams. You will see that we have assumed five subjects and intensive revision on three topics per subject. For a three-essay exam you should revise at least six topics well in case you really don't like the questions

Table 3.1 Sample timetable

	Monday	Tuesday	Wednesday	Thursday	Friday	Saturday	Sunday
9.00	Subject 1 Topic 1	Subject 2 Topic 2	Subject 3 Topic 1	Subject 4 Topic 2	Subject 5 Topic 1		
10.00 10.30	Subject 1 Topic 1 BREAK	Subject 1 Topic 3	Subject 4 Topic 1	Subject 3 Topic 3	Subject 5 Topic 2		
11.00 11.30	Subject 1 Topic 1 Subject 2 Topic 1	BREAK Subject 1 Topic 3	BREAK Subject 4 Topic 1	BREAK Subject 3 Topic 3	BREAK		
12.00	Subject 2 Topic 1	Subject 1 Topic 3	Subject 4 Topic 1		Subject 5 Topic 2		
12.30	BREAK	BREAK	BREAK	BREAK			
13.00 13.30	Subject 2 Topic 1	Subject 2 Topic 3	Subject 3 Topic 2	Subject 4 Topic 3	BREAK		
14.00 14.30 15.00	Subject 2 Topic 1 Subject 1 Topic 2	Subject 2 Topic 3 BREAK	Subject 3 Topic 2	Subject 4 Topic 3 BREAK	Subject 5 Topic 3		
15.30 16.00 16.30	BREAK Subject 1 Topic 2	Subject 2 Topic 3	BREAK Subject 4 Topic 2	Subject 4 Topic 3	Subject 5 Topic 3 Finish		
17.00	Subject 2 Topic 2	BREAK	Finish	Subject 5 Topic 1			
17.30 18.00 18.30 19.00	Subject 2 Topic 2 Finish	Subject 3 Topic 1 Finish		Finish			

on your favourite three. This means that the following week you would need to cover topics 4 to 6 for each subject area in the same way, assuming that you are to be examined in all five subjects (which may not be the case). During the intensive revision period make sure that you practise making essay plans using the questions on past papers and the essay-writing guidance provided in Chapter 1. Try to write one or two complete essays in the allotted time so that you are prepared for the real thing. Finally, whatever you do, be cautious about trying to revise a totally new topic the day before an exam. This can displace the knowledge you have already committed to your long-term memory and cause anxiety and confusion.

Remember that it is really important to take regular, short breaks as these improve concentration. Often students will shut themselves in a room for hours on end pretending to themselves and the world that they are working hard when in fact they are on their mobile phones, thinking about cake or just falling asleep. So, be smart and start as you mean to go on. Intersperse short spells of concentration with a bike ride, a walk, a coffee with a friend – anything to clear your head – then be disciplined and get back to work for another spell. This is far more likely to work than sitting at a desk for hours on end.

BOX 3.1 KEY REVISION POINTS

1. Revision really starts after the first week of your course.
2. The more you go over your notes the more you commit to your long-term memory.
3. Make clear, legible notes, but keep them short.
4. Be organised – get your exam timetables, past papers and notes together before you plan your revision schedule.
5. Use aide-memoires such as diagrams and mnemonics.
6. When intensive revision starts take regular breaks.
7. Don't try to learn a new topic the day before an exam.
8. Finish your revision early the night before an exam. Do some exercise or anything that will help you sleep.

DOING THE EXAMS

The day has arrived when your exams begin. This is where you get your opportunity to make all that hard work count. Before we get to the exams themselves here are some tips that should ensure everything goes smoothly – they may look like statements of the obvious, but then we know what always happens on the day … (see tips for a stress free start below).

Now to the really important bit: once you are told to turn over your paper the first thing you should do is make sure it is the correct paper (students are not the only ones who can get things wrong). Once you have established that you do have the correct paper look at the rubric (the instructions) as you will lose marks if you do not follow them. For example, there may be a compulsory question; there may be two sections from each of which you must select at least one question; there may be only one section with a free choice; you may have been given an article to critically evaluate, which will be attached to your paper. It is likely that your tutors will have given you information about the structure of the paper in advance, but (trust us, we're doctors) there are always students who lose marks because they have failed to follow the instructions. Note that in the event of the rubric being unclear you are allowed to clarify the instructions with your invigilator. The rubric may also inform you that you have been given extra time to read the questions, usually five to ten minutes.

Read all the questions carefully, preferably twice, before you select the ones to answer. Pay careful attention to the wording to be sure that you are clear about what you are being asked to do. If you are not, even if it is a topic you know well, you may be better off answering a question that makes more sense to you. Remember: answers of the 'vomit' variety (writing everything you know about a topic, without developing a clear, critical argument) will result in poor marks however much knowledge you display. Once you have selected the questions you are going to answer and the order in which you wish to answer them, DO NOT START YOUR ESSAY STRAIGHT AWAY. Instead go through the planning process outlined in the essay-writing skills chapter (Chapter 1). You can either do all of your plans first and then write all the essays, or do one plan and then write that essay, then make your next plan. Do whichever suits you best but do make a plan. In any event keep an eye on the time and try not to go over the time you have gauged for each question (usually about 45 minutes' writing time, depending on the length of the exam and number of questions). You will need to leave time to read through your answers and make minor corrections. Remember: you are still expected to write a proper, well-argued answer even though you are writing in exam conditions.

TIPS FOR A STRESS-FREE START

- Get up early. If you are travelling to campus set off earlier than usual, take the earlier bus or train.
- Eat something – even if it is only a banana.
- Don't forget your student ID, as this will usually be your passport into the examination room.
- Be sure you have the correct room number. If you are a student with learning support needs you are likely to be in a different room from most of your peers.

- Take plenty of water with you, as keeping hydrated will aid your concentration.
- Take plenty of pens (they invariably run out, and waiting for someone to see your hand up and find out what you want wastes valuable time and disrupts your flow).
- Once in the exam room put your pens, watch and water on your desk; then check your mobile phone is switched off, put it back in your bag and place your bag in the designated area.

EXAM ESSAY DOS AND DON'TS

DO:

- Read all the questions carefully and be sure you understand what is being asked.
- Make a plan for each essay.
- Begin your plan with a sentence or two which sums up your general argument in relation to the question.
- Think about your introduction and how you can use it to delimit the ground you will be covering.
- Identify no more than five clear points (remember PEE).
- Order these points logically and think about how they are linked to your argument.
- Refer to appropriate sources (dates are good but in general don't worry about page numbers).
- Pull your argument together with a strong conclusion – go out with a bang, not a damp squib.
- Remember quality not quantity.

DON'T:

- Miss out a question. This will have a devastating effect on your grade.
- Include irrelevant material.
- Scrawl – if tutors cannot read what you have written you won't get any marks.
- Leave the exam early – instead, use the time to check through your answers and make them the best they can be.

MINIMISING EXAMINATION STRESS

The revision skills and examination techniques that we have outlined in this chapter should also be the skills that will lead to a reduction in stress. Some stress is actually quite healthy, as it gives us the impetus to do well, but too much can be a problem (for those of you who have studied some psychology, you might know this as the Yerkes-Dodson law). Human beings are all different but in our competitive world exams seem to provoke anxiety in most students. It is the degree of anxiety that will vary. For most students anxiety levels can easily be reduced by following some simple advice. In some cases, however, more expert advice may be required. Usually your student support/counselling services will have someone who can help with these special cases of serious anxiety. Do not be afraid to ask for help. Look on your university noticeboards, as there are often classes available aimed at helping you have a stress-free examination period. Increasingly, universities provide mindfulness training, which has also been successful in some school settings.

We believe that one of the most important ways to reduce anxiety is to know how to assess your own strengths and weaknesses. When students receive their marked work there is a tendency to focus on the grade rather than on the feedback and advice they are given. There is also a tendency to focus on the grades of their peers. Our advice is to start with yourself. Look at your work and take the advice you are given in the feedback from your lecturers. If you are confused, make an appointment to see your tutor and try to address that confusion. When you are completing your next piece of work ask yourself whether you have taken account of the advice you have been given previously. If not, take another look at it and try to make some improvements. When your next piece of work is returned, compare your mark with your own previous mark. Do not compare yourself with your peers because your starting place is likely to have differed from theirs. If your own marks are improving, even if they are still lower than you had hoped, this is great. You will be surprised how much a shift of focus from competition with your peers to competition with yourself can improve your confidence. Your tutors really do spend a lot of time marking and providing you with advice that will help you improve. Remember: they have been through the processes that you are going through and they know what it is like, so don't be shy about approaching them. They want you to do well. Do your best but don't concern yourself with how you compare with others.

Your university will also provide revision sessions. These are usually really helpful and they can save you hours of individual planning. Any tips that you can get to make the task of doing exams less onerous will have a beneficial effect. We hope you have realised that writing an essay under exam conditions is a skill that you can develop through practice. The more you do, the better you become. So, as we said above, it is a good idea to get hold of old papers and work your way through some questions. Be an active learner; if you know that you are the sort of person who starts off with good intentions but ends up in a room doing not very much, then set yourself some little targets. When you have completed a task, such as planning an answer to an essay question, give yourself a treat. Go out and take your mind off revision, then return to it later. When you return to the task look through your notes and try to identify where your knowledge gaps are. This is a much more meaningful way to revise and therefore the information is more likely to stick.

Finally, it can often be useful to write down the things that cause you stress. Is it the sheer volume of work? Is it the setting that makes you nervous? Are you afraid of being unable to answer a question? Writing down your main anxieties is the first step in alleviating them. For example, if you get overwhelmed by the volume of work you have to do in preparation for exams and assignments, are you trying to read whole books when just a chapter will do? Are you writing too many unnecessary notes when a diagram may do? We hope that by going through the recommendations in this chapter you will be able to identify your own strengths and weaknesses, and thereby become confident examinees.

- Focus on your past successes and learn from your errors.
- Do not neglect your physical well-being: your mind and body work together; eat well, sleep well and exercise.
- Tackle revision in small sections and take regular breaks (think quality not quantity).
- Take advantage of relaxation sessions, mindfulness classes, revision and study skills classes.
- Avoid short-term calming strategies such as over-indulging in alcohol, coffee or chocolate.
- Remember: study skills are not for dummies but for the astute!

Stay focused, follow our guides and breathe deeply ...

NOTES

1 For freely available online mind maps see, for example: https://www.mindmup.com/ or https://bubbl.us/
2 Various online revision timetable tools exist. See, for example: https://getrevising.co.uk/planner or https://mystudylife.com/

Chapter 4

Presentation skills

GOALS OF THIS CHAPTER

At the end of reading this chapter and by completing the online resources that accompany it, you will:

1. be able to plan and prepare effective presentations;
2. have an appreciation of good practice in using visual aids in presentations;
3. understand what the audience and/or marker is likely to be looking for;
4. appreciate the value of developing good presentation skills.

INTRODUCTION

It is likely that at some point during your studies you will be required to give a presentation. You may be asked to give informal presentations during seminar sessions, or more formal presentations as part of your marked assessments. We know that some of you will squirm at the thought of presenting, but please don't be put off; when presenting in most university and academic contexts you are among friends. Developing good presentation skills is also an important life skill: the ability to convey information clearly is important. Developing your presentation skills now will set you in good stead for the future. Presentation skills have become more and more valued in the workplace too. For example, it has become increasingly common for employers to ask candidates to give a presentation as part of an interview and in recent years there has been a substantial shift towards giving presentations online.

It is completely normal to feel nervous about presenting. Proficient public speaking is not a skill that many people naturally possess, but the better you prepare and the more you do it, the better you get and the easier it becomes. Trust us: we have been where you are now!

In this chapter we take you through: planning for your presentation; preparing your content; visual aids; preparing your delivery; dealing with questions; and what the marker is looking for.

DOI: 10.4324/9781032645698-5

PLANNING (DOING YOUR RESEARCH)

In many ways, planning your presentation should be approached in the same way you approach planning an essay. If it has been a while since you read Chapter 1 of this book (writing skills and essay-writing skills), revisit it and think about how the lessons we consider there also apply to planning a presentation.

> ### FROM CHAPTER 1: WHAT IS THE QUESTION ASKING YOU TO DO?
>
> Before you begin to write, you must ensure that you are clear about what the question is asking you to do. You must also have done enough reading to enable you to answer the question in a logical and coherent fashion. One of the most common reasons for poor grades is the failure to provide a direct answer to the question. It is quite common for students to display a lot of knowledge about a topic without demonstrating the ability to analyse the sources they have used.

Referring back to Chapter 1, consider the following:

- What is the question asking you to do?
- What does the question entail?
- Reading 'smart'.
- Point, Evidence, Explain (PEE).
- Structure.

PREPARING YOUR CONTENT

By this stage you will have done much of your research. Next, you will need to think carefully about exactly what it is you are being asked to do.

- How long do you have?
- What are the assessment criteria?
- Who is the audience?
- What are your aims and objectives?
- How will you signpost your audience?

How long do you have?

You may be asked to choose a topic for your presentation, but often you are given a question to address. Even when you have been given a topic and/or a question to address, there is still a considerable amount for you to consider. For instance, the time allowance you are given is really important. It is never a good idea to try to deliver too much information in a presentation and, to avoid losing marks and receiving negative feedback, you must keep to time.

What are the assessment criteria?

If you are preparing for an assessed presentation, make sure you keep referring back to the assessment criteria. Do this regularly. It's amazing how easy it is to drift off track when preparing a presentation, and it's easier to ensure that you address the criteria as you go along, rather than needing to change things close to the day of the presentation.

Who is the audience?

Knowing who your audience is going to be can really help you prepare. Not only will it help you visualise the day and mentally prepare; knowing who your audience will be should help you pitch the content at the appropriate level. For example, if you are giving a presentation to fellow criminology students then you may be able to take some knowledge about a topic for granted. However, if you are giving a presentation about a criminology topic to students from a different course, you will not be able to assume any prior knowledge.

What are your aims and objectives?

As part of planning and preparing, you need to be clear about what your aims and objectives are. Focusing on the task you have been set, together with the assessment criteria, should inform your thinking about aims and objectives. What information do you need to cover in your presentation to answer the question(s)? What are the key messages you wish to convey to the audience? Take a look at the 'Visual aids' section below for example aims and objectives. These are taken from real student presentations that were prepared as part of the assessment in Box 4.1. Developing clear aims and objectives will help you organise your material in a logical way. Your presentation (just like an essay) should flow logically. There should be an introduction, a middle (which probably discusses key concepts, and critically analyses these) and a conclusion. Refer back to Chapter 1.

How will you signpost your audience?

Whoever your audience is, you need to signpost them through your presentation. By this we mean letting your audience know from the start what your presentation is about, what you will cover in your presentation, and what the key aims of the presentation are. Beginning with a brief overview and concluding with key messages from the presentation are really important in helping your audience follow what you are saying. If you find you are struggling to fit everything you want to cover into the allotted time, cut back some of the main body of your presentation – do not compromise how much signposting and summarising you do.

> ### BOX 4.1　ASSESSMENT EXAMPLE
>
> **Module: Qualitative Research Methods**
>
> **Assessment 1: Oral presentation**
> **Presentation during seminar sessions**
> **Submission date (visual aids):** Day before presentation
> **Weighting:** 30 per cent
> **Length:** 15 minutes per group
>
> **Task**
> The aim of this assessment is to support the development of your research process, and to enable you to critically reflect on your progress to date and development needs. It is hoped that the work you do and feedback you receive will help you in the writing of Assessment Two, the Report.
>
> In groups, students will present a reflective account of their research process and analysis to date, underpinned by the application of theories of interpretative methodology.
>
> You will reflect on the development of your interview guide, the conduct of your interview, transcription and thematic analysis to date. You should consider what challenges you have faced so far, how you have overcome them, and what you need to do next.
>
> Presentation: all members of the group must be actively involved in the presentation delivery
>
> All group members will receive a group mark
>
> We will be organising presentation groups in the first seminar week, so make sure you attend this so that you know who you will be working with. How you present the information is up to your group but you are expected to use a type of visual aid (PowerPoint or equivalent). You will be marked for your individual contribution as well as for how you work as a group. Use the resources on the virtual learning environment (VLE) as a useful starting point. Additionally you will each need to source at least two journal articles (found independently, not provided in the module resources) as evidence to support your presentation.

You must work as a group to select different articles and ensure that you are all making a different contribution to the overall presentation.

What to submit

- You will need to submit all slides relating to the group presentation. This must include a reference list detailing the independently sourced articles.

Slides should be submitted online (to the VLE) the day before your presentation (at the latest).

Assessment criteria

Your presentation will be marked based on the following criteria:

- *Academic content*: your ability to demonstrate understanding of the subject, evidence of thorough research, clear and concise arguments, using relevant and appropriate sources, and presentation structure.
- *Presentation style*: this reflects your ability to communicate your ideas to an audience, successful use of visual aids, and your ability to capture and maintain interest.
- *Personal qualities*: this element reflects your engagement with the audience and how you respond to questions.

The presentation is used to assess:

- Your understanding and application of research theory to your research topic.
- Evidence and understanding of the analysis of your interview data.
- Critical reflection on the research process to date.

STUDENT TASK

Read the assessment task in Box 4.1.

- How long do you have?
- What are the assessment criteria?
- Who is the audience?

VISUAL AIDS

Good visual aids can really enhance a presentation. It is helpful for your audience to see some of the key information you are discussing in your presentation, and visual aids should exist to help the audience follow the structure of your argument. We tend to use PowerPoint slides, but other good presentation software exists. For example, *Canva* is a graphic design platform that can also be used for presentations. It is less common now to give out handouts.

Think about your own experiences of watching presentations, or even being in lectures. Most people struggle to engage with too many visual aids, or visual aids that cram in too much information. Look at the two examples in Figure 4.1. What do you think of them?

These slides were developed by two different groups of students as part of the assessment outlined in Box 4.1.

Figure 4.1 (a) Example visual aid.

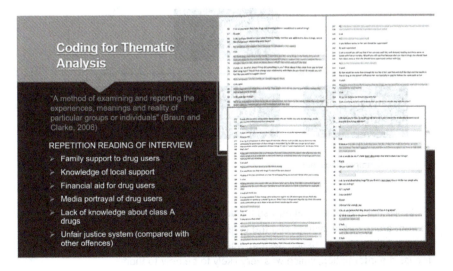

Figure 4.1 (b) Example visual aid.

Both of the slides are trying to do something similar: provide information about the themes the students elicited from coding the interview data. The first slide (Figure 4.1(a)) gives a succinct list of key themes, which the speakers then elaborated. In the second slide (Figure 4.1(b)), the speakers have tried to give an indication of the themes and also an insight into the coding process. Could there be a different way to present this information so the audience could more easily engage with it? The second slide provides a lot of information, making it challenging for the audience to digest it and listen to the speaker. It is also likely that the audience will not actually be able to physically see all of the words on this second slide unless the screen is very large. Slides should be clear and simple, and allow the speaker to talk around them.

It can also be helpful to provide visual aids to help explain complex points. Images or diagrams can be really useful here. Images can also be a good way of showing something that cannot be easily explained.

The slide in Figure 4.2 is taken from a talk given by one of the authors of this book, where she explained the structure of the criminal justice system in England and Wales to a group of criminologists in the United States.

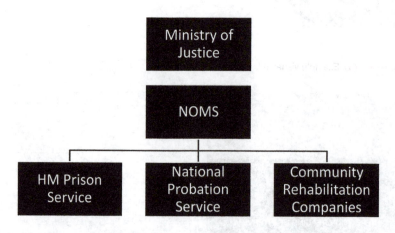

Figure 4.2 Example visual aid.

While not the most exciting visual aid, the diagram does clearly demonstrate the different areas of the system and the connections between them. Laura was able to talk about the criminal justice system while showing the slide to help the audience process the information, which was very likely to be new to them.

The slide shown in Figure 4.3 is taken from a talk Laura gave to a group of criminologists in the UK in 2023. Laura was discussing research she had conducted with a music programme run by a local Youth Justice Service. Laura could assume this audience had a good level of underlying knowledge about the UK criminal justice system, but that they would be unfamiliar with music programmes. Providing images enabled the audience to visualise the project and connect with the ideas being discussed.

Figure 4.3 Example visual aid.

Note that you must be aware of copyright issues when including images in talks. University libraries are often a useful source of information on copyright.

Earlier in this chapter we talked about signposting your audience (telling them what your talk will do, what you will discuss next and summarising what you have said) and being clear about your aims and objectives. You can do this in a number of ways, but beginning with an overview slide is an excellent idea. Take a look at the examples shown in Figures 4.4 and 4.5.

These examples allow the audience to understand what the presentation is going to cover.

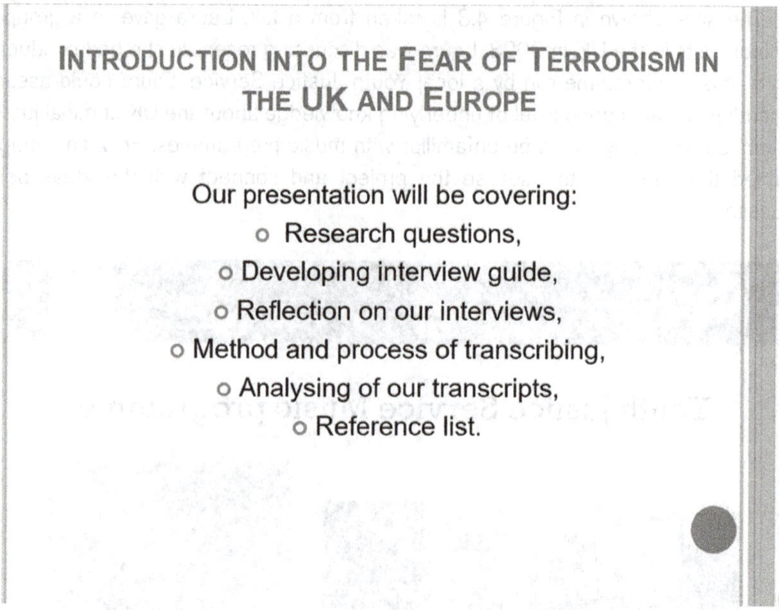

> **INTRODUCTION INTO THE FEAR OF TERRORISM IN THE UK AND EUROPE**
>
> Our presentation will be covering:
> - Research questions,
> - Developing interview guide,
> - Reflection on our interviews,
> - Method and process of transcribing,
> - Analysing of our transcripts,
> - Reference list.

Figure 4.4 Example visual aid.

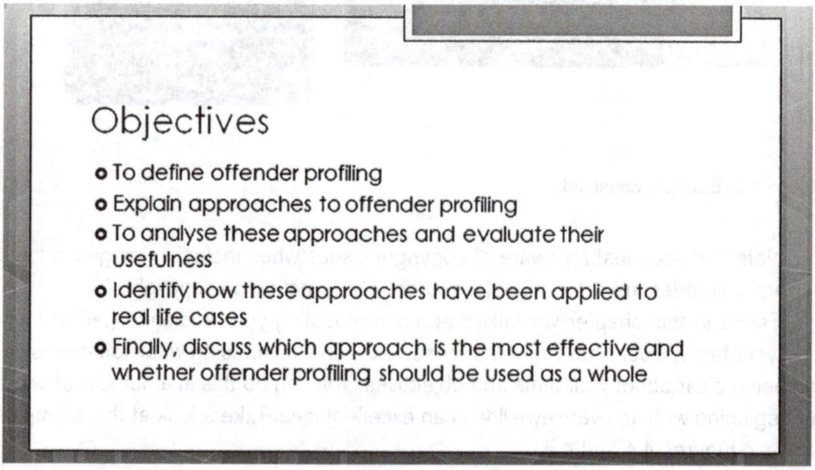

> ## Objectives
> - To define offender profiling
> - Explain approaches to offender profiling
> - To analyse these approaches and evaluate their usefulness
> - Identify how these approaches have been applied to real life cases
> - Finally, discuss which approach is the most effective and whether offender profiling should be used as a whole

Figure 4.5 Example visual aid.

PREPARING YOUR DELIVERY

By this stage you should have a clear idea of what you will cover, a well-structured argument (following our PEE guidance from Chapter 1), how you will introduce and conclude your presentation, and have drafted some visual aids. Hopefully you won't have too many slides, as you will be intending to talk around them and not read directly from them, allowing your audience to process the information on screen as you talk.

BOX 4.2   OUR TOP TEN PRESENTING TIPS

1   Watch and learn
    Attend other presentations and talks and focus on what you think the speaker does well, and what they don't do so well. What can you learn from this?

2   Prepare
    Do your research. Plan your content. Write your talk in full before you begin practising it.

3   Practice, practice, practice!
    Practise many times to iron out any parts of your talk that don't flow. Record yourself or practise in front of friends and family. Knowing your material well will help enormously with any nerves.

4   Don't try to cover too much material
    This applies to what you say and to any visual aids you use.

5   Keep your visual aids simple
    Remember: less is more. Your audience wants to listen to you, not read from a screen. While you might read a quote or key point from the screen, reading from your slides is best avoided.

6   Signpost your audience
    Start by explaining what are you going to cover today and what your audience should expect.

7   Use notes
    We don't recommend reading from a script, but neither do we recommend attempting to present without any notes at all. Flash cards with keywords are useful to help keep you on track.

8   Face your audience
    If there is a screen behind you, avoid turning to face it. If you don't want to look directly at your audience, focus your eyes on the back of the room.

9 Remember that your audience is supportive and sympathetic
   Most people feel nervous about public speaking. If your nerves show, your audience is more likely to feel respect for your courage, rather than view your nerves negatively.

10 Remember to breathe and take pauses when you need to
   This will help you pace your presentation. Having some water with you is a must.

Now you are ready to practise your presentation. If you can, it's a good idea to check out the room you are going to present in so that you can visualise the setting as you practise. Think of this stage as a dress rehearsal. Stand up and practise your presentation in full and do this many times. If you can get friends, fellow students and/or family to act as a mock audience, then so much the better. You will already have a clear structure, including introductory and conclusion elements, but don't forget to practise the transition between points. Think back to Chapter 1 where we talked about how to link paragraphs. You can apply the same principles here. The more you practise, the better you know your content, the more confident you become, and the better your presentation will go.

When thinking about timing, it is worth noting that nerves often make us talk a little faster. Be aware of this when planning and practising your presentation. Slow down and breathe – you and your audience will benefit from this. One thing we have seen students do over and over again is to forget to face the audience. It may sound odd, but when you have visual aids behind you it is easy to turn around to look at them or point to them, and then forget to turn back in full to your audience. Practise, and getting feedback from a mock audience, should help you avoid this.

The final piece of advice we have for you is to think about any notes you will have with you in your presentation. Some people write out a full script and read from this. Some people learn their entire presentation and don't use any notes at all. We recommend a mid-ground. Writing your presentation in full can be a really good idea, but we then suggest that as you begin to practise you transfer certain key points to notes pages or flash cards. We like to go into a presentation with a few flash cards that highlight the key points we are going to make. This will help keep you on track should you forget what comes next, and just having the notes there will help you feel more confident.

All of this has built up to the actual delivery of your presentation. The aim is that you will clearly communicate relevant and appropriate information to your audience. Good luck!

PRESENTING ONLINE

Much of the information in this chapter relates to presenting face-to-face or online. It is likely that if you are delivering a presentation as part of your course, you will be asked to do so in person. However, in most work and professional settings, being able to present online is now a key skill. Our advice is to undertake exactly the same planning process as a face-to-face presentation, but with these additional considerations:

- While giving an in-person presentation we suggest sticking to a few key slides; for online presentations you might want some additional content. This is because the audience won't have you to look at in the same way, as the screen will fill most of their view. The slides need to be engaging and not too full. Remember to ensure the audience has time to process what is on screen while also processing what you are saying.
- Practise, practise, practise! This applies just as much as it does to an in-person presentation, but when presenting online you should also ensure that you practise with the technology too. If using a platform like Microsoft Teams or Zoom, make sure you can share your screen to show your slides. The audience is unlikely to mind if you have some technical issues but it is likely to add to your stress levels. If giving a mock presentation to friends, family or other students, do so using the platform you'll be using in the real thing.
- As we have discussed earlier in this chapter, we recommend having notes to keep you on track during your presentation. When presenting online, we have noticed a tendency for people to present from scripts. This works much better online as long as you have practised your delivery well to ensure that it is engaging.

QUESTIONS

Most presentations end with the opportunity for the audience to ask questions. The sense of relief at having completed your presentation can quickly be replaced by some anxiety at not having control over the questions that may be asked. If you know your topic, remember to breathe and relax, and listen carefully to the question, then you will almost certainly be fine. Also remember that it is all right to admit that you don't know the answer, and better to admit this than to pretend otherwise. You should take time to think about your answer, and if you need to ask for the question to be repeated, then do so.

WHAT THE MARKER IS LOOKING FOR

The information below is a summary of what we (as markers of student presentations) look for. This also captures the things that an audience is likely to be looking for when listening to a presentation, and is what you should think about when preparing and practising your presentation. When practising your presentation, you could ask your mock audience to give you feedback on these points.

Website Instructor resource

Presentation mark sheet

ACADEMIC CONTENT

- Presentation well structured.
- Clear knowledge and understanding of the subject.
- Evidence of thorough research and preparation.
- Arguments clear and concise.
- Key points emphasised.
- Used relevant and appropriate academic materials.

PRESENTATION STYLE

- Presented at a steady pace.
- Voice clearly audible to the whole class.
- Captured my interest.
- Maintained my interest.
- Good communication of ideas.
- Good organisation.
- Enthusiasm shown for the subject.
- Successful use of visual aids.

PERSONAL QUALITIES

- Overcame nervousness.
- Responded well to questions.
- Engaged with the audience.

PART II
The importance of criminological research

Chapter 5

The context of criminological research
Power, knowledge, politics and values

GOALS OF THIS CHAPTER

At the end of reading this chapter and by completing the online resources that accompany it, you will be able to:

1. understand the relationship between the context and processes of research;
2. identify some of the constraints that affect the process of research;
3. interrogate the relationship between power and knowledge;
4. begin to explore the role of values in criminological research.

OVERVIEW

- The research process may be limited by external social, economic and political factors, which can constrain the limits of any given research project.
- Beginning researchers need to be mindful of the sorts of issues that can make the task of doing research difficult, such as gaining access to a research setting, obtaining sufficient funds and convincing the fund holders that their research is worthwhile.
- Alongside the external factors it is also important to consider how researchers' own social and cultural backgrounds, as well as their positions within any given organisation, may be of significance when it comes to the questions asked, the process of data gathering, the interpretation of the data and indeed when it comes to the ways in which the findings are received.
- For those who are new to criminological research it is common to assume that researchers do not bring values and preconceptions to the research process. Indeed, it is likely that given the status and **common-sense** understandings of science in our society (as we will see in Chapter 6), most people who are new to research will have the understandable but rather naive view that it is possible to carry out research without having to consider values at all.
- For the above reasons this chapter seeks to explain the relationship between power and knowledge in order to reveal the ways in which supposedly neutral research questions are shaped by political (both macro and micro) imperatives and financial constraints.

DOI: 10.4324/9781032645698-7

LEARNING FROM OTHERS

The context within which research takes place will have an impact upon the scope of the research as well as the questions that are asked. For this reason it is important that beginning researchers are taught to examine critically the research of others. Students should be encouraged to think about issues such as: economic and time constraints; the political climate in which research takes place; the imperatives of fund holders; the role of gatekeepers; and power dynamics between researchers and research participants.

There will always be problems associated with time and money at whatever level research takes place. However, for beginners to research, these limitations are especially relevant. It is therefore important that beginners think small. Most students who are starting research are unable to gain access to research funds. The positive aspect of this is that the problem of satisfying the priorities of fund holders is not usually something that impacts upon undergraduates and only impacts upon postgraduate students to a limited degree. This is an advantage for beginning researchers as they are often more free to explore issues that are of interest to themselves rather than to the fund holders. However, because students will experience economic and time constraints it is important to weigh up the merits of different forms of data collection, not only in terms of their ability to answer the research question/s in sufficient detail (see Chapter 10), but also in terms of cost and time and other practical considerations (see Chapter 11). For example, it may be possible to use the internet to access people rather than spend time and money on travelling to interview people in person (see Chapter 12). We also recommend you read Chapters 14 and 15 of this book to review the merits of working with existing, online and social media data sources.

More advanced researchers will have access to funding from four key areas: government departments, research councils, charitable foundations, and criminal justice agencies, such as police forces and prisons. While beginners are unlikely to gain funds from these bodies, it is important that early researchers examine different types of research in order to get an idea of the ways in which funders can impact upon the research process. For example, in the UK, Home Office-funded research will be more likely to constrain research questions in order to ensure that the political imperatives of the day are given priority. As King and Wincup (2008: 55) have pointed out, this should be no surprise, and although it is not, as they say, 'a scandal', it is something that should be borne in mind when applying for funding. If the desired end of a piece of research is to challenge policy in some way, then an application to the Home Office for funding may not be the smartest move. Indeed, other academics have gone much further; for example, Walters (2008: 12) has pointed to the wholly frustrating process of conducting Home Office-commissioned research where the Home Office ensures that it will almost always cherry-pick the answer it wants. He sees the research of the Home Office as a means to protect the interests of the government of the day, which, therefore, runs counter to the public good. Thus, while Home Office research is usually of a high quality, it is unlikely to reveal a full picture of crime in our society. Between 2020 and 2025 one of us has been running a large programme of research, funded by the Home Office but devolved to a regional Violence Reduction Unit (VRU), meaning that the decisions about the design of the research programme are taken at a regional level. While we have had more freedom over the research than might have been the case if the funding had been direct from the Home Office, tensions have arisen when we as the research team had different views about the focus from those of the VRU team and we 'had to present a challenge to the VRU at times' (Caulfield et al., 2023: 286). We have written relatively openly about our experiences (see Caulfield et al., 2023) but that does not always feel possible. For all researchers – new and experienced – it is therefore really important to understand how a research project has been funded to contextualise the findings that are presented.

King and Wincup (2008: 55), among many others, are right to spell out the relationship between Home Office research and development and the political party in power. The task of thinking critically about the assumptions that underpin policies is not one that is usually given to those who are in receipt of government funding. The use of closed-circuit television (CCTV) as a form of situational crime prevention is a case in point. Over a number of years this had been the topic of Home Office research, which had been quite costly, yet the results of such research were far from convincing. Fitz-Gibbon and Walklate (2017) and Walklate and Fitz-Gibbon (2023) have presented detailed discussions about the implementation of disclosure schemes which facilitate the sharing of information about people in contact with the criminal justice system, following the specific case of the murder of Clare Wood, a high-profile domestic violence case. The 2017 article examines the consultation period prior to the implementation of 'Clare's Law' in England and Wales and discusses the ways in which the experiences of an individual victim were used to justify the expansion of legislation and Criminal Justice Reform (Fitz-Gibbon and Walklate, 2017: 287). Here what is important is the political will to respond to an issue that is perceived to support 'public opinion'. Importantly, Fitz-Gibbon and Walklate explain that the law already allowed previous convictions to be disclosed where there was 'pressing need in order to prevent further crime' (2017: 288). They cite Kelly and Farthing (2012: 13) in order to draw attention to the need to guard against inappropriate disclosures as well as the possible excessive administrative burden that may undermine the effectiveness of the response of the police. Fitz-Gibbon and Walklate's consideration of the details of the Wood case led them to the conclusion that the changes made under Clare's Law would not have prevented her murder. The Independent Police Complaints Commission drew attention to the particular risks to women who are at the point of leaving violent partners and highlighted the need for 'better risk assessment and case management at the frontline policing stage' (Fitz-Gibbon and Walklate, 2017: 291), neither of which, the authors believe, is addressed by Clare's Law. Their analysis points to the context in which the law has been changed, a period of austerity, and concludes that the Clare's Law disclosure scheme may increase risks to women and therefore that there should be caution about adopting this or a similar policy elsewhere. Walklate and Fitz-Gibbon (2023: 170), reflecting several years after the introduction of disclosure schemes, note that they run 'the risk of encouraging victim blaming which simultaneously denies those potentially already victimised a sense of agency or control over their own lives'. However, it is particularly interesting to note that despite the absence of compelling evidence of the merits of Clare's Law, similar disclosure schemes were nevertheless quickly implemented in other comparable jurisdictions despite the paucity of evidence to support such schemes (e.g. Scotland, Ireland, parts of Canada, and New Zealand). Walklate and Fitz-Gibbon (2023: 166) suggest this 'is arguably illustrative of the wider public expectations associated with increasingly bureaucratised societies led and informed by information'.

In a different context but a similar vein, McAra (2017) and Hamilton (2023) have explored the rise of/return to 'penal populism' in governments in the UK, Europe and the United States. McAra, in her critical review of three phases of policy development in Scotland, points to evidence that 'Ministers will continue to play to populist pressures where this is perceived to have political traction' (2017: 774). She provides an example of the way in which the Cabinet Secretary for Justice decided to transform early release arrangements for long-term prisoners 'in the face of robust research evidence highlighting its likely damaging consequences'. She acknowledges that 'the capacity to shape policy has been determined by the extent to which evidence fits political vision' (McAra, 2017: 774). This leads her to suggest that criminologists should not simply be problem solvers but that they should also raise problems. Hamilton highlights that these issues 'urgently demand criminological attention' (2023: 902) and proposes that criminology is well placed to undertake research that moves beyond a simple critique of penal populism, contributing to a deeper understanding of the rise of authoritarian politics. Murray discusses how the findings of research that challenges political imperatives may be neutralised and undermined. She outlines the findings of a study carried out by the Scottish Centre for Crime and Justice Research on the use of stop and search to illustrate these processes while at the same time providing hope that media can 'act as conduit for critical findings' (Murray, 2017: 2).

> ### BOX 5.1 STUDENT ACTIVITY: POLITICS AND RESEARCH
>
>
> **Website Instructor PowerPoint slides**
>
> Read: Betts, P. (2022) 'Governing the Silence: The Institutionalisation of Evidence-Based Policing in Modern Britain', *Justice Power and Resistance*, 5: 9–27.
>
> 1 What does this article tell you about the ways in which academic research can be constrained, particularly from asking critical questions?
> 2 What does this article reveal about the context in which research takes place?
> 3 What does this article tell you about the relationship between power and knowledge?
>
> Now look at: Fitz-Gibbon, K. and Walklate, S. (2017) 'The Efficacy of Clare's Law in Domestic Violence Law Reform in England and Wales', *Criminology and Criminal Justice*, 17(3): 284–300.

1. Why do you think that the individual case of the murder of Clare Wood led to the introduction of the national domestic violence disclosure scheme in England and Wales?
2. What were the objectives of this scheme? How might the context in which the scheme was developed impact upon the likelihood of those objectives being achieved?

The activities outlined in Box 5.1 should not only enable you to start thinking about the context in which research takes place but they should also have given you an idea of the ways in which policies that have not been entirely successful may continue to attract funding and keep alternative responses off the agenda, which, as Lukes' (2005) work demonstrates, is an important dimension of power. There is a substantial history of government bodies 'cherry-picking' and manipulating research findings to support a particular policy or practice that might be more politically popular. As Murray (2017: 11) illustrates, 'officials sought to explain away stop and search, to reduce police practice to an everyday and non-controversial matter and to quietly push the research out of sight'.

The increasing **marketisation** of our universities is also a significant development that is relevant to our discussion of the context within which research takes place. Increasingly, some researchers may find themselves faced with the moral dilemma of whether to carry out 'safe' research that would be likely to attract funding and further their careers or to raise the challenging questions they would really like to answer through their research. Choosing the latter involves some risks insofar as it can be much more difficult to gain funding and public recognition – although we believe it is a risk worth taking in order to challenge the mounting constraints placed upon criminologists (see Hillyard et al., 2004; Currie, 2007). That said, as Murray points out, 'In putting ourselves on the line we may limit our career opportunities or access to professional networks, all of which is felt more acutely in a small country like Scotland, with its close-knit policy and academic circles' (2017: 14). For an interesting discussion see Smith (2012), which, while not directly linked to criminology, raises important issues for those entering the world of academic research.

Gatekeepers

Of course, all funding bodies have a gatekeeper role (gatekeepers are those who control access to the research we wish to carry out) as they are able to make decisions regarding the research topics they are or are not willing to support. This means that you will need to be informed about the objectives of these bodies and word applications in ways that marry with those desired outcomes. In all research, funded or small-scale unfunded, it is important to think carefully about the role of gatekeepers as they are part of the network of power relations within which research takes place. Gatekeepers will be concerned about the motives researchers may have in carrying out their research; they will want to know who and what it is for. Gatekeepers are often able to place limits on researchers' access to the people they may wish to interview or observe as part of their research. It is therefore important that you do some preliminary investigations about the agendas of any funding bodies to which you are considering making applications. Depending upon the type of research you wish to carry out, you will encounter gatekeepers not only when you are trying to secure funding but also when you are trying to secure access to participants. You will therefore need to think about how you will establish links with key individuals and build up relationships of trust. As Pole and Lampard (2002: 87) indicate, the relationship between researchers and gatekeepers can be key to the success of a study; therefore it is in the interests of researchers to build good relationships with these people. Gatekeepers who are working within criminal justice settings, for example, in a Youth Offending Team, may well be sensitive if you appear to be critical of their practices. One of our doctoral students, Paula McLean, was recently declined access to prisons to undertake research with black women, whose voices have largely been silenced within the criminal justice system. HM Prisons and Probation Service (HMPPS) did not feel that the proposed research fitted with their priorities. We can draw our own conclusions about why HMPPS, as gatekeepers, did not give approval for this research.

One of us was involved in interviewing social work, educational and police professionals as part of the process of doing a PhD on the ways in which agencies work together in child protection cases. The interviews took place at a time when social workers had been criticised severely by the press, as there had been a series of child abuse scandals during the 1980s. This wider context could not be ignored, as it meant that there was deep distrust of researchers on the part of professionals who were in constant fear of being accused of either acting too soon or too late. It was therefore important that the researcher worked hard to reassure the participants in the research that her purpose was not to find evidence that agencies were failing to work together (the received wisdom from the many reports of inquiries) but rather to gain in-depth data about the complexities of working together. Access to the police was particularly difficult to gain, as the gatekeeper (the Chief Constable in the area under study) would only allow one officer to be interviewed and permission was not granted for the interview to be recorded. While this meant that the data on police practices were very limited indeed, the actions of the gatekeeper also demonstrated the particular power of the police service to shape the knowledge that is produced about policing activities.

Similarly, in a later study, Hill (2007) gained access to young black people who had been in custody through gatekeepers within Youth Offending Teams and other youth organisations. The gatekeepers were professionals who had good working relationships with the young offenders and they provided an important bridge between the researcher and the participants. However, the researcher had to work hard to convince the gatekeepers that the interviews with the young people should not be carried out in the presence of a criminal justice worker and was not always successful in this. Again, this highlights one of the ways in which power and knowledge are intimately linked and it indicates the need for a reflective discussion about these processes in the writing up of research.

Blagden and Pemberton (2010) conducted research on sex offenders in HMP Whatton, which acted as a gatekeeping agency in relation to the research. They note that some researchers experience gatekeepers as obstructive, often using tactics to delay or frustrate the proposed research. While their experience of gatekeepers was largely positive, they were mindful of the way in which the discretion of the gatekeepers could influence which prisoners were identified as participants in the research and which were excluded from the process. It is important to note that research with some of the most vulnerable groups is most likely to be impacted by the discretion of gatekeepers. As Girling (2017: 45) has pointed out, it is in research with children in particular that gatekeepers have control over the research participants and settings. Indeed, it is in research with children that gatekeepers, like all adults, have the most power.

Some research into crime involves gaining access to participants through gatekeepers who themselves have criminal careers. See, for example, Wakeman (2014), whose PhD, *Rethinking Heroin: Use, Addiction and Policy in 'Austerity Britain'*, utilised ethnographic methods (see Chapter 12) and involved the recruitment of a user, 'Ryan', who introduced Wakeman to other users who became participants in the research. While the context of such research differs from the examples given above, there is nonetheless a power relationship which needs to be understood. Just as in the examples above, the gatekeepers who have access to criminal worlds still have the power to define what can and cannot be 'observed' or who can/cannot be interviewed. Although researchers can set agendas and control the foci of research, they are, as Pole and Lampard (2002: 87) have noted, both 'powerful and powerless'. As we will see in Chapter 7, such studies also give rise to ethical debates, which researchers need to think through before they embark upon their empirical research.

Power, protection and power dynamics

As mentioned above, researchers can be viewed as powerful and powerless. Do try to keep in mind that although gatekeepers are able to block research agendas that do not match with those of their organisation, their role often entails an analysis of how far researchers' proposals protect the interests of the proposed participants in their research. For example, it is now well known among social scientists in general that the powerful (usually white) research elites have historically defined those with less power in society as 'problems' without giving any consideration to the different conditions of existence within which many of those so defined live their lives. For example, debates about the right of white academics within social science to carry out work on behalf of the state in black and Latino communities developed during the 1960s in the United States (see Blauner and Wellman, 1998), so they are in no way new; yet the issues that were raised back then continue to surface in the poorest communities in many Western countries where associations are frequently made between rates of crime and 'people of colour'. It is therefore important that those who know and understand what life is like for some of the most excluded groups in society should be given a chance to talk about the 'problem of crime' as they experience it. Earlier in this chapter we mentioned a doctoral student – Paula McLean – who was denied access to prisons to undertake research on the experiences of black women. As a black woman who had experience working in the criminal justice system, Paula felt compelled to undertake research that challenged the absence of black women's voices in the criminal justice policy and research literature. She was able to work around HMPPS as gatekeepers by accessing women who had been released from prison, thereby highlighting their voice and experiences (McLean and Caulfield, 2023; McLean, 2024) and acknowledging the vital importance of ensuring silenced and excluded groups are given the chance to talk about their views and experiences. Some charitable foundations will favour proposals from those who demonstrate their proximity to the issues they wish to research. This is not an issue of bias but rather of balance. This is discussed further in Chapter 6. There has been a relatively recent move to working with community and peer researchers (people drawn from the communities themselves – see Rees et al., 2024) to ensure that research is able to reach different communities in more meaningful ways.

> ### BOX 5.2 LEARNING FROM EXPERIENCE
>
> Take a look at: Borges, G.M., Guerreiro, A. and Conde, L. (2023) 'Stroking Reflexivity into Practice: The Pros and Cons of Resorting to Gatekeepers to Conduct Qualitative Criminological Research', *Journal of Qualitative Criminal Justice & Criminology*, 12(2). https://doi.org/10.21428/88de04a1.31b36875
>
> This article examines the role of researcher reflexivity in overcoming some of the challenges involved in research where gatekeepers control access to participants. It draws on the experiences of two of the authors in two different pieces of sensitive qualitative research within the Portuguese criminal justice system. The first author's study aimed to analyse the reception conditions and integration practices in place for refugees in Portugal. The perceptions of professionals working, directly and indirectly, in the Portuguese asylum system were crucial to this task. The second author's study focused upon the perceptions of professionals from the Portuguese security forces regarding, first, the reasons why men and women joined organised criminal groups and, second, their understanding of these people's roles within those groups.
>
> The field notes of the first and the second authors highlight the complex and changing circumstances resulting from using gatekeepers to access participants for their criminological research. These reflections on the process of research are of importance to future researchers when considering ethical issues and when planning their modes of data gathering and analysis. Thus the issues raised in this article will be pertinent to our discussions in Chapter 7.

> **Questions for new researchers to consider**
>
> 1. In what ways did the reflections on the roles of the gatekeepers discussed in this article help you to identify strategies that are likely to create trust between researchers and powerful gatekeepers?
> 2. What do you think is important about the context in which this research took place?
> 3. Who might feel vulnerable in this kind of research? Why?

The authors of the article discussed in Box 5.2 identify some important issues that arose during the research process that not only affected the participants' willingness to take part but also caused stress and anxiety on the part of the researchers. Their discussion highlights the importance of researcher reflexivity on the whole of the research process as a way of identifying what might have gone wrong with the process. For example, on reflection the defensive behaviour of some participants was seen as a problem arising from the failure of gatekeepers to be clear about the research aims. Ultimately the gatekeepers' ability and willingness to do this rests upon their relationship with the researcher from the start. The authors believe that it is very important for a trusting relationship to develop between researchers and gatekeepers and there must be a concerted effort to be as open as possible about the research process. This means providing as much information as possible in the early stages about the ethical considerations and appropriateness of the methodology to the research aims. However, this openness must be continued throughout the whole of the research process and it is important that researchers demonstrate a willingness to reflect upon each stage of research and their role in it by making detailed field notes through which analysis may be honed and gatekeepers may remain informed. In this way a more professional and trusting relationship is more likely to be developed between researchers and gatekeepers and gatekeepers are more likely to remain on side and engaged.

In both pieces of research discussed in the article the topic areas were of political as well as social significance. In order to carry out such research the researchers needed access to people who would be willing to talk about sensitive information that had the potential to pose threats to the organisations that were dealing with the issues being researched. The researchers would have had to be mindful of the ways in which public concerns may have been impacting upon the political response to the topics being researched. In turn, they would have had to consider the pressures upon the professionals who agreed to be research participants to stay loyal to their organisation's goals as well as the power relationship between themselves and the gatekeepers. As we have discussed earlier in this chapter there are ways in which gatekeepers are able to limit what the identified participants will be able to say. There is thus a relationship between the context of research, the role of the gatekeepers and their relationships with researchers, and the extent to which participants and researchers may feel vulnerable. As we shall see in Chapter 7, this all suggests that ethical issues should remain on a researcher's radar throughout the process of research.

WHOSE VALUES? WHOSE JUDGEMENTS?

Stout, Yates and Williams (2008: 6) argue that as crime is such a political issue criminologists have an ethical duty to 'expose the relationship between governmental agendas and knowledge production'. Therefore consideration of the context of criminological research will inevitably involve engagement with the role of values in the research process. New researchers in the area of criminology need to develop the skill of identifying the values upon which researchers make their judgements about the reasons for crime in society, which will in turn help them to understand how different responses to crime are justified. Once those values are identified then it is possible to assess the strength of the arguments put forward in any given piece of research as well as to consider whether there are other values that may lead to different and perhaps better or more appropriate judgements about these issues. For example, a government that declares the only way to solve the problem of crime in society is to get tough with criminals may be operating with a theory that tough penalties serve to reduce crime by deterring criminals. However, it may be that politicians are responding to a perceived and perhaps media-led public disquiet about a supposed leniency towards criminals. In such a case the overriding value position has nothing to do with deterrence and reducing crime but has more to do with satisfying a more basic desire for retribution.

When considering the first question in Box 5.3 you will need to weigh up the evidence. As Carrabine et al. (2009: 296) have argued, while there is a long history of introducing severe penalties, 'the results are modest at best'. It may also be the case that there are alternatives, such as improving social conditions, that will produce the desired end in a better way. As Lilly, Cullen and Ball (2011: 200–201) put it, 'scaring people straight' overlooks the positive ways in which the conformity needed to reduce crime may be brought about. Those who undertake research into crime have a duty to consider alternatives and to raise critical questions about what we take for granted – not least because harsh penalties are costly.

BOX 5.3   IDENTIFYING VALUE POSITIONS

1. Do you think that harsher penalties are the most effective way to deter criminals?
2. Do you think that victims of crime are happier when offenders receive harsh sentences?
3. What are the sorts of crimes that are likely to create victims who are seriously harmed?
4. Are all crimes that result in serious harm responded to with harsh penalties?
5. Make a list of the reasons for your answers to these questions.

Your answers to the questions in Box 5.3 will reveal much about your own experiences as well as the extent of your studies on crime. If you think that going to prison, for example, is one of the worst things that can happen, then you might think that all people will think in the same way and therefore assume that prison is likely to be a good deterrent. However, if you have experienced prison in some way, directly or indirectly, you may be aware that these things are much less straightforward than they first appear. Similarly, if you have never been a victim of crime, or have little knowledge of victim perspectives, you may well think that a good reason for having tough penalties is to satisfy victims. When you begin to think about the answers to questions 3 and 4 in Box 5.3, the extent of your knowledge about crime and victimisation will come into play. For those of you who are already aware that not only do victims of corporate crime exceed those of conventional crimes but also that the offenders are much less likely to receive harsh punishments, it is likely that you may already be starting to ask questions about the circumstances in which politicians advocate harsh punishments. The severity of the punishment does not seem to follow the extent of harm when we consider that the numbers of people who die or are injured as a result of corporate offences far exceed those who are killed or injured as a result of 'conventional' crime. Gaining awareness of the different ways in which various groups of offenders and victims are constructed will provide you with the tools to go beyond ideas that at first sight appear to be 'common sense' and therefore 'self-evidently' sensible. Research in the areas of corporate crime and victimisation reveal that the interests of those with the most power (corporations) are often put before the interests of the victims, who in the case of these types of crime are often among the most disadvantaged in society (Tombs and Whyte, 2006).

Our understanding of the relationship between power, knowledge, politics and values would not be complete without an examination of the role official statistics play in our thinking about crime. In Britain the Home Office is the source of this important but, as we shall see, questionable information.

BOX 5.4 OFFICIAL KNOWLEDGE ABOUT CRIME: KEY QUESTIONS

1. How far do you think official crime statistics tell us the 'truth' about crime?
2. Are all crimes reported?
3. Do all reported crimes become official statistics?
4. Are all crimes recorded in the same way?
5. How would you explain the over-representation of some groups of people in prison?

Website Instructor PowerPoint slides

Hidden victims and the politics of crime research

When criminologists begin to raise questions about official crime statistics it becomes clear that they do not provide us with either a valid or reliable picture of crime (May, 2001; Carrabine et al., 2009; Savage, 2024). Before a criminal act becomes an officially recorded statistic, a series of processes has to be completed, starting with the reporting of a crime. There are many reasons why crimes are not reported, ranging from the failure of a victim to realise that a crime has taken place through to a lack of trust in the police. Even if a crime is reported it may not become a statistic for a variety of reasons, such as the discretion of police or indeed because of discriminatory practices. It is not the purpose of this chapter to examine these processes in any detail but rather to alert you to the reasons why researchers should treat statistics with some caution. Indeed, it could be argued that official statistics can never tell us the 'facts' about crime but rather that they can tell us a great deal about who is most likely to be defined as a criminal. As May (2001: 86–87) suggests, statistics are not independent of those who compile them, yet once a crime becomes a statistic a view of the world is generated that can be misleading and self-perpetuating. For example, if more black males are imprisoned for street crimes, the result of this can be that people understand this as an indicator of black males' greater propensity to commit such crimes when in fact the fear that the statistics generate may have led to increased reporting and increased policing of certain areas.

In recent years governments have taken an 'evidence-based' statistical approach to the study of crime within a performance target culture. Many of those who are concerned about crime and its impact upon society will want to do more than this by considering the complex and varying circumstances within which crimes take place. This has always been so within academic criminology. However, recent changes to the context of academic research have had the effect of relegating the role of theory to a subordinate position. As Tierney (2010: 330) has noted, a number of criminologists have pointed to this shift away from criminological theory and to the narrowing of the focus of criminological research. Indeed, it has been noted that there have been complaints that academic criminology has had little impact upon policy, although it is clear from Tierney's own historical account of the relationship between policy and research that the research that does impact policy is likely to be that which reflects the political imperatives of the time. This does not mean that all is lost, and there is currently a rising commitment to public criminology (Tierney 2010: 330–331) which aims to impact the way public opinion about crime is formed. However, it is not easy for academics to swim against the political tide, and Tierney cites Currie (2007), who articulates the powerful *disincentives* (Currie's emphasis) to raising public awareness through research that takes place within university research settings. As we have already shown in this chapter, academics may find it hard to challenge the politics of the day and may even be damaged by their efforts to do so because in order to gain their reputations as researchers they are reliant upon funding from bodies that have political allegiances.

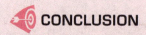

CONCLUSION

The processes of doing research are embroiled in relations of power, which should begin to alert us to the fallacy of notions of neutrality that surround debates about research. To say that there is a relationship between power and knowledge is not the same as saying that all knowledge produced within relationships of power should be dismissed. Rather, recognition of power/knowledge relationships should enable researchers to identify the ways in which issues are defined and in whose interests; it should enable researchers to question why some issues are given high priority (for example, street crime) and why others are consistently marginalised (for example, domestic violence or corporate crimes). Researchers must ask searching questions about the reasons why some important theorising is ignored. Is it necessarily because the evidence is weak? Or is there more to it? While there have been concerted efforts to take reports of domestic violence more seriously over recent years, there has been a simultaneous failure to address the problem. The fact that about two women per week are still killed in Britain at the hands of men is a poor reflection on our society and should be a source of some shame, yet this is not something that hits the headlines in a big way. Furthermore, the women who are often at the greatest risk are those whose partners or ex-partners have recently been released from prison. It is therefore not unreasonable to suggest that prison may not be the most appropriate response, or at least not the only response, that is needed to challenge this type of violence more generally.

The social location of researchers may serve to either increase or decrease the likelihood of being taken seriously by those who have the power to define 'the problem of crime'. For example, the issue of the way in which racial stereotypes are reproduced in political debates about crime can be explained by considering the ways in which the opinions of some researchers come to be seen as 'neutral' while those of other researchers are perceived to be 'biased' simply by virtue of the fact that they are put forward by a person who belongs to a minority group. In other words, it is important to understand how the views of those who have most power come to be perceived as 'normal' or even as representative of everyone in society, rather than of one group with one perspective among many.

 KEY LEARNING POINTS

- When assessing the research of others and planning your own research, you must be able to interrogate 'common sense'. In particular you should be able to identify the ways in which 'common sense' is constructed in media reporting about crime, as this often forms part of the contextual backdrop to policy research.
- You need to learn how to judge the strength of evidence that is presented to the public. When a crime has been committed there is often a sense of moral outrage that is frequently fuelled by the media. Politicians will want

- to be seen to be responding to such outrage and they are quite likely to support harsh and inappropriate responses to crime in such circumstances.
- It is your job as a researcher of crime to be mindful of the social processes outlined above and to identify, test out and question the theories that underpin responses to crime in society. Learning to critique the work of others (and by this is meant an assessment of the strengths and limitations of research) is an important first step in the process of doing research.
- Statistical evidence about crime rates is often the main way by which people are convinced that changes need to be made – yet many people are unable to assess statistical information and instead accept it in an uncritical way. Beginning researchers in criminology therefore need to be taught very early on how to raise important questions about the statistical information that often informs crime policy.
- Researchers should think carefully about where they will apply for funding, whether the questions they are asking are likely to be met with disapproval, and indeed whether they are sufficiently informed about their topic of concern to be considered the most appropriate person to carry out the research. When reading research publications, it is our job as researchers to consider how that research was funded and how that might contextualise the findings we see presented.
- Funders and the gatekeepers of research have the power to decide who should do what, where. They can promote the theories that are in keeping with their macro- and/or micro-political agendas as well as keep important issues off the agenda. Therefore a good strategy for all those researching crime is to assess the extent to which the ideals of the funding bodies match with their own theoretical assumptions. This means researching the agendas of the funding bodies before putting in applications. It will also be important to think through the feedback provided with unsuccessful applications in order to save time and energy in the future.

KNOWLEDGE CHECK

1. Why is it important that researchers understand the context in which their research is to take place?
2. Why is it important to understand the role of gatekeepers in the production of knowledge?
3. What other factors might constrain the processes of research?

REFERENCES

Betts, P. (2022) 'Governing the Silence: The Institutionalisation of Evidence-based Policing in Modern Britain', *Justice Power and Resistance*, 5: 9–27.

Blagden, N. and Pemberton, S. (2010) 'The Challenge in Conducting Qualitative Research with Convicted Sex Offenders', *Howard Journal of Criminal Justice*, 49(3): 269–281.

Blauner, R. and Wellman, D. (1998) 'Toward the Decolonization of Research', in J.A. Ladner (ed.) *The Death of White Sociology: Essays on Race and Culture*, Baltimore, MD: Black Classic Press.

Borges, G.M., Guerreiro, A. and Conde, L. (2023) 'Stroking Reflexivity into Practice: The Pros and Cons of Resorting to Gatekeepers to Conduct Qualitative Criminological Research', *Journal of Qualitative Criminal Justice & Criminology*, 12(2). https://doi.org/10.21428/88de04a1.31b36875

Carrabine, E., Lee, M., South, N., Cox, P. and Plummer, K. (2009) *Criminology: A Sociological Introduction*, London: Routledge.

Caulfield, L.S., Quigg. Z., Timpson, H., Wilson, S., and Adams-Quackenbush, N. (2023). Reflections on Good Practice in Evaluating Violence Reduction Units: Experiences from Across England and Wales. *Evaluation*, 29(3): 276–295.

Currie, E. (2007) 'Against Marginality: Arguments for a Public Criminology', *Theoretical Criminology*, 11(2): 175–190.

Fitz-Gibbon, K. and Walklate, S. (2017) 'The Efficacy of Clare's Law in Domestic Violence Law Reform in England and Wales', *Criminology and Criminal Justice*, 17(3): 284–300.

Girling, E. (2017) 'Doing Research with Children', in M. Cowburn, L. Gelsthorpe and A. Wahidin (eds) *Research Ethics in Criminology*, London: Routledge.

Hamilton, C. (2023) 'Radical Right Populism and the Sociology of Punishment: Towards a Research Agenda', *Punishment & Society*, 25(4): 888–908.

Hill, J. (2007) 'Daring to Dream: Towards an Understanding of Young Black People's Reflections Post-custody', *Youth Justice*, 7(1): 37–51.

Hillyard, P., Sim, J., Tombs, S. and Whyte, D. (2004) 'Leaving a Stain upon the Silence: Contemporary Criminology and the Politics of Dissent', *British Journal of Criminology*, 44(3): 369–390.

Kelly, R. and Farthing, S. (2012) *Liberty's Response to the Home Office Consultation on The Domestic Violence Disclosure Scheme*, London: Liberty.

King, R.D. and Wincup, E. (2008) 'The Process of Criminological Research', in R.D. King and E. Wincup (eds) *Doing Research on Crime and Justice*, Oxford: Oxford University Press.

Lilly, J.R., Cullen, F.T. and Ball, R.A. (2011) *Criminological Theory: Context and Consequences*, London: Sage.

Lukes, S. (2005) *Power: A Radical View*, second edition, Basingstoke: Palgrave Macmillan.

May, T. (2001) *Social Research: Issues, Methods and Process*, Buckingham: Open University Press.

McAra, L. (2017) 'Can Criminologists Change The World? Critical Reflections on the Politics, Performance and Effects of Criminal Justice', *British Journal of Criminology*, 57(4): 767–788.

McLean, P. (2024) *Reclaiming the Silenced Voices of Women in the Criminal Justice System*. PhD Thesis. University of Wolverhampton. Unpublished.

McLean, P. and Caulfield, L.S. (2023) 'Conspicuous by Their Absence – Reclaiming the Silenced Voices of Black Women in the Criminal Justice System', *British Journal of Community Justice*, 19: 36–54.

Murray, K. (2017) '"Why Have We Funded this Research?": On Politics, Research and Newsmaking Criminology', *Criminology and Criminal Justice*, 17(3): 1–19.

Pole, C. and Lampard, R. (2002) *Practical Social Investigation: Qualitative and Quantitative Methods in Social Research*, Harlow: Prentice Hall.

Rees, J., Caulfield, L. S., Booth, J., Kanjilal, M., Sojka, B., Spicksley, K., Blamire, J. and Arnull, E. (2024) 'The Opportunities, Challenges, and Rewards of "Community Peer Research": Reflections on Research Practice', *Qualitative Inquiry*. https://doi.org/10.1177/10778004241229789

Savage, J. (2024) *Measuring Violent Crime*, Oxford: Oxford Research Encyclopedia of Criminology.

Smith, K. (2012) 'Fools, Facilitators and Flexians: Academic Identities in Marketised Environments', *Higher Education Quarterly*, 66(2): 155–173.

Stout, B., Yates, J. and Williams, B. (2008) *Applied Criminology*, London: Sage.

Tierney, J. (2010) *Criminology: Theory and Context*, Harlow: Longman.

Tombs, S. and Whyte, D. (2006) 'Corporate Crime', in E. McLaughlin and J. Muncie (eds) *The Sage Dictionary of Criminology*, second edition, London: Sage.

Wakeman, S. (2014) *Rethinking Heroin: Use, Addiction and Policy in 'Austerity Britain'*, PhD thesis, University of Manchester.

Walklate, S. and Fitz-Gibbon, K. (2023) 'Domestic Violence Disclosure Schemes: The Opportunities and Limits of Technology and Information Sharing', in B. Harris and D. Woodlock (eds) *Technology and Domestic and Family Violence: Victimisation, Perpetration and Responses*, London and New York: Routledge, pp. 163–173.

Walters, R. (2008) 'Government Manipulation of Criminological Knowledge and Policies of Deceit', in T. Hope and R. Walters, *Critical Thinking about the Uses of Research*, London: Centre for Crime and Justice Studies.

Chapter 6

The significance of criminological research

Understanding the philosophical roots of our claims to know about crime in society

GOALS OF THIS CHAPTER

At the end of reading this chapter and by completing the online resources that accompany it, you will be able to:

1. identify different ways of producing knowledge about crime;
2. begin to identify the relationship between theories of knowledge (epistemologies), theories of crime and methods;
3. judge the strength of claims 'to know';
4. think critically about crime.

OVERVIEW

- Research on crime can be carried out from within three key traditions.
- These traditions allow us to study crime from a variety of perspectives.
- Crime is a political issue, therefore it does not make sense to claim 'neutrality'.
- Challenging neutrality is not a recipe for 'sloppy' research.
- For the above reasons we consider the importance of becoming a reflexive researcher and of thinking carefully about what is meant by 'objectivity'.
- The lessons from this chapter suggest that researchers need to think carefully about which knowledge claims are accepted, and which are subordinated and on what grounds, in order to challenge the stereotypes associated with stratifications such as ethnicity, gender, age and class.

In Chapter 5 we talked about the role of politics and values in research without mention of the different ways in which philosophical debates within social science in general have been divided on the issue of researcher neutrality. Many of you may well have thought that 'good' researchers must be neutral but you may not have thought about where that idea has come from or why you hold that view. This chapter seeks to ground our advice about how to do good-quality criminological research in a discussion of theories of knowledge (**epistemology**). Theories about the nature of the world in which crimes take place (**ontology**) are also very important to the task of carrying out research, and as you will see as you progress through the book as a whole, these two concepts are interrelated. We will talk about three basic theories of knowledge within which criminologists carry out their work: **positivism**, **interpretivism** and **critical criminological research**. We would include feminist criminological research under the heading of critical criminological research, with the exception of any approach that explains violence in terms of inherent biological differences, because these approaches seek to change the way we think about gendered places in society and hence about the ways we come to understand crime.

Sometimes methodology textbooks dilute debates about research to a binary opposition between interpretivism and positivism, which use, respectively, qualitative and quantitative methods. Other texts explain that the binary opposition between quantitative and qualitative methods hides the more nuanced views of many researchers these days, who use a variety of methods to obtain knowledge about the social world (see Chapter 12 for discussion of the use of mixed-methods). However, we believe that it is important to have a basic understanding of the assumptions that underpin the three key theories of knowledge before beginning research, as, even when researchers mix methods, they need to be clear about the assumptions they are making about the world they are researching and about the best way to carry out that research.

Website Student video

Part 2 values

BOX 6.1   WHAT ARE THE CHARACTERISTICS OF A 'GOOD' PIECE OF RESEARCH?

Use this box to list what you think are the key features of a good piece of research. Return to your answers at the end of the chapter and then again when you have read the whole book. Has your opinion changed?

My notes ...

POSITIVISM

Students who are new to research are likely to have some understanding of what is meant by positivism – even if they are not familiar with the term. Positivism refers to an approach to research which largely copies the approach of science. The key assumptions are that there is a real world 'out there' that can be discovered or known. Since positivists assume that it is possible to treat the social world in the same way as the natural world, then the logical deduction from that premise is that the methods social scientists use should be the same as the methods used by 'natural' scientists. Natural scientists sometimes claim that they begin their research with the collection of 'facts'. Once facts have been collected (e.g. numbers and types of people who commit burglary), then it is assumed that theories can be developed from the facts. For example, if it was observed in many different places at different times that the main characteristic of a burglar was 'thinness', we could keep checking this out until we were sure that we had enough information to convince us that this characteristic is so significant that we could conclude that 'all burglars are thin'. This is what is known as 'the principle of **induction**' (see Chalmers, 2004: 41). Of course, it is easy to see that this is a frivolous example, although early criminologists did try to identify the physical features that were common to criminals (some of you may have heard of Lombroso, for example, who wrote *L'Uomo Delinquente* [Criminal Man] (1876)). However, it may be that successful burglars do need to be reasonably slim and nimble in order to avoid being caught!

Induction involves a process of generalisation from a finite number of observations, which, as the philosopher of science Karl Popper (1980) realised, is based on flawed logic. For one thing, what one person defines as 'thin' may not be the same as another, so this means that in reality it is very difficult to observe in ways that exclude our values. More importantly, no matter how many times we confirm something we cannot really say that we have found 'the truth' because our next observation could always be the one that proves us wrong – the next burglar may be fat! Popper's view of science was therefore that researchers should maximise their chances of being proved wrong by setting up hypotheses and testing them out, rather than trying to gather evidence that confirms their theory. A method that begins with theory (rather than 'facts' or data) is called **deduction**. Popper did not think that we could collect facts that are free from values; we can say that 'facts' are always mediated by our values.

The criteria by which studies carried out in this framework are judged are reliability, representativeness, accuracy and validity (see also Chapter 13). It is assumed that research carried out within this framework can lead us to 'the objective truth' about crime and that it can explain why crimes occur. This approach to research will use quantitative methods, as it is largely concerned with measuring concepts and with **correlations** between variables. It rejects interpretation, as that is considered to be outside of science. This theory of knowledge also tends to take a deterministic approach which fails to acknowledge that human beings can act upon the world and are not simply acted upon. Thus, for example, early biological positivists believed that criminals were born 'bad' and that they could be identified by their features. The implication of this is that criminals cannot change. A small proportion of radical feminists also asserted that men were 'by nature' more violent than women. This led them to the belief that the solution was for women to radically separate themselves from men and take control of reproduction (see Firestone, 1970). This particular feminist perspective would not come under our definition of critical criminological research as this too denies the possibility of change and human agency. We call such assumptions *biological determinism*.

> ### BOX 6.2 KEY TERMS EXPLAINED
>
> **Reliability**: When positivists speak of reliability they are usually referring to the issue of whether the data are collected in the same way each time. In Chapter 5 we suggested that crime statistics are not collected in the same way in all areas. As a simple rule of thumb think about whether you have been given sufficient information about how data were gathered in any given study in order for you to repeat the study in exactly the same way and come up with the same results.
>
> **Representativeness**: This term relates to the issue of how far the data represent the group of people being researched. If researchers wish to generalise across the whole population of children and young people involved in crime in England, for example, it would be no use identifying a large group of 15-year-olds from one locality. Rather it would be necessary to specify what is meant by 'children and young people' (e.g. ages 12–18) and to survey a cross-section from different areas – urban, suburban, rural – and from different class and cultural groups.
>
> **Accuracy**: In order to have confidence in data collected we do need to know that researchers have made an effort to ensure that there are no mistakes in the mode of counting.
>
> **Validity**: In positivism this term refers to the issue of whether the data collected actually measure the concepts being investigated. For example, if you wanted to test the theory that improved lighting in car parks reduced theft you would need to show that you had examined the levels of theft prior to the changes to the lighting and you would need to take into account other factors (for instance, the installation of CCTV cameras) to make valid claims about the benefits of improved lighting.

Some positivists assert that knowledge gained according to the rules of positivism is superior knowledge because it is not tainted by values or opinions. They believe that knowledge so derived can be used to control events in the future. As we will see, and as we have already suggested to some extent in Chapter 5 (think back to those discussions about funding, politics, gatekeepers and power), the claims to superiority are open to question. This does not mean that studies carried out in this framework are not useful but rather that we need to be aware that, just like any other framework, it has limitations.

INTERPRETIVISM

As this name suggests, interpretivists challenge the idea of an objective reality that may be grasped through research. They are more concerned with people's subjective understanding because they assert that the subject matter of the social world is completely different from that of the natural world. Thus their ontological assumptions differ from positivists'. In sociology and social psychology, interpretivists have pointed out that as people are thinking and purposive beings it is entirely inappropriate to treat them as though they are 'things'. At its most extreme this framework asserts that reality can only be understood as consisting of those things of which we are conscious – the logic here being that if we are not conscious of something it does not exist in our experience. However, this extreme position is not held by everyone who works within this framework and we believe that such a position is problematic because things do exist beyond people's consciousness. For example, many of us may have been victims of crimes without knowing that a crime has taken place, such as the dilution of products like fresh juice or alcohol in a restaurant or bar. This sort of thing can happen on a grand scale and not be detected, but it does not mean that it has not happened. A more serious example is rape within marriage, which has only been a crime in England and Wales since 1992; yet women were being raped within marriage prior to that date and just because it was not then defined as a crime does not mean that their suffering was not a reality. However, a strength of the interpretivist approach is its ability to identify such suffering by speaking in depth to people and bringing the issue to light. (We will return to this when we consider the third approach: critical criminology.) Interpretivists have carried out important studies through which criminologists have gained knowledge about the ways in which those who break the law see the world. Some interesting examples are cited in relation to policing, with qualitative studies revealing how police officers become corrupt. Punch (2009: 179–181), for example, concludes from a range of international examples that corrupt cops rationalise their own criminality and construct their victims as deserving of their victimhood – in fact their rationalisations are just like those associated with the 'more usual' suspects. At the time of writing this third edition, this topic feels painfully relevant as a societal problem. Addo (2023: 52) undertook qualitative interviews with street-level Ghanian police officers and concluded that 'police officers adopt various neutralisation techniques to rationalise their involvement in corruption'.

Wakeman (2021: 4) provides a fascinating reflective commentary on his experiences of 'of doing research with people who use drugs, as someone who has a history of using drugs'. Wakeman's (2014: 710–11) autoethnographical insights, gained from his PhD research, enabled him to challenge theories, such as that developed by Becker and Murphy (1988) which depicted heroin users as rational actors who are able to make choices about their drug taking and who have ultimate control over their actions. Some of Wakeman's data actually reveal the irrationality and lack of control of some of the heroin users he observed who, while stating that they were in control and desisting from heroin use, paradoxically exhibited that this was not the case. In a second paper from the study, Wakeman (2015: 586) considers further the notion of drug users as 'rational choosers' to suggest that policy makers may need to take account of the 'cultural-economic order' that surrounds the use of heroin in 'austerity Britain' in order to increase the success of Heroin Assisted Treatment (HAT). It is, Wakeman argues, only by understanding the subjective realities of users' lives that barriers to the successful expansion of HAT may be identified. Writing in 2024, we can say that – despite the evidence base supporting the use of HAT to improve health and social outcomes, particularly for opioid users who have not fared well with traditional treatments (Riley et al., 2023) – England in particular has been slow to implement HAT.

Researchers operating within the interpretivist theory of knowledge contest the notion that knowledge derived from positivist epistemology is superior. Instead they would argue that positivistic knowledge is simply a different kind of knowledge from that gained using qualitative methods. For interpretivists it is important to access the life worlds of those being studied in order to understand the meaning of their actions to them. This seems to us to be quite important if we are to address the issue of crime in society. In an interesting article examining the role of emotion in British Muslim people's responses to counter-terrorism legislation, for example, Ahmed (2015) examines the ways in which emotions such as fear, powerlessness and injustice have the potential to lead to some increasingly marginalised Muslims being vulnerable to radicalisation. Ahmed is simply suggesting that there is something to be gained from examining the role of emotions in this area of criminology, as in other areas. She is also suggesting that given the emotive nature of a 'war on terror' its absence is surprising. Note that Ahmed is modest in her claims about this research and explicitly points out that it provides a 'small step in the direction of developing an understanding of how "war on terror" represents … the emotionality of law' (2015: 557). Ahmed posits a 'vicious cycle' of events following a terrorist attack in which the state (and we might add media) constructions of that attack feed into the terrorism discourse, justify the expansion of state control and increase fear and threats. The marginalisation of those who are perceived to be a threat in turn produces marginalisation, insecurity and helplessness, which in some cases may lead to the view that the only solution is to become a terrorist. Awan and Zempi (2017) also elicited data which suggested that some Muslim people were theorising that the radicalisation of young Muslims could be linked to their experiences of virtual and physical world abuse. They also outline the ways in which victims of these hate crimes become emotionally drained and may suffer from depression, paranoia and general insecurity, which shapes the way they view themselves and their world. Their study, perhaps rather predictably, also identifies the triggers which lead to an increase in hate crimes, these being terrorist attacks or 'national scandals' such as the grooming of young girls in Rotherham (Awan and Zempi, 2017: 369). These findings have been built upon by research across a range of countries and contexts in recent years (e.g. Germany: Grewal and Hamid, 2022; social media: Williams et al., 2019).

> **BOX 6.3   HALF A STORY?**
>
> Hargreaves (2015) has argued that scholars have focused too much on the victimisation and discrimination experienced by Muslims. Take a look at the arguments put forward in 'Half a Story? Missing Perspectives in the Criminological Accounts of British Muslim Communities, Crime and the Criminal Justice System', *British Journal of Criminology*, 55(1): 19–38.
>
> In the light of information gained in Chapter 5 and earlier in this chapter:
>
> 1. Do you agree with Hargreaves' assertion that scholars have focused too much upon the victimisation and discrimination experienced by Muslims in Britain? Why/why not?
> 2. Do you agree that the statistics examined by Hargreaves challenge what he calls the 'dominant narratives'?
> 3. Hargreaves argues that there is a need for a more nuanced criminological picture on this topic. How far do you think his recommendations will achieve this?
> 4. What do you think Hargreaves' recommendations reveal about his own attitude towards criminological research?

It is hard to carry out qualitative studies that are easily repeated. Criminologists who carry out studies within this framework prefer to talk to people in depth or to observe the life worlds of criminals, victims or people who are both criminals and victims. These data do not lend themselves to measurement; therefore it is not appropriate to judge them by the criteria used to judge quantitative data. When the term validity is used in **qualitative research** it does not refer to the issue of how far the researcher has measured what they set out to measure but rather the question of whether the researcher has managed to convey an authentic account from the viewpoint of those being researched and whether the conclusions drawn by the researcher are plausible. Within this perspective the important issue is not so much whether a research participant tells 'the whole truth' but rather how a participant constructs the truth in different circumstances. This can reveal quite a lot about the decision-making processes criminals go through prior to committing a crime. It can also reveal quite a lot about how criminals convince themselves that what they are doing is not wrong. Researchers can increase confidence in their findings if they are able to provide a detailed account of the ways in which their own role as the researcher may have impacted the findings. This is called **reflexivity** (see below).

CRITICAL CRIMINOLOGICAL RESEARCH

Critical criminologists are concerned with examining the ways in which we come to accept the world as it is. This means that the route to knowledge is via theoretical understanding of the mechanisms through which we make sense of our world. If we take the example of marital rape again, a concern of many feminists, it becomes apparent that there was for a long time an uncritical acceptance in society of men's rights to women's bodies once they were married. Without knowledge and understanding of the relations of power through which this view was maintained, the law would not have been changed because the notion of a 'conjugal right' was accepted by both men and women (although not all men and women). It was only after considerable campaigns by feminist writers that the laws in relation to rape were changed. As Oakley (2002) has argued, definitions of crime have largely been formed by middle-class males and, we might add, often in the interests of that same group. One of us (the oldest!) has been shocked in recent years to find that many students were not only unaware of the fact that rape within marriage is a crime but that they were also puzzled by the notion of rape within marriage. This is an indication of the ways in which attitudes can remain untouched long after the legislation has changed. The ways in which these attitudes are formed are therefore of interest to critical researchers who are concerned with the ways in which oppressions are both produced and reproduced in our everyday lives through socialisation processes and media representations, for example. Critical criminologists' ontological position is that the social world is multi-layered and has hidden structures through which oppressive practices are maintained. These structures have real effects on people's lives; therefore research has to expose them in order to bring about change. In Bows and Westmarland's (2017) study on the rape of older people in the UK the researchers sent Freedom of Information requests to all 46 UK police forces in order to discover:

> (1) The total number of recorded rape and sexual assault by penetration offences recorded by the force between 1 January 2009 and 31 December 2013, broken down by year and offence type; and (2) The number of rape and sexual assault offences involving a victim aged 60 or older at the time of the offence, recorded between the same period and again broken down by year and offence type.
>
> (Bows and Westmarland, 2017: 6)

In addition, the researchers required more details with regard to number 2 above; that is, they requested data on the gender of the victim and of the perpetrator, the age of the victim and offender at the time of the offence, the relationship between the offender and the victim, such as stranger, husband, acquaintance, the location where the offence took place, whether the offence was linked to any other offence, and finally whether the perpetrator was known as a serial sex offender. Of the approximately 130 cases of rape and sexual assault on older victims reported annually, 92 per cent of victims were female and the perpetrators were also more likely to be younger than their victims. The majority of the victims also knew the perpetrator as an acquaintance, husband or partner. Of these offences, 54 per cent took place in the victim's home, which included care homes. For our purposes here the important issue is that there has been a gap in the literature with regard to the intersection between gender and age in relation to sexual violence, despite there being feminist literature on the intersections between gender and other stratifications such as class and 'race'. Since the ageing society is largely female, Bows and Westmarland (2017: 13) point out that the need for research on sexual violence against 'older people' should actually take into account the *structured* (our emphasis) position of older women in society. Furthermore, the prevailing ideology that views rape as a biological response by men to young, attractive women may make it difficult for older female victims to perceive what has happened to them as rape. Bows and Westmarland (2017: 13) also note that the language used to describe such crimes is also an issue that should be highlighted; the term 'elder abuse' is gender neutral and therefore serves to hide the existence of such assaults on women; in turn this fails to challenge prevailing attitudes towards older women as 'frigid and asexual'. The study challenges media representations of cases of rape against older women as 'opportunistic' crimes committed in the course of committing a different offence. It also challenges the 'real rape' stereotype which depicts rape as a crime committed by a male stranger against young, attractive women in a public space (Bows and Westmarland, 2017: 14).

In the example above we can see that Bows and Westmarland were able to demonstrate that rape is not just a problem for younger women. In so doing they are able to make the case for the need for policies that support older victims of rape and to make their oppression visible.

Critical criminologists concern themselves with oppressive practices and so their research questions are likely to address issues such as why poor and ethnic minority groups are over-represented in prison; why the crimes of the powerful attract lesser punishments (or perhaps no real punishment at all); and why some victims are denied justice. This means that researchers within this perspective often take a longer, historical approach in order to examine the ways in which society has been organised over time and in whose interests. The ontological position is that reality is constructed in different ways in different times and places (so here they agree with interpretivists), but at the same time they try to show how these constructions have what we might call semi-permanence and how they impact people's lives; that is, these semi-permanent structures have real effects. In this sense there is, according to this view, a reality to discover, as positivists would assert – if for different purposes.

The purpose of critical criminology is to reveal the ways in which economic, political and social structures shape our definitions of crime (see White and Haines, 2004: 203). There is always an acknowledgement of the political and moral dimension to research in this approach; therefore critical criminologists are unashamed to speak up about the values they hold. When researchers are overt about their value position it is possible for others to understand the grounds upon which they make their judgements while remaining free to agree or disagree. Unlike those in the other research traditions which we have discussed, critical criminologists do not fight shy of speaking out about values – the ones they hold as well as those they believe to be problematic. Usually, critical criminological researchers draw a line under the values that produce or reproduce the oppression of those who have the least power in society. This means that research carried out within this framework will focus upon the crimes of the powerful as well as upon those of the less powerful. Critical criminology aims to explain the reasons why different types of crimes are committed within different social contexts and to explain why crimes are responded to differently according to where, when and who has committed them. These explanations serve to provide the justification for radical changes to the ways in which we define and respond to crime with the aim of creating a 'more humane and equal society' (White and Haines, 2004: 211).

BOX 6.4 USING RESEARCH TO INFLUENCE POLICY

With the above examples of differing approaches to research in mind and, in particular with reference to your consideration of the questions in Box 6.3 (Hargreaves, 2015), now read Alizai, H. (2023) 'European Approaches to Stopping Islamophobia Are Inadequate: Lessons for Canadians Combating Anti-Muslim Racism and Hatred', *Journal of Hate Studies*, 18(1): 63–79.

1. What are the key differences in research approach between Hargreaves and Alizai?
2. Are your original thoughts on Hargreaves' work changed by the evidence that is provided by Alizai? Give reasons for your answer, think about why you are/are not convinced.
3. Do you think that Alizai's work helps to provide a more complete picture of Islamophobia? Give reasons for your answer.
4. What do you understand by the view that Islamophobia is a by-product of unequal power relationships?

Website Student quiz

Theories of knowledge

Website Instructor PowerPoint slides

Values and research

BOX 6.5 KEY TERMS EXPLAINED: *EPISTEMOLOGY* AND *ONTOLOGY*

Epistemology is a rather grand way of referring to a theory of knowledge. Social scientists have theorised for many years about the best way to gather knowledge on the social world and in the early days it was thought that social scientists should copy natural scientists. Today it is accepted that there is more than one way to produce knowledge, and criminologists, like all social scientists, have to make decisions about the most appropriate way to obtain knowledge about the issue they wish to research. It is not useful to think about the different theories of knowledge as if they can be ordered from best to worst but instead it is a good idea to think about how each approach can lead to different types of knowledge that can help us gain a fuller understanding of crime in society.

Ontology is another grand term that refers to theorists' assumptions about the nature of the social world and the people in it. It is often defined as referring to the 'nature of being'.

The methods used by critical criminological researchers will reflect the concerns they have and the questions they ask. This means that the quantitative/qualitative split is challenged by this group of researchers in favour of an approach that attempts to break down and offer alternatives for our conceptualisations of and responses to crime. Critical criminological researchers may well combine methods but they will want to go beyond both statistical measures and individual meanings in order to enhance theoretical understanding. Such an approach is always committed to the ontological task of examining the relationship between how people act on the world (agency) to create social structures that appear (but are not totally) immutable. It assumes that positivism and interpretivism as ways of explaining our world are always incomplete.

OBJECTIVITY: THE SECRET WEAPON

In Chapter 5 we alluded to the ways in which notions of value-neutrality tend to be invoked as a way of demonstrating the superiority of some research over others. For researchers who do not carry out their research within a positivist framework it is important that they are able to defend their position when confronted with such comments. Edwards and Sheptycki (2009) have argued that criminologists need to understand both the politics and science of criminology; we believe that it is important to understand the relationship between these two issues, as the invocation of 'science' is often the tool by which knowledge that challenges the status quo is undermined. Positivists talk about objectivity in research but when they use this term they are often also signifying value-neutrality. If objectivity is deemed to be a sign of 'good' research then any research that can be labelled as 'subjective' will, by definition, be 'bad'.

Let us take a wander outside of criminology for a moment in order to borrow an analogy used by Lincoln and Cannella (2004) when considering the ways in which qualitative research in the United States, which aimed to expose inequalities along the lines of class, gender, 'race' and sexual orientation in social life and schooling, was discredited. Their argument begins with recognition of the fact that serious philosophers have discredited the pursuit of objectivity as a key criterion with which to judge social research precisely because objectivity (presumably defined as value-neutrality) is an illusion. However, they argue that despite this the notion of objectivity is used as both a weapon – with which to discredit *qualitative research* – and a shield with which to protect those who claim superiority for their 'objective' scientific research from criticism.

Within social research general debates about the need to challenge sexism and racism in society raised important questions about the ways in which knowledge is produced. In particular, research that aimed to challenge the subordination of women and ethnic minority groups in society asked searching questions regarding whose science dominant knowledge has been based upon. Sandra Harding (1991: 87) grappled with science's 'insistence on its own absolute authority'. She made a strong argument against claims of value freedom by pointing to the consequences of scientific knowledge. She notes that some 'pure scientists' claim to have carried out actions in the name of science in ignorance of their possible consequences, a claim which she sees as evidence of incompetence rather than of 'objectivity'. Harding (1991: 146) states that 'the best as well as the worst of the history of the natural sciences has been shaped by – or, more accurately, constructed through and within – political desires, interests and values'. It is therefore nonsensical to claim that objectivity can be achieved by *eliminating* values. Indeed, Harding implies that if we do not admit to this nonsense then scientists are simply being allowed to abrogate responsibility for whatever follows from their knowledge claims.

Following the insights of the science historian Donna Haraway, Harding explains that the logic of value-free objectivity (which she calls *weak* objectivity) is that the only knowledge which counts is that which is obtained from 'no place at all' (the assumption being that a scientist can be 'every place at once') (Harding 1991: 153), which, she explains, is why Haraway used the phrase 'the God trick'. To put this simply, since we cannot be all-seeing – like God – then we have to come at our research from different angles because we are all situated differently in society. So, the point is that those who have had most power to produce knowledge (historically this has been middle-class white men) have produced knowledge from one angle, which is not wide enough to gain a complete picture of our complex social lives. Therefore, if others with less power are allowed to do research from their angle, then it is possible to build up a more complete picture of this complexity. We think that Alizai's (2023) consideration of Islamophobia provides a good example of work where the values of the writer are clearly identified and in which it is possible to understand how she has made her judgements about the possibilities for better policy solutions.

It is interesting that the association of objectivity with value-neutrality is so strong that some research has been criticised on what we believe are flawed grounds. For example, Claire Alexander (2000) has commented on reactions to her ethnographic study of Asian gangs. She submitted an article about the negative media portrayals of Asian communities in Britain to the *Times Higher Education Supplement (THES)*. The article had been agreed in principle with the editor but because she was late she dropped the article off in person. At this point it became apparent to Claire Alexander that the editor had not thought 'Dr Claire Alexander' would be an Asian woman. After the meeting the editor's view appeared to change and Claire Alexander was informed that her research was 'too subjective' because she was 'too close' to her subject matter. This experience led Alexander to argue for the explicit partiality of the ethnographic voice. She asks why white researchers are not accused of being 'too subjective' when they research white people. She may also have asked why it is assumed that all people who are grouped under one label are assumed to be 'alike' when, if we think carefully about this, we are more likely to acknowledge that there is diversity within as well as between the different groups that we label in society. In the process of writing we wonder how many of you thought that Alizai was 'too close to her subject matter' and whether you might be reassessing that view.

When second-wave feminists of the 1960s, 1970s and 1980s asked 'What is the relationship between power and knowledge?' they were pointing to the fact that white men identified social problems and constructed research questions from their particular perspective. They thought that the knowledge they produced would help solve problems for women not just men. Feminist studies drew attention to the ways in which subjectivity is crucial to the research design because only women can know what it is like to experience gender oppression. Knowledge that is produced from a standpoint is less – not more – distorted than knowledge which tries to erase or deny its partiality. It was, of course, important that white middle-class women were sensitised to the ways in which their claims about women's experiences needed to take account of differences between women – the same tools that had been used to question (white) male-centred knowledge needed to be used to question white female knowledge (see debates in Somekh and Lewin, 2009; you may also want to look at original arguments by Sandra Harding, bell hooks and Patricia Hill Collins). It was as a result of dialogues between different feminists that white middle-class feminists were sensitised to the fact that they could not, and, we would argue, should not, try to speak on behalf of all women. Black women realised that their experiences were not the same as white women's experiences, even if there were some commonalities. In fact sexism was not usually the biggest problem for black women because the effects of racism in their lives often outweighed gender oppression. An illustration of this comes from the literature on the introduction of restorative justice in countries such as New Zealand, Australia and Canada where there are marginalised indigenous people. These studies have shown that Western-style traditional criminal justice systems consistently failed to address the needs of indigenous people whereas the restorative responses within their own communities worked significantly better. However, when it came to issues such as domestic violence it became clear that women could not get justice in either system; in the state systems they were met with racist attitudes but in their own communities the gender inequalities were increased (see Nancarrow, 2006; Cameron, 2006; Daly and Stubbs, 2006). Without research from the perspective of these women such issues would not be identified and therefore would not be addressed.

While the above provides a very over-simplified account of some complex arguments, we hope to have conveyed that objectivity and value-neutrality should be seen as analytically distinct. Harding (1991) calls this *strong* objectivity because it allows researchers to be clear about their standpoint and it also acknowledges that the perspective of the researcher influences the knowledge that is produced. This acknowledgement of the partiality of all research is, of course, discomfiting to those who have used their so-called 'neutral' science as a shield to protect them from critique and as a weapon with which to put down other forms of research. Studies that have aimed to address social problems, such as crime, have often left out the perspectives of the very people about whom they were supposedly concerned.

In the article 'Men Researching Men in Prison: The Challenges for Pro-feminist Research', Cowburn (2007) engages with important epistemological debates which suggest that it is not necessarily the gender (and, we could add, 'race'/ethnicity/age/disability, etc.) of the researcher which is important to the task of uncovering oppressive practices through research but rather it is the *attitude* of the researcher. Not all male researchers behave in oppressive ways towards women and nor do all white researchers behave in ways that oppress black people, although it is fair to say that many do not recognise their oppressive practices. This means that it is not enough to suggest that if research is carried out by a member of an oppressed group then that oppression will automatically be addressed. It is possible that some people who belong to groups whose voices are often subordinated to white males can reproduce their own oppression by failing to take a stand against some issues – and perhaps even by dismissing some issues as 'political correctness gone mad'. One of us has used this article in teaching and has been struck by the failure of some female as well as some male students to take issue with the fact that a senior officer in the prison said he would have to 'smack the bottom' of the female member of staff who allowed Cowburn to go unescorted to the lavatory (Cowburn, 2007: 283). Several students saw this as 'harmless' and said the inclusion of this incident in the article was evidence of 'bias' on the part of the researcher. How might you respond to the inclusion of such an example in research? We believe that such a response reveals the level of acceptance of some oppressive practices in society as well as a general misunderstanding of what is meant by bias. In fact Cowburn goes to great lengths to tell us about the way in which he carried out his research; he is a *reflexive* researcher.

Giri (2022) provides a more detailed and nuanced discussion of the ways in which men can do feminist fieldwork and research. Whilst, like Cowburn, Giri is committed to feminist principles in research, his focus on multiple identities enabled him to reveal the complexities of the power dynamics that surround research. His discussion of his interviews with research participants, such as Jamuna Rana and Radhika, demonstrate the insights gained through what he calls critical self- reflexivity.

BOX 6.6 STUDENT ACTIVITY: CAN MEN CARRY OUT PRO-FEMINIST RESEARCH?

Read Cowburn, M. (2007) 'Men Researching Men in Prison: The Challenges for Pro-feminist Research', *Howard Journal*, 46(3): 276–288.

Note down whether you agree/disagree with Cowburn as you read. Try to jot down the reasons why you agree or disagree.

Now read Giri, K. (2022) 'Can Men Do Feminist Research and Fieldwork?' *International Studies Review* 24(1). https://doi.org/10.1093/isr/viac004

Note down the key concepts introduced by Giri in his discussion of critical self-reflexivity.

1. Do you think that Giri's discussion takes us beyond Cowburn's discussion of reflexivity? If so how?
2. How were Giri's other characteristics, other than being a man, shown to be significant to the process of data gathering?

BOX 6.7 BECOMING A REFLEXIVE RESEARCHER

Recognising values in the work of others is an important element in the process of becoming a good reflexive researcher who has a heightened awareness of their own value positions. In everyday life people make decisions constantly that are shaped by the values they hold, but it is often the case that they are not conscious of where those values come from or even why they are held. Indeed, many people who are not involved in academic research have neither the time nor the inclination to reflect upon the values they hold, so researchers are privileged in this respect. Cowburn provides a detailed account of the way in which he carried out his research, what he assumed, how his values impacted the whole process, and how he made efforts to enable the reader to understand how and why he made his judgements.

Giri's research confirmed his commitment to feminist research principles which also enabled him to take account of 'intersectional identities'. It was through his constant questioning and attention to the multiple factors that produce insider and outsider status that he was able to reveal and sometimes overcome the different power dynamics produced in and through different social assumptions about identity. The notion of critical reflexivity has the end goal of producing better knowledge but, as Giri accepts, this is aways fluid and therefore open to constant questioning.

CAN/SHOULD WHITE PEOPLE DO RESEARCH ON BLACK PEOPLE?

The issues raised by Giri above alert us to the issues of intersectional identities. Just as there are differing views within feminist research about who can study women, so within anti-racist perspectives there are divergent views about who should do research on whom. Many black researchers have noted that being black does not necessarily mean that a researcher will challenge racial oppression. Indeed, an insight from feminism that has been relevant in researching race and racism is that people can reproduce their own oppressions. It is therefore more important that the researcher takes an overtly anti-racist stance (see, for example, Paula McLean's work, introduced in Chapter 5). As Giri's discussion reveals, assumptions about class, cast and education are also important aspects of the relationship between researchers and participants.

The experience of one of us researching black youth in the criminal justice system as part of a team of largely white researchers was problematic because it was difficult to gain access to the research participants (Hill, 2007). Furthermore, a small proportion of the participants displayed an open hostility to academics who were 'making money' from writing about them. It became clear from the data, however, that participants were not necessarily trusting of the black professionals with whom they had come into contact – they described black prison 'screws', for example, as worse than their white counterparts on some occasions. In interpreting such data, it is necessary to consider the ways in which black people may internalise racial oppression as well as the difficulties involved in challenging the received wisdom of those with most power.

BOX 6.8   ASSESSING YOUR UNDERSTANDING

How would you define the term bias?

Cowburn takes the position that if we are to address properly crimes of a sexual nature then we need to challenge sexism in society in general. Would you describe this as bias? Why/why not?

How might sexism impact female victims of rape?

Can you suggest reasons why it may be important to examine the intersections of racism, sexism and ageism when considering the issue of rape?

How do the concepts of intersectionality and critical self-reflexivity help you to consider your own role in the research process?

BOX 6.9   WHAT HAVE WE LEFT OUT?

As you will have gathered, the philosophical roots of criminological research are wide and expansive. It is impossible to cover all of it in a textbook such as this. However, you may also see references to postmodern research in some texts. Therefore, we wish to explain we have omitted detailed discussion of this whilst also giving you some food for thought should you wish to pursue it in the future. Postmodernism is a term which is usually used to refer to a movement that commented on late twentieth-century culture and challenged the over-**determinism** of some Marxist structuralism in the social sciences and notions of truth. It is because of the refusal of postmodernists to arbitrate between competing 'truths' that we do not believe that these perspectives go beyond the insights of interpretivism. Similarly, while postmodernism acknowledges the place of values in research, the assertion that all value positions are equal (see Neuman, 2006: 105) opens the door to oppression. We believe that postmodernism, while raising some important questions, is confusing in that it is characterised by extreme relativism that is simply not helpful when trying to understand and respond to the real problems that result from crime. As Harvey, MacDonald and Hill (2000) note, postmodernists act as sceptics rather than critics. However, we would admit that postmodernism has a radical edge and that this perspective, through both its ontological and epistemological scepticism (see Wheeldon, 2015 and discussion below), has highlighted some important issues. For example, despite the fact that criminology is carried out from a variety of epistemological and ontological positions, it was noted by Dooley (2010) that 'between 1951–2008 only 11% of the field's top peer reviewed outlets were qualitative' (cited in Wheeldon, 2015: 405) and, perhaps surprisingly given the growth of qualitative methods in criminology, this figure remained relatively stable between 2010 and 2019 at 11.3 per cent (Copes et al., 2020). Indeed, Wheeldon (2015) demonstrates that he is particularly concerned about the ways in which many articles are based on statistical manipulations, which fail to acknowledge either the epistemological and ontological assumptions that have been made or the limitations of focusing only upon numeric analysis. The philosophical literature is quite dense and the topic of postmodern pragmatism may therefore be one to which you may wish to return further on in your studies. It is not a topic that we believe to be helpful in the early stages of research.

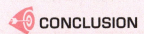

CONCLUSION

We have seen that criminological research may be carried out from within three key philosophical traditions, each of which produces different types of knowledge about our world. Criminology has been dominated by the positivist theory of knowledge but we have tried to show through our discussion of interpretivism and critical criminological research that this theory of knowledge has some significant limitations. This is not to say that positivism is bad and the other research traditions are good (they too have limitations) but rather to highlight the need to study the problem of crime in society from a variety of angles in order to gain a more complete picture of what is going on. Good researchers should be aware of the assumptions they are making and should provide reasons for their line of enquiry. This means that researchers should always take the time to reflect upon the judgements they have made during the process of their research and be prepared to challenge their own preconceptions on the basis of new evidence.

> ### ⭐ KEY LEARNING POINTS
>
> - There is a tendency for beginners to criminological research to take a rather narrow view about how knowledge should be gathered. This reveals quite a lot about the power of scientific discourse in society.
> - Criminological researchers must go beyond common-sense understandings of science in order to gain respect for their knowledge claims.
> - All research will have strengths and limitations; the confidence we have in any research should not depend upon the theory of knowledge that has informed the research but rather on the integrity of the researcher and her/his attention to detail about the research process.
> - It is important to raise questions about the ways in which we define crime in society, since definitions of crime reveal quite a lot about the moral values that underpin the law.
> - If criminological researchers were to put aside their values in the research process then bad laws would not be changed and new ones would not be developed, as, despite appearances, what counts as crime changes over time and from place to place. In other words, there is not total consensus about what is right and what is wrong or about who should be defined as a criminal. This means that it is important to take a critical position but this is not always a necessary condition for research.
> - It is interesting that critical approaches to social research in general and to criminological research in particular are often constructed as 'biased', yet research that blames oppressed groups for their social conditions without taking a look at the impact of wider social structures upon their lives could be said to hide behind a false neutrality.

REFERENCES

Addo, K.O. (2023) 'An Exploratory Study of Police Corruption in Ghana: Why Does it Exist?' *International Criminology*, 3: 52–62. https://doi.org/10.1007/s43576-022-00078-7

Ahmed, S. (2015) 'The Emotionalization of the "War on Terror": Counter-terrorism, Fear, Risk, Insecurity and Helplessness', *Criminology and Criminal Justice*, 15(5): 545–560.

Alexander, C. (2000) *The Asian Gang Ethnicity, Identity, Masculinity*, Oxford: Berg.

Alizai, H. (2023) 'European Approaches to Stopping Islamophobia Are Inadequate: Lessons for Canadians Combating Anti-Muslim Racism and Hatred', *Journal of Hate Studies*, 18(1): 63–79.

Awan, I. and Zempi, I. (2017) 'I Will Blow Your Face Off: Virtual and Physical World Anti-Muslim Hate Crime', *British Journal of Criminology*, 57(2): 362–380.

Becker, G.S. and Murphy, K.M. (1988) 'A Theory of Rational Addiction', *Journal of Political Economy*, 96(4): 675–700.

Bows, H. and Westmarland, N. (2017) 'Rape of Older People in the United Kingdom: Challenging the "Real Rape" Stereotype', *British Journal of Criminology*, 57(1): 1–17.

Cameron, A. (2006) 'Stopping the Violence: Canadian Feminist Debates on Restorative Justice and Intimate Violence', *Theoretical Criminology*, 10(1): 46–96.

Chalmers, A.F. (2004) *What Is This Thing Called Science?*, third edition. Buckingham: Open University Press.

Copes, H. Beaton, B. Ayeni, D. Dabney, D. Tewksbury, R. (2020) 'A Content Analysis of Qualitative Research Published in Top Criminology and Criminal Justice Journals from 2010 to 2019', *American Journal of Criminal Justice*, 45(1): 1060–1079. https://doi.10.1007/s12103-020-09540-6

Cowburn, M. (2007) 'Men Researching Men in Prison: The Challenges for Pro-feminist Research', *Howard Journal*, 46(3): 276–288.

Daly, K. and Stubbs, J. (2006) 'Feminist Engagement with Restorative Justice', *Theoretical Criminology*, 10(1): 9–28.

Edwards, A. and Sheptycki, J. (2009) 'Third Wave Criminology: Guns, Crime and Social Order', *Criminology and Criminal Justice*, 9(3): 379–397.

Firestone, S. (1970) *The Dialectic of Sex: The Case for Feminist Revolution*, New York: William Morrow and Company.

Giri, K. (2022) 'Can Men Do Feminist Research and Fieldwork?' *International Studies Review*, 24(1). https://doi.org/10.1093/isr/viac004

Grewal, S. and Hamid, S. (2022) 'Discrimination, Inclusion, and Anti-System Attitudes among Muslims in Germany', *American Journal of Political Science*, 68(2): 511–528. https://doi.org/10.1111/ajps.12735

Harding, S. (1991) *Whose Science? Whose Knowledge? Thinking from Women's Lives*, Buckingham: Open University Press.

Hargreaves, J. (2015) 'Half a Story? Missing Perspectives in the Criminological Accounts of British Muslim Communities, Crime and the Criminal Justice System', *British Journal of Criminology*, 55(1): 19–38.

Harvey, L., MacDonald, M. and Hill, J. (2000) *Theories and Methods*, London: Hodder and Stoughton.

Hill, J. (2007) 'Daring to Dream: Towards an Understanding of Young Black People's Reflections Post-custody', *Youth Justice*, 7(1): 37–51.

Lincoln, Y.S. and Cannella, G.S. (2004) 'Qualitative Research, Power and the Radical Right', *Qualitative Inquiry*, 10(2): 175–201.

Lombroso, C. (1876) *L'Uomo Delinquente*, fifth edition, Turrin: Bocca.

Nancarrow, H. (2006) 'In Search of Justice for Domestic and Family Violence: Indigenous and Non-indigenous Australian Women's Perspectives', *Theoretical Criminology*, 10(1): 87–106.

Neuman, W.L. (2006) *Social Research Methods*, sixth edition, Boston, MA: Pearson International.

Oakley, A. (2002) *Gender on Planet Earth*, Cambridge: Polity Press.

Popper, K.R. (1980) *The Logic of Scientific Discovery*, tenth impression (revised) edition, London: Unwin Hyman.

Punch, M. (2009) *Police Corruption: Deviance, Accountability and Reform in Policing*, Cullompton: Willan.

Riley, F. Harris, M. Poulter, H. Moore, H. Ahmed, D. Towl, G. Walker, T. (2023) '"*This Is Hardcore*": A Qualitative Study Exploring Service Users' Experiences of Heroin-Assisted Treatment (HAT) in Middlesbrough, England', *Harm Reduction Journal*, 20(66): 1–12. https://doi.org/10.1186/s12954-023-00785-y

Somekh, B. and Lewin, C. (2009) *Research Methods in the Social Sciences*, London: Sage.

Wakeman, S. (2014) 'Fieldwork, Biography and Emotion: Doing Criminological Autoethnography', *British Journal of Criminology*, 54(5): 705–721.

Wakeman, S. (2015) 'Prescribing Heroin for Addiction: Some Untapped Potentials and Unanswered Questions', *Criminology and Criminal Justice*, 15(5): 578–593.

Wakeman, S. (2021) 'Doing Autoethnographic Drugs Research: Some Notes from the Field', *International Journal of Drug Policy*, 98(1): 1–7. https://doi.org/10.1016/j.drugpo.2021.103504

Wheeldon, J. (2015) 'Ontology, Epistemology and Irony: Richard Rorty and Re-imagining Pragmatic Criminology', *Theoretical Criminology*, 19(3): 396–415.

White, R. and Haines, F. (2004) *Crime and Criminology: An Introduction*, third edition, Oxford: Oxford University Press.

Williams, M. Burnap, P. Javed, A. Liu, H. and Ozalp, S. (2019) 'Hate in the Machine: Anti-Black and Anti-Muslim Social Media Posts as Predictors of Offline Racially and Religiously Aggravated Crime', *British Journal of Criminology*, 60(1): 93–117. https://doi.org/10.1093/bjc/azz049

Chapter 7

The ethics of criminological research

GOALS OF THIS CHAPTER

At the end of reading this chapter and by completing the online resources that accompany it, you will:

1. be aware of key ethical principles and of the Codes of Practice of the British Society of Criminology and other related professional associations;
2. be able to understand why it is important to take ethics seriously;
3. be able to identify the different stances on ethics;
4. be able to make judgements about what you consider to be/not to be acceptable practices within the context of criminological research;
5. be able to make wise ethical decisions when carrying out your own research.

OVERVIEW

- Ethical principles have been developed for good reasons.
- Professional associations, such as the British Society of Criminology, provide important ethical guidance with which researchers should make themselves familiar. Researchers must engage with the ethics policies and procedures of their own university.
- However, blind adherence to a set of seemingly neutral principles can sometimes aid the concealment of personal and political motives that may run counter to the interests of research participants, researchers themselves or indeed to public interest in general.
- There are different stances on ethics that reflect the complexities of ethical decision making. Ethical decisions are underpinned by different value positions, so it is up to researchers to think carefully about and discuss their justifications for the conduct of their research process.
- New researchers should have knowledge and understanding of the bases upon which ethical judgements are made in the research of others in order to be better equipped to make the most appropriate ethical judgements themselves.

DOI: 10.4324/9781032645698-9

KEY ETHICAL PRINCIPLES

Since 'ethics is concerned with the attempt to formulate codes and principles of moral behaviour' (May, 2001: 59), it is bound to be underpinned by values about what is good or bad conduct in research.

In previous chapters we have encouraged you to think about the moral dilemmas which face criminologists who wish to carry out the sort of research that may challenge those who hold the most power in society. In this chapter we will encourage you to think about ethics in a similar way. That is, we hope that by the end of the chapter you will not just think of ethics as a set of 'neutral' principles or guidelines that are to be followed in all circumstances, but as a set of principles that are underpinned by values, which are always open to question because the context of research varies.

We begin by outlining the key ethical principles that underpin professional associations' guidance on research ethics. Later in the chapter we will develop a discussion about these key principles through which you will begin to gain more understanding of the complexities of ethical decision making. You can think of these principles in the first instance as a set of rules which should guide your research, but eventually we hope that you will gain a deeper understanding that will enable you to appreciate the different circumstances in which failure to adhere to some principles may be justified. There is an old saying which one of us likes to use: 'Rules are for the guidance of the wise and the observance of the foolish', which seems very pertinent to our discussion of ethics. We hope that you will eventually come to think of ethical principles as wise guidelines rather than as rules that should be followed blindly in all circumstances. However, as the British Sociological Association ethical statement suggests (point 4, page 1), any departures from the main ethical principles should 'be the result of deliberation not ignorance'.

You can find the British Society of Criminology's code of ethics at https://www.britsoccrim.org/ethics/. More detailed guidance may be obtained from the British Sociological Association (www.britsoc.co.uk/media/24310/bsa_statement_of_ethical_practice.pdf), from the British Psychological Society (www.bps.org.uk) and from the Social Research Association (http://the-sra.org.uk/research-ethics/ethics-guidelines/).

In general, criminological researchers must demonstrate that they are competent to carry out their chosen research project; that they have respect for everyone involved in the research process in any way; and that they act responsibly at all times in order to avoid harm to participants, the research community and society in general. The various professional ethical guidance documents for social scientists have converted this general guidance into some clear principles, which are outlined in Table 7.1. However, we stress that new researchers should always discuss ethical considerations with a lecturer/supervisor who will be able to offer guidance and a critical view. While we encourage you to think carefully about the ethical issues to which research gives rise we do not believe that it is appropriate to begin conducting research without having had the ethics of that research considered and approved by the lecturer/supervisor and, where appropriate, the university ethics committee.

Table 7.1 Upholding ethical principles

Principles	How to uphold them
Gain informed consent/avoid deceit	• Provide as much information as is possible about your research to the proposed participants bearing in mind that it might sometimes be appropriate to withhold some information in order to ensure that participants do not change their normal behaviour. • Ask the participants to sign a form which provides proof that they consented to their role in the research process. • Make special provision for children and vulnerable adults – see below. • Do not be coercive. • Think carefully about the relationship between your research question and the methods needed to answer it. If you are unable to answer your research questions using overt methods you will need to weigh up the risks of using covert methods against the benefits to society of the knowledge likely to be produced. • If you decide that deception is your only option then it may be important in situations where the 'subjects' of research could be damaged by the findings to debrief those observed at the end of the data-gathering process.
Maintain confidentiality	• Sign a statement of confidentiality and give it to your participants. • Use pseudonyms. • Be careful about how you store data and destroy them as soon as possible. • Ensure that the data you publish do not help to reveal the identity of your participants (for example by describing the geographical location too precisely or by using a quotation that would facilitate the identity of the setting or key individuals).
Safeguard those involved in/affected by the research – AVOID HARM	• Be aware of relevant laws, e.g. Human Rights Act, Data Protection Act. • Respect internet user agreements. • Provide information about help/support groups in research that is likely to raise sensitive issues. • Make sure that your participants are aware that they may withdraw at any time should the research begin to cause problems for them. • Do not take unnecessary risks that could result in avoidable physical or emotional harm to you, the research participants or the public in general. • Do not try to carry out research that takes you outside of your competence and could therefore bring disrepute to the community of researchers. • Do not accept funding from bodies that have objectives that differ from your own. • Use appropriate research techniques and do not make claims that go beyond your evidence. • Consider how your findings might be used/abused.

TAKING ETHICS SERIOUSLY

We need to take ethics seriously because no research should cause severe harm to human beings. If we are to continue to learn more about the problems that arise in our social world then it is important that researchers do their best to prevent any discredit to research communities. Unsurprisingly, then, the overriding justification that is usually provided for the development of ethical principles is that no one should be harmed by research. This means that, irrespective of the questions asked, it is generally accepted that the human beings taking part in our research come first, even before the pursuit of knowledge, which is at the heart of all science – natural or social. If your research is likely to cause harm of any kind then this should (at least in the first instance) indicate the need to think again. As Bryman (2015: 146) notes, ethical considerations impinge upon all scientific research but particularly in the social sciences.

In order to become an ethical researcher you will need to draw upon your own moral conscience and think about the consequences of the ways in which you are proposing to carry out your research. It will not be possible to second guess every eventuality that may arise in the process of your research at the proposal stage, but taking the time to think through the possible ethical dilemmas as early as possible will at least ensure that any harms are minimal. As we have suggested in earlier chapters, it is a good idea to look at other people's research in order to familiarise yourself with some of the pitfalls which have beset other studies, as this is a good way of avoiding similar mistakes in your own work. Reading about ethical decision making will also clarify your own moral values and thereby allow you to present justifications for the ethical decisions you make in your research.

Taking ethics seriously does not *just* mean making sure that you think about ethics at the planning stage of research. Despite researchers' best efforts, unforeseen ethical dilemmas may arise during the process of conducting research. These dilemmas arise precisely because no matter how hard we try we can never make accurate predictions in advance about human behaviour. Thus when an ethical dilemma arises mid-research the researcher will need to be careful to record the circumstances in which the dilemma arose, the decision she/he took and the justifications for that decision. As noted above, when researchers take the time to reflect upon and record their actions in relation to ethical dilemmas they will be helping new researchers to learn from their experiences.

Criminological research is a particularly thorny area because the issues criminologists wish to research are often highly sensitive and therefore the potential to harm is ever present. So far so good – but all this does beg the question of whether it is always possible to agree on what might constitute harm. Indeed, it may be necessary to construct what we might call a hierarchy of harms because some people may consider that certain (lesser) harms can be justified on the grounds that they reduce the likelihood of more serious harms occurring (or recurring) in the future. This implies that researchers need to be able to think through the consequences of their ethical decisions throughout the whole process of research in order to take account not just of the participants in the research but also of the group/s of people for whom the research is intended as well as the wider population which may be affected by the results. This means that making ethical decisions is a very complex process that, while guided by a set of principles, cannot be dealt with in a rule-bound way which assumes that these principles can be followed in the same way in all times, places and contexts.

BOX 7.1 LEARNING FROM THE PAST: REAL ETHICAL DILEMMAS

Background

Before looking at ethics specifically in criminological research we want to introduce you to a world-famous social scientific study on obedience by Milgram (1963). This study is mentioned in a wide variety of social science research texts because, although it is an old study, it continues to inform debates about ethics in social research.

Milgram chose methods that included deception. The participants in his study believed that their role was to administer electric shocks to other participants in the research ('learners') when they made mistakes. In fact the learners were 'in on the act', so they were not research participants. Nor did they receive electric shocks but they put on an act to convince the real participants that they had.

As a result of your consideration of this study we hope you will be better equipped to discuss and justify your own ethical decisions.

The context of Milgram's research

Milgram was interested to discover the extent to which people would obey an authority figure without question, even in circumstances where obedience would result in obvious harm to another human being. His interest in this topic was in part sparked by the seemingly 'blind obedience' of some German people during World War II who took part in Nazi atrocities.

Milgram made concerted efforts to weigh up the possible adverse effects of his chosen method of research. He sought advice from psychiatrists who were not of the opinion that the participants would be likely to administer the most severe 'shocks'. Milgram therefore decided that the psychological harm to the participants would be minimal. Milgram also ensured that he debriefed his participants and revealed his deceit so that he could minimise the ill-effects to the participants. A psychiatrist also saw the participants a year later and no problems were identified.

The participants' roles

Participants in Milgram's research were told that the study was about the effects of punishment on learning. Their role was to administer 'electric shocks' to learners (who, they were led to believe, were also participants in the research) each time they made a mistake in a given learning activity. The researcher explained to these participants that the shocks were to increase in severity following each mistake. In situations where the learner cried out in 'pain' or complained of a serious medical condition, the researcher ordered the participants to continue with the shocks, which caused the participants to show signs of stress, such as sweating, nail biting or trembling.

While the experiment itself was tension-producing, Milgram was happy that following the full debriefing sessions the ill-effects of the experiment were short-lived. He believed that his experiment was ethically justifiable. What do you think? Try to provide reasons for your answer.

Now take a look at the more recent study by Calvey (2020a). Is Calvey behaving ethically in his covert ethnography?

BOX 7.2   LEARNING FROM RECENT EXPERIENCES: CONSEQUENCES OF BREAKING ETHICS APPROVALS

It is not unheard of for whole research projects to be halted because of violations to ethical approvals. However, it is quite unusual to read about this in published work as getting research published typically relies on projects being successfully completed! Brewster, Bowers and Brooks (2024) provide a fascinating exception to this by sharing an example from a research project they were undertaking in prisons in California, United States. They had approval from each of the universities the team were based at and State of California Institutional Review Boards (IRB – note that ethics and research access approvals follow slightly different processes in the United States from those in the UK and elsewhere. An IRB in the United States is a panel of experts whose role is to oversee the ethical boundaries of research and, particularly, to ensure no human research participants are harmed, much like an ethics panel in a UK university). Brewster and colleagues were undertaking focus groups with people in prison to explore the impact of prison arts:

> Unfortunately, as we were wrapping up our nearly one-and-a-half-year focus-group study, we inadvertently violated IRB protocols when staff at one prison reversed our agreement to maintain the anonymity of participants by demanding to review the recordings. When we reported this to the University of California San Diego IRB, the Board withdrew its approval of our research, and launched a nearly one-year investigation to determine

any negative impact on the participating prisoners. The Board subsequently released their hold on our research, allowing us to continue our analysis of the focus group transcripts. We then notified the state IRB of our protocol violation and the positive outcome of UC San Diego's investigation, but they were unforgiving of our failure to notify them when we first committed the violation and denied our renewal application. This meant we were unable to complete our analysis of the focus group transcripts. Our transcript data was destroyed, and the research team disbanded.

(Brewster et al., 2024: 20)

The original issue had arisen when one prison had requested to have an officer present during the research focus groups. The research sub-team collecting data at that prison said no to the request as that would violate their ethics approvals, but as a compromise did agree to let officers listen to the recordings. The research team then failed to let the prisoner participants know about this change, and therefore the possibility that prison officers could potentially identify them from their voices on the recordings – this was the original violation of the IRB approval. The second issue was only notifying the university IRB and assuming, wrongly, that the university would notify the State IRB. If the researchers had notified the State IRB at the same time as the university IRB they might have been allowed to continue the research. The investigation concluded no harm, but even so they were not allowed to continue. Advice from one of the research team is 'cover all bases, real and imagined!' (Email from Larry Brewster to Laura Caulfield, May 2024).

The above example might seem quite shocking – the whole research project was abandoned after 18 months of work. In this case we suspect political motivations behind the decision and a territorial issue causing the State IRB to feel angry at not being immediately informed. We can't know the answer to this but it does provide us with an insight into the relations of power within which research takes place. It also points to the need to adhere to the strict protocols regarding how data is stored. Ethical violations are, quite rightly, taken very seriously, therefore every effort should be taken to ensure adherence to the agreed protocols. As this case demonstrates, this does not only protect the participants but it also protects the reputations of researchers and the institutions to which they belong.

ETHICAL STANCES (OPENING CANS OF WORMS)

We have already hinted that there is more to ethics than following a set of rules. Having set out key principles and guidelines, we are now going to explain why we believe that researchers should always consider the ethics of each individual piece of research on a case-by-case basis. This is sometimes called situated ethics or **consequentialism**. We prefer the latter term, as it signals the need to consider the consequences of our ethical decisions, a process which allows us to weigh up benefits against harms. We hold this view because we are aware that in some contexts accepted ethical principles can not only serve to prevent the production of important knowledge (see Calvey, 2008, 2020b) but also to maintain the interests of those who are already most powerful in society.

Some methodology textbooks go into long explanations about the different stances on ethics, which can serve to over-complicate the debates for those who are new to research. We prefer to think about a continuum, one end of which represents a universal position, in which it is assumed that the agreed ethical principles should be followed at all times as though they are inviolable rules, while the other end represents a position in which ethical principles can be thrown to the wind in the interests of knowledge production.

We do not believe that either of these positions at the extremes is tenable but, as we have already indicated, rather, we do think that there are contexts in which it may be justifiable to question the merits of some generally agreed ethical principles. Our position is underpinned by the belief that researchers should always be mindful of the consequences of their ethical decisions. We might assume that this is also the position of the largest social research funding council in the UK, the Economic and Social Research Council (ESRC), since its Research Ethics guidance acknowledges that there are situations in which covert observation (a method of data collection which involves deception) may be justified:

> The broad principle should be that covert or deceptive research should not be undertaken lightly or routinely. It is only justified if important issues are being addressed and if matters of social and/or scientific significance are likely to be discovered which cannot be uncovered in other ways.
>
> (ESRC, 2024)

However, we are inclined to agree with Calvey's belief that covert research is stigmatised (2017) because in practice the proliferation of ethics committees, increased fears about risks and the increasing regulation of research have all served to privilege some forms of research over others rather than to alert new researchers to the situations in which any one of the generally agreed ethical principles may need to be questioned. As Carrabine et al. (2009: 42) have asked, 'is a criminologist working within tight ethical codes still able to conduct effective research into closed worlds … such as the closed worlds of child sexual abuse, people trafficking or corporate crime?' We believe that new researchers should be taught to think critically about the contexts in which their research takes place so that they may be enabled to make wise ethical decisions.

Figure 7.1 Ethics continuum.

Informed consent

With the above discussion in mind, we now wish to examine the principle of informed consent. While most research methods do not, at least overtly, challenge this principle, research which relies upon covert observational methods makes the notion of informed consent redundant. As some readers may be aware, much research on crime and 'deviance' has relied upon covert methods. For example, over the years covert observational studies have allowed researchers to reveal, among other things, detailed information about juvenile gangs (Parker, 1974); salesmen on the fiddle (Ditton, 1977); police practices (Holdaway, 1983); crack dealers (Jacobs, 2006); people working in the night-time economy (Calvey, 2020a); and trafficking in body parts (Scheper-Hughes, 2004). Unerring compliance with the principle of informed consent would rule out such research, which, we hope you will agree, would be detrimental to the study of crime. Instead we wish to draw attention to some situations in which we believe adherence to this principle should be maintained while pointing to other situations where we believe the opposite position to be true. Furthermore, we wish to point out that the apparent adherence to the ethical principle of informed consent may serve to obscure the messiness, or what Calvey (2008: 907) calls the 'blurred reality', of fieldwork.

Quantitative techniques of data gathering lend themselves much more readily to the ethical principle of informed consent. In situations where researchers set up experiments in order to try to find out about the limits of human behaviour, for example, if a psychological study aimed to gain deeper understanding of the situations in which human beings will become violent, they may well be able to gain meaningful consent, but if the participants were to be *fully* informed they may change their behaviour and thereby invalidate the experiment. In such circumstances the researcher has to weigh up whether/how far the deceit will result in harm to research participants, researchers or the public interest in general. Beins (2004: 44) states that 'there is good reason to believe that keeping participants ignorant of some aspects of the research has negligible effects on them in general'. Indeed, the ESRC (2024) recognises that there are situations where formal written consent is not necessary. We can deduce from this that there are degrees of deception, the most extreme of which are likely to occur in covert studies. Calvey, whose work we mention in Box 7.1 and above, has written extensively on the use of deception in various forms of social research, and correctly highlights that 'Deception occupies a classic love or loathe position in social research, which often results in extreme and hyper responses from its audiences on both sides' (Calvey, 2020b). Beins (2004) makes a useful distinction between active and passive deception in which the latter is seen as more justifiable, since it does not involve the researcher in telling lies about what is going on (as in Milgram's study, see Box 7.1), but rather it involves withholding some information in order to avoid the problem of research participants changing their normal modes of behaviour (see, for example, Cowburn, 2007). Passive deception can occur in any form of research but it is most likely to occur when qualitative methods, such as in-depth interviewing or overt observation, are utilised. This is the case because in situations where researchers are trying to access the meanings that participants give to their actions and possibly theorise about how these meanings may have come about (say, through consideration of their acceptance of racist or sexist assumptions), revealing the full purpose of their study would very likely compromise the data. Where the research topic suggests that meaningful and useful data could not be gained other than through the use of covert methods, researchers should try as far as possible to weigh up the risks involved in carrying out their chosen study. When this method of data gathering is chosen it is especially important that the researcher should be more acutely aware of the ethical dilemmas that may arise in the process of their research. Furthermore, they should be capable of defending their actions. Note that the most common defence of the use of covert methods relies upon adherence to another ethical principle, confidentiality, which we discuss below.

Website Student video

Part 1 Ethics discussion

BOX 7.3 STUDENT ACTIVITY: INFORMED CONSENT

Take another look at Cowburn's (2007) research on men in prison, to which we referred in Chapter 6.

Consider whether the participants in his research should have been informed about his concern with sexism. Try to provide ethical justifications for your view on this issue. In order to do this you should think about how far the means of research justified the ends and consider the extent to which other important ethical principles have been applied.

Informed consent can only be gained, of course, when the participants are capable of providing it. Researchers therefore need to think about how they will deal with a situation in which the subjects of their research are unable to understand what the research is all about or what the consequences may be for them; that is, special provision must be made to protect the rights of children and vulnerable adults by gaining consent from someone who has their interests at heart. Linda Moore (2011) provides a good discussion of her research with children in custody which outlines some of the difficulties involved in gaining consent from children. Where doubts about a child's ability to give meaningful consent arise she advises that researchers seek the advice of professionals. In our research with children involved in the criminal justice system we actively sought children's consent but also the consent of their youth justice caseworkers (Caulfield et al., 2022). However, Girling (2017: 44) has noted that young people may sometimes be over-researched in fairly narrow policy areas while being neglected beyond the realm of government objectives. This may mean that because, as we noted in Chapter 5, the professionals who are the gatekeepers of research on young people are able to have control over the participants and settings, there is a possibility that important aspects of young people's experiences as victims, offenders or both are excluded from research processes. Girling (2017: 50) identifies the paradox of children being simultaneously ubiquitous and hard to reach. They are hard to reach not because of their own desire to be 'hidden' but 'because of the architecture of gatekeeping, surveillance and control that governs their everyday and institutional lives'. Informed consent constitutes an important aspect of many types of research but there is no doubt that there are situations in which the gaining of consent may render the research ineffective.

> ### BOX 7.4 STUDENT ACTIVITY: COVERT, INVISIBLE, NON-PARTICIPATORY OBSERVATION (Pollock, 2009)
>
> In a world where hatred is promulgated online a space opened up for researchers to investigate typically hard-to-reach deviant subcultures. An interesting example is a large-scale study online by Pollock (2009) into white supremacy and racial hatred put forward by news groups. His description of his role as a covert invisible researcher reflects the ability of online observers to remain 'hidden' in the virtual world of the internet. Putting aside other methodological issues, consider how far a study of this type will need to conform to ethical guidelines.
>
> Pollock, E. (2009) 'Researching White Supremacists On Line: Methodological Concerns of Researching Hate "Speech"', *Internet Journal of Criminology*. Available at www.internetjournalofcriminology.com

Producing an informed consent form

In studies where it is appropriate to gain informed consent, you will need to produce a form which you and your participants should sign. In general your form should include the following:

- the title of your study;
- name/s and contact details of the researchers;
- a clear and concise description of the purpose of your research;
- an outline of the possible benefits or risks of taking part;
- your guarantee of anonymity and confidentiality (note that you will need to remember to store the form safely in order to maintain anonymity);
- your guarantee to respect the participants' rights to withdraw at any time (which you should sign);
- agreement sections which relate to the collection and storage of data.

Some people produce two forms: one which informs the participants and the other a consent form. We think it makes things clearer if the information is on one form, but follow your university's guidance on this point. Most universities will provide students with guidance on producing a consent form. We also recommend that you look at the examples we have provided in the support material.

Website Student guide to ...
Consent forms

Of course, as discussed above, it is possible that your research may involve the participation of children or vulnerable adults. In these circumstances it is not possible to gain their informed consent so you will need to consider who can be approached to give consent on their behalf. Sometimes organisations will have their own rules and procedures, and it is your duty as a researcher to find out what these are and make sure that you follow them. It is also your responsibility to undergo a Disclosure and Barring Service (DBS) check when conducting research with children or vulnerable adults.

Note that as your research progresses you may realise that the original purpose of your study has changed (this is why good researchers keep a reflexive journal or reflective diary so that they can record the reasons for any shifts in purpose or perspective – see Chapter 19). In such circumstances you should consider whether you would need to produce another consent form for your research participants. While **reflexivity** about ethics is seen as a must for those carrying out covert studies, as Calvey (2008: 909) points out, 'covert practices are routinely glossed over in sanitised overt accounts'.

Website Student guide to ...
Informing participants and interview protocols

Confidentiality and anonymity

We have seen above that the principle of informed consent is not applied in a universal way to all research. Where informed consent is obtained, it is usual for the researcher to guarantee confidentiality and anonymity in order to ensure that participants and, where applicable, the organisations to which they belong cannot be harmed as a result of taking part in the research. When using covert methods, a researcher will not have provided any such guarantee but this does not mean that s/he can ignore the issue of confidentiality and anonymity. Indeed, this principle may well be even more important in such circumstances, since the topics of covert research are far more likely to reveal information that could impact negatively the 'subjects' of the research as well as the researchers involved in the study, those who belong to the wider research community and, where applicable, the organisation in which the research is taking place. It is therefore incumbent upon researchers to try to identify as far as possible any situations in which they think confidentiality could be compromised.

The discussions to which the cases in Box 7.5 give rise illustrate the ethical dilemmas which beset social researchers. They also illustrate that the ethical principles with which researchers are encouraged to operate cannot be viewed as a 'one-size-fits-all' way of addressing these dilemmas. It can be seen from these examples that the context of the research must always be at the forefront of the researcher's mind when making ethical decisions. The context of the research is key to the process of ethical decision making. In the first example the methods chosen by the researcher would make no difference to the freely chosen actions of those being observed, as the setting is a public place. In both studies it is safe to assume that the people being observed would be involved in those activities whether the researcher was there or not. Berg (2004: 52) suggests that if the research project itself does not increase or cause risk to the participants then it may be considered ethical. In the second study the researchers are involved in the grey/illegal activities and it could be argued this could bring disrepute to research communities in general. Researchers may decide that research of this nature is not for them, as there may be risks to researchers or their families that they are not prepared to take. This is completely fine but we believe that if decisions were to be taken by ethics committees that some subjects are inappropriate for academic study it would rule out much important research on crime and indeed would serve to maintain inequalities of power.

BOX 7.5 RESEARCHING DRUG MARKETS: CONSIDERING CONFIDENTIALITY, ANONYMITY AND PARTICIPATION

There have been several covert studies in which researchers have recorded their observations of illegal drug supply. Consider these two studies and decide whether the decisions made by the researchers were ethical:

1   One such study, which one of us has often discussed with students, is Sanders' (2005) study of the supply and use of ecstasy in a London nightclub which used the method of covert participant observation. Sanders witnessed bouncers supplying ecstasy to punters in the club – but he was not involved in this activity himself. As this was a covert study there was no formal agreement to maintain confidentiality, although Sanders chose to do so. Was this a good ethical decision? Why/why not?
2   More recently, researchers have begun to use covert methods to study online drug sales. As several States in the United States legalised cannabis, Miller and Miller (2021) used covert participant observation to research cannabis grey markets in Las Vegas, Nevada. While cannabis is legal in Nevada, it is regulated, and an interesting impact of this has been the emergence of grey markets that skirt the line between legal and illegal sales. Miller and Miller conclude that 'grey market marijuana delivery operators ... are simply drug dealers hiding in plain sight' (2021: 1029) yet they purchased cannabis from these operators on multiple occasions. What are the ethical arguments for and against Miller and Miller's participation in these activities? Give reasons for your answer, particularly considering potential risks to the researchers.

In the first study in Box 7.5, the researcher maintained confidentiality and anonymity. However, there is a world of difference between maintaining the confidentiality of someone who is observed breaking the law in public and breaking the confidentiality of a child who has disclosed abuse to a researcher in the process of participating in research. Piper and Simons (2005) discussed the issue of confidentiality in a study on the topic of children harming animals. Their discussion reflects upon a dispute that arose at the steering group phase of the study when the question of what should be done if a child, who had been promised anonymity and confidentiality, disclosed that they harmed animals because they were being abused. Most of the group agreed that in such a case confidentiality should not be maintained. In this case we must look again to the research context; this time the important issue is that the participants are children. It would not be ethical for a researcher to maintain confidentiality when confronted with the disclosure of abuse from a child. This is because any harm that may subsequently come to that child as a result of inaction on the part of the researcher would not be justifiable, since responsible adults who are working with children have a statutory responsibility to report suspected abuse. When the participants in research are children, then the adults who are involved in the research must intervene to protect the child. However, when constructing the consent form it is a good idea to include a paragraph that spells out the situations in which breaches of confidentiality would be permitted. In the research the following phrase was used:

> I can promise confidentiality on anything you may tell me except on anything that leads me to be concerned for your own or another's safety, in which case I must do whatever is necessary to ensure that you or the person being harmed is protected.
>
> (Piper and Simons, 2005: 60)

In this particular piece of research, confidentiality was maintained with regard to children's disclosures of any harms done to animals. While, as Piper and Simons (2005) acknowledge, some members of the RSPCA did not agree with this at first, it was decided that it would be unethical to get children to admit to doing something wrong, only to end up reporting them. It is important to note that some organisations may require exceptions to maintaining confidentiality. For example, HM Prison Service stipulates that researchers report criminal activity, self-harm and any breaking of prison rules to a member of prison staff. Ashleigh, one of our PhD students, is currently undertaking research in an adult men's prison, investigating the needs of older prisoners. Ashleigh produced a participant information sheet that was approved by the University of Wolverhampton faculty ethics committee and also met HM Prison Service requirements for boundaries around confidentiality by including the following statement:

> The information you provide will be confidential, with only myself and my research supervisors having access to it. However, if you tell me about a crime that has been committed that the prison service does not know about or should you disclose either the intention to harm yourself, harm another individual, attempt to escape, or act in any way that may result in a breach of security, or break any prison rules, I am required to tell the prison service. Other than in these areas however, none of the information gathered will be shared in a way that can identify you by anyone outside of the study.
>
> (Ashleigh Whitwell, 2024)

Blagden and Pemberton (2010) have discussed the issue of confidentiality in relation to their interviews with sexual offenders in prison. They were duty bound to report to prison officers if the participants revealed their intentions to put anyone at risk, thereby limiting their promises of confidentiality, and they acknowledged the limitations of their role at the outset of the research. They refer to this as a 'dual role dichotomy', since their desire to protect the anonymity of their participants must be overridden by the moral duty to protect (possible) future victims from harm. As they tell us, this is in line with the British Society of Criminology's guidelines and the guidelines of the British Psychological Society.

Avoiding harm

> The potential for harm can be emotional, physical and financial. While in some situations there is clear guidance and a universal understanding about how to avoid harm, in others the circumstances are less clear cut, and researchers need to make subjective judgements about acceptable risks. In part, any understanding about 'avoiding harm' depends on different viewpoints.....The researcher has an ethical responsibility to consider...potentially conflicting perspectives, and make a balanced and reasoned judgement about what are acceptable risks for everyone involved.
>
> (SRA, 2021: 3)

In order to avoid harm, researchers must do two key things:

1 At the design stage think through and identify the harms to which their chosen methods of study may give rise and ensure that all practical steps are taken to demonstrate that their choice of actions can be justified ethically by avoiding undue harm. (Refer to Table 7.1.)
2 When/if unforeseen ethical dilemmas arise in the process of research, the decisions that are made in response to these dilemmas should be documented and reflected upon in the research methodology, as this will help others make wise ethical decisions in the future.

BOX 7.6   CAN COVERT OBSERVATIONAL RESEARCH BE CARRIED OUT ETHICALLY?

The BBC's *Panorama* programme has an extensive history of carrying out undercover investigations. In 2022 an episode highlighted abuse at a mental health unit in the north of England. Organisations like Mind (one of the UK's leading mental health charities) immediately called for a public inquiry. Some staff were sacked and an independent review was undertaken of the individual mental health unit and the wider Mental Health NHS Foundation Trust (Shanley, 2024). The report concluded that there were significant problems across the unit and wider Trust, including 'repeated missed opportunities to act on concerns raised' (Shanley, 2024: 8), 'Poor leadership visibility in the service, as well as weak governance processes and a practice of suppressing "bad news" in the organisation' (9) and 'a closed culture, including an absence of psychological safety, incivility between staff, poor leadership, and a lack of teamworking' (9).

This and other similar *Panorama* investigations build on a case in 2012, where 11 care home workers were convicted of ill treating patients in the Winterbourne View private care home. These convictions were made possible by undercover filming of abuse, which when made public on BBC's *Panorama* in 2011 was distressing for the families of those who were abused. However, as Ramesh (2012) reports, as a result of this undercover investigation by the BBC the abuses have come to be understood as 'disability hate crimes' and the Care Quality Commission, the National Health Service Regulator, has made changes which should improve the response to complaints about abuse to patients and has facilitated the setting up of a specialist whistle-blowing team.

Calvey (2017: 8) has noted that there is a huge public appetite for covert documentaries. He suggests that 'such undercover journalistic work, although sensitive, can clearly be seen to be in the public interest' (9) but argues that at the same time academics within the social sciences are being increasingly regulated.

1   Why do you think this is?
2   Should covert observational methods be used as 'teaching material for cases of failed or bad ethics' (Calvey, 2008: 914)? Or instead should teachers be encouraging students to think carefully about the ethical issues to which different covert observational studies have given rise in order that they may carry out important criminological studies using this method in the most ethical way possible?
3   How might an academic go about researching disability hate crimes using covert observation?
4   What are the ethical dilemmas to which such a study might lead?
5   How might these dilemmas be resolved?

We have seen from our discussion thus far that the avoidance of harm may require us to challenge some well-established ethical principles. This does not mean that these principles are not important but rather that our adherence to them should be context dependent. Gaining knowledge and understanding of the contexts in which ethical principles may be breached justifiably will avoid complacency among researchers that is sometimes (albeit inadvertently) encouraged by a 'tick-box' approach to ethics. As May (2001: 67) has noted, the drawing up of and conformity with ethical guidelines is a beginning. From these beginnings many debates will continue to flow. As a general rule we would say that a simple guiding mantra for ethical research is to follow the principles unless to do so would incur undue harms. In such circumstances researchers need to ensure that they justify their actions by explaining how ethical principles may sometimes come into conflict with each other. They should demonstrate the ways in which their decision to breach a principle will reduce harm. Murphy and Dingwall (2001: 340 cited in Flick, 2009: 38), for example, have argued that ethical codes that are not method sensitive may not only constrain research but may also increase the risk of harm to participants by 'blunting the ethnographers' sensitivities to the method-specific issues which do arise'.

Earlier we asked you to consider Pollock's (2009) covert invisible non-participatory observational research. Now that you have almost come to the end of the chapter take a look at your responses to the question asked in Box 7.4. Pollock discusses the ethical issues and decides that the nature of his research enables him to be sure that the ethical principles do not apply to his chosen research method for the following reasons. First, participants in the news groups are aware that anyone can see what they are posting. They are anonymous themselves but they are also aware that they could be being monitored by various authorities. Pollock therefore deduces that his research does not invade privacy. While many covert observational studies transgress the advice regarding informed consent, there is no such transgression to consider in this case, again because those being observed are knowingly posting comments in a public space. It does not make sense for a researcher to be required to gain consent to view the posts when anyone is able to do so if they wish. Pollock does point to the difference between viewing posts online for purposes such as amusement or pleasure and viewing posts with the explicit purpose of using them in a research study, but he says the decision to use the data must 'remain with the moral conscience of the researcher'. For Pollock the salient justificatory issue is the paucity of data on 'hard-to-reach' groups which usually refuse access to researchers. He does, however, issue a warning that should harm come to any of the people whose 'hate speech' has been used in the research the researcher will be deemed more culpable if s/he has not gained informed consent. Because the identity of these news group members did not appear online and because he was observing archives rather than live chats, Pollock presumably felt confident that no harm would come to either himself or to the people who had contributed to the news group discussions. He does warn, however, that the observation of live chats would not be as safe. Research in this mode does indicate that there is a safe space within which early researchers may pursue some exciting criminological topics.

PAUSE TO THINK ...

Now read Rambukkana's (2019) discussion of the use of online data in research on the 'alt-right'. Rambukkana poses six key questions to help us think through the ethical considerations relevant to using what he terms 'gray data' ('research data that have their provenance in the gray area between found texts and the products of participants', Rambukkana, 2019: 312).

- How does this type of research fit with recent trends in social research to undertake research *with* rather than *on* participants?

Rambukkana, N. (2019) 'The Politics of Gray Data: Digital Methods, Intimate Proximity, and Research Ethics for Work on the "Alt-Right"', *Qualitative Inquiry*, 25(3): 312–323.

Universities will have their own ethical guidelines and committees. It is up to researchers to convince these committees that they have thought carefully about how they will avoid undue harm in their research. While harm to participants is a particularly important issue, harms to academic institutions, to wider social organisations, to public interests and indeed to the researchers themselves should all be considered. As the guidance in Table 7.1 demonstrates, researchers can avoid undue harm by being as informed as possible in advance of their studies. In criminological research, where there is a strong likelihood that the research will be of a sensitive nature, it is important to acknowledge that even when participants give their consent to trawl over difficult events the researcher has a duty to have access to identified organisations or professionals which can be called upon if any participants suffer from ill effects as a result of their participation. This signals that you have gone beyond simple compliance with an ethical principle.

Avoiding harm – a spotlight on researcher well-being

When we think about avoiding harm, this also extends to us as researchers. In Chapter 11 we explore some practical considerations around keeping physically safe as a researcher. Undertaking criminological and many other kinds of social and psychological research can present challenges to our own well-being. Spending considerable amounts of time engaging with difficult issues, and potentially speaking with people about their own traumatic experiences, can take its toll. Our experiences on ethics committees suggest that researchers will sometimes downplay the risk of harm to themselves. However, it is important to note that in such circumstances this may cause difficulties for the research institution, as research managers and universities may ultimately be held responsible for something that happens to a researcher. However, all research will involve some degree of risk and if ethical codes become inviolable rules then the 'flavour' of research will be vanilla.

When undertaking research there can also be a desire from researchers to want to support people who share their own difficult experiences and it is important to draw boundaries around this. As a novice researcher it is vital that you engage with your supervisor concerning any choice of research topic. This is also true for very experienced researchers who should always have someone with whom they can debrief and explore their own feelings (while maintaining appropriate confidentiality and anonymity of course). For example, Laura is currently leading a project exploring how musicians working in prisons and detention settings are supported (The Artists Care project). The project involves interviewing musicians about their experiences and it is possible that they will raise things that have been difficult for them. The researcher who will be conducting the interviews understands the boundaries around her role as a researcher and that while she can provide contact details for sources of support for participants (as we noted above), she cannot be a source of support for them. She has regular, informal catch-ups with Laura (who in this instance is the research supervisor) to talk about how the data collection is going, but also to ensure there is space to discuss any difficult issues arising from the research. In this situation both people are part of the project research team so there are no concerns around confidentiality. It is really important to make these arrangements, whether with a researcher supervisor or, at a minimum, ensuring you have someone to talk to about how you are feeling throughout the research process.

CONCLUSION

Criminological research raises some particularly complex ethical issues. We have tried to convey the importance of the development of ethical principles in the research process while at the same time suggesting that an overly rule-bound approach to ethics may be counter-productive in some contexts. We have suggested that it is useful to think of a continuum of ethical stances and we hope to have conveyed that there are problems for criminological research at both extremes. The research examples we have provided should have helped you identify the circumstances in which ethical principles may conflict with each other, which in turn should enable you to develop the skills of justifying your own ethical decisions and critiquing the decisions made by other researchers.

Website Instructor activity

Identifying ethical issues in research

Website Student quiz

Ethics

KEY LEARNING POINTS

- It is very important that researchers reduce the possibility of undue harm resulting from their research. For this reason researchers should be familiar with ethical principles.
- There are different stances on ethics but we have suggested that the consequentialist stance enables researchers to be cognisant of the ways in which ethical principles may conflict with each other in some contexts.
- The research examples demonstrate that there are particular concerns about covert research methods because these are said to negate the principle of informed consent and to be based on deceit. However, unless we examine the *context* of research these concerns cannot be understood properly.
- From the above it follows that ethical principles have been developed with good reason but also that it is unwise to follow them in a rule-bound way, as this will rule out some research methods through which important knowledge about crime has been produced.

REFERENCES

Beins, B.C. (2004) *Research Methods: A Tool for Life*, London: Pearson Education.
Berg, B.L. (2004) *Qualitative Research Methods for the Social Sciences*, fifth edition, London: Pearson.
Blagden, N. and Pemberton, S. (2010) 'The Challenge in Conducting Qualitative Research with Convicted Sex Offenders', *Howard Journal of Criminal Justice*, 49(3): 269–281.
Brewster, L., Bowers, J. and Brooks, L. (2024) 'New Theoretical Frameworks for Designing and Evaluating Arts-in-corrections Programs', in M. Gardner and L.S. Caulfield (eds) *Arts in Criminal Justice and Corrections: International Perspectives on Methods, Journeys, and Challenges*, London: Routledge.
Bryman, A. (2015) *Social Research Methods*, fifth edition, Oxford: Oxford University Press.
Calvey, D. (2008) 'The Art and Politics of Covert Research: Doing Situated Ethics in the Field', *Sociology*, 42(5): 905–918.
Calvey, D. (2017) *Covert Research: The Art, Ethics and Politics of Undercover Fieldwork*, London: Sage.
Calvey, D. (2020a) 'Being on Both Sides: Covert Ethnography and Partisanship with Bouncers in the Night-time Economy', *Journal of Organisational Ethnography*, 10(1). https://doi.org/10.1108/JOE-09-2020-0037.
Calvey, D. (2020b) 'Deception', in R. Iphofen (ed.) *Handbook of Research Ethics and Scientific Integrity*, Cham: Springer. https://doi.org/10.1007/978-3-030-16759-2_15
Carrabine, E., Lee, M., South, N., Cox, P. and Plummer, K. (2009) *Criminology: A Sociological Introduction*, London: Routledge.
Caulfield, L. Jolly, A. Simpson, E. and Devi-McGleish, Y. (2022) '"It's Not Just Music, It Helps You from Inside": Mixing Methods to Understand the Impact of Music on Young People in Contact with the Criminal Justice System', *Youth Justice*, 22(1): 67–84. https://doi.org/10.1177/1473225420938151
Cowburn, M. (2007) 'Men Researching Men in Prison: The Challenges for Pro-feminist Research', *Howard Journal*, 46(3): 276–288.
Ditton, J. (1977) *Part-time Crime*, London: Macmillan.
Economic and Social Research Council (ESRC). (2024) *Consent*. [Online], UK Research and Innovation (UKRI). Available at: https://www.ukri.org/councils/esrc/guidance-for-applicants/research-ethics-guidance/consent/
Flick, U. (2009) *An Introduction to Qualitative Research*, fourth edition, London: Sage.
Girling, E. (2017) 'Doing Research with Children', in M. Cowburn, L. Gelsthorpe and A. Wahidin (eds) *Research Ethics in Criminology*, London: Routledge.
Holdaway, S. (1983) *Inside the British Police: A Force at Work*, Oxford: Blackwell.
Jacobs, B.J. (2006) 'The Case for Dangerous Fieldwork', in D. Hobbs and R. Wright (eds) *The Sage Handbook of Fieldwork*, London: Sage.
May, T. (2001) *Social Research: Issues, Methods and Process*, Buckingham: Open University Press.
Milgram, S. (1963) 'Behavioral Study of Obedience', *Journal of Abnormal and Social Psychology*, 67(4): 371–378.
Miller, J. and Miller, H. (2021) 'Beating the House: Ethnographic Insights into a Web-Based Marijuana Grey Market', *American Journal of Criminal Justice*, 46: 1018–1033. [Online]. Available at: https://link.springer.com/article/10.1007/s12103-021-09661-6
Moore, L. (2011) 'The Convention on the Rights of the Child Comes of Age: Assessing Progress in Meeting the Rights of Children in Custody in Northern Ireland', *Northern Ireland Legal Quarterly*, 62(2): 217–234.

Parker, H. (1974) *View from the Boys*, Newton Abbott: David and Charles.

Piper, H. and Simons, H. (2005) 'Ethical Responsibility in Social Research', in B. Somekh and C. Lewin (eds) *Research Methods in the Social Sciences*, London: SAGE.

Pollock, E. (2009) 'Researching White Supremacists On Line: Methodological Concerns of Researching Hate "Speech"', *Internet Journal of Criminology*. Available at www.internetjournalofcriminology.com

Rambukkana, N. (2019) 'The Politics of Gray Data: Digital Methods, Intimate Proximity, and Research Ethics for Work on the "Alt-Right"', *Qualitative Inquiry*, 25(3): 312–323.

Ramesh, R. (2012) 'Winterbourne View Abuse: Last Staff Member Pleads Guilty', *Guardian*, 12 August.

Sanders, B. (2005) 'In the Club: Ecstasy Use and Supply in a London Nightclub', *Sociology*, 39(2): 241–258.

Scheper-Hughes, N. (2004) 'Parts Unknown: Undercover Ethnography of the Organs-trafficking Underworld', *Ethnography*, 5(1): 29–73.

Shanley, O. (2024) 'Independent Review of Greater Manchester Mental Health NHS Foundation Trust' [Online], NHS England. Available at: https://www.england.nhs.uk/north-west/wp-content/uploads/sites/48/2024/01/Final-Report-Independent-Review-of-GMMH-January-2024.pdf

Social Research Association (SRA). (2021) *Research Ethics Guidance* [Online], sra.org.uk. Available at: https://the-sra.org.uk/common/Uploaded%20files/Resources/SRA%20Research%20Ethics%20guidance%202021.pdf

PART III
Getting going with criminological research

Chapter 8

Planning

Where do research ideas come from?
How do we 'fine-tune' them?

GOALS OF THIS CHAPTER

At the end of reading this chapter and by completing the online resources that accompany it, you will:

1. begin to recognise where your own ideas originate;
2. be aware of the ways in which you theorise about crime in your everyday lives and reflect upon those theories;
3. be able to specify general concepts;
4. be aware of the importance of background reading;
5. begin to translate your ideas into research questions;
6. be aware of the purposes of a literature review;
7. turn your plans into a formal research proposal.

OVERVIEW

- This chapter will encourage you to think about from where your ideas about crime originate. What we choose to research is likely to be influenced by our own life experiences. We may have been a victim of crime in the past or we may even have been involved in the perpetration of crime in either a direct or an indirect way. The ideas we hold about what is right or wrong are influenced by our families, the friends we keep, our level of education, etc. The questions we choose to ask will be influenced by what we think we know and by what we believe already.
- However, good researchers need to demonstrate that they have more than 'everyday' or 'common-sense' knowledge about their chosen topic of research; therefore it is important that you examine the work of others in order to reflect upon and refine your own ideas for research.
- Once you have done some initial background reading you will have expanded your knowledge of your chosen research topic. It is also likely that in the light of the new knowledge encountered through the first stage of the literature review process you may discover that you are beginning to challenge the views you held previously. This is just the beginning of your exploration.

DOI: 10.4324/9781032645698-11

- It is likely that at some point during your studies you will be required to write a research proposal. Often a research proposal is a credit-bearing part of a dissertation or research methods module. Writing a research proposal is a vital part of the research process, ensuring you have really thought through your ideas and plans and can explain them clearly enough for others to understand. Getting feedback from your lecturers or supervisors is also a really important part of the development of your research project.

GETTING STARTED: IDEAS (CONCEPTS) AND THEORIES

In Chapter 6 we introduced you to the different theories of knowledge within which criminological research has been carried out. We demonstrated that the ways in which researchers' theories about how the social world should be defined and about what is the best way to gather knowledge on the social world will influence the questions that we seek to answer through our research. In this chapter we are concerned with where our ideas (or concepts) come from and the relationship of these ideas to lower levels of theory – what we might call specific theories – about crime.

Crime is a social problem; therefore you do not need to be a criminology student to have opinions about crime. However, as a serious researcher you will need to have a good understanding of where your ideas have come from and you will need to reflect upon the reasons you hold particular viewpoints. A research idea may develop from a profound personal experience, such as being the victim of a violent crime or from a wider concern with an issue that you feel strongly about, for example, trafficking in nuclear arms. However, it is important to be realistic about what can and cannot be achieved within a research project. It is better to 'think small' in the early days of research, as in this way it will be easier to demonstrate that you can do a competent study which you are able to defend.

To carry out a competent study you must demonstrate your understanding of theory. While the word 'theory' may make some students feel anxious, it is good to remember that theorising is a common feature of our lives; it is not just something academics do. However, unlike laypeople, academics try to produce convincing evidence to support their theories and they learn how to identify the strengths and limitations of existing evidence by critiquing the available literature, through which they demonstrate their knowledge of their chosen research area – more of this later. As we have suggested, very often our research ideas take root from our day-to-day experiences. For example, we may be travelling on a bus or a train and overhear someone say something like: 'families are not the same as they used to be, couples are not committed to each other anymore and that's why we see so many kids getting into trouble' or 'crime has increased in our area ever since we started letting all these foreigners come to work here'. Whether we agree with such ideas or not will depend upon many factors, such as whom we associate with, where we live, what newspapers we read and our level of education. We hear these sorts of things because people in their everyday lives are trying to make sense of what is happening in their world. However, such explanations of different types of crime are not usually based on systematic theorising; rather, they have often been gleaned from relatively similar and often unreliable sources.

As a new researcher you will need to think about how you can move from the unsystematic form of theorising that is often a feature of everyday life, to what is a more 'privileged' form of theorising (after all, most people do not have the time to think about things in the way that academics can) that takes place within an academic setting.

In academic research a sound theory is usually based on a set of ideas that we have about something. Criminologists use theories in order to attempt to find explanations for the phenomena that we refer to collectively as 'crime', yet the term 'crime' encompasses many forms of lawbreaking, from individual illegal drug use to organised corporate crime. Those who study crime may be concerned with why different crimes happen but they may also be concerned with the reasons why some behaviours come to be defined as criminal. For example, who decides that using the drug cannabis is illegal but using the drugs alcohol or tobacco is not? On what basis is such a decision made? Contrary to what many people think, it does not necessarily have to be on the basis of harm, as Nutt (2009) has argued, yet even his scientific evidence was not enough to convince politicians. Nutt struggled to explain that the view expressed by many politicians, namely that you cannot compare the harms of an illegal substance with those of a legal one, is illogical. Indeed, Professor Nutt was sacked in 2009 by the then Home Secretary Alan Johnson because his evidence did not 'fit' with political imperatives, yet these same politicians are likely to call for 'a more scientific' approach to research when social scientists carry out **qualitative research** on drug use in society. It is interesting to reflect on the legalisation and decriminalisation of cannabis in many countries in recent years, and to consider why and how laws are made and unmade. Researchers therefore need to become mindful of the ways in which our understanding of crime in society may be shaped by an often ill-informed public perception, frequently gained from biased or partial media reporting and a perceived need on the part of politicians to respond to that public perception.

The above discussion suggests that it is important for criminological researchers to break crime down into several categories in order to provide more meaningful knowledge of and explanations for the many acts that constitute crime in society. For example, in everyday life when people say things like 'crime has got worse', there is an assumption that we all know what is meant by this because there is a tendency to understand the term 'crime' to mean street crimes. Researchers have to be much more precise than this so that there can be no doubt about the phenomenon which they wish to study. This is important because in general people get their ideas about crime from various media, which focus more on street crimes. This skews our thinking about crime and serves to mystify the many other crimes which should cause us concern. Once we understand this we can quickly see the need to break down our ideas more precisely in order to improve our research design. As Neuman (2011: 57) puts it, 'simple is better'.

To illustrate how you can make the move from everyday to academic theorising it is helpful to have an example. Let us start with an idea that has taken hold in society, such as the linkage of family breakdown with crime. This is an idea that has been taken up by politicians across the political spectrum; for example, family breakdown remains an indicator of risk in the assessment tools used by Youth Justice Services (HM Inspectorate of Probation, 2023) and it is an assumption embodied in the statement used in the Conservative policy document 'Breakthrough Britain' (Social Justice Policy Group, 2007) that crime is strongly correlated with family breakdown.

> **BOX 8.1 BREAKING DOWN CONCEPTS**
>
> Crime and family breakdown are two key concepts that might inform a piece of research. Try to think how you could clarify these concepts in order to make research aims clear.

As a starting point for the exercise in Box 8.1 we might expect that you would have interrogated the concept of crime itself since, as we have already demonstrated in Chapter 6, crime changes over time and across space, so the concept (or idea) of crime is best understood as a **social construction**. It is therefore a good idea to specify the types of crime that are being linked to family breakdown rather than to speak of crime in general. Through the process of breaking crime down into categories (for example, street theft), you will be able to pave the way for theory testing. Similarly we might expect that family breakdown would need to be more clearly defined. Families 'break down' for a variety of reasons: there could be a death in the family; a family member comes to need full-time care, a divorce or separation. The reasons for divorce or separation may also vary; for example, you might suppose that if a couple split up because of violence it could be more likely that the children would become involved in violent crime. This is a process that can help you narrow down your area of research. The more you clarify your ideas in this way, the better placed you will be to identify the focus of your research and test out your ideas. In qualitative research this process of conceptualising is ongoing; researchers will often come up with new definitions of concepts in the process of analysis (see Chapter 17). In **quantitative research** this process is important because clear definitions are needed in order to operationalise concepts; that is, to make them measurable (see Chapter 13).

THE INFORMAL LITERATURE REVIEW: BACKGROUND READING

Researchers always demonstrate that they are familiar with the existing knowledge surrounding their research topic. You should begin the process of reviewing the literature on your chosen topic as soon as possible, as this will enable you to avoid replicating things that have been done already (unless a replication study is the aim – replications of quantitative studies have become increasingly popular in psychology in recent years in order to further test findings – but we won't explore that here). By the time you get to the end of the full process of review you should be in a position to construct your final question for research. But where do you start? At first it is likely that your research ideas are rather vague and you may well need to discuss these with your supervisor in order to avoid starting the impossible or just to get an idea of where to look in the first instance. There is such an array of literature that it can be very bewildering at first and your interest in a topic may start with the sort of literature that is not usually associated with academia, such as television programmes. Your study may well benefit from 'literature' gained from films or TV, especially as crime is such a popular entertainment topic. There will also be plentiful news media resources. However, it is important to review academic journals (academic journals are almost always refereed – that is, the research is reviewed by other academics as a quality assurance measure), academic books, official documents, organisational documents (sometimes called 'grey' literature) – for instance, documents that you might find from an organisation like the National Association for the Care and Resettlement of Offenders (NACRO).

Website Student activity

Getting started with summarising

Tips for sifting the literature

The most obvious place to begin is with the title of a resource, which will usually tell you quite a lot about the content. Here is a good example: 'Domestic and Family Violence Leave Across Australian Workplaces: Examining Victim-survivor Experiences of Workplace Supports and the Importance of Cultural Change' (an article by Kate Fitz-Gibbon and colleagues (2023) in the *Journal of Criminology*). Of course, as you become familiar with different writers you will also begin to get an idea of the perspective of those authors. For example, Kate Fitz-Gibbon can be said to write from a feminist perspective. A quick Google search would reveal that she has written frequently with Sandra Walklate, which means that you would immediately have an idea about the perspective of this writer as well. Such a search could then lead you to search for single-authored publications by Sandra Walklate as well as for any other joint-authored publications by this author.

You will often find a précis on the back cover of books and a summary with e-book versions, which will help you ascertain its relevance to your study. You can also scan the index to identify the topics that may be most useful to you. A refereed journal article will always include an abstract that will provide details of the study's purpose, methods and findings. You might also look at the introduction and conclusion to assess its relevance.

REMINDER

As we noted in Chapter 1, the internet is a wonderful source of information but you must be discerning. You need to ensure that the sources you cite are reputable; at worst you could be accessing sites that are operated by hate groups (Berg, 2004), so take care. Here are some tips to help you be discerning: Look

> for the author's name – if there isn't one be very cautious; if there is, have you heard of them? If not, look that person up to find out what else they have written. Can you discern the agenda of the author? For example, are there assumptions about gender or ethnicity that you find worrying or offensive? Can you find out the reason the internet site exists and how long it has existed? Also when was it last updated? Does the author mention other writers that you have heard of and provide evidence to back up what is being said?

Where shall I start?

We think that it is helpful for students to be given an idea of what is involved in the process of refining research ideas, and this is indeed what many lecturers do when they talk about their own research or when they encourage postgraduate research students to speak to undergraduates about their progress in research. Those who are new to research are inclined to think of the process in a linear way when in reality the process is quite messy. In order to demonstrate how this process might begin we are going to return to the example used above in which we started to think about a statement in the policy document 'Breakthrough Britain' (also see Box 8.2), which almost 20 years ago asserted an association between family breakdown and crime as part of a justification for supporting marriage through changes to state support.

We would like you to imagine that you heard something in the news about a new report called 'Two Nations' published by the centre that originally authored 'Breakdown Britain' and 'Breakthrough Britain'. 'Two Nations' (Centre for Social Justice, 2023) builds on ideas promoted by the Centre for Social Justice in 2006/2007 about crime/family breakdown and this sparked an interest for you in the topic, which you thought you might pursue as part of your course – note that interest in a topic can be ignited for a variety of reasons: for example, because you agreed with the connections that were being made or because you thought there were some problems with attributing crime to 'family breakdown' and you wanted to find out more. It is often worth looking at documents of this kind because they tell us quite a lot about which crimes are constructed by governments as the most pressing as well as about the ways in which those who are involved in certain crimes are perceived. As Radzinowicz (1999: 469, cited in Garland and Sparks, 2000: 192) pointed out, there is a disturbing gap between criminology and criminal policy. Unfortunately, despite the wealth of criminological knowledge, a relatively populist political approach holds sway (McAra, 2017; Hamilton, 2023) There is a constant need for criminologists to challenge the assumptions made by politicians and for them to question the grounds upon which policies are implemented (refer back to Chapter 5 and the discussion of knowledge and politics).

Your initial thinking, as is revealed through Box 8.1, will depend on your own experiences and/or on some previous reading. It is always useful to do an exercise such as the one above with others because when we compare our thoughts with those of other people we often start to identify the ideas that we take for granted. The initial reading of the document should have enabled you to identify the evidence provided by the authors and the ways in which that evidence is used to justify policy proposals.

BOX 8.2 SPECIFYING CONCEPTS AND IDENTIFYING VARIABLES

Take a look at McAlinden, A.M., Farmer, M. and Maruna, S. (2016) 'Desistance from Sexual Offending: Do Mainstream Theories Apply?', *Criminology and Criminal Justice*, 17(3): 266–283.

This article provides a good description of the way in which the concept of desistance is operationalised.

Using the insights gained from the exercise in Box 8.1, specify what you mean by the concept of family breakdown and jot down some of the crimes that you think may be linked to it. Try to give reasons for the association. Next, try to think of other variables that might help to explain the crimes you believe to be linked with family breakdown (as you have defined it).

Now take a look at the Centre for Social Justice (CSJ) website. 'The CSJ is best known for its major "Breakdown Britain" (2006) and "Breakthrough Britain" (2007) reports, which identified the five Pathways to Poverty – family breakdown, educational failure, worklessness, addiction and crime, and problem debt and housing' (Centre for Social Justice, 2024). You will find these reports under the 'Family' heading, available at https://www.centreforsocialjustice.org.uk/about/the-five-pathways/family

In 'Breakdown Britain' (2006) the chapter entitled 'Fractured Families' points to statistics that indicated at that time that 70 per cent of young offenders were from lone-parent families and that levels of all anti-social behaviour and delinquency were higher in children from separated families.

'Breakthrough Britain' (2007: 14) states that 'strong and stable families are indispensable to a strong and stable society' and that the consequences of a broken family are children's behavioural problems, the increased likelihood of early sexual activity, becoming pregnant, higher levels of smoking, drinking and other drug use (17). This report stated that there is a strong correlation between crime and family breakdown.

'Two Nations' (2023) does not significantly challenge the assumptions about family embodied in the earlier reports although there are some important insights into the ways in which poverty and economic vulnerability has divided Britain.

- How is family defined in all three of these documents? Would you define family in the same way?

- Would your definition of family lead you to question the usefulness of the concept of family breakdown to our understanding of some forms of youth crime and anti-social behaviour?
- How would you assess the strength of the evidence provided for the theories about crime embodied within these reports?

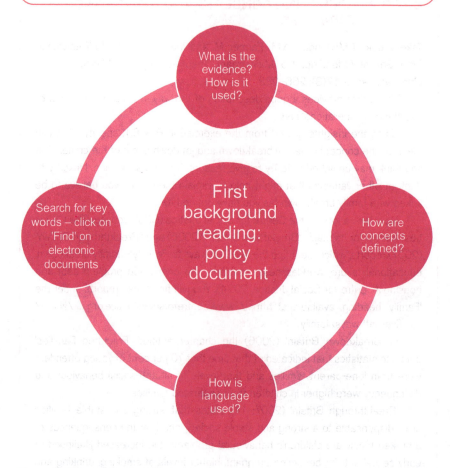

Figure 8.1 Interrogating your literature sources: policy documents.

Some of you may have used the 'find' facility on the computer as a quick way of identifying where the key concepts (crime and family breakdown) that are of interest to you are used in the document. This should also have enabled you to discern the ways in which the concepts were defined.

Where next?

You are only just getting into the research process, having pursued one idea by looking at a policy document. There is a whole lot more background reading to do before your ideas can become concrete. It is important to remember that doing research is a creative enterprise (Berg, 2004). If you are following a thread of ideas that you find interesting, the chances are that you will enjoy reading around the topic until your 'criminological imagination' is developed. A useful next step may be to search for further statistical information – but remember the caution we recommended in Chapter 5 in relation to official crime statistics – or for responses to the document. For example, Gingerbread, Barnardo's and Child Poverty Action Group provided a joint response to 'Breakthrough Britain' (www.gingerbread.org.uk/uploads/media/17/6863.pdf), which, while welcoming some aspects of the report, challenged the assumption that the tax and benefit system favours lone parents; the view that lone parenthood of itself leads to poor outcomes for children suggests that where there is conflict in families separation may lead to better outcomes for children. These 'snippets' of information are useful, as they give you some idea of other issues or variables that may need to be considered in your study; for example, having looked at the evidence provided in this document you may deduce that poverty or conflict could be more significant indicators of crime-related problems than family breakdown.

PAUSE TO THINK ...

In fact the documents discussed above don't tell us directly that much about crime but it is possible to 'read between the lines' by looking carefully at the ways in which language is used in the documents. Ostensibly the Centre for Social Justice Think Tank working party was concerned with five pathways to poverty, yet there were no social scientists involved in that working group, according to Slater (2011). The focus upon marriage in the documents, however, signals that some families are more likely to be perceived as a problem than others; the concern with 'dad-lessness' implies that lone motherhood is a concern. It appears that many of the ills of society are being placed squarely within 'dysfunctional' family relationships but what does that term mean? Is a definition of a 'functional' family provided or hinted at? Which crimes is the report concerned about? Which family members are the foci of concern? Are there any contradictions in the arguments? If you raised questions for yourself in this way you can give yourself a pat on the back, as this means that you are already starting to read critically.

It is also important that you recognise that despite the CSJ's claim to be independent the document is political; therefore you need to think about what you have read in context. Might it be that 'family' is being used in an ideological way to support a particular view of welfare? Do you think that family breakdown is the key issue?

Take a look at the London School of Economics' blog post 'Government and "Independent Expertise": Think Tanks Represent a Blind Spot for Critical Analysis' (Pautz and Heins, 2016). In what ways might your reading of this impact upon the way in which you review reports in the future?

> Of course, just because you are embarking upon a piece of criminological research, this does not mean that you will not have political views yourself, but these views should not prevent you from thinking carefully about the strength of the evidence provided to justify policies that purport (at least in part) to reduce crime in society – whichever party is putting them forward. As Denscombe (2002: 35) says, 'personal interest should not act as a blinker that unduly narrows the focus of research'. It will be important to look for the source of the evidence used in the document you have read and to think about how it has been collected and used rather than to accept it because you think you agree with what is being said.

It is always interesting to consider what might be gained from moving away from the theory of knowledge underpinning the research that has been adopted in policies. For example, the variables that have been associated with delinquency in positivistic research were translated into risk factors that are still used in some assessments within the Youth Justice System to predict where intervention should take place (the Risk Factors Prevention Paradigm (RFPP)). Most notably in the UK this approach informed an assessment called Asset, the default tool for assessing the risk-related needs of children in contact with the youth justice system. If you were to pursue further background reading on this issue you would soon discover that there are differing perspectives on the merits of attempts to predict risk. For example, if you were to search *Youth Justice* you might find an article by O'Mahony, P. (2009) 'The Risk Factors Prevention Paradigm and the Causes of Youth Crime: A Deceptively Useful Analysis?' in which he discusses some of the problems with using scientific approaches within the social sciences where constructs are imprecise and culturally variable. O'Mahony points to the importance of challenging notions of 'culture-free' risk factors because the ways in which gender and 'race' are socially constructed are very important to our understanding of why some (young) people get involved in crime. There is thus a suggestion that it may be important to carry out studies from within an interpretivist framework in order to gain a more nuanced understanding of the reasons young people turn to crime. Furthermore, O'Mahony (2009: 112) points to the ways in which the RFPP fails to take account of adult onset offending such as white-collar crimes and domestic violence (a discovery which, at this early stage of research, could take you off in another direction completely). If you then wanted to find out more about current thinking about risk-based approaches to youth justice and searched *Risk Factors Prevention Paradigm* you might find a report by Wigzell (2021) 'Explaining Desistance: Looking Forward, Not Backwards'. In this report Wigzell highlights some of the debates around the recent shift from thinking about risk, to thinking about desistance – noting that while this is probably a positive shift, by placing more emphasis on strengths than risks, 'the desistance paradigm has been transplanted into youth justice from the adult arena with remarkably little academic critique about its transferability and application to children (2021: 2). Desistance approaches, and in particular a move to 'Child First' approaches to UK youth justice (where children are

PLANNING CRIMINOLOGICAL RESEARCH   121

viewed as children, not offenders), reflect a move away from risk-based positivistic approaches towards a more nuanced understanding of children (although we note that at the time of writing Asset was still being used, even in the context of the new Child First approach – presently something of a conflict).

> **BOX 8.3   DEVELOPING YOUR RESEARCH IDEAS**
>
> Think of a topic that interests you; then go to your university library page and conduct a search of the *British Journal of Criminology* that may help you gain more information about it. What did you find? How did you decide which articles might be useful? When you have completed the task, look at the inverted checklist below to see whether you missed anything out.

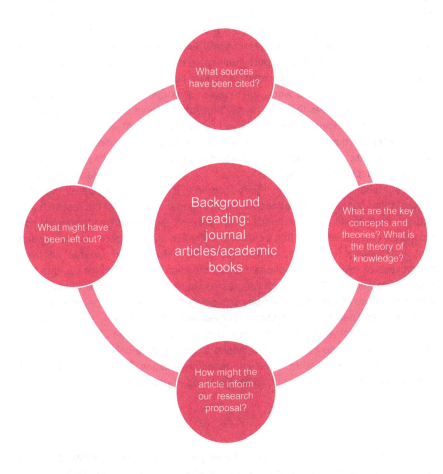

Figure 8.2 Interrogating your literature sources: academic texts.

> **Checklist**
>
> You should have:
>
> - browsed the abstracts in order to identify the most relevant literature;
> - read the chosen articles carefully, highlighted key concepts, identified the theories being used, discussed or developed and identified the theory of knowledge within which the study was carried out;
> - looked at the citations that were included, as they could lead to more ideas to follow up for your own study.

TRANSLATING IDEAS INTO QUESTIONS

Eventually we hope that through the process of careful background reading you will be equipped to raise quite a few questions about the studies you have looked at, which will in turn enable you to construct some research aims. You could decide, for example, that your aim is to explore the reasons why more boys than girls get involved in delinquent activities or to critically examine the way in which the term 'family breakdown' is used to support youth crime policies. Both of these aims could have emerged from some of the literature that we have mentioned above. Eventually, in your attempts to fulfil your aims, your research question/s will emerge; for example, we could ask, 'How does the term "family breakdown" serve to mystify more salient reasons for youth crimes?' Alternatively, you could decide to set up a **hypothesis** (to test a theory) such as 'youth crime will be lower in local communities where there is affordable leisure'. This implies that you would need to carry out multi-variate analysis in order to ascertain whether the **independent variable** 'affordable leisure' is significant (see Chapters 10 and 13). A decision to look at boys compared with girls suggests that gender constructions will be an important element of the research and that you have found some materials which question the use of gender-neutral risk categories (see above). Note that a critical examination does not necessarily imply that your study belongs to what we have termed 'the critical theory of knowledge', although the process of taking a concept apart (deconstruction) may well move you into that research tradition as the research progresses (hence the importance of keeping a reflexive journal). However, if your study explicitly sets out to explain the ways in which a concept might serve to hide relations of power and oppression, you will be operating overtly with a set of values that will form part of your analysis (see Chapter 6). As you continue to review the literature and indeed begin the data-collection process you may find that you will need to refine your research question. This is a normal part of research and any refinements should be discussed in your methodology.

WRITING A RESEARCH PROPOSAL

It is likely that at some point during your studies you will be required to write a research proposal. A research proposal is an outline of what you intend to research, why this research is needed, and how you plan to undertake the research.

Often a research proposal is a credit-bearing part of a dissertation or research methods module that you will have to submit and gain feedback on before commencing with your research project. Even if you are not required to write a formal proposal, you will likely be asked to produce an informal proposal for discussion with your tutor or dissertation supervisor. Your university module guidance will make it clear which applies to you. Writing a research proposal is a vital part of the research process, ensuring you have really thought through your ideas and plans and can explain them clearly enough for others to understand. Getting feedback from your lecturers or supervisors is also a really important part of the development of your research project. Both novice and experienced researchers need to produce research proposals: whether planning an undergraduate project, writing a proposal for doctoral-level study, or writing a proposal to a funding body for a grant to undertake the research. Articulating your idea and the reason the research is needed is vital to a successful research project. Things don't always go completely to plan in research projects (see Chapter 11 for more on this) but by planning well you will undoubtedly have a smoother experience.

Everything you have learnt so far in this chapter will feed directly into preparing your research proposal. In fact, now that you have completed the rest of the chapter you can directly turn the learning from your reading, thinking and the activities you have completed into a proposal.

What, why and how

What: The first step is to identify a topic. Think back to the start of this chapter and where your own interests and ideas come from. As we noted, what we choose to research is likely to be influenced by our own life experiences. The questions we choose to ask will be influenced by what we think we know and by what we believe already. However, a good researcher needs to demonstrate that they have more than 'everyday' or 'common-sense' knowledge about their chosen topic of research; therefore it is important that you examine the work of others in order to reflect upon and refine your own ideas for research. Once you have done some initial background reading you will have expanded your knowledge of your chosen research topic. The task here is to ensure it is clear to anyone reading your proposal that you are familiar with the existing research on your chosen topic. This early thinking and reading will have prepared you for translating your ideas into questions.

Why: Why is this research important? Is this a topic where there is limited current research? Or have previous studies highlighted questions suitable for further investigation? As a novice researcher you are not expected to undertake highly original research or make a significant contribution to the field of criminology, but you do need to be clear about why this particular research is needed. A good way to find inspiration is, when doing your initial reading, to look at the discussion and conclusion section to see what the authors propose as sensible questions for future research.

How: How will you undertake this research? This is where you will need to outline your approach and methods. You will need to choose research methods that are appropriate to answer your research questions (see Part IV of this book), but also methods that are feasible within the constraints within which you are working (i.e.

realistic in terms of time, funding, access to participants – also see Chapter 11 for a discussion of real-world research). Your proposal should include the research methods you intend to use, research tools (e.g. surveys, questionnaires), intended participants and procedures for collecting any data. You will also need to write about the ethical considerations of your approach (see Chapter 7), although seeking full ethics approval will come later. Whether you intend to collect new data (see Chapters 12 and 13), work with exiting data sources (see Chapters 13 and 14) or undertake a critical literature review (see Chapter 9), you will still need to state your approach and methods clearly.

You might follow the guidance from this chapter and elsewhere in this book through the following steps to write your research proposal:

1. Identify a topic of interest.
2. Refine your thinking through initial reading about the topic.
3. Translate your initial thinking into questions.
4. Consider which methods are appropriate to start to investigate your research questions.

BOX 8.4 RESEARCH PROPOSAL FORMAT

Below is an example research proposal format. While the exact format of a research proposal varies depending on the level of study, it typically includes: introduction, literature review, methodology and reference list. Your own university is likely to have a preferred format, especially if you are writing a proposal that will be submitted as part of a credit-bearing module. Let's assume that this proposal is around 1,000 words for an undergraduate dissertation:

Introduction

This is the first part of your proposal where you should provide a clear and succinct summary of what the research is about (the topic and your questions), why it is important (the 'so what?' question). You should provide some background and context in this section. For example:

- Is this a topic of current interest to policymakers, research, the public?
- What is the scale of the issue (can you find any current statistics to help make the case?)?
- What is already known about the topic?
- What is missing from current research?
- What are the aims/objectives/research questions of your proposal research project?
- How will exploring these questions help to address the issue you have identified and contribute to the field (keeping in mind that the expectations to contribute to knowledge are greater the higher the level of study you are at)?

Literature review

You'll write a fuller literature review in your research report or dissertation, but your research proposal should include an overview of key literature relevant to your topic. This section makes it clear that you are familiar with existing research on your chosen topic and that your proposed research is grounded in what is already known.

- What has current research stated about the topic/issue?
- What are the key theoretical approaches guiding existing research on this topic?
- What are the key debates in the existing literature?
- What are the strengths and limitations of existing research?
- What are the key gaps in the existing research literature?
- How will your research fit within the context of the answers to the above questions?
- What are the aims/objectives/research questions of this proposal research project?

Methodology

You will need to outline your overall approach and the practical stages of the proposed research. The proposal must make it clear that the proposed research is feasible for the level of research experience you have and the resources available to you.

- Will you collect new data or work with existing data sources?
- If you collect new data, will you take a quantitative, qualitative or mixed-methods approach?
- Why is this method appropriate to answering your research questions?
- How will you select and access participants and/or data sources?
- What are the key ethical considerations and how will you seek ethics approval?
- What data collection tools will you use (e.g. survey, interviews, systematic review of data/literature)?
- What methods will you use to analyse the data?
- What practical challenges do you foresee and how will you plan for those?

You might also be given the space to write a Conclusion. This is where you should summarise the key points outlined in your proposal and clearly make the case for the feasibility and value of your proposed research.

Reference list

Your proposal must include citations and references in the same way as an essay or other assignment (see Chapter 2).

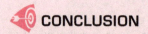 **CONCLUSION**

Research is a creative enterprise insofar as you need to think 'outside the box' in order to raise interesting questions that may not have been asked before. This chapter should have enabled you to start thinking about your own views on crime and why you hold them. It is hoped that it has also encouraged you to start talking to others about their views, as this is a good way of identifying the ways in which your own life experiences might influence the way you think. It is a good idea to start practising writing clear definitions of the concepts that are of concern to you so that by the time you carry out your own research project you will be able to make the limits of your concerns apparent. It is extremely important that you begin background reading as early as possible and that you become adept at discerning reliable sources. Your background reading will help you to construct questions for research, and even though your question may eventually shift a little this process will lead to the more focused reading that is needed to write the formal literature review. In other words, by the time you have done your background reading you should have a good idea of what you are trying to achieve and how you will achieve it. If you are required to write a research proposal, the learning from this chapter will have prepared you well for that – and the feedback you receive on your research proposal will be an important part of developing your research study.

 KEY LEARNING POINTS

- Think small when you begin research, as this will help ensure that you stay focused.
- Reflect upon your own viewpoints and try to articulate why you hold specific views.
- Always try to go beyond common-sense knowledge by reading around the subject in a critical manner.
- Use short cuts, such as reading abstracts, to assess the relevance of your sources.
- Keep good records of your sources and don't forget to record page numbers if you are writing down direct quotations.
- Be methodical when making notes using the headings suggested to organise your thinking.
- sRemember that although your review comes first in the presentation of your final research, in reality you will find that you are 'tweaking' it throughout the whole research process.

REFERENCES

Berg, B.L. (2004) *Qualitative Research Methods for the Social Sciences*, fifth edition, London: Pearson.

Centre for Social Justice. (2023) 'Two Nations' [Online], The Centre for Social Justice. Available at: https://url6.mailanyone.net/scanner?m=1syIGQ-00000002oWx-322I&d=4%7Cmail%2F90%2F1728424800%2F1syIGQ-00000002oWx-322I%7Cin6q%7C57e1b682%7C10977208%7C9441127%7C6705ABA2629C6B687A607882606A9949&o=t.wweenrwcasfojcilrooiusge.rtcku.&s=uvtdJhs2AY2cLkp5gi-k9IUbq

Centre for Social Justice. (2024) 'The Five Pathways' [Online], The Centre for Social Justice. Available at: https://www.centreforsocialjustice.org.uk/about/the-five-pathways (accessed 21 May 2024).

Denscombe, M. (2002) *Ground Rules for Good Research: A Ten-point Guide for Social Researchers*, Buckingham: Open University Press.

Fitz-Gibbon, K., Pfitzner, N. and McNicol, E. (2023) 'Domestic and Family Violence Leave Across Australian Workplaces: Examining Victim-survivor Experiences of Workplace Supports and the Importance of Cultural Change', *Journal of Criminology*, 56 (2–3): 294–312. https://doi.org/10.1177/26338076221148203

Garland, D. and Sparks, R. (2000) 'Criminology, Social Theory and the Challenge of our Times', *British Journal of Criminology*, 40(2): 189–204.

Hamilton, C. (2023) 'Radical Right Populism and the Sociology of Punishment: Towards a Research Agenda', *Punishment and Society*, 25(4): 888–908. https://doi.org/10.1177/14624745221114802

HM Inspectorate of Probation. (2023) 'Assessment' [Online], HM Inspectorate of Probation. Available at: https://www.justiceinspectorates.gov.uk/hmiprobation/research/the-evidence-base-youth-offending-services/supervision/assessment/

McAlinden, A.M., Farmer, M. and Maruna, S. (2016) 'Desistance from Sexual Offending: Do Mainstream Theories Apply?', *Criminology and Criminal Justice*, 17(3): 266–283.

McAra, L. (2017) 'Can Criminologists Change The World? Critical Reflections on the Politics, Performance and Effects of Criminal Justice', *British Journal of Criminology*, 57(4): 767–788.

Neuman, W.L. (2011) *Social Research Methods*, seventh edition, Boston, MA: Pearson International.

Nutt, D. (2009) 'Estimating Drug Harms: A Risky Business?', Eve Saville Lecture Centre for Crime and Justice Studies, October. Available at: https://www.crimeandjustice.org.uk/publications/estimating-drug-harms-risky-business (accessed 3 April 2024).

O'Mahony, P. (2009) 'The Risk Factors Prevention Paradigm and the Causes of Youth Crime: A Deceptively Useful Analysis?', *Youth Justice*, 9(2): 99–114.

Pautz, H. and Heins, E. (2016) 'Government and "Independent Expertise": Think Tanks Represent a Blind Spot for Critical Analysis', *London School of Economics Policy and Politics blog*. Available at http://blogs.lse.ac.uk/politicsandpolicy/52710-2/ (accessed 3 April 2024).

Slater, T. (2011) 'From "Criminality" to Marginality: Rioting Against a Broken State', *Human Geography*, 4(3): 106–115.

Social Justice Policy Group (2007) 'Breakthrough Britain: Ending the Costs of Social Breakdown'. Available at www.centreforsocialjustice.org.uk/core/wp-content/uploads/2016/08/BB_third-sector.pdf (accessed 8 August 2017).

Wigzell, A. (2021) 'Explaining Desistance: Looking Forward, Not Backwards' [Online], NAYJ Briefing. Available at: https://thenayj.org.uk/cmsAdmin/uploads/explaining-desistance-briefing-feb-2021-final.pdf (accessed 21 May 2024).

Chapter 9

Critiquing the literature and the process of writing your formal review

GOALS OF THIS CHAPTER

At the end of reading this chapter and by completing the online resources that accompany it, you will:

1. be able to distinguish between different types of literature;
2. understand what it means to **critique** the literature;
3. be aware of the ways in which researchers use different theoretical perspectives;
4. be aware of the need to make your own standpoint clear through your discussion of the standpoints of others;
5. be able to write your review in a coherent, structured and appropriate style;
6. be aware of the importance of **reflexivity** in the process of writing a review.

OVERVIEW

- The process of writing a review is ongoing throughout research in the sense that it will constantly be refined as your ideas develop.
- The quality of a review is enhanced by a researcher's ability to distinguish between different types of literature – empirical, theoretical and methodological. It is therefore important that researchers continue to develop the skill of critical reading.
- Familiarity with the work of others enables researchers to establish and justify their own standpoints on their chosen topics of research.

CRITIQUING THE LITERATURE

Researchers carry out a review of the literature to inform and refine their research questions, as discussed in Chapter 8, and also because they need to demonstrate their awareness of the state of knowledge on their chosen topic. It is really crucial that reviews are critical, as this will ensure that you demonstrate your ability to *analyse* the sources you have identified as important as opposed to just describing them. As Bell and Opie (2002: 137, citing Haywood and Wragg, 1982: 2, our emphasis) point out, it is relatively easy to produce a descriptive review but it is quite another thing to produce a review which demonstrates 'that the writer has studied existing work in the field *with insight*'. In practice this means that when you are preparing to write your review notes you should not simply outline what has been said but you should also record your own response to what has been said, such as what might be missing or which authors disagree with that position.

We now turn to the task of helping you read more critically, as this in turn will enable you to make the move from descriptive to analytical writing. You will need to read theoretical literature as well as empirical studies so that you become familiar with the ways in which researchers use theory in their research. Empirical studies will, of course, include discussions of methodology as well. It's good to get int the habit of noting down these references as you will need to chase up some of these so that you will eventually be able to justify your own methodological approach (more on this in Chapter 10).

In our experience it is all too easy to read lots of interesting studies, only to forget some of the key points when you come to writing your literature. This is why we think it is a good idea to produce a table on which to record the key information gained from each piece of literature. Having a structured way to record your notes not only helps you write your literature review, but is a great way of prompting you to ask critical questions of studies as you read them. You should record your own thoughts on each piece – even if you shift your position after further reading, these comments will be a useful start to the writing process. We suggest that you use the following headings:

1. Literature source
2. Key concepts
3. Theoretical perspectives
4. Key quotations/ideas
5. Methods used (where relevant)
6. Theory of knowledge
7. Political standpoints (if relevant) and context
8. Research questions
9. Key findings
10. Your own critical comments

TIP

Make sure that if your review notes include direct quotations/key ideas you also keep a record of the page number where the quotation/idea appears. You don't want to be accused of **plagiarism**; nor will you want to be chasing up page numbers later on when you have returned books or lost articles, etc.

Cowburn (2007) provided a synthesised account of the theoretical, empirical and methodological literature that has influenced his work on sex offenders. He demonstrated the importance of including a discussion of these key elements in any piece of research, since such details enable those who are reading the research to understand the basis on which judgements were made in the research process. Although the article is actually concerned with the difficulties encountered by male researchers in the data-collection process, it is a useful article to review because it provides such a lot of details about the assumptions behind his previous research, and in particular it provides a very detailed account of the reasons why he has chosen a critical epistemological approach. This article certainly demonstrates the importance of the three key aspects of literature that should be included in a review.

> ### BOX 9.1 CRITICAL READING
>
> Referring back to the article considered in Chapter 6 on whether men can do Feminist fieldwork and research (Giri, 2022), did you make any notes that you can relate to the headings above? Do you think that you read actively? That is, did you ask yourself questions about what you were reading as you went along? For example, what literature sources were cited by Giri? How did Giri's discussion of the literature help you to understand what he was trying to do? How did he go about it? What were his key considerations? Did you agree with them? Why/why not? Did you identify any aspects of the reading that confused you or with which you were unfamiliar? If so, this would signal that you need to chase up some further references to gain deeper understanding.
>
> It is likely that you will identify some gaps in your knowledge, but everyone will come to this task with different levels of information. For example, those readers who have studied debates within feminism about how, when or whether men can do research on women may be familiar with the differences between radical feminists who agree that men can do some pro-feminist research and those that have taken an essentialist position in which they advocate radical separation from men. Giri (2022: 5) tells us that 'it is the nature of the research and the way it is done, which sets it apart as a feminist, rather than the sex of the researcher (Morgan 1981, 86–87; Harding 1987; Ackerly and True 2010)'. This challenges early standpoint feminism, which did not take account of the fact that the category 'female' is diverse. Similarly, Giri points out, the category male is also diverse.
>
> Giri goes on to tell us how and why he moved from his original plan to carry out a quantitative study, through which he realised he would be reducing the data to categories and numbers, to a qualitative study. He wanted to listen to the women's complex accounts and thereby reveal the 'multifarious reality of war' through women's varied experiences and their different standpoints derived from their own positionality in their social worlds. Furthermore Giri considered the impact of what he refers to as his own axes of power (positionality) such as class, ethnicity, language, gender etc. on the data collection process.

CRITIQUING THE LITERATURE AND WRITING YOUR FORMAL REVIEW 131

Table 9.1 How to keep records of your reading

Literature source	Theoretical framework	Research aims/ questions	Research methodology	Key findings	Strengths	Limitations
Goldthorpe et al. (2022). *An Evaluation of the Lancashire Violence Reduction Network's Trauma Informed Lancashire Communities Early Adopters*. London: National Institute for Health Research.	Normalisation Process Theory (NPT) – NPT is a theory of implementation that has been used to support evaluations of complex interventions by exploring how new ways of working are embedded across groups of people and organisations. NPT focuses on four constructs: Coherence (understanding new ways of working); Cognitive Participation (linking new ways of working to existing knowledge); Collective Action (operationalising new ways of working); and Reflexive Monitoring (appraising and reflecting on new ways of working).	Research questions: explore the extent to which staff from Lancashire Violence Reduction Network (LVRN) and partner organisations understand and implement Trauma Informed (TI) approaches and to identify training needs, explore how TI approaches support LVRN clients and explore how data collection systems can be developed and improved to support sustainable, long-term evaluation that results in improvements to LVRN service delivery.	A total of 52 people from a range of organisations took part in interviews and focus groups. This resulted in four case studies: DIVERT Programme; Emergency Department Navigators; TI Education; and TI training and workforce development. Secondary data was also analysed where it was available.	Explores the extent to which staff from LVRN and partner organisations understand and implement trauma informed approaches and to identify training needs; explores how TI approaches support LVRN clients and explores how data collection systems can be developed and improved to support sustainable, long-term evaluation that results in improvements to LVRN service delivery.	Research design facilitated the engagement of a range of professionals; success in recruiting and training staff from the football trusts to work in TI ways.	The short timescale for the research meant that some people may not have been able to participate before the fieldwork had to be completed. There were also some gaps in the data collected and participants from key organisations – exacerbated by the Covid-19 pandemic. A final limitation was that secondary data about programme activity was not always available.

Reading critically entails thinking, questioning and some 'chasing up' in order that you can come to your own conclusions about the strengths and weaknesses of what you have read. In turn this will help you to justify the reasons for the user rejection of specific aspects of the wider literature in your own research project.

Table 9.1 gives suggested headings to help you keep track of your reading. One of our doctoral students, Amy Fenn, is undertaking research focused on violence reduction and prevention. She has written a literature review on research evidence concerning violence reduction initiatives and in Table 9.1 we have included an example of how she has made notes about one report that she included, among many others, in her literature review.

STUDENT ACTIVITY

Referring to the headings in Table 9.1, choose an article on a topic you are currently interested in. Perhaps it relates to a module you are studying or a research project/dissertation idea you are considering. Read the article and make a record of your reading. After you have completed reading the article and making notes, consider how the headings in the table helped you to read the article more closely and to enhance your critical thinking.

CASE STUDY: SAMANTHA'S PROGRESS

Samantha is an (imaginary) student who has already read a good deal of literature on the topic of undertaking research with people in prisons convicted of sex offences. She has made notes on everything she has read, using the headings we provide in Table 9.1. She has underlined comments made in key articles published during the past 20 years (Blagden and Pemberton, 2010; Cowburn, 2007; Kitson-Boyce et al., 2018; Lacombe, 2008; Mann, 2012; Pandey, 2023). She has noted that Blagden and Pemberton (2010), Cowburn (2007), Mann (2012) and Pandey (2023) have included useful discussions about some of the practical and ethical issues relating to carrying out research in prison, and she has noted that this will be useful when she discusses her methodology. There is an asterisk in her margin reminding her to discuss the issue of confidentiality (see Chapter 7) in her methodology chapter. Samantha notes that in some of the studies she has read the authors were concerned with the issue of offenders taking responsibility for their actions, even though in some senses Blagden and Pemberton (2010) saw the offenders as vulnerable. She compared this article with Lacombe's (2008) critique of the treatment of sex offenders in a risk society, and with Kitson-Boyce et al.'s finding that there were differences between those desisting from sex offending and those still actively offending, with desisters taking more responsibility and identifying 'this responsibility-taking for their own behaviour and actions as a general turning point in their lives' (2018: 304). She noted that Lacombe's (2008) historical account of the treatment of sex offenders referred to the now 'discredited' view that offenders were monsters who could not control their behaviour; yet the therapy involved their acceptance of the view 'once a sex offender always a sex offender'. She made a note that she was unsure about this. She read with interest about relatively recent prison-based models of Circles of Support and Accountability (that previously had been only community based) and made a note that she felt unsure how successful such a programme might be, needing to read more than one study to feel confident about any findings. To address this, she tasked herself with searching for any more recent studies on such prison programmes.

Samantha was interested to see that in both Mann's (2012) and Blagden and Pemberton's (2010) accounts of their interviews with sex offenders there was evidence that the offenders tried to justify or minimise the effects of their crimes. This set her thinking about *why* they might do this and she was reminded of something she had read in Cowburn's (2007) article – the view that sex offending has its roots in 'normal' society. This is a view that she found challenging but interesting and to some extent at odds with the significant stigma in society towards those who have committed sex offences (Kitson-Boyce et al., 2018). She chased up this idea by exploring the feminist literature. She spoke to some of her lecturers and eventually one of them suggested that she might find an old but quite important piece of feminist literature helpful. The article was MacLeod, M. and Saraga, E. (1988) 'Challenging the Orthodoxy: Towards Feminist Theory and Praxis', *Feminist Review*, 28(spring): 16–55, which Samantha thought was relevant to the point that Cowburn was making. She discovered that the authors had documented some of the ways in which male professionals constructed men as biologically driven rather than as responsible for their actions. In some cases child sexual abuse was explained as a result of family dysfunction – where dysfunction stood for problems with *maternal* behaviour, such as losing the desire to have sex. Samantha made a critical comment about this in her table as it didn't really make sense to her. She was aware of the 'bad press' that feminism often gets and up until this point she thought she agreed with some of the criticisms. The more she read, the more she came to understand that the idea that men are biologically driven was coming largely from men who were trying to explain sexual violence. This seemed strange to her as she had a recollection that some feminists were criticised for the mantra 'all men are rapists' but this was certainly not what the feminist writers she was reading seemed to be saying. Rather, they were saying that men *can* control their urges but if they grow up believing that they cannot, then perhaps it is no surprise that some men will try to excuse their behaviour.

With very little searching, Samantha also found references to Carol Smart (1989: 67), who documented the ways in which in courts sexual abuse was often put down to women's frigidity. A quick Google search enabled her to find reports of how Judge Cassell, in his summing up of a case of child sexual abuse in 1990, suggested that as the abuser's wife was pregnant and not having sex with her husband, the husband was 'understandably driven' to have sex with his 12-year-old stepdaughter. Samantha was quite shocked by this and raised the following question in her notes: 'Were these the same men who resisted feminist theorising? They are assuming men can't help it.' She spoke to her supervisor about this, who explained that there were several different feminist perspectives. One of the most radical perspectives suggested the separation of men from women on the grounds that men are 'naturally' more violent than women. He went on to explain that this reasoning was based on a biologically determinist premise that was criticised by most feminists. He also told Samantha that he thought she was correct to note that the male theorists who explained abuse in terms of *women's* failure to satisfy men were making the same error. Thus, from this, Samantha gained a more nuanced understanding of different feminist perspectives, and her supervisor explained that media representations of feminists were usually based on a caricature image of the most extreme (although small in number) feminists.

Samantha chased up the references to Jeff Hearn's (1998) work, cited by Cowburn (2007), and found that he had similar concerns to those of the feminist writers. His work, influenced by feminism, alerted her to the fact that gender should include discussions of masculinity as well as femininity. Samantha also looked up some of the literature on child abuse and found Nigel Parton's work in her university library in which she discovered a quotation that she thought was important: in Parliament on 27 April 1989, David Hinchcliffe stated that the roots of sexual violence were 'not so much in deviant family and sexual values but in "normal" ones ... we need to address in particular male socialisation, sexual attitudes and expectations of women in society' (cited in Parton, 1991: 166). Samantha came to the conclusion that this older literature was highly relevant to her research, as the little evidence that was available suggested that the same justifications are being made today by sex offenders.

Samantha decided to carry out life history interviews that explored with the offenders the ways in which they constructed their masculinity. She thought that although some interviews had been carried out in prison with sex offenders, none of them had sufficiently explored the relationship between their constructions of masculinity and their offending. She also decided that Matza's (1964) concept of neutralisation was still relevant today when considering sex offences.

KEY TERM

Critique: This term should not be confused with criticism. Rather, critique means identifying the strengths and weaknesses, and it usually involves making your own original points that are based on your wider knowledge of the topic.

Website Instructor activity

Critiquing a research article

BOX 9.2 STUDENT ACTIVITY

Identify the key elements of Samantha's progress with her literature review. Do you think she left anything important out of the process? When you have finished reading this chapter, follow up on some of the references provided in the case study above and make some critical comments of your own. How would you have proceeded with research on this topic?

Website Student activity

Planning a review

GETTING DOWN TO WRITING

Like any other piece of work, a literature review has an introduction, a main body and a conclusion (see Chapter 1). We suggest that you provide an introduction which explains why you think your chosen research area is important; for example, in the case study we outlined above, 'Samantha' could have decided that the official programmes open to sex offenders fail to take account of the meanings they give to their offending behaviour but instead *impose* meaning upon their behaviour, which they have to accept (see Lacombe, 2008). However, we think that the best introductions are often written at the end of the writing process so we would not necessarily recommend that you begin this task before you have written the main body of the review. This does not negate the need to have a good idea of why you think your chosen topic is worthy of research.

Website Student guide to …

Reviewing articles

The case study included above outlined, albeit very briefly, some key elements in the process of writing the main body of a review. The key to a good review lies in the writer's ability to compare and contrast the literature and to make sensible critical comments on the strengths and limitations of the different literatures. Do not think that the first draft will be adequate. Good writers revise and reconsider their critical comments as they move back and forth between new and old – but relevant – studies. This isn't a task that can be carried out quickly; rather it requires much thought and reflection. The more you read and reread the literature, the more your knowledge expands and the more your understanding improves. Ultimately this lengthy process will increase the likelihood of you being able to produce a final draft with sensible and appropriate critical comments.

Once you have got to the stage where you feel very familiar with the literature, you should be able to organise it in a logical way and start writing. There are several ways to do this but in general you will start by setting the scene and then you will work your way from broadly related research, through which you set the context, through to the specific research that has influenced your study most so that you finally end up with the formulation of your own clear statement of the research aims. This will involve a clear statement about the ways in which your research relates to and goes beyond existing studies. This is usually referred to as the 'inverted pyramid' approach (see Chapter 19, Figure 19.3, for a visual representation of this). Always keep your own purposes in mind, as this will ensure coherence of structure and logical justifications.

A straightforward chronological approach may be ideal when you are taking a historical approach to your study, perhaps in a situation where you are looking at something like the circumstances in which laws change in relation to specific issues such as drug use, for example. You will need to make a judgement depending on your chosen topic but often a chronological account can lead to a boring and somewhat incoherent review. Within the inverted pyramid approach it is also possible to organise the literature thematically. Try to take the time to identify key ideas which you can then group together and discuss critically – preferably in order of importance. It is also quite helpful to use headings which act as 'signposts' for the reader.

> **TIP**
>
> Colour code the key ideas you have identified in each of the articles in order to help you organise your review more coherently into key themes.

Remember that it is not a good idea to spend a long time discussing something that has only limited application to your research; in other words, the length of your discussion on each theme should be proportionate to the importance of the topic. In practice this means that your review is far more than a summary of the state of knowledge in your chosen area. Rather it should provide a synthesis of ideas that perhaps have not been linked before. Note that although you will have a separate methodology chapter/section to your research you will need to discuss the significance of researching the same topic in different ways within your review. As we have indicated already, research only *appears* to be a linear process, so, although the review comes before methods, you do need to display your knowledge of methodology literature in your review.

Once you have made your decision about the structure of your review you should take another look at your critical comments. When you present the different literatures you should spell out the implications of the knowledge you are including and you should try to identify what you think is missing and how your research might fill that gap. Ensure that you make links between those perspectives that are similar – you can use words or phrases like 'similarly', 'in the same vein', 'additionally', etc. When you introduce studies that present different views you should use words like 'however' or 'conversely'. We think it is also very important that you make your own 'voice' clear. So, although at this stage in the research you are writing about the views of others, you should nevertheless make comments as you go from which the reader will be able to identify your perspective. This is why it is so important to read critically and to make notes about your own response to the materials you are reading as you go along. For example, you may have identified that the literature provides relatively conflicting knowledge on your chosen topic. You therefore need to comment on the reasons why there is such conflicting evidence and explain the reasons why you are more convinced by some than by others. *Don't sit on the fence!* As Denscombe (2002: 51) has reminded us, the literature review is your opportunity to 'enhance the credibility of your research in the eyes of those who read it and who might be influenced by its findings'.

Your conclusion should sum up the major agreements and disagreements as well as your general conclusions about the research that has had the most influence on your research design. You should end up with a clear statement about where your own study is going and how it will add to the existing knowledge.

Finally, don't forget:

- that it's OK to use headings in a review – in fact it often helps;
- to write clearly and succinctly – imagine the reader knows nothing;
- to proof-read;
- to check that all your references are included;
- to revisit and review your own critical comments throughout the process of carrying out and writing up your research.

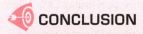

CONCLUSION

In order to write a convincing literature review you should ensure that you consult relevant texts through which you demonstrate your knowledge of your chosen research topic. A good review will not simply describe the existing state of knowledge but it will also critique that knowledge in a way that makes the researcher's perspective explicit. In order to write critically it is necessary to read critically; that is, to make notes of your thoughts and responses to the reading materials as you go along. It is worth putting time and effort into the preparation of the review, as it is this process that will help you consolidate your own ideas.

> ### ⭐ KEY LEARNING POINTS
>
> - There are three key types of literature: empirical, theoretical and methodological.
> - Critique involves the identification of strengths as well as weaknesses.
> - It is important to develop strategies to help you write your review in a methodical way. We have recommended that you produce a table in which to record key aspects of the literature that you have identified as important to your research.
> - You will produce the first draft of your review relatively early in the research process but don't forget that it is very important to continue reading as your research progresses. You will need to revisit and revise your review before you finally complete your research.

REFERENCES

Ackerly, B. and True, J. (2010) *Doing Feminist Research in Political and Social Science*, New York: Palgrave Macmillan.

Bell, J. and Opie, C. (2002) *Learning from Research*, fifth edition, Buckingham: Open University Press.

Blagden, N. and Pemberton, S. (2010) 'The Challenge in Conducting Qualitative Research with Convicted Sex Offenders', *Howard Journal of Criminal Justice*, 49(3): 269–281.

Cowburn, M. (2007) 'Men Researching Men in Prison: The Challenges for Pro-feminist Research', *Howard Journal*, 46(3): 276–288.

Denscombe, M. (2002) *Ground Rules for Good Research: A Ten-point Guide for Social Researchers*, Buckingham: Open University Press.

Giri, K. (2022) 'Can Men do Feminist Research and Fieldwork?', *International Studies Review*, 24(1). https://doi.org/10.1093/isr/viac004

Goldthorpe, J., Khan, K., Stewart, H. and Wheeler, P. (2022) *An Evaluation of the Lancashire Violence Reduction Network's Trauma Informed Lancashire Communities Early Adopters*. London: National Institute for Health Research.

Harding, S. (1987) *Feminism and Methodology*, Bloomington: Indiana University Press.

Hearn, J. (1998) 'Theorizing Men and Men's Theorizing: Varieties of Discursive Practices in Men's Theorizing of Men', *Theory and Society*, 27(6): 781–816.

Kitson-Boyce, R., Blagden, N., Winder, B. and Dillon, G. (2018) 'A Prison-model of CoSA: The Potential to Offer "Through the Gate" Support and Accountability, *Journal of Sexual Aggression*, 24(3): 294–310. https://doi.org/10.1080/13552600.2018.1509575

Lacombe, D. (2008) 'Consumed with Sex: The Treatment of Sex Offenders in Risk Society', *British Journal of Criminology*, 48(1): 55–74.

MacLeod, M. and Saraga, E. (1988) 'Challenging the Orthodoxy: Towards Feminist Theory and Praxis', *Feminist Review*, 28(spring): 16–55.

Mann, N. (2012) 'Ageing Child Sex Offenders in Prison: Denial, Manipulation and Community', *Howard Journal of Criminal Justice*, 51(4): 345–358.

Matza, D. (1964) *Delinquency and Drift*, New York: Wiley.

Morgan, D. (1981) 'Men, Masculinity and the Process of Sociological Enquiry' in H. Roberts (ed.) *Doing Feminist Research*, London: Routledge and Kegan Paul, pp. 83–113.

Pandey, M. (2023) 'Interviews with Men Convicted of Rape: Reflections and Lessons of a Female Researcher in a Male Delhi Prison', *Gender a výzkum / Gender and Research*, 24(1): 135–158. https://doi.org/10.13060/gav.2023.009

Parton, N. (1991) *Governing the Family*, London: Macmillan.

Smart, C. (1989) *Feminism and the Power of the Law*, London: Routledge.

Chapter 10

Theories, methods and their relationships to theories of knowledge

GOALS OF THIS CHAPTER

At the end of reading this chapter and by completing the online resources that accompany it, you will be:

1 familiar with different theories about crime and with the assumptions that underpin them;
2 able to understand the relationship between theories of crime, theories of knowledge and methods;
3 able to identify the methods that are most appropriate to the research questions you may wish to answer;
4 able to understand the difference between methods (the *how* of research) and *methodology* (not just the *how* but also the *why*).

OVERVIEW

- This chapter will help you pull together the knowledge you have gained through your reading of the early chapters in this text in order that you will be ready to 'get going' with research.
- It will focus specifically on some of the key criminological theories that have been developed over time.
- Through a series of practical exercises it will help you understand the relationship between theories of crime, theories of knowledge and their relationship to the methods of criminological research.
- By the end of the chapter you should have the ability to identify the methods that are appropriate to your own research questions and to justify your choices.

DEVELOPING A METHODOLOGICAL APPROACH TO THE STUDY OF CRIME

Most criminological textbooks provide expansive discussions of different theories of crime, but it is true to say that more often than not theories are discussed with

DOI: 10.4324/9781032645698-13

very little reference to either theories of knowledge or methods. Where methods are discussed it is usually in a chapter that is separate from the discussion of theory. The relationship between theories and methods, therefore, is quite often ignored and can lead to the false impression that the methods researchers use are unrelated to the questions they ask.

Criminology has been influenced by a range of disciplines within medicine and social science. Garland (1994) spoke of three key perspectives: sociological, psychoanalytic and administrative criminology. Sociological criminology is concerned with the relationship between the individual and society. Psychoanalytic criminology draws upon the work of Freud and the role of the unconscious and conscious mind. This approach focuses upon individuals and the ways in which the development of personality might influence the propensity to commit crimes. Administrative criminology focuses largely upon crime prevention strategies rather than on the individuals who commit crimes. This perspective treats individuals as rational calculators who will weigh up the pros and cons of criminal acts. Each of these broad strands is influenced by a set of assumptions about the nature of the social world in which crimes take place as well as about human 'nature'. In turn these assumptions will influence the questions researchers ask as well as their decisions about the most appropriate way to gather knowledge that will help them answer those questions – as we saw in Chapter 6. Our main task in this chapter is to enable you to identify the assumptions which underpin various criminological theories. Once you are able to unpick these underlying assumptions you will soon be able to understand how they in turn have influenced the types of research projects in which criminologists have been involved. It is this process that will enable you to understand why research has been carried out in a particular way, but, more importantly, it should help you to think about your own research purposes in a deeper way.

THE DIMENSIONS OF CRIMINOLOGICAL RESEARCH

Burrell and Morgan (1992), in their book *Sociological Paradigms and Organisational Analysis*, developed a matrix onto which they mapped perspectives within sociological thought along two axes. We have adapted this here in order to enable you to identify the underlying assumptions of key *criminological* theories and related penal and victim theories. Burrell and Morgan identified four sociological paradigms (or frameworks) which we believe to be helpful to the task of understanding the philosophical assumptions behind the three key criminological perspectives. However, we also wish to reveal the importance of moving in and out of frameworks as a device through which to confirm or challenge what we (think we) know. This process helps us to work out not only what our views are but also why we hold them and our reasons for changing them. Once you are able to do this you should also be able to produce better critiques of the work of others and more convincing justifications for your own research. As we noted in Chapter 5, crime is a political concept; therefore, as Stout Yates and Williams (2008: 6) so eloquently put it, criminology should not just be about problem solving on behalf of the state (administrative criminology) but it should also be about different ways of raising issues for debate that may challenge the state. In order for researchers to carry out both of these important tasks it is essential that they gain an understanding of the ways in which assumptions about what in general any social science is/should be – and indeed what society is/should be – shape the knowledge about crime that is produced.

The study of crime is largely influenced by sociological and psychological theorising, and through these disciplines our knowledge and understanding of crime has been widened considerably. It is for this reason that criminologists need to have an awareness of the assumptions that have underpinned this theorising. Sociology, as the name suggests, is concerned with the social, whereas psychology is largely concerned with individuals (although note that there are different perspectives within psychology and also that social psychology and interactionist sociology have much in common). Sociology has frequently been discussed in relation to two key concepts: order and change, both of which are relevant to any discussion of crime in society. Early social theorists grappled with two key questions: How does change come about? And how is order maintained? For change to come about, human beings have to be considered capable of acting on their social world. For order to be maintained there has to be some acceptance of social regulation. The concepts of order and change have often been perceived as polar opposites (as the two extremes in the change/regulation continuum shown in Figure 10.1). The key questions about order and change are linked to, but separate from, another set of assumptions relating to four important debates about **ontology**, **epistemology**, human nature and methodology that together make up the subjective/objective continuum in Figure 10.1. Researchers need to decide:

- whether or not they think that there is a tangible social world that can be discovered through research (ontology);
- whether or not they think that science provides the appropriate tools with which to research the social world and, if so, what form of science they are talking about. Some key questions we raised in Chapter 6, for example, were: What do we mean when we talk about objectivity? Can it be achieved? If so, how? Is science inductive, deductive, or both? (epistemology);
- whether human beings may be said to have free will. If so, to what extent? (human nature debates);
- what sorts of methods are appropriate to their aims and research question/s? (methods debates).

These are all questions with which social scientists in general are familiar and which will therefore underpin any research into crime. Following Burrell and Morgan (1992), we can represent the questions embodied within the subjective/objective continuum as shown in Figure 10.1.

While you will see that, like Burrell and Morgan, we have set up oppositional concepts, it is our intention to demonstrate that as criminological research has progressed the debates that have ensued have facilitated ways of overcoming

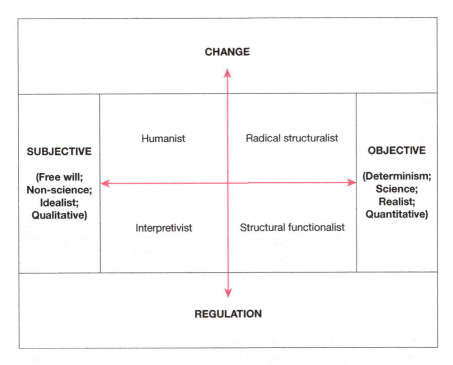

Figure 10.1 The dimensions of criminological research frameworks (adapted from Burrell and Morgan, 1992).

oppositional modes of thinking. However, the frameworks do provide us with a useful heuristic device through which researchers can become aware of the assumptions they are making and thereby become more logical in their arguments and research decisions.

The sociologist Anthony Giddens (1979) attempted to overcome the polarisation of structure and action. These concepts are linked to our consideration of the regulation/change continuum. Giddens (1979) pointed out that structure does not simply constrain action; rather it is involved in action. An example we might use when discussing research on crime is the way in which the structure of the law may actually lead people to question why a given act is defined as criminal. In a later work (1990: 221) Giddens explained that human activities often take place within institutional settings, which can either mobilise or limit the human capacity to act. Furthermore, he explained how the more institutions are grounded in our everyday routines the more difficult they are to change. Finally, and perhaps most importantly for criminologists, Giddens noted the ways in which sanctions are used to limit people's options. Thus, as we explained in Chapter 5, crimes are defined and responded to within relations of power, which result in the constraint of only some people's actions; for example, if we think about the often assumed relationship between family breakdown and crime, why is it that those involved in corporate crimes escape being defined as members of 'dysfunctional' families? What we hope you will soon realise is that this does not mean that the functionalist paradigm produced knowledge that was 'wrong' or of no use but rather that it produced only partial knowledge that led to important further debates. As we saw in Chapter 6, such insights are key to **critical criminological researchers**, as they are concerned with bringing about change and therefore with the need to understand and reveal the relations of power within which crimes are defined and within which crimes and society's response to them take place.

Idealism	ONTOLOGY	Realism
Anti-science	EPISTEMOLOGY	Pro-science (however defined)
Free will	HUMAN 'NATURE'	Determinism
Unstructured (e.g. ethnographic interviews and observation)	METHODS	Structured (e.g. experiments and large-scale surveys)

Subjective ←――――――――――――――――――――→ Objective

Figure 10.2 The subjective/objective continuum (adapted from Burrell and Morgan, 1992).

We can plot different types of research at various points between the two extremes of the regulation/change continuum. To do this it is necessary to ascertain whether the researcher's main concern is with the maintenance of social order in society as it is, or with the development of a more equal society. Thus we can see that doing research involves questions not just about methods – *how* we do research – but also about why we have chosen to do our research in a particular way. A *methodological* approach to criminological research therefore involves the need to understand the relationship between theories of crime, theories of knowledge and methods. Research into crime has most commonly been concerned with order and regulation in society; after all, if some behaviour is defined as a problem to society then it is logical to want to regulate that behaviour. However, what we know is that there is not always agreement about the sorts of behaviours that should be defined as a problem. For example, homosexuality was once defined as illegal in the UK and continues to be illegal in some countries. It was only as a result of wider debates within social science that attitudes towards homosexuality were changed. Without the acknowledgement of the human capacity to change the way we think about things that we take for granted, there would be little chance that the way we define and respond to crime could ever change. The history of crime, however, demonstrates that in fact the way we define and respond to crime *does* change – even if changes may come about rather more slowly than some researchers would like. This does seem to indicate that it is not logical to polarise regulation and change but rather to examine the issues that may inhibit or facilitate change, and to examine the contexts in which change may be more appropriate than adherence to the status quo.

You may have already deduced from your reading of Chapter 6 that discussions of **interpretivism** and **positivism** are often centred on another polarisation, namely objectivity and subjectivity, or we might say science or anti-science. We attempted to show how it might be helpful to see the constant interplay between objectivity and subjectivity by being more precise about what we mean by objectivity and by keeping this concept separate from the concept of value-neutrality. We did this in order to include the third theory of knowledge, critical criminological research, within our discussion. When you start plotting the assumptions made by different theorists on the matrix shown in Figure 10.1 we hope you will be able to identify a pattern which will enable you to discuss the assumptions that this group of theorists tend to make. Keep in mind the fact that debates about theories of knowledge centre on (1) the extent to which the social world can be studied in the same way as the natural world, and (2) the issue of what is understood by the term 'truth'.

PAUSE TO THINK ...

- Can we find 'the truth' about crime once and for all?
- Is truth always mediated by our experiences and therefore a relative concept? (Refer back to Chapter 6.)

Once you get the hang of identifying the philosophical assumptions that theorists make you should begin to understand that the delineations between the different research traditions are not as neat as many 'standard textbooks' suggest. Furthermore, the exercises outlined below should help you identify some of the contradictions and flaws that can always be found in theories. Once you are able to do this you will in turn be able to make and express judgements about the reasons why some theories are stronger or more convincing than others. Thus, when you come to do your own research you will be far better equipped to:

- make suitable choices about the literature that is to inform your study;
- discuss the theories that have informed your own studies;
- comment upon the strengths as well as the limitations of the theories that have informed your work in order to explain the ways in which your research will address the gaps in existing knowledge;
- express the reasons why the methods you have chosen are appropriate to the questions you want to answer. (This means that as well as being able to *describe* the methods you use in your own research you should also be able to *justify* your choice of methods and explain why you carried out your research in a particular way.)

THE BEGINNINGS OF CRIMINOLOGY: CLASSICISM AND POSITIVISM

You will be able to find detailed accounts of early criminology in many of the textbooks available from your university library. Furthermore, it is highly likely that your degree course will have begun with an outline of the main criminological theories. Our aim here is not to reiterate those theories in detail but instead to get you thinking about what they assume. The two sets of ideas outlined in brief in Box 10.1 both continue to influence the ways in which crime is researched today. This first mapping exercise will have shown you (quite quickly, we hope) that they represent opposite ends of the free will/determinism continuum. **Classicism** assumes that because human beings are rational beings they are all equally capable of making decisions that are in their best interests – but we might want to add the caveat 'not in circumstances of their own choosing' to invoke Karl Marx. It is not necessary to be a Marxist to acknowledge that it may be very important to know something about the circumstances in which people commit crimes, but since the pleasure/pain principle of classicism did not take account of social inequalities in society, many criminologists today see the theory as incomplete. According to classicist theories, all criminals should be treated in the same way irrespective of what we would call extenuating circumstances. Thus someone who stole food because his/her family was starving would be treated in the same way as someone who stole food despite having plenty. At heart the classicists expressed a theory of *punishment* which they viewed as deterrence; theories of crime causation were not their concern, nor were the motivations of criminals. Instead classicists reduced criminals to calculators of risk.

In opposition to classicism, the early positivists (we like to refer to these as *biological or individual positivists*) did not assume that human beings were in control of their actions because they theorised that crimes were only committed by those who were somehow 'defective'. In other words, the causes of crime lay not in the way in which society was organised – or, as in the case of the classicist argument, in the way in which people were controlled – but rather in the biological make-up of each person. Thus experts were required to identify those people who, as prisoners of their own biology, could not be held responsible for their crimes. Of course, this also implies that they could not be reformed and therefore this perspective was used to justify, at best, shutting prisoners away indefinitely in poor conditions or, at worst, the death penalty. While Lombroso's focus on physical characteristics became the focus of critique (including in his own work), biologically deterministic theories continued into the twentieth century. The shift in focus to supposed hereditary mental conditions became known as the eugenics movement, a science defined by Galton (1883) as 'the science of improving stock' (cited in Valier, 2002: 19). As a result of this approach some of the most brutal forms of social control were justified; for example, in the United States there were mass sterilisations of people defined as 'feebleminded' and in some states 'psychosurgeries' (Lilly, Cullen and Ball, 2019) such as frontal lobotomies and electric shock treatment were permitted up until the 1970s. For Europeans the worst examples of the impact of the study of inherited characteristics were seen in Nazi Germany. Today drug treatments are used to control behaviour in children as young as 2.

BOX 10.1 EARLY THEORIES OF CRIME AND PUNISHMENT

Using the knowledge gained in Chapter 6, read up on the theories of the Italian economists Beccaria and Lombroso.

- Where would you 'map' the two sets of ideas put forward by these theorists in terms of their assumptions about free will/**determinism**? Try to give reasons for the position you choose.
- What theory of knowledge is implied by each set of ideas?
- Where would you place each set of ideas on the regulation/change continuum? Why?
- What are the implications of all the above for the choice of research methods?
- What do these theories leave out?

BOX 10.2 CLASSICIST IDEAS IN USE TODAY

Look up rational choice theory and situational crime prevention, both of which come under the heading of administrative criminology.

- What do these perspectives assume about both criminals and victims?
- Do these assumptions take account sufficiently of people's different life experiences?
- What types of research methods can be used to support rational choice theory?
- What would be the likely attitude of such researchers to the official crime statistics?
- What are the strengths and limitations of such research?

As the biological positivist theory of knowledge assumes that the (social) problem of crime may be understood best by copying the methods of natural science, it can be seen that there is a clear relationship between this assumption and the ways in which early positivists chose to treat their subject matter (criminals). While criminals, like non-criminals, are thinking, conscious human beings there is an assumption that they should be treated as if they are 'things' (or non-human) for the purposes of research. That is, their feelings and motives are excluded from the process of study (see Chapter 12). Thus you should be able to discern the relationship between ontology, epistemology and the choice of research methods made by early positivists who assumed that motives lie outside the enterprise of science.

While classicism focused upon individuals' free will and their ability to make choices, it too failed to focus upon people's explanations of their crimes. Rather, classicism assumed that there is an abstract human nature that is inherently selfish and hedonistic. For this reason classicists focused upon crime prevention. Early classicism assumed that crime would be prevented if controls were not so restricting as to cause rebellion. Put simply, the more restrictions there are in society the less pleasure people would have and the more laws would be broken, an idea which is summed up in Lilly et al.'s (2019) phrase 'bad laws make bad people'. This said, in cases of serious violent crime, it was argued that punishment should be meted out quickly and that citizens should be aware of the crimes that carry harsh punishments so as to ensure that they would be clear about the certainty of the punishment following such crimes. While on the one hand the classicists' focus upon free will seems in stark contrast to the determinism of biological positivism, on the other hand, when we explore the assumptions that classicists held about 'human nature' it is possible to discern determinism, albeit in a different guise, since 'human nature' was assumed to be universally selfish and hedonistic, and therefore in need of constant control. Classicists believed that it was necessary for states to be open about the moral codes that underpinned the laws in society and that there should be consensus about the need for the laws that exist. Their concern was not to explain crime but rather to prevent it by ensuring that most people adhered to the social controls.

PAUSE TO THINK ...

Do those who break the law always act out of self-interest? Can you think of examples of crimes that may be said to stem from different motivations?

LEARNING FROM THE PAST

The early biological and sociological positivists have to be understood in the context of their time and place. The idea that social issues could be studied in the same way as natural science stemmed from the success of science in solving problems in the natural world. Indeed, the word 'positivism' represents the optimistic view that the world could be changed for the better ... but did this mean for the better of all? When we examine the work of early theorists it is possible to discern a whole host of assumptions that we may wish to challenge in our current society. For example, what we would now understand as sexist, classist and racist assumptions may be seen in hindsight to have underpinned the work of Lombroso (1920: 151):

> Women have many traits in common with children; that their moral sense is deficient; that they are revengeful, jealous .... In ordinary cases these defects are neutralised by piety, maternity, want of passion, sexual coldness, weakness, and an underdeveloped conscience.

For Lombroso, white middle-class males were assumed to be at the pinnacle of evolution; therefore any characteristics that were not held in common with these men were thought to be the ones that would facilitate the identification of the criminal classes. When explaining female crime Lombroso believed that the further removed a woman was from white, middle-class definitions of 'femininity' the more likely she was to be criminal. This is a view that was also present in the work of psychologists such as Thomas (1907) and Freud (1920) (see discussion by Klein, 1973), which is evident in the words of Thomas (1907: 112, cited in Klein, 1973):

> What we look for most in the female is femininity, and when we find the opposite in her we must conclude, as a rule, that there must be some anomaly. ... Virility was one of the special features of the savage woman ... in the portraits of red Indian and Negro beauties, whom it is difficult to recognise for women, so huge are their jaws and cheekbones, so hard and coarse their features, and the same is often the case in their crania and brains.

PAUSE TO THINK ...

Examine newspaper reports of female-perpetrated crimes.

- Can you identify some of the assumptions of early positivists in the ways in which female criminality is reported today?
- How might criminological researchers challenge such ideas?

The sociologist Émile Durkheim is famous for the way in which he applied the methods of science to the study of social life. His important study of suicide (1970) provides us with a very detailed account of how he arrived at the view that suicide, which seems like one of the most individual acts that can be committed, is caused by forces that are outside of the individual. Note that in Durkheim's time (1858–1917) suicide was against the law, which is no longer the case in the UK, although in around 20 countries worldwide suicide is still considered a crime. In this study Durkheim tried to follow the rules of natural science very closely and it took him a great deal of time to come up with the conclusion that lack of integration in society was the cause of what he called *egoistic* suicide; lack of security about the rules that govern society was the external cause of what Durkheim called *anomic* suicide. These were the two forms of suicide which, according to Durkheim, were prevalent in modern industrial societies. It is interesting to research the debates on the study of suicide because they reveal the ways in which studies from different epistemological positions widen our understanding of this phenomenon.

While we have suggested that positivism implied some optimism about the possibility of manipulating causal variables in an attempt to reduce crime in society, we have also seen that a focus on the individual's characteristics (biological positivism) can lead to the justification of drastic measures to control behaviour.

> ### BOX 10.3 WERE BIOLOGICAL POSITIVISTS ABLE TO AVOID THE USE OF VALUES IN THEIR RESEARCH INTO CRIME?
>
> Do some further reading about:
>
> 1. how Lombroso explained female criminality;
> 2. the 'types' of people who were identified as in need of treatment by scientists in the eugenics movement.
>
> What was assumed by these theorists?
>
> Look up critiques of Wilson and Herrnstein's (1985) *Crime and Human Nature* and Herrnstein and Murray's (1994) *The Bell Curve: Intelligence and Class Structure in American Life*. Did these much later studies suggest that the authors were able to carry out their work in such a way as to exclude their ideological views?

> ### BOX 10.4 THE STUDY OF SUICIDE
>
> Research the debates about Durkheim's method in the study of suicide.
>
> - Do you think he managed to keep his values out of the research process? Provide reasons for your answer and make an evaluative comment.
> - What assumptions did Durkheim make about the official statistics on suicide?
> - Have all those who have researched suicide made the same assumptions about the official statistics?
> - Choose a specific crime and identify the official statistics on the prevalence of this crime. Think of a research question that relates to this particular type of crime and try to articulate the way in which your research question will shape your perspective on the official statistics.
>
> Hint: You may need to refer to Chapter 5 in order to refresh your memory about the different assumptions that theorists have made about official statistics.

A focus on social conditions led to entirely different solutions to the problem of crime, which involved the manipulation of social variables, such as widening access to education or action against poverty. Durkheim, who is considered to be an archetypal positivist, for example, assumed that crime is a normal, indeed healthy, aspect of social life (Durkheim, 1982). For Durkheim, crime served a positive function because laws signal the moral values of society. When individuals break laws the social response serves to maintain the 'moral' society. However, there may be occasions, especially when groups break the law, when the social response is to question the morality of the law (rather than the lawbreakers). In these cases crime functions to change the status quo and to change perceptions of what is/is not moral. As Carrabine et al. (2020) point out, this is the paradox of functionalism. We believe, however, that this paradox demonstrates the fallacy of labelling a *theorist* because the whole reason for developing theories is to test them out and revise them in the light of new information – this is the nature of research and it means that theorists can provide more nuanced explanations or shift their ground in the light of new evidence (if you are interested you may want to look at Durkheim's work as a whole and consider to what extent it is appropriate to refer to him as 'a positivist').

Researchers take account of and build on the work of others. The influential American sociologist Robert Merton, for example, drew upon the work of Durkheim to develop a theory of crime that he linked to the strains of living in the American society of his time. As Tierney (2010) has pointed out, Merton posited a link between the lack of legitimate opportunities to achieve the American dream of material success and the incidences of crime. It follows from this that if the legitimate means of success are improved – say, through wider access to further education – then crimes will be reduced. However, the theory has several shortcomings; for example, many crimes are committed by those who have achieved material success; there are differences of opinion about what are the most important cultural values; violent crimes cannot be explained by Merton's theory and, as we shall see shortly, as cultural criminology has highlighted, some crimes may give the perpetrators pleasure – or 'a buzz' as we might say colloquially. This said, Box (1983) argued that if Merton's anomie theory was applied to the study of corporate crimes some of the most well-known criticisms would be addressed.

POSITIVISM TODAY

We have seen thus far that the focus of analysis for biological positivism was the individual mind or body. These perspectives generally failed to take account of the impact of the social context of crime. Later positivistic schools of thought shifted the focus of attention from individuals to the social conditions in which crimes are committed. This did not necessarily signal a shift away from determinism but rather a shift in theorising about what the determining factors leading to crime might be. To put this in more formal language, there was a shift in the theories of causation; that is, a shift from a focus on the individual to a focus on society, but not a shift in the *epistemological* or *ontological* positions. For some commentators a problem with sociological positivism's assumption that the causes of crime lie outside of the individual is that it allows criminals to abrogate responsibility for their actions. This is why many social researchers today talk about reasons rather than causes because it is only through an examination of the *relationship* between individuals and society that we are able to get a more nuanced understanding of why different forms of crime are committed. The assumptions of such researchers challenge the notion of causation (whether social or individual) and instead assume that it is important to look at the interplay between the individual and society in order to assess the weight that should be given to each before attempting to change policy or suggest 'treatment'. That is, such researchers try not to fall into the trap of operating under the assumption that individuals are either completely determined by their biology or by the social order but they see the merit in using quantitative methods that are associated with natural science.

Researchers operating within the positivist theory of knowledge usually start out by examining the relationship between two variables – a '**bivariate relationship**' (e.g. poverty and crime; intelligence and crime) – and to do this they need to think about which variable is dependent upon the other. In these examples crime is the **dependent variable** but sometimes it may be hard to know which variable is the dependent one; for example, with the variables illegal drugs and crime does illegal drug use necessarily lead to crime? Can involvement with other crimes actually be a factor that leads to drug use? It is important to think about these issues in order for the research to be fair as well as to think about other possible variables that might challenge the relationship we have found (this moves us on to 'multi-variate analysis', as in Durkheim's study of suicide). As we saw in Chapter 8, there are several variables that may be related to crime. Furthermore, we saw that we need to be quite clear about the sorts of crimes we are talking about in our studies; that is, we need to operationalise crime. Individual researchers will not be able to test out all possible variables alone but they will be able to look at other studies in order to see what has been suggested already. They will also be able to decide whether a relationship is **spurious** (leading us up the garden path, as it were) or not. For example, claims that there is a relationship between low intelligence and crime can be challenged by a shift in focus onto crimes such as corporate crime or crimes that take place in the private sphere. Even when there is evidence that may be quite convincing, it is important that researchers specify the circumstances in which their theories hold true. For example, if poverty is found to be an indicator of certain types of crime, does this relationship hold true in all circumstances? We may want to compare rural areas with urban areas, for example, to decide whether we need to qualify the conditions in which poverty is a significant factor. Furthermore, we may identify other independent variables that are equally significant and each of these may suggest different types of policy response. Researchers using positivist assumptions will always need to discuss their samples (see Chapter 16) in order to demonstrate that they have done everything possible to avoid sample bias. They must also show understanding of 'sampling error', which can always occur simply because criminological researchers cannot ever study the whole population of those involved in particular types of crimes. This is why it is important to carry out tests of statistical significance (see Chapters 13 and 16).

It is important that criminological researchers today continue to look for **correlations** between variables, but we suggest that it is equally important to challenge the assumptions of early positivists who, in our view, mistakenly conflated causes and correlations. We believe that it is because of this conflation that extreme determinism was a feature of early positivistic research which, in turn, made it possible to justify some of the most worrying measures to prevent crime that we have discussed above. We need to be alert to the ways in which some researchers today may use what we believe are outmoded assumptions about science in general and causation in particular to try to implement policies that go beyond the findings of their research.

INTERPRETIVISM: WHERE SOCIOLOGY AND SOCIAL PSYCHOLOGY COLLIDE

As we pointed out at the beginning of this book, crime is a socially constructed concept and crimes take place in different social contexts. To understand crime more completely, therefore, it is also important to carry out research in a way that takes account of people's subjective accounts of their motivations. Theories within this perspective challenge the idea that people can be treated as if they are 'things' and instead focus upon the ways in which people come to understand themselves in relation to others. One perspective within the interpretivist theory of knowledge, interactionism, developed from the work of the sociologist Georg Simmel (1908) and the social psychologist George Herbert Mead (1934). Mead's work influenced the **symbolic interactionist** perspective, which was concerned with social processes. In criminology the concern with the social processes that lead to the status of criminal is usually referred to as the labelling perspective. The impact of labelling has been a key idea in the study of crime because, as Kitsuse (1962) noted in his discussion of deviance, it is only at the point where a person places a label on another that behaviour comes to be seen as problematic. In other words, it is the social reaction to an act that is significant rather than the act itself. The ways in which others react to our behaviour shape our sense of who we are – a 'kind' person, a 'happy' person, an 'eccentric' person ... a 'criminal'. Labels of any kind are likely to affect the ways in which people subsequently perceive themselves and act, so this suggests that studying the interaction between individuals and others in the wider society may expand our understanding of crime. This said, it is important to be mindful that people react to labels in different ways; therefore it may be important to work out when and in what circumstances a negative label might produce a positive response.

The person who influenced criminological thinking most with regard to labelling was Howard Becker. In his book *Outsiders* (1963), one issue he examined was the way in which the development of laws in relation to the use of marijuana in 1930s' America created a climate in which the young people who used this drug came to be perceived as a risk to society. Once this process has taken place those labelled become outsiders and – so the theory goes – develop their own cultural norms, which they see as being counter to the general culture of society. Young (1971), in a similar vein, discussed the way in which the police reaction to the use of marijuana in Britain gave rise to what he called a 'fantasy crime wave' which served to amplify this form of 'deviance' as the drug users lived up to the stereotypes that were a feature of newspaper reports. The media outrage created political pressures, which in turn gave rise to heavier policing and harsher sentences. As Valier (2002: 93) states, there was a tendency for policymakers to mistake the changes which were caused, in Young's view, by the social reaction as further evidence of the problematic nature of *all* drug users.

BOX 10.5 LIVING UP TO AND CHALLENGING LABELS

Violent crime is frequently associated with a specific view of what it is to be a male. Ideas about labelling have been developed in research that focuses on discourse (see Chapter 12) – how men explain their violence. Take a look at Heber, A. (2017) 'You Thought You Were Superman: Violence, Victimisation and Masculinities', *British Journal of Criminology*, 57(1): 61–78.

1. Look at the data on page 66. Do the data demonstrate the ways in which labels shape people's sense of who they are?
2. How does Heber's focus on different discourses challenge traditional assumptions about gender? Why might this be useful to the task of widening our understanding of crime and desistance from crime?
3. What does this study tell you about the ways in which theories are developed and expanded?

BOX 10.6 THE ASSUMPTIONS OF THE LABELLING PERSPECTIVE

Plot the position of labelling theorists on the matrix in Figure 10.1. Think about the following questions before you decide on their position on the matrix:

- What would be the attitude of labelling theorists to official crime statistics?
- What does this perspective assume about human nature and the social structure?
- What questions do you think criminologists who are influenced by this perspective are likely to ask?
- What methods are most appropriate to this perspective?

THE THRILL OF CRIME

Many explanations of crime have tended to over-predict crime among the working class and people living in poverty. This is partly because, in general, criminologists have focused less on the crimes of the powerful than they have on the crimes of those with least power. However, we know that some conventional crimes, for example, shoplifting, are not committed solely by the poor; therefore this knowledge leads to the questioning of explanations that link shoplifting to determining variables, such as the boring jobs carried out by the working classes or people's basic need for more resources in order to live. As O'Malley (2010) has pointed out, this was a point made by Jack Katz in his book *Seductions of Crime* (1988). Katz therefore shifted his attention to the lived experiences of those committing crimes and identified the thrill associated with the risk as a reason for crimes. This shift of focus can explain why those who are not poor might engage in shoplifting; indeed, it was theorised that the thrill might be greater the more a person had to lose. The only way we can find out whether this theory may be important is to talk to criminals or to enter their worlds through participant observational studies. O'Malley (2010: 9) refers to the ways in which cultural theorists pointed to the normality of thrill and risk in the modern culture of the consumer society where 'the boundary between legitimate and illegitimate is becoming more volatile and ambiguous'. Cultural criminology acknowledges that while some criminals may be rational calculators of risk and reward there are also other constructions of risk that may be relevant to our understanding of crime precisely because they reject this calculating form of rationality. This means that the role of emotion becomes an important element in the search to widen knowledge of criminal behaviour. There is also a sense in which recent developments in cultural theory fit with the **dialectical** (see below) analysis associated with critical criminology, although it has also been criticised for not taking sufficient account of the social structures within which crimes are carried out (Chamberlain, 2015: 138–139). You should have deduced that here the assumption of free will is central to the way in which research within this perspective is carried out.

MARXIST THEORIES AND CRIMINOLOGY

In general, Marxist criminologists were critical of attempts to see the causes of crime as evidence of individual pathology and they maintained that this was a way of perpetuating the idea that criminals can be distinguished from non-criminals. These conflict theorists argued that the conventional study of crime was tied to the capitalist economic system and indeed that the laws supported that system. A key moment for criminology was the publication of a book called *The New Criminology* (Taylor, Walton and Young, 1973), in which a thorough critique of existing criminological theories was presented. Some of the main issues to which they pointed were: the failure of criminologists to ask questions about control as well as about crime; the over-determinism of some explanations (this critique also included those Marxist theories which implied that the capitalist system would have to be overthrown in order to solve the problem of crime) at the expense of recognising the purposive actions of human beings; and the inadequacy of some theories of knowledge. Indeed, Muncie (1998) stated that this book transformed criminology from a science of social control into a struggle for social justice. The book also led to a focus on the crimes of the powerful. In a sense, conflict theorists assumed that the law produced criminals (see Lilly et al., 2019) because in their view laws served to conceal the crimes of those who had the most power. These ideas challenged the value-neutrality that (supposedly) was a feature of positivism and the assumption that society was characterised by consensus, which was an assumption of mainstream criminology, as in Durkheim's view. However, *The New Criminology* (1973) was an important book not because it provided a 'blueprint' for research but more because the huge intra-left debates and divisions between idealists and realists to which it gave rise, as well as the critiques from the opposite ('right') end of the political spectrum which were sparked by this book, were significant to the task of doing research, as they signalled the need to be ever-mindful of the assumptions *all* researchers make as well as of the strengths and limitations of their evidence.

BOX 10.7 RESEARCHING THE CRIMES OF THE POWERFUL

Corporate crimes have been explained in various ways using the insights of many of the theorists to whom we have referred. Imagine that having done some reading about corporate crime you have become interested in the relationship of this type of crime to the political economy and that you want to do some research that uses this knowledge. Try to do the following:

- Outline your philosophical assumptions.
- Define the type of corporate crime upon which you will focus your study.
- Outline the main aim/s of your research.
- Construct a research question that relates to your aims.
- Identify the most appropriate method/s.
- Suggest some outcomes.

BOX 10.8 CORPORATE DENIAL: THE POWER OF ORGANISATIONS

Now look at Schoultz, I. and Flyghed, J. (2020) 'From "We Didn't Do It" to "We've Learned Our Lesson": Development of a Typology of Neutralizations of Corporate Crime', *Critical Criminology*, 28: 739–757.

What do Schoultz and Flyghed say about the ways that organisations seek to 'neutralise' corporate crime? Does this help you to understand why it is difficult to challenge corporate power?

Compare your answers to the activities in Box 10.7 with the research described in this article.

MAINTAINING THE LEGITIMACY OF THE STATE

Hall et al.'s (1978) *Policing the Crisis* provides us with a good example of a study that attempted to explain a panic about street crimes (referred to in the press as 'muggings') in Britain. You will find accounts of this study in several texts (e.g. Valier,

2002; Downes and Rock, 2007). Briefly, this study challenged the notion that there was a new crime (mugging) by providing historical evidence of the existence of similar street crimes across several time periods. The researchers spent 13 months trawling through the press coverage of 'mugging' and they demonstrated that several types of street crime were conflated under this heading, thereby giving rise to fear and moral panic. Their research into the incidences of street crimes, as revealed through official statistical records, suggested that the social reaction was out of proportion.

This led the researchers to ask how this came about. They explained how the media and judiciary interacted in such a way as to present a (false/exaggerated) picture of the increasingly unsafe British streets that were supposedly becoming like those of their US counterparts. Crucially, attention was drawn to the way in which the term 'mugging' was used to refer to incidences of crimes that involved black perpetrators and white victims. Hall et al. (1978) developed a theoretical explanation of the panic surrounding mugging, which was grounded in their analysis of the social and economic changes that were challenging the prosperity and full employment of the working classes for the first time since World War II. Their analysis suggested that black youth became a scapegoat, the means by which attention was deflected from the crisis that challenged the legitimacy of the state and united the public against the perceived threat of black youth. This process divided the white and black working classes by constructing the 'enemies' as youth, crime and 'race' (see Downes and Rock, 2007) and facilitated the practice of 'stop and search', which in turn gave rise to the amplification of street crimes perpetrated by young black males. The point made by Hall et al. (1978) is that this whole process takes place *without* coercion. They use Gramsci's (an early Italian Marxist) concept of **hegemony** to provide understanding of the ways in which states in crisis need to unite their citizens, without coercion, against a common 'threat' in order to legitimate and sustain their control.

BOX 10.9 POLICING THE CRISIS

Plot the different assumptions underpinning the study by Hall et al. (1978) on the matrix in Figure 10.1.

- Can you discern what this study assumed about regulation?
- How do you imagine the authors thought about the issue of objectivity?
- What methods were used in this study? And what was their attitude to official crime statistics?
- Now, look up 'left realism'. How do you think left realists might respond to Hall et al.?

To avoid confusion between what we have called a critical epistemology and Marxism in general we believe it is important to remind you that *critical criminological research* refers to a theory of knowledge characterised by an effort to overcome some of the binary oppositions to which we have referred in this chapter. While much of radical criminology is influenced by the ideas of Marx, it is the *dialectical* elements of Marx's work that underpin the theory of knowledge which we refer to as critical criminology. Harvey, MacDonald and Hill (2000: 85) define **dialectical analysis** as 'a process of locating events or actions in a wider social and historical context and involves conceptually moving backwards and forwards between the specific part and the whole'.

ANTI-DISCRIMINATION

In recent years criminologists have been concerned with the ways in which concepts such as gender, ethnicity, sexuality and religion may be relevant to our study of crime, especially those crimes that appear to be motivated by hatred. However, as a discipline, criminology was slow to confront feminist insights in research. In general, debates within feminism have informed research that has been concerned with both sexism and racism, but as Heidensohn (1985: 162) argued, it was necessary to 'step outside the confines of criminological theory altogether and seek models from other sources in order to achieve a better understanding of women and crime'. This said, the influence of black feminist thought on criminology at that time was 'almost nil' (Daly and Stephens, 1995). What is of interest here, given that the focus of our discussion is the relationship between theories and methods in the research process, is that criminology has been for the most part historically dominated by white males. For many years male criminologists made unproblematic generalisations about *all* criminals, which were based on a male 'norm'. Furthermore, despite men's use of methods, such as in-depth ethnographic interviews (see Chapter 12), that have in more recent years come to be associated with 'feminist' research, the gaze of the (predominantly male) criminologist has been on criminal men's crimes against other men.

It was feminists who raised the question of violence against women and children in the private sphere and black men and women who identified the need to question, among other issues, why more black people in general were policed and incarcerated than white people; why racist violence was overlooked. Feminists who were concerned with the victimisation of women (as opposed to women's lawbreaking) led the way in terms of advocating methods that involved the subjects of research in research design. Any criminological research that is concerned with the unequal treatment of victims is likely to use a variety of methods such as in-depth ethnographic interviews and participant observation as a way of 'telling it like it is' from the perspective of those who have found it hard to obtain justice (see, for example, McLean and Caulfield, 2023). Such studies are often criticised because they are small in scale and therefore generalisations cannot be made. However, it is important for researchers to be mindful of the fact that the purpose of such studies is *not* to make generalisations but rather to gain in-depth knowledge and understanding of an issue from the perspective of those who are affected by it. For those feminists who were concerned with women's lawbreaking, the focus of study was often centred on the ways in which assumptions about 'proper' gender roles, especially as represented in the press, impacted the processes of sentencing (see e.g. Lloyd, 1995; Jewkes, 2011) or on the different conditions of existence in which women carried out crimes (Carlen, 1992). Feminist debates in turn led to gender research carried out by men, which was concerned with explaining the different ways in which men come to understand their masculinity. Such research suggested that many violent crimes, but especially those against women, can be linked to the perpetrators' understandings of their gender roles.

Increasing worries about crimes that are motivated by fear – or, more accurately, hatred – of lesbian, gay, bisexual, trans, queer or questioning (LGBTQ+) people who do not fit into the so-called heterosexual norm and media-led fear of some religious groups suggested that research into crime needed also to examine the victims of crime. Questions concerning when, where and upon whom the status of victim is conferred became important to those who wished to change the ways in which we think not only about criminals but also about victims. Research in this area has led to improvements in policing (see e.g. Herek, Cogan and Gillis, 2003) and to changes in sentencing practices (see Dodd, 2017).

The main value underpinning critical criminological research is the need to overcome oppressive practices that serve to maintain unequal relationships. Hence critical criminology is open about its value positions and is quite eclectic in its choice of methods. Anti-sexist and anti-racist perspectives as well as those that take account of social class and the diversity of culture will all therefore come under this heading. As we saw in Chapter 6, critical criminology does not seek only to find causes of crime, nor does it simply attempt to reveal the ways in which those committing crimes interpret and account for their own actions; rather critical criminology attempts to provide theoretical understanding of specific crimes as well as of the response to those crimes. In order to do this, critical criminological researchers, whether they call themselves Marxists or not, will be concerned to follow Marx's example of attempting to 'dig below the surface' in order to challenge everyday perceptions. It is through this process that they are able to go beyond causation *and* beyond interpretation in order to provide analyses of the many ways in which the law may be seen to operate in the interests of those with the most wealth and power.

BOX 10.10 USING A MIXED METHODS CRITICAL APPROACH TO RESEARCH IN ORDER TO INFLUENCE POLICY

Re-visit the article by Alizai (2023) discussed in Chapter 6.

Alizai specifically states that she aims to identify, analyse and assess approaches to addressing Islamophobia. She does this by taking a 'qualitative case study approach' through which she examines approaches to tackling Islamophobia in France, the UK and Spain. She also reveals in her citation of Bayrakli and Hafez (2018: 64) that she concurs with the view that the 'legal and political recognition of Islamophobia would, ideally, lead to policies and interventions that would prevent the manifold manifestation of this phenomenon'.

Now consider the following questions and jot down reasons for all your answers.

1. Where do your ideas about the concept of Islamophobia come from?
2. How far do you think that Alizai reveals her value position on the issue she has researched? Do you think that this helped you to assess the strength of the judgements that she has made?
3. How does Alizai counter notions of the 'Islamification' of Europe?
4. What suggestions does Alizai make about the different ways in which different research methods could be used to uncover the reasons why Islamophobia is perpetuated, despite policies that aim to prevent it?
5. In what ways do you think that crimes of violence against Muslims could be reduced most successfully? What do you think might be some other positive outcomes of such a reduction?

Website Instructor PowerPoint slides

Epistemologies and real-life research

QUESTIONS FOR DISCUSSION

Our brief examination of some of the key theories of crime with which you will be gaining familiarity demonstrates that the history of criminological debates remains relevant to research in the present. Use the questions below to form the basis of discussions with your peers:

- Why is it important to define the terms that we use as clearly as possible?
- The determinism of positivism has been criticised by many and some have described positivist studies as futile (see Tierney, 2010). How far do you agree?
- What has been learned from the intra-left debates about crime and society?
- What has the mapping exercise (Box 10.1) demonstrated to you about the progress of research?
- How did Herrnstein and Murray (1994) explain crimes in deprived areas and on what grounds was their study discredited?
- By what criteria should research that is not carried out within the positivist framework be judged? Why is it important to be aware of these criteria?

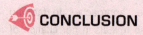

CONCLUSION

It is important to have a general overview of the history of criminological theorising because it is through the processes of peer review that our knowledge and understanding grow. It is also through the process of moving from one theory of knowledge to another that researchers are able to gain a more thorough understanding of crime in society and of the strengths and limitations of each perspective. In reality, criminologists need to explain the circumstances that are most likely to lead to specific types of crimes; to question the definitions of crime that hold sway at any given time; to understand the different reasons why people turn to specific types of crime; to reveal the processes through which some crimes stay off the political agenda, despite the seriousness of their effects and through which some (oftentimes lesser) crimes create moral concerns that result in the acceptance of harsher punishments. All of these issues should be important to criminologists in order to guard against the dangers of policies that appeal to a misguided 'common-sense' approach to crime which fails to take account of the complexity of our lives. To admit that there are no definitive 'right' answers to the problem of crime should not prevent us from looking for the best answers we can find. If we forget what has been said before, then we may fail to challenge the reproduction of ideas that have been refuted.

KEY LEARNING POINTS

Website Student video

Part 3 – students talking about their own research

- The big question for researchers, if we wish to be taken seriously, is 'How can we make sure that our work is as convincing as possible?'
- We need to demonstrate that we are aware of the assumptions we have made in our research by providing an explanation not only of *what* we did but *why* we did it.
- We need to show awareness of the ways in which theories imply methods.
- Whether we choose a 'scientific' approach or not should not really be the important issue; rather the key issue should be how well our research questions are answered.
- We need to remember the lessons learned from the processes of critique – for example, despite powerful critiques of biological determinism it continues to rear its head in political debates about 'the crime problem' as well as serving, as Lilly et al. (2019) note, to maintain the invisibility of many forms of victimisation. Knowledge and understanding of the strengths and limitations of previous research is the hallmark of a good study.
- If we provide insufficient detail of our research, we fail to allow others to understand how and why we have made our judgements.
- If we stay stuck with an attitude that science is either the best or conversely the most inappropriate way to do criminological research, we will close our minds to many important questions that fall between these extremes. Furthermore, such polarised positions can lead to the sorts of conclusions to which administrative criminologists came when they abandoned the

> search for explanations of crime altogether in favour of the more limited concern of reducing the opportunities for crime.
> - Administrative criminology concentrated on manipulating the social environment rather than the social conditions of existence. The role of theory in such research is minimised, as the assumption that we all know what it means to act rationally reduces the research enterprise to the need to measure the impact of any given crime prevention strategy.

REFERENCES

Alizai, H. (2023) 'European Approaches to Stopping Islamophobia are Inadequate: Lessons for Canadians Combating Anti-Muslim Racism and Hatred', *Journal of Hate Studies*, 18(1): 63–79.

Bayrakli, E. and Hafez, F. (eds). (2018) European Islamophobia report: 2017. Seta Foundation, Leopold Weiss Institute. https://setav.org/en/assets/uploads/2018/07/EIR_2017.pdf

Becker, H.S. (1963) *Outsiders: Studies in the Sociology of Deviance*, London: Macmillan.

Box, S. (1983) *Crime, Power and Mystification*, London: Routledge.

Burrell, G. and Morgan, G. (1992) *Sociological Paradigms and Organisational Analysis*, Aldershot: Ashgate Publishing.

Carlen, P. (1992) 'Criminal Women and Criminal Justice: The Limits to, and Potential of, Feminist and Left Realist Perspectives', in J. Young and R. Matthews (eds) *Issues in Realist Criminology*, London: Sage.

Carrabine, E., Cox, P., Crowhurst, I., Di Ronco, A., Fussey, P., Sergi, A., South, N., Thiel, D. and Turton, J. (2020) *Criminology: A Sociological Introduction*, 4th edition, London: Routledge.

Chamberlain, J.M. (2015) *Criminological Theory in Context*, London: Sage.

Daly, K. and Stephens, D.J. (1995) 'The Dark Figure of Criminology: Towards a Black and Multiethnic Feminist Agenda for Theory and Research', in N.H. Rafter and F. Heidensohn (eds) *International Feminist Perspectives in Criminology: Engendering a Discipline*, Buckingham: Open University Press.

Dodd, V. (2017) 'Crackdown on Social Media Hate Crimes', *Guardian*, 21 August. Available at www.theguardian.com/society/2017/aug/21/cps-to-crack-down-on-social-media-hate-says-alison-saunders (accessed 21 August 2017).

Downes, D. and Rock, P. (2007) *Understanding Deviance*, fifth edition, Oxford: Oxford University Press.

Durkheim, É. (1970) *Suicide: A Study in Sociology*, London: Routledge and Kegan Paul.

Durkheim, É. (1982) *The Rules of Sociological Method*, ed. S. Lukes, London: Macmillan.

Galton, F. (1883) *Inquiries into Human Faculty and its Development*, London: Macmillan.

Garland, D. (1994) 'Of Crimes and Criminals: The Development of Criminology in Britain', in M. Maguire, R. Morgan and R. Reiner (eds) *The Oxford Handbook of Criminology*, Oxford: Clarendon Press.

Giddens, A. (1979) *Central Problems in Social Theory*, London: Macmillan.

Giddens, A. (1990) *Essays in Social Theory*, Cambridge: Polity Press.

Hall, S., Criticher, C., Clarke, J. and Roberts, B. (1978) *Policing the Crisis: Mugging, the State and Law and Order*, London: Macmillan.

Harvey, L., MacDonald, M. and Hill, J. (2000) *Theories and Methods*, London: Hodder and Stoughton.

Heber, A. (2017) 'You Thought You Were Superman: Violence, Victimisation and Masculinities', *British Journal of Criminology*, 57(1): 61–78.

Heidensohn, F. (1985) *Women and Crime*, New York: New York University Press.

Herek, G.M., Cogan, J.C. and Gillis, R.J. (2003) 'Victim Experiences in Hate Crime Based on Sexual Orientation', in B. Perry (ed.) *Hate and Bias Crimes: A Reader*, London: Routledge, pp. 243–259.

Herrnstein, R.J. and Murray, C. (1994) *The Bell Curve: Intelligence and Class Structure in American Life*, New York: Free Press Publications.

Jewkes, Y. (2011) *Crime and the Media*, second edition, London: Sage.

Katz, J. (1988) *Seductions of Crime*, New York: Basic Books.

Kitsuse, J. (1962) 'Social Reaction to Deviance: Problems of Theory and Method', *Social Problems*, 9: 247–256.

Klein, D. (1973) 'The Etiology of Female Crime', reproduced in J. Muncie, E. McLaughlin and M. Langan (eds) (1996) *Criminological Perspectives: A Reader*, London: Sage.

Lilly, J.R., Cullen, F.T. and Ball, R.A. (2019) *Criminological Theory: Context and Consequences*, seventh edition, Los Angeles: Sage.

Lloyd, A. (1995) *Doubly Deviant, Doubly Damned: Society's Treatment of Violent Women*, London: Penguin Books.

Lombroso, C. (1920) *The Female Offender*, New York: Appleton.

McLean, P. and Caulfield, L.S. (2023) 'Conspicuous by Their Absence – Reclaiming the Silenced Voices of Black Women in the Criminal Justice System', *British Journal of Community Justice*, 19: 36–54.

Mead, G.H. (1934) *Mind, Self and Society*, London and Chicago, IL: Chicago University Press.

Muncie, J. (1998) 'Reassessing Competing Paradigms in Criminological Theory', in P. Walton and J. Young (eds) *The New Criminology Revisited*, Basingstoke: Macmillan.

O'Malley, P. (2010) *Crime and Risk*, London: Sage.

Schoultz, I., Flyghed, J. (2020) 'From "We Didn't Do It" to "We've Learned Our Lesson": Development of a Typology of Neutralizations of Corporate Crime', *Critical Criminology* 28: 739–757.

Simmel, G. (1908) *The Metropolis and Mental Life*, Dresden: Peterman.

Stout, B., Yates, J. and Williams, B. (2008) *Applied Criminology*, London: Sage.

Taylor, I., Walton, P. and Young, J. (1973) *The New Criminology: For a Social Theory of Deviance*, London: Routledge.

Tierney, J. (2010) *Criminology: Theory and Context*, Harlow: Longman.

Valier, C. (2002) *Theories of Crime and Punishment*, Harlow: Longman.

Wilson, J.Q. and Herrnstein, R.J. (1985) *Crime and Human Nature*, New York: Simon & Schuster.

Young, J. (1971) *The Drugtakers: The Social Meaning of Drug Use*, London: Paladin.

Chapter 11

Preparing for the practical challenges of 'real-world' crime research

GOALS OF THIS CHAPTER

At the end of reading this chapter and by completing the online resources that accompany it, you will be able to:

1. make an informed decision about whether 'real-world' research is appropriate for your research topic;
2. consider the range of places and types of participants that may be involved in 'real-world' criminological research;
3. understand the importance of good research design and pilot studies in 'real-world' criminological research;
4. appreciate the significance of researcher safety in 'real-world' criminological research;
5. demonstrate an awareness of some of the practical issues faced in 'real-world' criminological research, and how to overcome these issues.

OVERVIEW

Website Instructor PowerPoint Slides

Preparing for the practical challenges of 'real-world' crime research

- Real-world' criminological research typically involves participants with real experiences of crime and the criminal justice system.
- Criminologists conduct research with prisoners, people who have been in prison, people serving community sentences, victims, the public, and staff and volunteers working within the criminal justice system or relevant third-sector organisations, including victim charities.
- Conducting criminological research in the real world can be challenging and time-consuming, but highly rewarding if there are likely to be significant benefits for practice and understanding within the criminal justice system and/or relevant third-sector organisations.
- Good research design is important in any research, but perhaps even more so when conducting research within the criminal justice system. Often, researchers will be dealing with an inherently vulnerable group of individuals and, because access to prisons and other agencies in the criminal justice system for research

DOI: 10.4324/9781032645698-14

is notoriously difficult, once access is gained things must be done correctly, as it is often impossible to return to the research site(s).
- For the above reasons, piloting research should be the first stage of any data gathering in order to overcome potential problems before taking the research larger scale.
- Once you have recruited participants, it is important to manage your relationship with them carefully, as drop-out rates can be high.
- Ensuring the safety of researchers and research participants is paramount. Issues of researcher safety should be taken very seriously and thoroughly considered with your research supervisor and your university ethics committee.
- It is important to fully consider the practical issues that can affect real-world criminological research. Potential issues may be varied and numerous, but by learning from more experienced researchers it is possible to overcome some of the common pitfalls.
- Some of the lessons from this chapter apply to all research, not just to 'real-world' criminological research. For example, the ability to successfully manage your participants is a skill which all researchers need to develop.

INTRODUCTION

We preface this chapter by noting that it is simply not practical for most undergraduate students to conduct research with agencies of the criminal justice system. The issues around this are discussed throughout this chapter. However, this chapter offers many lessons that are applicable to all criminological research and will also provide you with a greater depth of understanding of the practical challenges involved in much of the research you read about as a student of criminology. This will provide you with further knowledge and understanding that will allow you to develop your ability to think critically about the research you encounter elsewhere in your studies.

Unlike the other chapters in this book, this chapter has been developed around particular case studies of research in prisons, which we hope will provide you with interesting insights into the practice and challenges of conducting research in criminal justice settings. The prison-based research examples are supplemented with examples of research in other areas that are broadly applicable to criminological research. While, as noted above, this type of research is typically not practical for students, for those who may progress to postgraduate and professional research careers, we encourage you to return to the guidance in this chapter again at that point. We hope that this chapter may also help inspire some readers to pursue this type of research in the future.

SHOULD I DO 'REAL-WORLD' RESEARCH?

As a student of criminology, your research focus may include either victims or perpetrators of crime, or those working within and around the criminal justice system. It may be that secondary research or research on student populations can tell you what you need to know for your research, and this is explored elsewhere in this book, but you could consider the benefits of 'real-world' research. We use the term 'real world' here to refer to research outside of the university setting, involving people with real experiences of crime and criminal justice.

The answer to whether you should do real-world research depends on a few things. Ask yourself the following questions:

- Would I be able to answer my research questions better by conducting 'real-world' research or through secondary or student participant-based research? Refer to Chapter 14 of this book for further information that will help you answer this question.
- Would any research I conduct in the real world be beneficial to both academic knowledge and practice?[11]
- Do I work/volunteer in an organisation where I could easily and ethically access a group of participants?
- Do I have contacts, or do my lecturers have contacts, in relevant organisations where I could easily and ethically access a group of participants?

If you can answer 'yes' to questions 1 and 2, and either question 3 or 4, then you could consider conducting research in the real world. Whatever your decision, you should thoroughly discuss this with your supervisor and gain their approval before beginning to plan any research.

Remember: a key principle in conducting real-world research is not how useful will this be for your research project or dissertation, but whether the research is relevant to the needs of that particular group of individuals or organisation. Keeping this in mind is fundamental to ensuring that all research participants are treated with respect. Many excellent research studies that fully address clearly defined research questions are conducted using secondary data sources (see Chapter 14 for more on this subject). While the advent of internet-mediated research has in some ways blurred the boundaries (see Chapter 15), the same considerations apply whether working with participants face to face or online.

WHERE DO CRIMINOLOGISTS DO 'REAL-WORLD' RESEARCH?

Criminological research can take place in any number of settings and with a wide variety of research populations. These range from victims of crime, to people in prison and on probation, people who have been in prison, to those working within the criminal justice system or relevant third-sector organisations. The authors of this book conduct research primarily with prisoners and people serving community sentences.

A key point to note for student researchers is the time it can take to get research access agreed, particularly in agencies of the criminal justice system. If you already work within the criminal justice system or have contacts, the process may be slightly quicker, but you will still need to follow formal research application procedures, even if you have had your research agreed informally. At the time of writing this edition, the Ministry of Justice National Research Committee will not accept research applications from undergraduate students, due to the volume of research applications they receive.

When aiming to do research within the Probation Service/Probation Regions or within His Majesty's Prison and Probation Service (HMPPS) Headquarters, researchers must apply for research approval to the HMPPS National Research Committee (NRC) through an online form. If the proposed research also involves health and social care bodies, researchers should apply through the Integrated Research Application System (IRAS) (www.myresearchproject.org.uk/). If research approval is granted through an IRAS application, separate NRC is not required.

The Ministry of Justice (2024) outlines that the NRC application process 'exists to ensure:

- the research applicant, Ministry of Justice (MOJ) and HMPPS attain best value from the research conducted
- the resource implications and impact of the research on operational delivery is considered
- the robustness and relevance of the research is adequately assessed
- matters of data protection/security and **research ethics** are dealt with in a consistent manner'.

When assessing research applications, the NRC need to feel sure that the proposed research will be of sufficient value to HMPPS compared with the resource implications and that it is methodologically and ethically sound. In addition, note that you are typically expected to have gained ethics approval for your research from your university prior to making a formal IRAS application. The main aims of the application process are to protect individuals and ensure that resources are used effectively. Even with all of this addressed in the research design, it is wise to have had prior contact with the organisation you aim to work with so that they know to expect the formal research application. Later in this chapter (Box 11.2) you can read about Ashleigh Whitwell's PhD research – Ashleigh designed her research in direct consultation with the prison governor and feels sure that this helped when her NRC application was considered. However, here we refer you back to Chapter 5 and the discussion of gatekeepers. Remember the example we gave of another PhD student who was declined access to prisons to undertake research with black women, whose voices have largely been silenced within the criminal justice system. HM Prisons and Probation Service (HMPPS) did not feel that the proposed research fitted with their priorities.

Other researchers work with the police, people serving community sentences, victims of crime, the courts, the probation service, the NHS and more. The NHS research application and ethics procedures, through IRAS, are particularly complex and lengthy, and so we advise you to avoid embarking on this route unless you have a great deal of time available. Other organisations where you might access a sample, such as community and voluntary groups, typically have no formal application processes and so the time between first making contact and conducting your research may be shorter.

> **KEY TERMS EXPLORED: RESEARCH ETHICS OR RESEARCH ACCESS?**
>
> As discussed in Chapter 7, university **ethics** committees are the primary port of call for ethical review for researchers studying issues in crime and criminal justice. Once university ethics approval has been granted, researchers might need to seek further ethical approval – for example, in the UK the Health Research Authority provides ethics review for research involving patients and healthcare. As discussed in this chapter, when it comes to undertaking research in prisons and probation settings, in the UK permission is sought from HMPPS NRC. Each country around the world will have its own processes. For example, as explored in Chapter 7, in the United States there are state-level institutional review boards.
>
> An important point to note here is that the NRC gives approval for access to undertake the research and takes consideration of ethical practices, but it is not an ethics review committee – a point that we find is often misunderstood. We have two recent PhD graduates who successfully gained ethics approval for prison research but were turned down by HMPPS NRC for their planned programmes of research. In this way the NRC is a gatekeeper to research (see Chapter 5). Both students went on to undertake excellent research and graduated with doctoral degrees, but they had to be prepared to be flexible and work to redefine their research programme.

RESEARCH DESIGN

Good research design is important in all research, but this is even more apparent when aiming to conduct research with prisoners, those on community sentences, people who have been in prison or victims. Carlen and Worrall (2004) document two main reasons for this: first, because researchers will be dealing with an inherently vulnerable group of individuals; and second, because access to prisons and other agencies of the criminal justice system for research is notoriously difficult, once access is gained things must be done right as it is often impossible to return to the research site(s). Doing research in prisons, for example, is qualitatively different from other forms of research, often related to the safety and security concerns of the institution (Crighton, 2006). However, 'a good research design outside a prison will often be a good research design within a prison' (Crighton, 2006: 8).

Over five decades ago, in 1970, Matza highlighted that research into crime had become too far removed from the key players: people convicted of crimes. Despite this acknowledgement, many researchers in the area often rely solely on impersonal statistical data. While there are numerous cases where this is appropriate to address specific research questions, it is clear that those directly involved in criminal activity can tell us much about their own lives and the crimes they have committed, just as can those who have been the victims of crime or who work with these groups. We cannot expect to obtain a full picture of the thoughts, experiences, development and needs of any group of people without speaking with them directly. As Nee (2004: 4) states: 'If we can show that we can research offenders' understandings of their own behaviour reliably ... then surely a grounded approach to research, using the offender as expert, is a method we ignore at our peril.' When done well, the information gleaned from interviews with those involved in the criminal justice system can provide us with a wealth of information that is simply not available through official records. Indeed, Sapsford and Jupp (1996) suggest that self-report methods provide researchers with the opportunity to collect information free from the restrictions of official data (both practical and political) – as discussed in Chapters 5 and 10. While today we might feel we know quite a lot about some groups, there remain groups whose voices and experiences have remained largely absent from the policy and research literature (McLean and Caulfield, 2023). However, it is important to note that there are numerous reasons why self-report data from interviews may not always be entirely accurate. The reliability of self-report data relies on the honesty of respondents' accounts, and there is always a risk that these accounts will provide 'an imaginative organization of experiences that imposes a distortion of truth ... a mixture of fiction and non-fiction ... about life and particular lived experiences' (Denzin, 1989: 24). In an attempt to combat this, a 'triangulation' of data has typically been found to be the best approach to increase validity. While all information should be taken seriously, researchers should check stories wherever possible.

Official records held by HM Prison Service and the probation service, such as Offender Assessment System (OASys – see Box 11.1) records, may be used to cross-check some of the information provided by people in prison and serving community sentences and allows the likely accuracy of the self-report data to be assessed. The use of such records also allows for the collection of demographic and other data that do not require explanation by the individual. This then allows more time for discussion of more pertinent issues during contact with participants. Given the time pressures faced by researchers in prison settings in particular, the ability to save time in this way during an interview is invaluable. While a typical rule of thumb is to begin with records before moving on to data collection with the individual (King, 2000), the rights of informed consent and privacy of all individuals must be adhered to, meaning that it may not be possible to review records prior to interviews, as interviewees should give written permission for the researcher to view their individual documents.

> **BOX 11.1 KEY TERM EXPLAINED: OFFENDER ASSESSMENT SYSTEM**
>
> The **Offender Assessment System (OASys)** was developed by the probation service and prison service in England and Wales as a standardised measure to provide a consistent and in-depth assessment measure of areas of need for individual offenders, and to provide a risk of reconviction score. The OASys was piloted three times from 1999, and in 2001 the decision was made to implement the assessment throughout England and Wales' prison and probation services. The OASys consists of 13 sections that assess offenders' criminogenic needs, risk of harm and likelihood of reconviction based on areas covered in the widely used Level of Service Inventory-Revised (LSI-R: Andrews and Bonta, 1995). The first 12 sections relate to risk of reconviction, while section 13 is used when considering suitability of interventions. Assessment is carried out at the beginning, end, and throughout the sentence, and has been designed to highlight areas of risk and need, to trigger further assessments, as the basis for sentence planning, and to measure change. In order to predict the likelihood of reconviction, sections 1 to 12 of the OASys examine offending history and current offence, social and economic factors, and personal factors. Data are collected from a range of sources, including the probation service, courts and prison service. From a research perspective, the measure provides a useful tool from which to obtain demographic data collected about people in prison and serving community sentences and to cross-check sections of interview data.

Remember: even if you gain access to conduct research with prisoners or those serving community sentences, there is no obligation for the criminal justice system or an individual to let you see their records.

DATA-COLLECTION METHODS: CONSIDERATIONS WHEN INTERVIEWING VULNERABLE GROUPS

While a full discussion of interviews as a method of data collection may be found in Chapter 12, there are a number of specific issues relevant to conducting interviews with vulnerable groups that warrant discussion in this chapter.

Prison staff in particular often note the problems experienced when researchers have attempted to use questionnaires with prisoners. Issues with literacy and the length and complexity of some questionnaires often result in prison staff being needed to help prisoners work through questionnaires. This has obvious time and resource implications, and removes anonymity from participants – and this level of staff resource requirement may well not be available, certainly within prisons in England and Wales at the current time. Staff often report being much happier having prisoners interviewed by researchers to avoid the above issues. Researchers must also be mindful of potential issues with literacy outside of prison settings and ensure that the language used in data-collection tools is clear and appropriate. When involving young people and children in research, this need may be even greater. Experienced researchers will tell you that a great deal of sensitivity is needed in offering to read questions to someone you suspect may have literacy problems. Aside from such practical issues, the benefits of interviews have been espoused by many, being one of the most widely used **qualitative research** methods, as discussed in Chapter 12. There is the opportunity for researchers to increase rapport with interviewees, thereby hopefully increasing openness. As King and Wincup (2008) note, establishing rapport with research participants is one of the keys to successful interviewing in prisons.

BOX 11.2 RESEARCH IN ACTION: PILOTING RESEARCH WITH PEOPLE WHO HAVE BEEN IN PRISON

Background

We suggest that the first stage of any data gathering should involve a pilot study in order to overcome any potential problems before taking the research full scale. This is particularly important in prison research – such as that described below – where once access to prisons has been granted it is important to get things right. However, you should note that the pilot study described below is taken from a piece of postgraduate research and thus is larger than would be expected from undergraduate researchers. Nonetheless, there are important lessons to be taken from this real-world example.

Between 2007 and 2011 one of the authors of this book conducted a study across three women's prisons in England (see Caulfield, 2012, 2016). Prior to conducting semi-structured interviews with incarcerated women, a small number of pilot interviews were conducted with a sample of women who had previously been in prison. While the pilot sample differed from the main research sample as the women were not now in prison, their status as women UK citizens who had been in prison meant that they had been through similar experiences and understood the relevant issues. It is, however, vital to be aware that the differences between actually living in prison and in the community are significant and so will have had some impact upon the interviews. Nonetheless, this stage formed an important part of the research development.

Pilot interviews are also useful to ensure that appropriate language and terms of reference are being used within the research. Within Caulfield's study the purpose of the interviews was primarily to assess the appropriateness of the questions being asked in the interview, and also in part as a 'practice run' to iron out any problems and to enhance familiarity with the interview schedule. The pilot also acted as a forum to check the language used in the consent form and participant information form. In an ideal world these pilot interviews would have been best conducted in a prison with current prisoners to allow the pilot to be as similar to the 'real' situation as possible. However, given the difficulties of accessing a prison sample, interviewing people who had previously been in prison provided a suitable pilot sample.

Prison Link

The pilot sample was recruited from a charity organisation 'Prison Link'. Prison Link was a Birmingham-based charity, run primarily by volunteers, which worked with prisoners and their families. Prison Link assisted members of the community in maintaining family ties through assisted visits and a family support network. They also offered one-to-one support and befriending to members of the black community in Birmingham who were serving a custodial sentence. Prison Link 'aims to empower and support prisoners and ex-offenders and their families and children by offering a range of services designed to maintain family links and stability and encourage positive change' (Prison Link, 2007).

The researcher contacted Prison Link and discussed the aims of the research with them. Prison Link believed the research was likely to be of benefit in understanding the needs of women in prison and so agreed to help recruit participants for the pilot study. Volunteer staff within Prison Link liaised with women who had previously been in prison who were in contact with the charity to recruit a pilot sample for this research. Four women were identified and all agreed to take part. Their experiences of imprisonment ranged from five to twenty years ago, with three women having been in prison over the past ten years. While being in prison such a considerable time ago made this sample different from the main target sample for this research, the pilot interviews were useful in testing the interview schedule. The researcher conducted interviews at the Prison Link premises. Participants were offered payment of £20 for their time. (See the discussion of whether or not you should pay your participants later in this chapter.)

Findings from the pilot study

One of the interviews from the pilot exercise was transcribed in order to test out the transcription process. Rather than analyse the specific content of the interviews that took place, the aim of the pilot interviews was to practise interview techniques and the interview schedule, and to get feedback on the experience from participants. It is always surprising how different conducting a real interview is from reading the interview questions at home beforehand. As discussed in Chapter 12, you may need more prompts than you think and you may feel that some questions are difficult to ask. This is particularly the case if the research topic is of a sensitive nature.

The interviews included questions about participants' past experiences, about which all four women spoke at length. While the structure of the interview schedule flowed well – beginning with broad background questions before approaching any questions of a sensitive nature – when probed, feedback from three participants was that the interviewer could be more direct with some sensitive topics. This feedback was useful in developing a balance between trying to avoid offending participants with very personal questions, and also encouraging them to speak about their experiences in these areas. An example of this is questions about childhood experiences, where the researcher was initially reluctant to ask outright about negative childhood experiences. However, the interviewees felt that as long as interviewees did not feel pressured to respond, the interviewer could be more direct with such lines of questioning.

After completing the interview, interviewees were asked to discuss their experience of the interview, and specifically how they felt about the questions they were asked. All four women reported feeling at ease during the interview, and three reported enjoying the opportunity to express their experiences and how they had rebuilt their lives after prison. Of note was that two of the women felt that the time taken to discuss the research prior to the interview had been important in helping them understand why their part in the research was important. It is possible that because of this they were more open and willing to discuss their past experiences.

Overall, the pilot interview process significantly increased the researcher's familiarity and confidence with the interview schedule. While these interviews were not able to prepare the interviewer fully for the experience of interviewing women in prison, they were vital to the task of developing appropriate language and confidence for the main study.

In Box 11.2 we give an example of piloting research in the community before going in to prison. It is though important to acknowledge that valuable research can be conducted in the community about prisons and people who have been in them. As noted above and in Chapter 5, Paula McLean's PhD research was not granted prison NRC approval. She therefore redesigned her work to be undertaken with women in the community who had previously been in prison. Although the design needed amendments to consider how to work with people in the community and how their experiences and needs might differ from those currently in prison, Paula conducted highly valuable work that has highlighted the voices of black women who have experienced prison.

Those with experience of interviewing vulnerable groups have also commented that it is preferable, wherever possible, to use individual rather than group interviews (Nee, 2004). As with many other types of research, group interviews or focus groups can be useful in the initial stages 'in order to identify salient issues, tighten research questions and clarify terminology' (Nee, 2004: 11) but issues such as poor literacy, communication and social skills can result in some participants failing to express themselves and thus limiting the validity of the data collected. In an individual interview, the interviewer is more able to work around literacy problems and, as above, build a rapport with the interviewee, in an attempt to overcome communication issues.

Asking research participants to talk openly about their life experiences will undoubtedly result in sensitive issues being broached. As mentioned earlier, building a rapport with research participants is vital, particularly when seeking openness about sensitive topics. In addition, Harvey (2008) reports that in a low-trust environment such as a prison, emphasising independence and social remoteness from the prison establishment encourages the disclosure of information.

RECRUITING A SAMPLE

Recruiting organisations

If you work within an agency of the criminal justice system or a voluntary organisation, or have good contacts, it is usually best to informally discuss your research initially. If you don't have such contacts, you may also find that an initial informal approach works best. First, try making contact via a phone call, and once contact has been established and some discussion had concerning the research, you should send an email outlining the research. However, we do highlight here that it is always best to try and find someone from your own networks (including talking to your tutors and lecturers) to make an introduction, as agencies of the criminal justice system and charity and voluntary sector agencies are typically over-stretched and may be unable to consider research requests from people unknown to them. If you do go ahead with more of a 'cold call' approach, at the phone call stage it will probably be clear that some organisations are not able or willing to participate. This may be due to limited time to help with research, or perhaps a belief that the research would not be beneficial to them. It is also worthy of note that some organisations prefer to work only with postgraduate and professional researchers, typically for good reason to ensure the research has enough benefit for their organisation and the people they support.

A key element of research recruitment is benefit selling, whether this is to the organisation as a whole, staff who you wish to help in identifying participants or participants themselves, and it is important to ensure that the particular benefit and value to each group is made clear. Staff within an organisation may be the gatekeepers to your research participants, or indeed the participants themselves, and so it is vital that you try to engage them with your research. In order to protect and inform colleagues, all those either involved with the research or likely to be asked about the research should be informed of the nature of the study and given the opportunity to discuss this with you. This may be through a formal presentation you give to staff where they are able to ask questions and discuss the research, or it may be that you provide relevant staff with non-technical written materials explaining the research, and give them the opportunity to discuss the study with you on an informal basis.

Participant recruitment

Once access has been granted from the organisations, you may need to develop a range of participant recruitment activities to get a suitable sample. These will depend on the type of organisation, but we suggest some tried-and-tested approaches in Table 11.1. As noted previously, ensuring that potential participants are aware of the benefits of the research is essential.

Table 11.1 Participant recruitment strategies

Strategy	Pros	Cons
Posters	Easy to produce Good to raise awareness of the research Does not take much staff time	Does not result in high recruitment Other strategies needed Need to be highly visible to the target population
Letters/emails	Easy to produce Personal so better response rate A tear-off slip in prisons and easy return instructions help increase responses to letters	Relies on having contact details/staff may be needed to deliver them in some settings May be ethical concerns – discuss with your supervisor and ethics committee Literacy issues might mean that some potential participants are excluded
Media (for example, an interview or advert in the organisation's newsletter, a prison TV/radio station interview) / social media	If targeted well, can be high impact Good if followed up with a letter (in prison) or email	Not always possible in a prison setting
Staff directly approach potential participants (including colleagues, victims, prisoners and so on)	They can 'sell' the benefits on your behalf Results in high recruitment	Staff need to fully understand the benefit of the research and be engaged Potential for misunderstandings to be communicated Staff may be too busy to do this
Through a community group meeting	You can 'sell' the benefits of the research Potential participants can ask questions Results in high recruitment You may be able to arrange data collection straight away	None in our experience

MANAGING YOUR PARTICIPANTS

Recruiting participants is only half of the challenge. Any experienced researcher will tell you that drop-out rates are often high between contacting participants and collecting the data. Once you get to the point of meeting with participants for data collection, drop-out rates are very low, so it is what you do between first contacting a participant and meeting them to collect data that is often important.

Our keys tips are as follows:

- 'Strike while the iron's hot!': the sooner you can conduct your data collection the better. You must ensure that potential participants have time to consider taking part, but the sooner you can collect data the less time you have to lose track of participants.
- Keep track of them: if you are going to be conducting research with people in the community but won't be collecting the data immediately, phone/email/message (check what form of communication they prefer) your participants to check they are still happy to take part on the date you agreed.
- Re-confirm visits close to the time: the time and travel involved in real-world research is wasted if you turn up to a research visit but your participant does not. This has happened to most researchers, but you can minimise this risk by calling participants the day before or on the day to re-confirm your meeting.

Even with all of the above, you should still be prepared for things to go wrong on the day. We have driven for hours to meet interviewees that didn't show up, or arrived at a prison to find that our assigned staff member wasn't there and so we couldn't speak with any prisoners. These things happen, so it is really important to do what you can to keep participants engaged but also plan extra time into your research schedule (see Box 11.2 below for quite a dramatic example of a research student needing extra time).

RESEARCHER SAFETY

Ensuring your own safety, and the safety of anyone else involved in your research, is paramount. Issues of researcher safety should be taken very seriously, and thoroughly considered with your research supervisor and your university ethics committee. Below we discuss some issues to consider and provide some tips on ensuring researcher safety. Also refer to Chapter 7 and the discussion of 'Avoiding harm – a spotlight on researcher well-being'.

As a researcher you should think very carefully about where you meet research participants to collect data. If you have gained access to your participants through the probation service or a charity or community group, see if they can provide a space for you to meet with participants. If that is not practical, arrange to meet participants in a public area such as a coffee shop. You should avoid meeting research participants in their home if possible. Wherever data is being collected, many researchers use what we term a 'call-in system' when conducting research in the community. Our advice is to go out to conduct research in pairs where this is appropriate, but at the very least make use of the call-in system.

BOX 11.3   THE 'CALL-IN SYSTEM' EXPLAINED

The 'call-in system' is an approach to researcher safety used by many researchers who conduct research in the community. This system should be used when working with all participants in the community. The basic principle is this: that a nominated 'research buddy' knows where you are at all times during data collection, and that your research buddy knows what to do if they cannot contact you.

A step-by-step guide to the call-in system

1. Nominate a 'research buddy': this can be any responsible adult; just make sure it is someone you can rely on.
2. Let your research buddy know the time you have agreed to meet the research participant, exact details of where you are meeting and how long you expect the data collection to take.
3. Call your research buddy when you arrive at the research destination and then call them again when you leave.
4. If you do not call your research buddy within the time discussed, they should try to call you. If you do not answer, they should continue to try.
5. If your research buddy cannot contact you within ten minutes they should call the police.

Thankfully, most research experiences are positive and safe ones, and we have never been in a situation where we have needed to use point 5 of the call-in system. However, using this system helps ensure that you are protected and safe.

If you find yourself in a position where you are conducting research in prisons, there are other safety issues to consider. Fundamentally, prisons are places concerned with security, and so the likelihood is that your safety as a researcher will have been considered. However, you should not take this for granted, and if you feel concerned or uncomfortable in any way you should alert your research contact in the prison.

If you are discussing sensitive issues with prisoners it may be important to have somewhere private within each establishment to conduct your research. In closed prisons in particular this may pose an issue concerning researcher safety. It is perfectly acceptable for you to ask your research contact at the prison, or another member of prison staff, about the psychological and behavioural state of individual prisoners with whom you will be in contact. While prison staff may not anticipate any problems, it is good practice to either conduct the interview in a room with a safety alarm or provide researchers with a personal attack alarm. It is unwise to take any unnecessary risks and it is important to always respect any safety concerns of prison staff.

PRACTICAL ISSUES

It is important to fully consider the practical issues that can affect 'real-world' criminological research. Potential issues may be varied and numerous, but by learning from more experienced researchers it is possible to avoid some of the common pitfalls. We consider some of these issues below. While you can consider many issues in detail prior to beginning the research, you should also be prepared to be flexible in your approach and able to respond to issues as they arise.

Accessing official reports

You may encounter particular issues if you plan to access official reports as part of your research, particularly those that may be held by the criminal justice system about individuals. Access to large group datasets, such as the Crime Survey for England and Wales, is covered in Chapters 13 and 14. The benefits of accessing individual data – such as OASys records – were discussed earlier in this chapter. You must first ensure that each organisation involved in your research has given permission to access records for each participant, provided that the individual participant concerned gives consent. In every instance individual participants should also give their consent and it must be very clear why gathering individual data is important to the research. The principles of informed consent apply equally to all participants and 'there are no grounds for not addressing issues of consent from prisoners' (Crighton, 2006: 11) or others involved in the criminal justice system.

Given the importance of security and anonymity, issues may occur when attempting to transfer information from official documents into Word, Excel or IBM SPSS Statistics software ("SPSS"). The prison and probation services in particular have high levels of IT security, meaning information cannot be saved and taken outside of the prison. In our experience, the best course of action is to print paper copies of each record and anonymise these prior to leaving the prison, probation, charity or other offices. Alternatively, if you only need part of the information stored in official records, it may be better to copy information into a notebook. You can then manually transfer the data into an Excel or SPSS file at a later date. Two things are important here: first, ensure you mention your wish to access official data early on in your discussions about possible research access; second, carry a black marker pen with you for anonymising records.

One of the authors of this book (Laura) recently worked with a local Youth Justice Service (YJS), analysing data on young people's engagement with their community sentences. The data Laura accessed were stored on a system called Careworks, and approval to access the data was given to Laura by the senior management of the YJS. However, despite support from staff working face to face with young people, and from senior management, there were many delays in accessing the data. The data held on the Careworks system were vital to the research, but the information technology officer assigned to help with the research was too busy to provide access. While not an entirely unusual situation, there are lessons to be learned here. Perhaps Laura could have checked that the officer had been given a time allowance for helping with the research. It may also have been possible in advance to arrange for Laura to access the data on site, rather than relying on the information technology officer.

Should you hold keys if you are conducting research in prisons?

Few student researchers will be faced with this question, as typically prison staff escort researchers around the prison. However, when conducting postgraduate research we and our PhD students (including Ashleigh whose work is discussed in Box 11.2) have been offered keys, and so it is worth considering this issue.

Many researchers have discussed the issue of researchers holding keys within a prison (Liebling, 1992; Genders and Player, 1995; Sparks, Bottoms and Hay, 1996; King, 2000; Mills, 2004; King and Liebling, 2008). King (2000), for example, argues that researchers should not hold keys to the prison, as in the eyes of the prisoners this puts researchers too close to the position of staff and thus decreases trust, while Mills (2004) discusses issues of personal safety, particularly for female researchers holding keys. While some have commented that 'if the prison want you to do the research, then it is their responsibility to ensure your safety, and to escort you around the prison' (Cowburn, 2004), the issue is rarely this straightforward. Gaining access to prisons is never guaranteed, and researchers must be flexible and willing to work around the prison staff and prison regimes. An important factor is that holding keys considerably limits the burden on prison staff, primarily by drastically reducing the need for escorts. Anecdotally, we have heard that prisons now favour this approach and, pragmatically, the only sensible decision seems to be to do what each individual establishment suggests: if they wish researchers to hold keys, then researchers should hold keys. Holding keys has the added benefit of increasing researchers' sense of independence within the prison and the ability to control their own time to some extent.

Working around the organisation of prisons

If you are conducting research in prisons, a member of staff may be identified as your 'research liaison officer'. This may be a prison officer or prison psychologist appointed by the governor to take overall responsibility for recruiting participants, ensuring that suitable space is available for data collection, and generally making sure that the research runs smoothly. This can help significantly with participant recruitment and arranging interview times. However, be aware that participants will not always be available when they are called up. This clearly highlights some of the challenges faced when conducting research within the prison service. Not only is it difficult to gain initial access, but researchers must be constantly aware of the regimes within prison that dictate when prisoners are available. This is both a practical consideration, but also an important point to highlight when applying to conduct prison research, as a willingness to be flexible and the ability to work around the demands of the prison should be made clear right from the initial application.

An awareness of the practical issues of prison research and planning around the prison day is vital. Carlen and Worrall (2004: 185) have highlighted the importance of working to suit the prison, noting that prison staff can often be 'wary of researchers, especially of any who fail to show their appreciation of prison staff priorities or institutional concerns'. Furthermore, while most prisoners who have agreed to participate in research will find it a welcome change, and therefore the imposition is minimal, there are likely to be greater time consequences for staff members who are already very busy. These points also apply when conducting research in community settings. Laura's recent research with children involved with a Youth Justice Service required a great deal of flexibility in order to be available when the young people were available to be interviewed for the research (Caulfield et al., 2022).

Involvement with research participants

While the majority of research relationships are uncomplicated, on occasion researchers have found themselves very involved with participants. It is wise for all researchers to be aware of this, particularly when undertaking research of a sensitive or emotional nature. In such situations it is easy to see how researchers can find it difficult to walk away from participants and their problems at the end of the research. It is hard not to be affected emotionally by participants who open up to you as a researcher (Smith and Wincup, 2000), and this has certainly been the case on a number of occasions during our research over the years. This highlights how important it is for researchers investigating sensitive issues to ensure that they have some kind of debriefing process in place. Whether this is formalised with your supervisor, or an informal arrangement with a partner or close friend, it is good practice to have some system in place to deal with these emotional issues. Remember: while you may suggest further sources of support for participants on your participant information form, it is not appropriate for you to attempt to provide either subsequent support or friendship.

Payment, payback and feedback

There has been considerable debate concerning the payment of research participants, with some suggesting that payment is potentially coercive (McNeil, 1997). Much of the debate around this issue stems from the medical sciences, where ethical debate centres on the capability of participants to assess risk accurately when financial incentives are offered. While these issues also apply to the social sciences, where considerations of risk to participants are paramount in assessing the ethical nature of research, many social scientists argue that participants should be adequately and appropriately reimbursed for their time (cf. Carlen and Worrall, 2004). We agree with this view, and furthermore, many charity and community organisations expect this (see e.g. Box 11.2). Indeed, large research funders have recently moved towards this approach. The National Institute for Health and Care Research (NIHR: 2024), for example, which funds a good deal of work in and around the criminal justice system, state that:

> Paying people for their involvement in research helps to support more equal partnerships between researchers and members of the public. It helps to support the inclusion of people who might not otherwise be able to get involved, whether for financial or other reasons relating to access. Consequently, it widens the potential pool of people who might influence the course of research. and offer detailed guidance for researchers on this subject.

Within prison establishments it is in no way appropriate to provide prisoners who participate in research with rewards for their participation, be this monetary or affecting standards of care, privileges or parole. It is often the case, however, that research participation can be a welcome break for prisoners and so the most a researcher can do, other than thank individuals verbally for their participation, is to make the process as comfortable as possible and be considerate to any needs the prisoner may have as a result of participation. While it is typically not viable or advisable to provide participants with individual feedback, you may wish to advise participants that they can receive general feedback from the researcher via the contact details provided in the participant information form. Where possible, we offer participants the option to receive a copy of the final research report. Remember to only give out your university contact details, not your personal ones.

You should also consider the role of the people who have helped you identify research participants or helped facilitate your research visits. In addition to being respectful, polite and courteous, you could consider sending 'thank you' cards for their help and support. It is often a good idea to send organisations an overview of the research findings.

Table 11.2 provides an example of research undertaken with older men in a prison in England by PhD student Ashleigh Whitwell. Note that this was as an advanced postgraduate piece of research and was larger and more involved than undergraduate research. However, this provides an example of the stages involved in the research process. Ashleigh's research happened throughout the Covid-19 pandemic and provides an example of just how many challenges there can be that are outside of the researcher's control. Note that not all of the challenges that Ashleigh encountered were due to the pandemic and delays are likely when working in prisons. Ashleigh worked hard to overcome these challenges, being flexible and keeping good lines of communication open with the research. With perseverance she completed her data collection and at the time of writing this edition, is writing up her thesis and a set of findings and recommendations for the prison.

Table 11.2 Research in action: a summary of the research process in a men's prison in England (Ashleigh Whitwell, 2024)

1. Beginning of PhD study November 2019–March 2020	Familiarisation of the fundamentals of PhD research, university practices and reintegration to academia.
Covid-19 Outbreak in March 2020 – UK Government announces nationwide lockdown. Prisons no longer accessible for researchers for foreseeable future. Both university and HMPPS ethics committees closed to new submissions for foreseeable future.	
2. Introductory visit to research site: HMP Stafford April 2020	Cancelled due to Covid-19 outbreak.
3. Change in Governor at research site August 2020	A change in leadership at the research site meant that project reintroductions had to take place. Initially, this had to be done virtually as Covid-19 restrictions still in place.
4. Introduction visit to research site October 2020	A slight change in Covid-19 restrictions meant an in-person visit to HMP Stafford was able to take place. Discussions around project scope, participant recruitment and the potential barriers caused by continued impact of Covid-19. Also allowed familiarisation of environment.
Between April 2020 and September 2021, researcher carried out written work around Literature Review and Methodology chapters, with first drafts submitted for both of these. Unable to progress with data collection as ethic committees still closed to submissions.	
5. Ethics forms submitted to university for approval November 2021	University ethics committee re-opened for submission. Forms, included draft information sheets and consent forms, submitted immediately.
6. Change in governor at research site and reintroduction visit January 2022	A second change in leadership took place at the research site. Another visit was made to site by researcher and supervisory team to reintroduce the project, again, and receive an update on Covid-19 restrictions surrounding the prison estate.
7. Ethical approval received from university July 2022	After some delay, caused by the impact of Covid-19, ethical approval finally granted by the university.
8. Ethics forms submitted to HMPPS ethics committee November 2023	HMPPS ethics committee re-opened for submission. All forms approved by the university were submitted.
9. Ethical approval received from HMPPS June 2023	After some delay, caused by a change in practice from the impact of Covid-19, ethical approval is finally granted by HMPPS and the research is notified.

Continued

Table 11.2 Continued

Between July 2022 and May 2023, researcher revised Methodology chapter and began planning for participant recruitment and data collection, ready for when ethical approval was granted.	
10. Change in governor at research site June 2023	For a third time, a change in leadership at the research site was announced. Previous governor handed project over to a member of the Senior Leadership Team. Meeting took place between researcher and new point of contact, project reintroduced.
11. Attendance at Equalities meeting at research site July 2023	Research introduced project to wider staff and prisoner population, as well as new governor. Plans made to begin process of participant recruitment.
Between July 2023 and August 2023, researcher visited the research site to advertised project to potential prisoner and staff participants. This involved face-to-face conversations, distribution of information sheets and small meetings.	
12. Completion of data collection with prisoner participants August–September 2023	Three separate focus groups conducted with 5–8 prisoner participants in each group. Each focus group lasted between 1 and 1.5 hours. Recorded using a recording device.
Between September 2023 and November 2023, researcher transcribed prisoner focus groups and begins to group data thematically, reflecting on comparisons/differences to conclusions from the Literature Review.	
13. Staff participant data collection	Expected to be completed January 2024, but continued until April.
ONGOING – research redrafts and edits Methodology chapter to reflect challenges and changes in data collection period.	

BOX 11.4 CRITICAL ACTIVITY

Think about a piece of real-world criminological research you would like to conduct. First, work through this chapter and list any practical considerations and issues you may face with your chosen topic. Second, next to each consideration or issue, identify at least one way in which you could overcome this. If you are planning your final-year research project or dissertation in a 'real-world' setting, this will go a long way towards the smooth running of your research. We encourage you to show your supervisor and ethics committee that you have considered these factors.

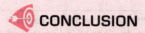 **CONCLUSION**

This chapter has outlined some of the benefits and challenges of conducting what we have referred to as 'real-world' research. While most undergraduate researchers will conduct research using secondary data sources, or with student/public samples, many of the lessons involved in conducting research involving agencies of the criminal justice system apply to all criminological research. Whatever type of 'real-world' research is being conducted, the research should be relevant to the needs of that particular group of individuals or organisation. Keep in mind that it may well be possible to address your research questions using secondary data sources.

 KEY LEARNING POINTS

- After considering the range of factors presented in this chapter, you should now be in a position to make an informed decision about whether real-world research is right for you and the type of research you would like to conduct.
- It is important to note how vital good research design is in conducting criminological research in the real world.
- There are numerous considerations when conducting research with prisoners in particular that make the use of a research pilot study an important consideration.
- Numerous tried-and-tested strategies exist for recruiting a research sample. There are pros and cons of most methods, so researchers should decide what is appropriate for their particular research.
- Following the guidance in this chapter on researcher safety and discussing these issues with your research supervisor and ethics committee will go a long way towards ensuring that you are kept safe throughout the entire research process.

NOTE

1 Broadly defined, to include agencies of the criminal justice system, prisoners, victims, those serving community sentences, people who have been in prison, the public, staff and volunteers, and/or relevant governing bodies.

REFERENCES

Andrews, D.A. and Bonta, J. (1995) *The Level of Service Inventory – Revised*, Toronto: Multi-Health Systems.

Carlen, P. and Worrall, A. (2004) *Analysing Women's Imprisonment*, Cullompton: Willan.

Caulfield, L. Jolly, A. Simpson, E. and Devi-McGleish, Y. (2022) '"It's Not Just Music, It Helps You from Inside": Mixing Methods to Understand the Impact of Music on Young People in Contact with the Criminal Justice System', *Youth Justice*, 22(1): 67–84. https://doi.org/10.1177/1473225420938151

Caulfield, L.S. (2012) *Life Histories of Women Who Offend: A Study of Women in English Prisons*, PhD thesis, Loughborough University.

Caulfield, L.S. (2016) 'Counterintuitive Findings from a Qualitative Study of Mental Health in English Women's Prisons', *International Journal of Prisoner Health*, 12(4): 216–229.

Cowburn, M. (2004) Quote cited in Mills, J. (2004) '"There's a Lot in Those Keys Isn't There?" The Experience of a Female Researcher Researching Rape in a Male Prison Undertaking the Research as a Key Holder', in G. Mesko, M. Pagon and B. Dobovsek (eds) *Policing in Central and Eastern Europe – Dilemmas of Contemporary Criminal Justice*, Ljubljana: Faculty of Criminal Justice, University of Maribor.

Crighton, D. (2006) 'Methodological Issues in Psychological Research in Prisons', in G.J. Towl (ed.) *Psychological Research in Prisons*, Oxford: BPS Blackwell.

Denzin, N.K. (1989) *Interpretive Biography*, Newbury Park, CA: Sage.

Genders, E. and Player, E. (1995) *Grendon: A Therapeutic Prison*, Oxford: Clarendon Press.

Harvey, J. (2008) 'An Embedded Multimethod Approach to Prison Research', in R.D. King and E. Wincup (eds) *Doing Research on Crime and Justice*, Oxford: Oxford University Press.

King, R.D. (2000) 'Doing Research in Prisons', in R.D. King and E. Wincup (eds) *Doing Research on Crime and Justice*, Oxford: Oxford University Press.

King, R.D. and Liebling, A. (2008) 'Doing Research in Prisons', in R.D. King and E. Wincup (eds) *Doing Research on Crime and Justice*, Oxford: Oxford University Press.

King, R.D. and Wincup, E. (2008) 'The Process of Criminological Research', in R.D. King and E. Wincup (eds) *Doing Research on Crime and Justice*, Oxford: Oxford University Press.

Liebling, A. (1992) *Suicides in Prison*, London: Routledge.

McLean, P. and Caulfield, L.S. (2023) 'Conspicuous by Their Absence – Reclaiming the Silenced Voices of Black Women in the Criminal Justice System', *British Journal of Community Justice*, 19: 36–54.

McNeil, P. (1997) 'Paying People to Participate in Research: Why Not?', *Bioethics*, 11: 390–396.

Mills, J. (2004) *'There's a Lot in Those Keys Isn't There?' The Experience of a Female Researcher Researching Rape in a Male Prison Undertaking the Research as a Key Holder*, National Criminal Justice Reference Service, US Department of Justice.

Ministry of Justice. (2024) 'Apply to Conduct Research in Prisons, Probation or HMPPS Headquarters' (online). Gov.uk. Available at https://apply-for-hmpps-research.service.justice.gov.uk/Introduction-and-Guidance/#:~:text=The%20NRC (accessed 30 May 2024).

Nee, C. (2004) 'The Offender's Perspective on Crime: Methods and Principles in Data Collection', in A. Needs and G. Towl (eds) *Applying Psychology to Forensic Practice*, Oxford: BPS Blackwell.

NIHR. (2024). *Payment Guidance for Members of the Public Considering Involvement in Research* (online). NIHR National Institute for Health and Care Research. Available at https://www.nihr.ac.uk/documents/payment-guidance-for-members-of-the-public-considering-involvement-in-research/27372 (accessed 30 May 2024).

Prison Link (2007) *Prison Link homepage*. Available at http://prisonlink.co.uk/ (accessed 3 August 2013).

Sapsford, R. and Jupp, V. (1996) *Data Collection and Analysis*, London: Sage.

Smith, C. and Wincup, E. (2000) 'Breaking In: Researching Criminal Justice Institutions for Women', in R.D. King and E. Wincup (eds) *Doing Research on Crime and Justice*, Oxford: Oxford University Press.

Sparks, R., Bottoms, A.E. and Hay, W. (1996) *Prisons and the Problem of Order*, Oxford: Clarendon Press.

Whitwell, A (in preparation, 2024) *The physical, psychological, and practical needs of older prisoners.* PhD Thesis. University of Wolverhampton. Unpublished.

PART IV

Doing criminological research: data collection

Chapter 12

Qualitative approaches to research

GOALS OF THIS CHAPTER

At the end of reading this chapter and by completing the online resources that accompany it, you will be able to:

1. identify the settings in which in-depth interviews are appropriate;
2. explain the differences between the various forms of in-depth interview;
3. choose appropriate techniques and interviewer 'roles';
4. carry out in-depth interviews;
5. understand when focus group discussions might be a suitable method;
6. identify the settings in which the collection of observational data is appropriate;
7. understand the different philosophical underpinnings of observational studies;
8. explain mixed-methods approaches;
9. justify your chosen method and technique;
10. be aware of emerging and future directions in qualitative research.

OVERVIEW

- A qualitative approach to criminological research involves in-depth, detailed descriptions of criminal behaviour and lifestyles as well as of the processes involved in responding to crime.
- Detailed description is obtained via in-depth qualitative interviews, focus groups, and/or observational techniques.
- There are several ways in which qualitative interviews may be carried out.
- Your chosen technique should reflect the philosophical assumptions that underpin your research and be appropriate to the questions you wish to answer.
- Similarly, observational studies can be carried out in different ways depending upon the philosophical assumptions you make.
- You should always be able to discuss the relationship between your choice of method and your research question/s.

DOI: 10.4324/9781032645698-16

INTRODUCTION

Within this chapter we cover some of the most widely used qualitative data collection techniques: interviews, focus groups and observations. It is very likely that you will have read research studies that have used these techniques and, if you're planning your own research project, you might consider one of these methods. As we'll explore in this chapter, it's not unusual for researchers – certainly advanced researchers working on large-scale projects – to use a combination of methods. In recent years we have also seen a range of really interesting developments in qualitative research approaches, using innovative and perhaps sometimes more accessible methods of data collection that build on these traditional approaches.

IN-DEPTH INTERVIEWS

Types of in-depth interviews

There are two main types of in-depth interview: guided (sometimes called semi-structured) and unstructured. Guided interviews reflect the fact that researchers usually have an idea of the topics they would like to explore with the research participants in advance of carrying out the interviews. They are easier to manage than the more conversational unstructured form; however, the unstructured approach is particularly useful when carrying out life histories or case studies. It is important to be clear about the aims of your research, as these will enable you to make clear decisions about the most appropriate form of interview. The data should be as relevant as possible to the desired aims and outcomes of the research; otherwise the task of analysing the data will become very daunting because of the large quantities of data that will be generated.

Life history interviews (note: life histories may also involve participants writing autobiographical accounts) may also be either guided or unstructured. The decision about the style of interview depends upon whether the researcher simply wishes to access in-depth knowledge about a life/lives in order to show what that life was like or whether the researcher is trying to do more than this by developing theories about the relationship between individual acts and the society in which people live their lives. A life history approach may simply serve to provide a detailed narrative that does no more than present one person's 'story'. However, a researcher may also use narratives in order to attempt an explanation of why something may have happened. A guided approach to life history interviews will be more likely to be underpinned by a particular theoretical perspective. For example, one of us (Hill, 2007), in a study of young black people's reflections on their offending, used a life history approach to interviewing in order to explore the conditions in which the young offenders had lived their lives prior to and during custody in order to make sense of their post-custody decisions and attitudes.

When to use in-depth interviews

Many methodology texts provide students with a simple 'advantages/disadvantages' table which compares structured (quantitative) approaches with semi- or unstructured (qualitative) approaches to interviewing. We do not intend to begin in this way, as we do not think it is helpful to compare techniques that have different purposes. For example, the fact that it is possible to generalise from a large-scale survey but not from 20 in-depth interviews is not relevant to a discussion of an in-depth study that does not claim to make any generalisations. Indeed, to list this as a disadvantage of **qualitative research** is quite meaningless, just as it would be meaningless to say that a disadvantage of a structured survey is the failure to gain in-depth detail. If a researcher chooses an in-depth method of interviewing it should be because this fits with the purposes of the research.

If you take time to look at research reports you will soon get the hang of identifying the different in-depth qualitative methods of data gathering. Perhaps what is more difficult is being clear about the criteria by which this kind of research should be evaluated since, as we have seen, it is often the case that qualitative research may be viewed as inferior to, rather than simply different from, **quantitative research**.

BOX 12.1 STUDENT ACTIVITY: WHEN SHOULD I USE IN-DEPTH INTERVIEWING METHODS?

Which of the following research aims indicate the use of in-depth interviews? Give reasons for your answers.

- To explore the conditions in which women are engaged in prostitution (see Phoenix, 2000).
- To investigate the extent of gang membership in the UK (see Bennett and Holloway, 2004).
- To measure the relationship between lack of street lighting and incidents of violent crime.
- To explore the issues that women face when they end a violent relationship (see Humphreys and Thiara, 2003).
- To study the personal relationship between female offenders and their co-defendants (see Jones, 2008).
- To identify the trends in violent crime across England and Wales.
- To understand the processes through which criminal careers are developed.
- To test for a relationship between alcohol use and aggression (see Newberry, Williams and Caulfield, 2013).
- To explore the ways in which men who have both engaged in and been exposed to violence view gender in relation to this violence (see Heber, 2017).
- To explore black women's experiences of the criminal justice system (see McLean and Caulfield, 2023).

Conducting in-depth interviews

Our own experiences as researchers, as well as our experiences as teachers of research, have demonstrated to us that carrying out interviews is often considered to be an easy task by beginners to research. This is largely because interviews are seen as an extension of what we do in our everyday conversations as we go about our daily lives. The reality of doing in-depth interviews is quite different from our first expectations precisely because interviews are not the same as conversations. That said, it is actually quite important to try to reproduce the conditions of a 'natural' conversation when carrying out an in-depth interview, so it is really important that researchers prepare carefully before carrying out any kind of interview. You should refer back to Chapters 7, 8 and 9 in order to refresh your memory about gaining access, ethical considerations, and how to review literature and translate your ideas into questions. There are also some practical decisions that must be considered, such as whether or not to carry out the interview face to face or via a telephone or online (see later in this chapter), which involves, in turn, consideration of whether the setting of the interview is appropriate and safe; the type and reliability of the recording instrument; whether or not to use a note taker in a face-to-face interview in order to record facial reactions/gestures (this means that the interviewer can avoid the distraction of note taking); and how to deal with a participant who is distressed.

In addition to these practical issues, researchers must consider their own social location in society in relation to their interviewees (research participants) in order to take account of the impact this may have on the data collected. For example, Hill (2007), a white, late middle-aged woman, interviewed young black people who had been in custody and therefore it was vital that she considered the impact her own characteristics might have upon the research participants prior to the interviews (also refer back to the discussion of Giri's work (2022) in Chapter 9). In particular, she needed to think of ways in which she could gain the trust of the young people she was to interview. It is always a good idea, especially when the research topic is sensitive, to ask some very general questions that put the participants at their ease and which allow them to develop a rapport with you. Bilby, Caulfield and Ridley (2013: 59) decided, in their research with prisoners and young people in contact with Youth Offending Teams, to avoid formal words like 'interview' altogether, and instead spoke about 'conversations with a purpose'.

PAUSE TO THINK ...

- Try to list your ideas about the ways in which you think interviewers should conduct themselves. Give reasons for your answer.
- How might a researcher's philosophical assumptions influence their interview style and stance on the relevance of interviewer/interviewee 'matching'?

- Can you think of some examples of research that we have discussed already in this book that may help you to justify your own future decisions about the roles you might choose to take during the interview process?

Research beginners will often grasp the different purposes of qualitative research as compared with the purposes of quantitative research; yet when it comes to their thoughts about the *process* of in-depth interviewing, they may hold on to the positivist idea of value-neutrality. It is likely that many of you will have suggested that interviewers should remain remote from the research participants and that they should not offer their own views or discuss any aspect of their own personal biography with a research participant. We hope that your reading of this text thus far has enabled you to think about the ways in which different research contexts may suggest different interviewing styles. For example, in situations where criminological researchers are concerned with sensitive issues, such as rape, it will be wholly appropriate to put the participant at their ease and to express some views that may increase their trust in you as a researcher. The existing literature indicates that assumptions are made about the sexuality of men who are raped and that this makes it difficult for male victims to speak out, especially if they are gay (for a good review of some of the salient literature see Rumney, 2008). This suggests that if male survivors of rape consent to be interviewed in depth then researchers would not only need to show sensitivity and compassion but it would also be appropriate for them to comment from time to time. For example, if a male rape victim spoke about the difficulties involved in getting people to believe him it would be important for the interviewer to allude to their wider knowledge of other men and women who have had the same experience. Indeed, Berg (2004: 99) mentions the fact that some researchers share their own experiences within the interview setting; for example, Patricia Gagné talked about her own experiences of domestic violence when carrying out a study with Tewkesbury (Tewkesbury and Gagné, 1997) which concerned Appalachian women's experiences of domestic violence. Feminist researchers have called this type of exchange within interviews a dialogic approach. It is a style of interviewing that many feminists use as it challenges the 'scientific' impersonal approach advocated by those who assume the possibility of complete value-neutrality. This also challenges standard views of the interviewer/interviewee relationship where one person gathers information from another and treats the subject more like an object.

PAUSE TO THINK ...

- Does a **dialogic interview** style increase or decrease the validity of the interview data? Give reasons for your answer.
- How might the validity of qualitative data in general be improved?

Hint: refer to Chapter 6 if you have forgotten what validity means in the context of qualitative research.

While we want readers to see the benefits of interviews to which researchers make an 'active contribution' (see Enosh and Buchbinder, 2005), it is not always appropriate to assume such an interviewer role. For example, let us say you had gained permission to interview people convicted of violent crimes. It is likely that you would want to get at the participants' 'subjective' truths as opposed to the actual truth of the criminal act. Heber (2017), for example, focuses on men as both victims and perpetrators of violence in her study of violent men. She uses discourse analysis of in-depth semi-structured interviews (see Chapter 17) in order to develop an understanding about the ways and the contexts in which these men renegotiate gender norms. If we wish to further our knowledge of why criminals act in particular ways then interviewers will need to allow the participants to speak in their own terms in order to expand understanding of the ways in which criminals justify their actions to themselves. It is through this process that researchers are able to reveal more information about the conditions in which people will break the law or indeed, as in the research by McAlinden, Farmer and Maruna (2016), will desist. Researchers may find this difficult at times, as they may have to listen to things which they find abhorrent without showing their feelings. This does not mean that they need to rid themselves of their own value position, but rather that they should act in a way that maximises their participants' ability to speak openly. We can sum this up by stating that some researchers will focus on achieving authenticity while others will try to explain why and how participants make sense of things in particular ways.

Website Student document

Reading about interview styles

BOX 12.2 POWER AND THE INTERVIEW PROCESS

Take another look at Giri's reflections upon his interviews in the article to which we referred in Chapter 6.

- In what ways did Giri's reflections upon aspects of his own identity reveal the power relationships between the researcher and the subjects of his research?
- How far do you think that an understanding of the concept of 'multiplex subjectivity' will enable you to develop more productive criminological research?
- Why/why not?

It is also useful to carry out interviews with victims of crimes, since this information can tell criminologists about the circumstances under which some crimes are committed. For example, in the late 2010s the UK government was keen to tackle hate crime on social media. Significantly, the Crown Prosecution Service figures demonstrated the ways in which crimes motivated by hatred of religion increased significantly following the terrorist attack in Manchester in May 2017 (Dodd, 2017). These statistics gave strength to the findings of Awan and Zempi (2017), which indicated the significance of 'trigger attacks' to the perpetration of both physical and virtual anti-Muslim hate crimes. While Awan and Zempi's study was expressly very small, it also revealed victims' processes of theorising about the reasons why some young British Muslims may be radicalised. It is important to note that hate crimes against Muslims (like hate crimes against gay people or black people, etc.) are, as Awan and Zempi (2017: 373) explain, profound in their effects, since such crimes are against their whole identity. Therefore it is important to gain more knowledge about people's experiences of hate crimes in order to address the harmful consequences specific to these types of crime.

While interviews are an exciting part of research that new researchers are usually keen to carry out, it requires skill and practice to become an effective interviewer. Our own early experiences as interviewers as well as our knowledge of our students' first attempts at interviewing have taught us that in practice it is important to try out interviewing skills on some willing 'guinea-pigs' before embarking upon the real thing. The most common problem is that participants' answers will be too brief if an interviewer does not think in advance of some ways to draw out more in-depth responses. The most important task for an interviewer is to put the participant at their ease by establishing a rapport at the beginning of an interview. You might tell the participant about something funny that happened on your way to meet them, or perhaps mention and discuss a topical news event as a way of breaking the ice. It is especially important to make participants feel comfortable with you when the research topic is sensitive, so it is a good idea to leave the most sensitive questions until towards the end of your interviews. We liken this process to dipping your toe in a bath tub to ensure that the water is not too hot before jumping in. It is often useful to use **vignettes** in circumstances where your research aims to access participants' attitudes towards sensitive issues. A vignette is a short summary of a scenario designed in such a way as to invite comment. Vignettes are often followed by some questions designed to draw out the participants' views.

EXAMPLE VIGNETTE

Here is an example vignette:

> Jackson was raped at the age of 18. He told his friend, Jake, whose response suggested to Jackson that Jake did not believe it was rape. Jake said that because Jackson was gay he must have wanted sex. Jackson failed to report the offence to the police for fear that they would not believe him.

- What do you think about Jake's response to Jackson?
- What would your advice have been?
- What would your advice have been if the victim was heterosexual?

In general, do remember to keep professional 'jargon' to a minimum, unless of course you are interviewing professionals who will understand it. It is most important that the participants in your research do not feel intimidated by the language you use, so try to make sure that you speak in plain English. Furthermore, you should ensure that you do not upset participants by using language that may be offensive; therefore you will need to make sure that you are culturally sensitive. Table 12.1 provides you with a

Table 12.1 Data gathering via interviews and focus groups

Type of interview	Reasons for choice	Issues to consider
Unstructured	To allow the participants to reveal the meaning of their actions or the reasons for their attitudes in their own terms.	How can you gain the trust of the participants in your research? Have you considered the power relationships within the interview process and the role you will assume? (Note that you will need to be reflexive throughout the whole process of research.) How far will you divulge your aims? How can you ensure that when you do ask questions they are clear? Have you identified some possible probes? How can you ensure the validity of the data? How will you record the data? (Don't forget to gain permission.) How will you maintain confidentiality? Will the location of the interview be safe for the participants and researcher?
Guided (semi-structured)	Usually when the researcher has identified specific areas that they wish to explore in order to develop a particular theory.	As above plus: Do the topics you have identified help you to answer the research questions? Have you allowed the participants sufficient flexibility to raise issues that you may have omitted?
Life history (guided, unstructured)	In situations where the researcher wishes to explore the relationship of key points in an individual's life to particular social norms and events; where the researcher seeks to identify the life events that brought about specific actions or changes to behaviour and/or attitudes; where thick description helps others to understand what it is like to be in a particular situation. Some researchers may wish to check accounts against historical 'facts'.	As above (Unstructured and Guided) plus: Consider the role of chronology – is it the most important thing or is it the significance of events that is important?
Focus group	Can be a way of collecting qualitative data from a large number when resources are short. Allows differences of view and contradictions to emerge.	As 1 and 2 above plus: How will you deal with group dynamics? What are the specific problems relating to data recording focus group interviews?

quick checklist of things to consider before making your final choice about your style of interview.

Designing an in-depth interview schedule

It is really helpful for any researcher planning on conducting interviews to have a clearly designed interview schedule. When designing an interview schedule you should consider the points we have covered so far in this chapter. How you decide upon the key topics to be covered in the interview schedule and the exact questions you ask will be informed by the literature review and the over-arching research questions (see Chapter 9). Remember, with any form of data collection you must ask yourself whether the questions you ask will enable you to address your research questions.

Below we have provided an example interview schedule. We find it useful to work from a template that covers key elements like a reminder to discuss the participant information and consent forms (see Chapter 7), some introductory questions (remembering what we said above about building rapport and leaving sensitive/personal questions until later in the interview) and a note at the end thanking participants for speaking with us. The example below is a semi-structured interview schedule and so includes key topics, key questions and prompts. Note that prompts are especially useful for interviewees who need encouragement to say more – although quite often interviewees will talk at length with no prompts and your job as interviewer is to be prepared for both situations. Either by encouraging less communicative participants to say more or gently steering very communicative participants back on topic. This is one of the reasons why earlier in this chapter we encourage you to practice your interview schedule. It will not only allow you to refine your technique, and perhaps your questions, but will also allow you to gain confidence in dealing with different types of participants.

BOX 12.3 A SEMI-STRUCTURED INTERVIEW SCHEDULE

The interview guide below is taken from a research project that involved an assessment of the development of an innovative programme for people in prison who are eligible for Release on Temporary Licence (ROTL).[1] The programme sought to match people in prison with placement employment opportunities in arts and cultural organisations (such as theatres and music venues). The researchers wanted to find out about how this innovative programme had been developed, any challenges there had been for the people involved (prisoners, prison staff, placement providers), and what the impact had been on prisoners who had taken part in the project. The interview guide below was designed for prisoners taking part in a ROTL placement. The novel nature of the project meant that, although we had key things we wanted to learn about, we kept the interview schedule relatively open. We designed a semi-structured schedule with key questions supported by potential prompts.

You can watch a short film about the project and our research report on this website: www.geese.co.uk/what-we-do/creative-licence/

INTERVIEW GUIDE: CREATIVE LICENCE

Discuss participant information form and ask participant to sign consent form.

Introduction

We would like to speak to you about your views and any impact on you of taking part in Creative Licence. Thank you for agreeing to take part in this interview and for signing the consent form.

The interview should last approximately 45 minutes, depending on how much you would like to say. Please remember, we can take a break or stop the interview at any time if you feel the need to do so – just let me know. Are you happy to begin?

(A) Opening section

- Firstly, could you please tell me about your role within this arts organisation (the placement)?

- Can you talk me through the timeline of your involvement with this placement?
    - Initial conversations in the prison – how did you hear about the opportunity?
    - What happened after you agreed? Talk me through the practicalities and timing from expressing an interest to starting the placement.
    - Tell me about the placement: what work have you been doing, with which teams, over what timeframe? *(Please assume I know nothing.)*

(B) Expectations and experiences

- Can you tell me about what you expected from the placement?
    - Has it lived up to this?
- Can you highlight anything about the opportunity that attracted you initially?

(C) Impact

- Can you tell me about what you feel your contribution to the placement organisation has been?

- What have the benefits been to you?
  - Have you learnt new things/skills?
- Have you spoken to other people about the placement?
  - What have you told them about? (What are you most proud of?)
- Has the placement/experience had an impact on your plans for the future?

(D) Challenges

- Have there been any barriers/challenges that you've had to work through?
  - What were these and how did you/the prison/the placement organisation address them?
  - Practical issues? (e.g. travel?)
  - Are there barriers you're experiencing currently?
- Have there been any barriers for you that you can advise ACE/Geese Theatre/the prison to address?
  - What are these and how could they be addressed?

(E) Learning for the future

To help with our key learning to share with other prisons and placement providers:

- In your view could Creative Licence be improved in any way?
  - What? Why? How? Who?

(F) Close

- Is there anything else you would like to add that we haven't already talked about?

Thank you very much for giving your time to share your experiences and views.

(Adapted from Caulfield and Puttick, 2024.)

Conducting interviews online

If you are developing and practising your interviewing skills through a research methods module, it is likely you will be doing this in person with fellow students. However, it has become more and more common in a range of research projects to conduct interviews online. There are pros and cons to this. It is often possible to offer potential interviewees more flexibility around the timings of interviews if you/they do not need to travel, and this might mean that people are more likely to participate. In terms of time and resources (e.g. travel expenses) this can be quite efficient. However, in our experience conducting interviews online makes building a rapport more challenging and so it is important to really focus on this at the beginning of the online session because building trust and rapport is so crucial to the interview process. You might be quite familiar with platforms such as Microsoft Teams, Zoom, and Google Meet, which can be set up easily in order to conduct interviews. As we discuss in Chapter 17, these platforms can also offer helpful recording and (basic) transcription capabilities.

> ### BOX 12.4   STUDENT ACTIVITY: CRITICAL QUALITATIVE RESEARCH
>
> Read: Hill, J. (2007) 'Daring to Dream: Towards an Understanding of Young Black People's Reflections Post-custody', *Youth Justice*, 7(1): 37–51.
>
> - How far do you think that the type of interview used in this study exposed the interplay between (1) the conditions in which offences were committed and responded to; and (2) the meanings that the young offenders gave to their actions?
> - How far do you think that such an analysis may be useful?
>
> Tierney (1999: 309) states that the challenge for researchers is 'not to make the individual into a cohesive self, but instead to create methodological and narrative strategies that will do justice to … multiple identities'.
>
> - How far do you think Hill's study achieves this aim? Give reasons for your answers.
> - Do you think your own identity has influenced your answer to this question?
> - If so, how important do you think it is for a researcher to discuss their identity?
>
> Prepare to carry out a life history interview with young black offenders who have been released from custody. Decide whether or not you want to adopt a guided approach and give reasons for your decision.
>
> - List the issues you think you will need to consider before you begin the interviews.

FOCUS GROUPS

Some researchers make use of focus groups (sometimes called focus group interviews), an interviewing method that has its origins in market research. These too can vary in terms of how far they are guided by the issues which the researcher seeks to explore. When there is a semi-structured approach it is usual for a facilitator to identify some key topics for participants to consider. Participants will often be divided into several quite small groups. They may be asked to jot down their individual thoughts on each topic before sharing their thoughts within their group. The next stage would be for the groups to summarise their views before sharing with the other groups present. Focus groups may also be used in a less structured way. In these cases they are often a precursor to quantitative data-gathering processes. As Pole and Lampard (2002) have noted, they can provide a degree of synthesis between quantitative and qualitative approaches.

Focus groups are particularly useful following individual in-depth interviews when researchers may want to explore the ways in which participants' views, as expressed in individual interviews, may change in the context of the focus group interview. Here the task of the researcher is to assess whether these changes are the result of group pressure, which may serve to create a false consensus (see Somekh and Lewin, 2009: 43), or whether in fact, especially in cases where the participants have similar experiences, they are the result of an individual participant's ability to force a meaningful discussion that leads to greater honesty. In the process of carrying out research for a PhD on inter-agency cooperation in child protection work, for example, one of us (Hill, 1999) used a focus group interview following in-depth interviews with social work professionals in order to explore the differences between what participants were prepared to say when alone and when in a group. The fieldwork was carried out at a time when there was great anxiety among professionals responding to child abuse; therefore professionals were, at least at first, often at pains to state their knowledge of statutory guidelines and their unfailing adherence to them. It was during a focus group interview that one participant expressed some of his worries about aspects of the procedural response, and this enabled the other professionals to speak more honestly about some of their own concerns.

In many ways the process of designing a focus group schedule is similar to designing an interview schedule (see earlier in this chapter). If designing a semi-structured focus group schedule you are likely to have identified key topics/lines of inquiry from your reading of the research literature and development of your research questions (see Chapter 9). Remember, with any form of data collection you must ask yourself whether the questions you ask will enable you to address your research questions. We have included an example focus group moderator guide in the support material to help you develop your own.

Website Student guide to …

Moderating focus groups

It doesn't have to be an either/or

There are many innovative variations on the focus group in-depth interviewing continuum. In practice there tends to be a process of moving back and forth between different techniques of data gathering in much qualitative research. Deuchar, Miller and Barrow (2015), for example, provide a detailed account of the ways in which they used discussions with experienced youth workers to identify issues that had been raised by young people with whom they had worked over the years. These professionals acted as gatekeepers to some disillusioned young people who were in varying degrees of 'trouble'. The researchers' ethnographical approach with the young people involved in the study also employed what Clifford Geertz referred to as 'deep hanging out' – getting to know them in their own 'safe' space at the Youth Project (1973, cited by Deuchar et al., 2015). Their informal conversations with the young people helped them identify the young people's thoughts on the local community as well as their relationships with residents and police. Interviews were also carried out with the local community Police Inspector as well as with the campus Police Officer at the local school. Local residents were harder to access but they did manage to identify three local people through a process of snowball sampling. The participants were eventually brought together in a series of workshops, the content of which was influenced by data from all the different stakeholders obtained prior to the workshops. All stakeholders were valued and took it in turns to take the lead in proceedings. After the workshops the researchers carried out follow-up interviews through which they developed their discussion of the ways in which their findings might be used to test out how far 'integration initiatives based on the concept of praxis' (Deuchar et al., 2015: 72) brought theory and practice together to produce relationships of trust. This sort of research is of particular importance when researchers are keen to empower people in their local settings.

OBSERVATION

Ethnography is usually the term used to describe complete participant observation in which the researcher takes on a covert role. For this reason this type of observational research is relatively rare within criminology owing to the ethical issues to which it gives rise (see Chapter 7). However, as Yates (2004) has stated, it has made a considerable contribution to our criminological understanding and for this reason it is important for new researchers to have knowledge of observational methods and to understand the assumptions that underpin them. Yates (2004) also admits that it is important to note that most observational research within the field of criminology has been focused on those with least power in society; therefore it is incumbent upon researchers to be clear about the reasons for their study and we would add that it is important to ensure that stereotypical representations are not reproduced in such research.

New researchers in criminology are unlikely to be guided towards research that involves complete participant observation and so the section below on conducting observational studies will be less detailed in this regard. However, the 'covert invisible non-participatory observation' outlined by Pollock (2009) may be an area which will be attractive to new researchers as it is relatively safe and easily and cheaply accessible.

Types of observation

Pole and Lampard (2002: 71) characterise observation as 'the first-hand involvement of the researcher(s) with the social action as it occurs', which describes all forms of observation whether or not that be the complete immersion of a researcher within a particular setting over a protracted period. While the term 'ethnography' is often restricted to complete participant observation we do not believe that this is a particularly useful distinction, especially when observation is used in conjunction with ethnographic interviewing. Observation may be overt or covert. Overt observation gives rise to fewer ethical concerns, although there is perhaps more chance that the observer will have an impact upon the data collected than in covert studies. Many methodology texts also speak of participant or non-participant (sometimes referred to as simple) observation (see e.g. Flick, 2009; Matthews and Ross, 2010). Gold (1958) is frequently cited in general social science methodology texts which discuss different types of observational data collection. He spoke of four key roles that researchers may choose to take in the process of carrying out observational studies, which are defined by the degree of detachment or involvement a researcher has with the subjects of the research. We can represent this as a continuum as shown in Figure 12.1.

Complete participant; Participant as observer; Observer as participant; Participant as detatched observer

---

Subjective ←--→ **Objective**

Figure 12.1 Researcher roles in observation studies.

Given that we have tried to challenge oppositional modes of thinking in this text it will come as no surprise to discover that, in reality, we do not believe it is helpful to think of these researcher roles as discrete or ideal types. Researchers may move in and out of the first three roles during the process of research, although we think it is unlikely that criminological researchers would be able to carry out a complete and, by implication, covert observer role, as this suggests the treatment of human beings as if they are inanimate objects. Towards the objective end of the continuum it is likely that observations will be more structured. Structured observations may be used in combination with in-depth interviews and non-structured observations, especially by critical criminologists who may wish to use quantitative strategies as a way of explaining the relationship between structure and meaning.

When to use observational methods

In simple terms criminological researchers should choose observational methods when they wish to gain insider understanding of people involved in criminal activities or indeed of those who are involved in responding to criminal activities. For example, it is possible to use observation from the perspective of an **ethnomethodologist** (a researcher who tries to identify people's methods of making sense of situations). In such research, decision-making processes, such as jury decisions, will be the focus of the observation and the researcher/s will try to identify what assumptions underpin people's decisions. While observational studies are most often described as qualitative, observational methods may also be used in a quantitative way. As May (2001: 151) says, 'there is a central ethnographic component to successful survey work, while numbers may equally appear in the representation of ethnographic studies'. This means that it may sometimes be appropriate to count the number of times a particular decision is made and to record the details. For example, if there were a concern about bias in sentencing, an observation schedule would be appropriate to record such things as the age, gender and ethnicity of the offender. As in all decisions about methods, researchers need to ensure that their choice of observational method is suited to the aims of their study. As we indicated in Chapter 7, however, we suggest that caution is needed when assuming a complete participant researcher role because of the special ethical concerns to which it gives rise. That said, if you can justify your ethical decisions and it seems highly unlikely that it would be possible to gain important data in any other way, then we are certainly not against this method, but we would suggest that it requires a higher level of expertise than other forms of observation.

PAUSE TO THINK ...

Refer back to Box 12.1 and think about whether any of the listed research aims may also indicate the use of observational methods.

BOX 12.5 OBSERVATION AND THEORIES OF KNOWLEDGE

Consider the following.

Conventional ethnography

A research team decides to observe groups that define themselves as a gang in several different areas. The researchers gained access to the gangs through trusted local individuals. They produced detailed descriptions of what they saw in as neutral a way as possible and compared what they had recorded. As a result of this process they developed a **hypothesis** – 'the sense of belonging of which gang members speak is more tenuous for male gang members than for female members' – which they tested out by further observations of the gangs.

- What role did theory play in the first set of observations?
- What theory of knowledge does the development of a hypothesis usually imply?
- What is the role of theory in the subsequent observations in this study?
- How can the concept of belonging be made measurable?
- How could researchers be sure that the key **dependent variable** is gender?
- How is this similar to and different from **positivism**?

Interpretivist ethnography

A research team aims to observe young people in an area designated as 'high risk' in terms of crime. The researchers wish to access what life is like in this area from the perspectives of the young people who live there. Two members of the team have become involved with a voluntary organisation working with young people in the community who have been in trouble with the police. They move into the community and through their voluntary work they have an opportunity to get to know the young people and to observe them in their everyday lives. They are participant observers who choose to be covert about the fact that they are recording their observations for the purposes of research. They wish to provide insights into what these young people thought they were doing and why they were doing it. In other words, they were trying to uncover the meanings that actions had for the young people in order to widen understanding of their risk-taking behaviours.

- What role does theory play in the data-collection process?
- What do you think are the strengths and limitations of this approach for criminologists?
- Would the results have been better had the researchers chosen to be overt about their observation?

Critical ethnography

A research team aims to observe young people in an area designated as 'high risk' in terms of crime. The researchers wish to access what life is like in this area from the perspectives of the young people who live there. Two members of the team have become involved with a voluntary organisation working with young people in the community who have been in trouble with the police. They move into the community and through their voluntary work they have an opportunity to get to know the young people and to observe them in their everyday lives. They are in effect participant observers while being covert about the fact that they are recording their observations for the purposes of research. However, these two members of the research team are able to introduce the other members of their team to some key young people in the area. They explain to the young people that their 'friends' (i.e. the other members of the research team) would like them to help them with some research they are doing in areas of high deprivation. They ask the young people whether they would be willing to be trained in videoing skills so that they could make a film depicting everyday life in their neighbourhood. The plan is to show the films in several key places in order to raise awareness of the social conditions in which some young people are identified as a problem to society and to facilitate discussions through which

Website Instructor activity

Workshop – ethnographic research on children

understanding of the relationship between meaning and structure is exposed. In this way the researchers are demonstrating that the meanings the young people give to their actions are not the whole of the story because their actions take place within a particular social context. This social context interacts with the meanings the young people give to their actions and therefore these meanings cannot be understood in isolation.

- What role does theory play in the data-collection process?
- Do you think that relations of power shape meanings in people's lives? Give reasons for your answer.
- Do you think there could be a role for hypothesis testing in this type of ethnography? Give reasons for your answer.

As Box 12.5 indicates, the theoretical assumptions that underpin the choice of observational methods will vary in the same way that our choice of interviewing method and the researcher role will vary. As we have stressed throughout this book, it is important that you are clear about your own assumptions and that you are consistent. That said, some researchers do attempt 'theoretical' (as opposed to method) triangulation. This is where researchers try to analyse an issue from different standpoints, such as an interpretivist account of why a crime is committed compared with a structuralist Marxist approach, for example. This kind of analysis actually takes place within a literature review but it is more usual to use the review to justify why one position is deemed more appropriate than the others that are being discussed. We think that theoretical triangulation is quite complex for beginners and indeed we are uncertain as to the merits of such triangulation, as it assumes that it is possible to arbitrate between competing accounts. So theoretical triangulation rather goes against the position we have taken throughout this text because we have tried to convey the ways in which different theories of knowledge provide us with different types of knowledge that are all important if we wish to have a more rounded understanding of a social phenomenon such as crime.

Website Student activity

Getting started with ethnographic research

Ethnographic researchers will often use a combination of in-depth interviews and observation. Overt observation may be used in situations where a researcher has already had access to a setting, say, in order to carry out interviews. Having gained trust, the researcher may subsequently obtain permission to observe an important meeting, for example, a case conference. However, it may be that a researcher will gain permission to observe a particular setting in advance of interviewing as a way of identifying some key topics for interviews. Covert observation, as we suggested in Chapter 7, is best used when the data cannot be generated via any other method.

Doing observation

Like interviewing, observation is often believed to be an easy option when in fact this is far from the case. Apart from the fact that observation is a very time-consuming activity it can also be quite a risky activity. Criminological researchers who choose to become complete participants must consider their personal safety, the safety of those they are researching, what they will do if they witness a crime and the reputation of the research institution (refer back to Chapter 7). They will also need to think about the best way to record their data. When researchers are completely immersed in the research setting it is often hard to know what to record at first. It is often also practically difficult to make notes without blowing one's cover, so researchers will need to develop strategies that enable them to 'jog' their memories at a later time, such as making brief, covert notes from time to time while still 'in the field'. The detailed notes should be made as soon as possible and should include descriptions as well as reflexive comments about the researcher's own reactions to what has been seen and heard. It can take some considerable time for the main focus of the research to emerge from the large amounts of data. This means that the process is largely inductive (although, as we have suggested throughout this text, no observation can be completely free from theory). In reality, as beginners in research, most of you will be unlikely to be thinking about this type of observation as yet.

Where the researcher's role is overt the researcher must consider how they may put the people being observed at their ease in the same way that this issue must be considered within an interview. After the observation has taken place the researcher will need to think carefully about their impact upon the behaviour of those being observed. As Pole and Lampard (2002) suggest, researchers may actually be directly responsible for some of the things being observed. Where the researcher is already a part of and therefore accepted in the research setting the impact of the researcher may be less than when they are an outsider.

It is increasingly likely that researchers will choose to make audio and/or visual recordings in order to have an accurate record of their observations. However, this may well impact negatively the data gathered and be overly intrusive. Consequently, some researchers may involve the participants in their research in recording their own activities, which may overcome the problem of the researcher having too great an impact upon the data because this fits with the purposes of the research. Take a look at Table 12.2 and consider whether in-depth interviewing methods are likely to fit with the topics listed.

Overt observation may be structured or unstructured (or somewhere in between). If a structured approach is chosen, then theory will inform the process from the start. It may be the case that an unstructured approach is followed up by structured observation once certain kinds of behaviour have emerged from the initial unstructured process. In reality, researchers will be influenced by their review of existing knowledge but the 'thick' data gained through observation may cause them to reconsider their initial focus. This is why research journals recording when, where, why and how a research aim was modified are of the utmost importance when writing up one's methodology.

Autoethnography with heroin users

Criminologists who have embraced the merits of ethnographic research have often had a hard time justifying their epistemological position, as we have seen.

Table 12.2 Data gathering via observation

Type of observation	Reason for choice	Issues to consider
Complete participant (covert)	To get an insider view that it would be impossible to gain in any other way – the setting is not artificial.	What are the ethical problems associated with covert research? (See Chapter 7.) How will you reflect upon your own role? How will you record your data? Can you counter criticisms such as 'researcher lack of objectivity'? How will you leave the field sensitively?
Participant as observer (overt)	To study in detail a setting in which you are already a member. Your role as a researcher is known to those in this setting, so you will not be running the risk of being morally compromised.	You may need to consider how much detail about your research you will reveal. How will you reflect upon the impact of your own role?
Observer as participant (overt)	To gain legitimate access to a specific setting whilst maintaining an element of detachment.	How will you make your presence as unobtrusive as possible? How can you be sure that your presence has not affected the data? Will your observations be structured?
Complete observer (covert)	This is not really appropriate in criminological research as it suggests a 'social experiment'.	

In particular it has been especially difficult for criminologists to involve 'the self' in their research such has been the strength of the scientific discourse (see Jewkes, 2012). While in the sociological and feminist research literature the self was seen as an important aspect of researching social life, for one of the authors of this book the move from a department of sociology into a department of criminology (both in the school of social science at that time) revealed the resistance among many criminologists to the unashamed inclusion of the self in research. Wakeman's (2014, 2021) consideration of his own past heroin and crack cocaine addiction provided the space within which to consider how the intersections of biography and fieldwork can facilitate the generation of new knowledge. His 'deep' descriptions tell us what it is like to be a heroin addict. This introduction of the human detail (as opposed to the in-human detachment) opens up different ways of thinking about the best response to problem drug use in society.

> **BOX 12.6 BIOGRAPHICAL CONGRUENCE**
>
> Read: Wakeman, S. (2021) 'Doing Autoethnographic Drugs Research: Some Notes from the Field', *International Journal of Drug Policy*, 98(1): 1–7 (Online). Available at: https://doi.org/10.1016/j.drugpo.2021.103504
>
> - What are the positive elements of congruence according to Wakeman? Do you agree with Wakeman's position? Why?/Why not?
> - What are the negative elements of congruence? Are the risks worth taking? Give reasons for your answers.

MIXED-METHODS

In this book we have separated out qualitative and quantitative methods of data collection and analysis. However, you might have noticed when reading research articles that it is not uncommon for qualitative *and* quantitative methods to be used in the same study. As you will come to understand more fully throughout this book, qualitative and quantitative methods – and indeed secondary data analysis (see Chapter 14) – can all give important insights into a topic. It is therefore not surprising that using more than one approach to investigate a topic can be powerful. While some researchers have viewed one approach as 'better' than another, our view is that when well thought through, taking a mixed-methods approach (the term used for applying more than one method) can, when used appropriately, tell us much more about a topic than using one approach alone. For example, we might want to get a sense from research participants about the elements of key issues on a particular topic that are important to them, so conduct interviews or focus groups to understand this. The key themes (see Chapter 17) we take from analysis of this qualitative data might then inform the development of a survey or questionnaire (see Chapter 13) to collect data on more specific issues with a larger number of participants.

The key with mixed-methods approaches is to ensure that the use of different methods is complementary and that you are clear about what you seek to gain from each method. For example, in research with children in contact with the youth justice system, we took a mixed-methods approach to investigating the impact of a music programme so that we could do two key things: 1. understand the impact on officially recorded sentence engagement of all children who had taken part in the programme; 2. gain an in-depth understanding of how children experienced the programme and what was most meaningful to them (Caulfield et al., 2022). We addressed the first point by accessing records held by the youth justice service of children's engagement with their youth justice sentence and compared this against a comparison group of records of children who had not taken part in the music programme. In this case, quantitative methods allowed us to analyse a relatively large data set to answer one specific research question. However, the quantitative data could not tell us anything about why the programme might have had an impact and how children experienced this. We therefore undertook semi-structured interviews with a sample of children who had taken part in the programme. The combination of these two data sets allowed us to conclude that the programme had an impact, to offer insights into why the programme might have achieved this, and share information on how the children experienced the programme.

> ### CASE STUDY: TECH4PRISONLEAVERS: A MIXED-METHODS APPROACH TO UNDERSTANDING THE IMPACT OF A DIGITAL SUPPORT PROGRAMME FOR MEN LEAVING PRISON
>
> One of the authors of this book undertook a mixed-methods study to explore a project working with men who had recently left prison.
>
> *Project aims*: Led by the Digital Poverty Alliance, the project aimed to implement and test a digital support programme for men leaving prison. The project – called Tech4PrisonLeavers – aimed to provide 'digital and employability skills training to 20–25 male former prisoners aged 18–44. The project focused on improving participants' digital skills and enhancing their employment opportunities, leading to sustainable employment and a brighter future for themselves, their families, and their communities' (Digital Poverty Alliance, 2023).
>
> The project aimed to be part of the solution to the problem that limited access to technology can increase the distance between prisoners and society in a rapidly changing digital world. The research literature presents a picture of people with experience of the criminal justice system having inconsistent and often inadequate access to education both before and during prison, with inadequate access to technology exacerbating the educational award gap and its impact on employability (Grierson et al., 2022; Barreiro-Gen and Novo-Corti, 2015).
>
> As a novel pilot project it was important to understand whether the project was successful. Therefore, a research team was involved with the pilot from the beginning to examine if the project met its aims.
>
> *Project delivery*: Men who had recently left prison were referred to the project. They attended a launch event where they were provided with digital devices. Over a three-month period the men engaged with a series of online and virtual workshops focused on employability skills, with support from a mentor. The men also undertook mini courses focused on digital skills development. Finally, they attended a graduation and award ceremony.

Research aims: The research took a **mixed-methods** approach to investigate how far the project met its aims, including looking at: employment outcomes; changes in the confidence, skills, and well-being of participants — including their digital skills and confidence, aspirations and perceived ability to find employment.

Research methods: The research used quantitative measures of the primary outcomes (well-being; perceived competence with finding future employment; aspirations; digital literacy — see Chapter 13 for a closer look at this), extended through qualitative exploration of participants' experiences and project implementation from the perspective of participants, staff and volunteers.

Why a mixed-methods approach was useful in this research: The quantitative measures allowed us to assess the impact on participants of taking part in the project. However, quantitative methods alone would not have allowed us to understand participants' experiences, the role of mentors and volunteers, what all of these groups felt had been good about this new project and areas that might need to be improved or developed. It was important to us as a research team not only to be able to provide evidence about whether the project had 'worked' but to be able to offer deeper insights. Taking a mixed-methods approach meant that we could show whether the project had an impact (as demonstrated through the quantitative measures) but also allowed us, through the qualitative data, to understand what it was about the project that made it a success from the viewpoints of project participants and those involved in delivering the project. The qualitative data also enabled us to make some useful recommendations about ways the project could be developed in the future.

The Digital Poverty Alliance have published a white paper based on our research, calling for the UK Ministry of Justice to look at a wider programme of support for prison leavers with access to devices, connectivity and digital skills training. You can read the white paper here: https://digitalpovertyalliance.org/projects/tech4prisonleavers/

In Chapter 13 we revisit this case study to focus in more detail on the quantitative elements of the study.

CURRENT TRENDS IN QUALITATIVE RESEARCH

While it's important for novice researchers to get to grips with the traditional qualitative methods covered in this chapter, it is also useful to be aware of the range of methods being developed and used by researchers. More advanced readers may want to consider utilising some of these methods in their own research.

Current trends in the development of qualitative methods have often been driven by an acknowledgement that traditional methods are not always the best way of working with all participant groups. No matter how relaxed and inclusive we make an interview or focus group, and how much energy we put to building trust and rapport with participants, not everyone will feel comfortable. We explore some examples below focused on creative data collection approaches for working with children in and adults in criminal justice. We have not intended this section of the chapter to be exhaustive, but instead to offer inspiration and suggestions for further reading around these emerging trends.

Creative approaches with children in youth justice

When working with children in any setting, but particularly so in youth justice settings, conducting traditional interviews or focus group discussions might not be the best way to allow children to feel relaxed and comfortable being open with researchers. Some researchers have therefore moved to more relaxed, arts-based methods to gather data with children.

Dr Vicky Meaby undertook extensive work with children – some involved with youth justice services and some not – exploring their experiences of loss. Meaby (2019: 104) notes that that 'When considering issues of loss, young people's lack of voice is evident (Ribbens McCarthy, 2006; McCarthy and Jessop, 2005), especially marginalised young people, including those who offend (Beyond Youth Custody, 2017).' It was therefore important for Meaby to find a method of working with young people, exploring a challenging issue, that would allow their voices to be heard. Meaby utilised an approach that combines ethnography and arts-based approaches, called ethno-mimesis (O'Neil et al., 2002). Meaby worked with children during art sessions over multiple sessions, engaging them through ethno-mimesis:

> Taking an ethno-mimetic approach therefore offered me multiple opportunities to gain insight into the lives of young people, through words, through action and through art. In the first instance, young people's experiences were explored through their own narratives of personhood, place and space. This was enabled during one to one work by a series of story book cards depicting key themes that had emerged from young people as the research progressed.
>
> Where the young person wanted to, narratives were then collaboratively (re) presented via art, photography or creative writing. This also worked in reverse, with stories emerging from young people's creative work. Additionally, I was also able to observe the process of art making, as well as exploring young people's rationales for the stories they shared and the creative work produced. Ethno-mimesis therefore, in its synthesis of creative methodology and ethnographic work, helped me to engage and build relationships with participants, illustrate quantitative data (King and Roberts, 2014) and break down hierarchical structures of researcher and researched (O'Neill, Roberts and Sparkes, 2014).
>
> (Meaby, 2019: 104–105)

Dr Mary-Rose Puttick writes about an arts-based focus group she designed when working with children in contact with the youth justice service in 2024. Mary-Rose was involved in a project learning about Child First approaches to youth justice and wanted to hear directly from the children about their experiences. The use of in-person, arts-based focus groups was chosen as a culturally sensitive, therapeutic approach to use with the children's participant group. The plan was to use a form of visual metaphorical map-making, to help build an understanding of the contextual and emotional realms of experience, in this case experiences of the Youth Justice Service, that could be challenging to explain through textual, or indeed oral, mediums (Bagnoli, 2009). The participant group were invited to create a collective multi-layered visual map, with the intention to follow the same step-by-step process used by Jackson Foster, Deafenbaugh and Miller (2018) in their use of group map-making to explore the community factors affecting children's emotional health and stress: starting with individual surveys, followed by metaphor image drawing, following by linking and ranking images.

Mary-Rose has written the following summary of the method for us to include in this book:

> In terms of practical delivery of this approach, it is important to allow time at the start for sitting with the children and supporting them to feel at ease with the researchers and the process. Start with sharing names and some general chat, perhaps with some refreshments. The researchers can then talk about the overall project, its aims, data collection phases and participant groups, in child-friendly, accessible language, and allow time for the children to ask any questions about the project as a whole. Following this, the researchers introduce the arts-based focus group approach and why this approach has been chosen, such as for its flexibility, inclusivity and the way in which it opens up space for alternative forms of conversation about potentially challenging issues that can then be represented in visual and symbolic formats. Explain that as well as being open and less structured in order to adapt to the group dynamics, there will also be some guidance and direction to help the children think about different issues and experiences. It is useful to have some key prompt questions displayed on flipchart paper and also to give some concrete examples of what metaphorical images might look like (e.g. draw a river and explain this could represent a journey, and/or that they could use more obvious symbols such as emojis for feelings, such as a heart to represent love or a face with different expressions on). If you have photographs from other projects you could show those too. It is important that children know that art skills are not important and that there are no right or wrong answers and that you hope they will enjoy this process of remembering and sharing. Again, allow time for questions and comments before doing the consent process with the children, which will have been simplified accordingly to suit the age group.
>
> Children are then guided to work through the different phases, with timings planned in advance by the researchers and researchers prepared to adapt the phases as necessary. The idea is to build up children's thinking about the issues

gradually, and their confidence in sharing, until they add to the group map. First, start with an individual task which is printed on paper – such as considering what activities they have been involved with (in this case with the Youth Justice Service) and the positives and challenges of their interactions/experiences. Guide the children to then add the ones which they feel are most important to post-it notes. Following this, invite the children to come together in a small group and encourage them to look at their lists and to share some of the words in the group and to think of some symbols/images together for how they want to represent them – and start to build up a visual group map. Ask them to also work together to rank their post-it notes in terms of what they feel are most important and to place them on the map wherever they want to. The researchers can ask questions to the group to support this process and also remind the groups about the key question prompts around the room. Towards the end of the session, if appropriate, the small groups can come together as one whole group to share and talk about their maps and ask each other questions or as an alternative the maps can be displayed on the walls and the other groups can look at other maps and add post-it notes (in a different colour) to add textual or visual responses or questions to their peers' maps.

(With thanks to Dr Mary-Rose Puttick for the above description.)

Narrative arts approaches with criminal justice practitioners

Dr Ella Simpson (Simpson, 2024; Simpson, Morgan and Caulfield, 2019) has developed an innovative creative narrative research method. Simpson argued that the voices, experiences and life stories of some practitioners working in criminal justice had not been heard. From this Simpson developed a method to allow practitioners to 'share their authentic stories' (2024: 143). Building on narrative criminology (to read more about this see, for example, Presser and Sandberg, 2015), which prioritises stories when considering issues around crime and justice, Simpson wanted to create a method that let practitioners tell their life story, without too much interference or interpretation from the researcher, thus aiming to minimise some of the power dynamics that might be apparent between researcher and participant (see Chapter 5). Simpson arrived at a storyboard approach, arguing that creative data collection techniques can allow 'participants a greater degree of freedom to explore and communicate their stories' and also 'because the visual aspects of the method have been considered an effective way to 'disrupt the power imbalances between researchers and participants and aid the empowerment of participants (Wang and Burris, 1994)" (p. 144)

Simpson writes:

> I used techniques developed from my own creative work in prisons, with the aim of foregrounding participants' narratives. The storyboards could contain words as well as pictures in whatever combination a participant felt best communicated and validated their experiences.

Table 12.3 Example structure for an arts-based focus group

Format:	Activity:	Timing:
Whole group	Researchers: • Explain the purpose and aims of the research. • Go through consent process – emphasise confidentiality for them and the people they are working with; safe space; can stop at any time; complete consent forms. • Overview of what we're going to be doing in the workshop – explain building map up in layers, starting with an individual task which we'll be collecting afterwards but they don't have to share all of it on the group map if don't want to.	15 mins
Individual	• Complete individual task 1 with example shown first – the individuals and groups they engage with through the Service and types of activities. Task 1: Individuals to think about the following questions: 'These questions are to build up a picture of who you meet and what you do at the youth justice service.' What *individual people* do you meet with through the Service? How often do you see them? What kinds of things do you do with them? Next... What *groups* are you part of through the Service? How often do you meet? What kinds of things do you do in the groups? • Complete individual task 2 – the positive and negative factors of young people in general at the Service. Task 2: Individuals to pick what they think are the most important positive and negative factors from task 1 and write each on a post-it note (two different coloured post-its – green and red). 'Now please think about the positive and negative factors (people, places, events, experiences) for children and young people at the youth justice service.'	10 mins 10 mins 5 mins
Small group	• Work in groups of 3–4 – put out flipchart paper, coloured pens and post-its. • Ask them to put a circle with Youth Justice Service at the Centre and to add lines/circles coming out of it with any individuals or groups they interact with (from individual task 1). • Ask them to look at the words they wrote on their list in individual task 2 and think of an image (literal or metaphorical) to represent that word (show examples) and to draw them on the map wherever they want to put it ... and they can add any additional words or images if they think of more. • Ask them to look at the words they wrote on their post-it notes and to put their post-its together and rank them according to what they think are the most important positive and negative factors and to place them on the map. • Ask questions about their choices (researcher to make notes).	30 mins
Whole group	Whole group come together to share their maps (if they want to) and take part in a wider discussion – reflecting on overall experiences and feelings towards the Service and asking peers questions about their images/maps if they want to (researcher to make notes).	20 mins

The eight-frame storyboard technique is a simple A4 sheet of paper divided into eight squares with space for the author to write the title of their story. The presentation is suggestive of a story captured as a film. Each square or frame represents one episode in a participant's journey. In Figure 12.2 Simpson has completed the storyboard as an example of their own journey through life, from working in prisons to becoming a researcher.

Figure 12.2 Simpson's eight frame storyboard (from Simpson, 2024).

Simpson (2024: 144) asked

> practitioners' participating in my research to use text, images, or a combination of the two to narrate their story of how they came to work in prison. This event forms the content of the final and eighth frame of the storyboard, which participants are asked to fill in first. … By beginning with the final frame, participants create a pause in the forward trajectory of their lives from which to reflect upon how particular circumstance came to be. Participants fill and connect the preceding seven frames with whatever events, memories or reflections are most relevant in whatever order they choose. In this way, participants are the authors of their own authentic, autobiographical stories.

Using objects and images to understand and explain stories in criminal justice

As noted above, narrative criminology prioritises stories when seeking to understand and explain issues around crime and justice, and this is largely explored through verbal tales. However, Copes and Ragland (2016: 271) highlight that photographs can 'capture and produce stories' that can 'either reinforce or challenge dominant cultural narratives depending on what is included and excluded in the frame, and how the image is captioned'. Copes and Ragland note that 'each viewer will interpret the story told by the ... image differently. Although these interpretations can be stigmatizing, they also can humanize people ... thereby facilitating more complex, implicit narratives' (2016: 271).

Photographs and objects can serve as a research tool in their own right but also as a usual part of a methodological 'toolkit'. For example, Dr Paula McLean (2024), as part of her doctoral research, undertook in-depth interviews with black women who had previously been in prison. McLean undertook a series of three interviews and invited participants to bring a photograph or object to the second interview:

> In the first interview in preparation for the second interview, all participants were invited to provide any images or objects to supplement and support their narratives. Object elicitation is very empowering and enhances the collaborative nature of this research as it invites participants to select something of significant meaning that relates to their lived experience and contextualises their storytelling (Silver, 2013). It was through this and the lens of black feminism that the objects were analysed. Objects can evoke powerful emotions and latent memories which enhances engagement by shaping the direction of the interview and to reinforce the equity and inclusivity in the researcher/participant relationship which was an integral part of the research. Furthermore, objects/images add more nuance and elaboration to the data beyond the realm of narratives alone (Banks, 2018; Harper, 2002; Sheridan & Chamberlain, 2011).
>
> Participants welcomed the opportunity to select objects and whilst a couple were unsure of what they could select, they still grasped the opportunity to consider it. They were informed that the objects could be whatever they thought would supplement their story such as photographs, documents, a collage, storyboard and so forth.
>
> A rationale for using object elicitation was that because of the trauma that id often experienced by Black people throughout the CJS journey, memories can get buried to negate the pain and trauma and an object can help to draw on these memories. In using objects in research with terminally ill cancer patients, Willig (2016: 7) found that they elicited 'unrehearsed, in the moment' reflections spoken for the first time, and this allowed both researcher and participant to share in the experience of looking at the object simultaneously and reflecting on what it signifies for the participant. Making sense of what had happened to them and the meaning of it in their current lives was also very attached to the objects. It was found they often represented a journey with peaks and troughs, and it was quite an experience to be a part of this with them. Willig described it as 'meaning making' and how it is important to take the time to collaboratively savour these moments in the interview process. I could identify with Willig's experiences with my own participants and their chosen objects.
>
> (McLean, 2024: 149–151)

CONCLUSION

Qualitative research is concerned with gaining 'thick' description of aspects of the social world. In criminology knowledge about the lives of those involved in crime has been important to the task of understanding criminal behaviour and challenging some of the social conditions that may contribute to that behaviour. We have noted, however, that in criminology much research has been aimed at the most powerless members of society. This means that researchers need to present their data in ways that challenge stereotypical representations of 'criminal types'. It is important to be mindful of both the practical and philosophical issues that will necessarily impinge upon the process of data gathering. In this way you will be able to justify your research decisions and maintain consistency.

KEY LEARNING POINTS

- In-depth qualitative methods require careful preparation in order to elicit the depth of data needed to access the meanings which participants give to their lived experiences. You should familiarise yourself with the practical skills that will enable you to carry out effective interviews, focus groups and observations.
- You should apply your knowledge and understanding of the philosophical assumptions that underpin different research traditions to your discussion of your choice of interviewing and observation methods. You should also apply this knowledge to your discussion of your chosen researcher role.
- Ethnography is concerned with meanings that are normally associated with an interpretivist theory of knowledge.
- The data you collect should be relevant to your research aims. Note that critical social research will attempt to explain the relationship between meaning and structure, and may therefore use a variety of methods in order to fulfil the research aims.

NOTE

1. Release on Temporary Licence (ROTL) means being able to leave the prison for a short time for a limited number of reasons, including to take part in paid or unpaid work and to help individuals to settle back into the community. Only some people in prison are eligible for ROTL and all individuals who are eligible for ROTL must meet strict risk criteria. A key aim of ROTL is to support successful resettlement into the community.

REFERENCES

Awan, I. and Zempi, I. (2017) 'I Will Blow Your Face Off: Virtual and Physical World Anti-Muslim Hate Crime', *British Journal of Criminology*, 57(2): 362–380.

Bagnoli, A. (2009) 'Beyond the Standard Interview: The Use of Graphic Elicitation and Arts-Based Methods', *Qualitative Research*, 9(5): 547–570

Banks, M. (2018) *Using Visual Data in Qualitative Research*, London: Sage.

Barreiro-Gen, M. and Novo-Corti, I. (2015) 'Collaborative Learning in Environments with Restricted Access to the Internet: Policies to Bridge the Digital Divide and Exclusion in Prisons through the Development of the Skills of Inmates', *Computers in Human Behaviour*, 51: 1172–1176.

Bennett, T. and Holloway, K. (2004) 'Gang Membership, Drugs and Crime in the UK', *British Journal of Criminology*, 44(3): 305–323.

Berg, B.L. (2004) *Qualitative Research Methods for the Social Sciences*, fifth edition, London: Pearson.

Beyond Youth Custody. (2017) Trauma, Beyond Youth Custody. Available at http://www.beyondyouthcustody.net/tag/trauma/.

Bilby, C., Caulfield, L.S. and Ridley, L. (2013) *Re-imagining Futures: Exploring Arts Interventions and the Process of Desistance*. Final grant report for the Arts Alliance.

Caulfield, L.S., Jolly, A., Simpson, E. and Devi-McGleish, Y. (2022) '"It's Not Just Music, It Helps You from Inside": Mixing Methods to Understand the Impact of Music on Young People in Contact with the Criminal Justice System', *Youth Justice*, 22: 67–84.

Copes, H. and Ragland, J. (2016) 'Considering the Implicit Meanings in Photographs in Narrative Criminology', *Crime, Media, Culture*, 12(2): 271 (online). Available at https://doi.org/10.1177/1741659015623599 (accessed 30 May 2024).

Deuchar, R., Miller, J. and Barrow, M. (2015) 'Breaking down Barriers with the Usual Suspects: Findings from a Research-informed Intervention with Police, Young People and Residents in the West of Scotland', *Youth Justice*, 15(1): 57–75.

Digital Poverty Alliance (2023). *Tech4PrisonLeavers: Project Overview*. Available at https://digitalpovertyalliance.org/projects/tech4prisonleavers/

Dodd, V. (2017) 'Crackdown on Social Media Hate Crimes', *Guardian*, 21 August. Available at www.theguardian.com/society/2017/aug/21/cps-to-crack-down-on-social-media-hate-says-alison-saunders (accessed 21 August 2017).

Enosh, G. and Buchbinder, E. (2005) 'The Interactive Construction of Narrative Styles in Sensitive Interviews: The Case of Domestic Violence Research', *Qualitative Inquiry*, 11(4): 588–617.

Flick, U. (2009) *An Introduction to Qualitative Research*, fourth edition, London: Sage.

Giri, K. (2022) 'Can Men Do Feminist Research and Fieldwork?' *International Studies Review*, 24(1).

Gold, R. (1958) 'Roles in Sociological Field Observation', *Social Forces*, 36(3): 217–223.

Grierson, M., Bolton, M., Varghese, D. and Olivier, P. (2022) 'Design Considerations for a Digital Service to Support Prison Leavers', *Designing Interactive Systems Conference* (pp. 1–13). New York.

Harper, D. (2002) 'Talking about Pictures: A Case for Photo Elicitation', *Visual Studies*, 17: 13–26.

Heber, A. (2017) 'You Thought You Were Superman: Violence, Victimisation and Masculinities', *British Journal of Criminology*, 57(1): 61–78.

Hill, J. (1999) *The Discourse of Inter-agency Co-operation: Towards Critical Understanding of the Theory and Practice of Child Protection Work*, PhD thesis, University of Keele.

Hill, J. (2007) 'Daring to Dream: Towards an Understanding of Young Black People's Reflections Post-custody', *Youth Justice*, 7(1): 37–51.

Humphreys, C. and Thiara, R.K. (2003) 'Neither Justice nor Protection: Women's Experiences of Post-separation Violence', *Journal of Social Welfare and Family Law*, 25(3): 195–214.

Jackson Foster, L.J., Deafenbaugh, L. and Miller, E. (2018) 'Group Metaphor Map Making: Application to Integrated Arts-Based Focus Groups', *Qualitative Social Work*, 17(2): 305–322.

Jewkes, Y. (2012) 'Autoethnography and Emotion as Intellectual Resources: Doing Research in Prison Differently', *Qualitative Inquiry*, 18(1): 63–75.

Jones, S. (2008) 'Partners in Crime: A Study of Female Offenders and their Co-defendants', *Criminology and Criminal Justice*, 8(2): 147–164.

King, H. and Roberts, B. (2014) 'Biographical Research, Longitudinal Study and Theorisation', in O'Neill, M., Roberts, B., and Sparkes, A. (eds) *Advances in Biographical Methods: Creative Applications*, Oxon: Routledge, pp. 106–123.

Lemos, G. (2011) *Create-Ability: The Changing Meaning of Art and Artistry*. London: Lemos and Crane. Available at https://www.lemosandcrane.co.uk/home/index.php?id=213533 (accessed 27 October 2020).

Matthews, B. and Ross, L. (2010) *Research Methods: A Practical Guide for the Social Sciences*, London: Longman.

May, T. (2001) *Social Research: Issues, Methods and Process*, Buckingham: Open University Press.

McAlinden, A.M., Farmer, M. and Maruna, S. (2016) 'Desistance from Sexual Offending: Do Mainstream Theories Apply?', *Criminology and Criminal Justice*, 17(3): 266–283.

McCarthy, J. and Jessop, J. (2005) *The Impact of Bereavement and Loss on Young People: A Wide-Ranging Review of the Literature on the Implications of Bereavement for Young People's Lives*, London: Joseph Rowntree Foundation.

McLean, P. (2024) *Reclaiming the Silenced Voices of Women in the Criminal Justice System*. PhD Thesis. University of Wolverhampton. Unpublished.

McLean, P. and Caulfield, L.S. (2023) 'Conspicuous by Their Absence – Reclaiming the Silenced Voices of Black Women in the Criminal Justice System', *British Journal of Community Justice*, 19: 36–54.

Meaby, V. (2019) *Nothing to Lose? A Constructed Grounded Theory of Loss in the Lives of Young People Who Offend*. PhD Thesis, Durham University. Published.

Newberry, M., Williams, N. and Caulfield, L.S. (2013) 'Aggression in Females: Does Alcohol Consumption Make a Difference?', *Aggressive Behaviors*, 38(3): 1844–1851.

O'Neill, M. et al. (2002) 'Renewed Methodologies for Social Research: Ethno-Mimesis as Performative Praxis', *Sociological Review*, 50(1): 69–88.

O'Neill, M., Roberts, B. and Sparkes, A. (2014) *Advances in Biographical Methods: Creative Applications*, London: Routledge.

Phoenix, J. (2000) 'Prostitute Identities: Men, Women and Violence', *British Journal of Criminology*, 40(1): 37–55.

Pole, C. and Lampard, R. (2002) *Practical Social Investigation: Qualitative and Quantitative Methods in Social Research*, Harlow: Prentice Hall.

Pollock, E. (2009) 'Researching White Supremacists on Line: Methodological Concerns of Researching Hate "Speech"', *Internet Journal of Criminology*. Available at www.internetjournalofcriminology.com (accessed 6 June 2024).

Presser, L. and Sandberg, S. (2015) *Narrative Criminology: Understanding the Stories of Crime*. New York and London: New York University Press.

Ribbens McCarthy, J. (2006) *Young People's Experiences of Loss and Bereavement Towards an Interdisciplinary Approach*, Berkshire: Open University Press.

Rumney, P. (2008) 'Policing Male Rape and Sexual Assault', *Journal of Criminal Law*, 72(1): 67–86.

Sheridan, J. and Chamberlain, K. (2011) 'The Power of Things', *Qualitative Research in Psychology*, 8(4): 315–332.

Silver, J. (2013) 'Visual Methods', In C. Willig (ed.) *Introducing Qualitative Research in Psychology*, third edition, Maidenhead: McGraw Hill/Open University Press, pp. 156–167.

Simpson, E. (2024) 'Making the Story Count: An Argument for the Development of a Narrative Evaluation Tool in the Arts in the Criminal Justice Sector', in M. Gardner and L.S. Caulfield (eds) *Arts in Criminal Justice and Corrections: International Perspectives on Methods, Journeys, and Challenges*, London: Routledge.

Simpson, E., Morgan, C. and Caulfield, L. (2019) 'From the Outside In: Narratives of Creative Arts Practitioners Working in the Criminal Justice System', *The Howard Journal of Criminal Justice*, 58(3): 384–403. Available at: https://doi.org/10.1111/hojo.12318 (accessed 28 May 2024).

Somekh, B. and Lewin, C. (2009) *Research Methods in the Social Sciences*, London: Sage.

Tewkesbury, R. and Gagné, P. (1997) 'Assumed and Presumed Identities: Problems of Self-presentation in Field Research', *Sociological Spectrum*, 17: 127–155.

Tierney, W. (1999) 'Writing Life's History', *Qualitative Inquiry*, 5(3): 307–312.

Wakeman, S. (2014) 'Fieldwork, Biography and Emotion: Doing Criminological Autoethnography', *British Journal of Criminology*, 54(5): 705–721.

Wakeman, S. (2021) 'Doing Autoethnographic Drugs Research: Some Notes from the Field', *International Journal of Drug Policy*, 98(1): 1–7. Available at: https://doi.org/10.1016/j.drugpo.2021.103504

Willig, C. (2016) 'Reflections on the Use of Object Elicitation', *Qualitative Psychology*, City University of London, pp. 211–222.

Yates, J. (2004) *Criminological Ethnography: Risks, Dilemmas and their Negotiation*, Document 208043, National Criminal Justice Reference Service (accessed 3 March 2013).

Chapter 13

Questionnaires and surveys

GOALS OF THIS CHAPTER

At the end of reading this chapter and by completing the online resources that accompany it, you will be able to:

1. demonstrate an understanding of the advantages and disadvantages of using questionnaires and surveys in criminological research;
2. appreciate the importance of selecting appropriate samples;
3. design questionnaires using robust and appropriate question structures;
4. appreciate the importance of sensitivity when using questionnaires.

OVERVIEW

- Questionnaires are widely used in criminological research and when designed well they can provide a useful tool for collecting data on large samples using a standard set of questions.
- One of the best-known questionnaire/survey methods in criminological research is the Crime Survey for England and Wales (formerly known as the British Crime Survey).
- As with all methods of data collection, there are advantages and disadvantages to questionnaires. In addition, there are a number of different methods of collecting questionnaire data – in person, by telephone, web-based surveys and postal surveys – and the merits of each method should be considered by researchers.
- The structure and wording of questions within a questionnaire are extremely important to get right and this chapter provides guidance on this.
- Criminological research often addresses sensitive topics; therefore, it is essential to consider sensitivity in using questionnaires in any criminological research.

WHAT ARE QUESTIONNAIRES AND SURVEYS?

The use of questionnaires and surveys is widespread in criminological research and, while the terms are often used interchangeably, there are some differences in meaning. While the content may be similar, surveys are sometimes longer and often used on a larger scale, as we will discuss in more detail below. For ease, we will primarily refer to the term 'questionnaire' throughout this chapter.

When designed well, questionnaires provide a useful way of answering research questions or addressing hypotheses. Their purpose includes: gaining factual demographic data on specific groups of people or population samples; obtaining general information relevant to specific issues in order to understand or examine what is not currently known; and gaining a range of insights on specific issues and experiences. As explored later in this chapter, it is also possible to apply specific types of **validated** questionnaire measures to people's thoughts and behaviours and how these change over time.

Questionnaires are used at all levels of criminological research, from undergraduate research projects to national crime surveys such as the Crime Survey for England and Wales (discussed later in this chapter and in Chapter 14). They comprise sets of questions that when answered will enable the researcher to address their research questions and/or hypotheses, typically through statistical analysis. We will examine the types of questions that can make up a questionnaire later in this chapter, but most questionnaires consist of **closed questions** where respondents must choose from one of a predefined set of answers. This enables statistical comparison of the answers of large numbers of respondents. However, some questionnaires include one or more **open questions** in addition to closed questions so that participants can provide some individual responses. Unlike interviews or focus groups, questionnaires typically exist in a standard and non-variable format so that all respondents are asked exactly the same questions in exactly the same order.

As all respondents are presented with a standard questionnaire, typically a list of questions, it is vital to ensure that the questionnaire is well designed. A badly designed questionnaire is likely to result in useless data that cannot answer the research questions, and so you will need to ensure that your questionnaire measures the concepts you have set out to measure. Piloting your questionnaire on a small sample may help in testing this. Good design also includes appropriate consideration of your intended participants and how the questionnaire will be completed: participant self-completion; face to face with a researcher; or by telephone. For these reasons you should pay particularly close attention to the section on questionnaire design later in this chapter.

HOW ARE QUESTIONNAIRES AND SURVEYS USED IN CRIMINOLOGICAL RESEARCH?

First used in 1982, the Crime Survey for England and Wales (known until 2012 as the British Crime Survey) is the largest-scale example of criminological survey research in England and Wales. The survey aims to provide information representative of the entire population of England and Wales about their experiences of crime during the past year (including crime not reported to the police). As the survey is not reliant on official statistics, it is regarded by some as a good indicator of the real extent of crime in England and Wales. For a discussion of the potential problems with official statistics, see Chapter 5. However, as discussed elsewhere in this book, it is also important to be aware of potential issues with self-report data.

The Crime Survey for England and Wales includes anonymised data from approximately 50,000 people. Most are aged 16 and over living in England and Wales. However, there is also a – much shorter – version of the Crime Survey for 10- to 15-year-olds. Given that young people are more likely than adults to be victims of some types of crime, these data are likely to be useful. The survey needs to be large scale to better ensure that the data collected can be generalised to the whole population. However, if the respondents were 50,000 students or 50,000 people living in rural areas, for example, then the data could not be said to be representative of the broader population. This is a good example of why choosing your sample appropriately is vital and you can find more information about this in the 'Selecting participants' section below. The survey uses a random sample of households from Royal Mail's address list. Recipients receive an invitation letter and information leaflet. According to Kantar Public – who, at the time of writing, administer the survey for the Office for National Statistics – around three out of four households invited take part. The survey is administered face to face by interviewers who ask questions about experiences of crime and views on government crime policy, who then enter each answer into a laptop computer. The only exception to this is a self-completion part of the survey that respondents are asked to complete individually about their own behaviour. This section includes potentially sensitive topics, such as personal drug and alcohol use, where respondents may be more likely to be honest than if reporting the answers to these questions to the interviewer.

You can find information and data on the Crime Survey for England and Wales at www.crimesurvey.co.uk

Questionnaires are not only useful for such large-scale data collection but are often used for much smaller scale research. For example, in research on a recent project aimed at men who had recently left prison, undertaken by one of the authors of this book – see Case Study Part 1 (also see Chapter 12).

CASE STUDY PART 1: TECH4PRISONLEAVERS

Project aims: Led by the Digital Poverty Alliance, the project aimed to implement and test a digital support programme for men leaving prison. The project – called Tech4PrisonLeavers – aimed to provide 'digital and employability skills training to 20–25 male former prisoners aged 18–44. The project focused on improving participants' digital skills and enhancing their employment opportunities, leading to sustainable employment and a brighter future for themselves, their families, and their communities' (Digital Poverty Alliance, 2023).

The project aimed to be part of the solution to the problem that limited access to technology can increase the distance between prisoners and society in a rapidly changing digital world. The research literature presents a picture of people with experience of the criminal justice system having inconsistent and often inadequate access to education both before and during prison, with inadequate access to technology exacerbating the educational award gap and its impact on employability (Grierson et al., 2022; Barreiro-Gen and Novo-Corti, 2015).

As a novel pilot project it was important to understand whether the project was successful. Therefore, a research team was involved with the pilot project from the beginning to examine if the pilot met its aims.

Project delivery: Men who had recently left prison were referred to the project. They attended a launch event where they were provided with digital devices. Over a three-month period the men engaged with a series of online and virtual workshops focused on employability skills, with support from a mentor. The men also undertook mini courses focused on digital skills development. Finally, they attended a graduation and award ceremony.

Research aims: The research took a **mixed-methods** (see Chapter 12) approach to investigate how far the project met its aims, including looking at: employment outcomes; changes in the confidence, skills, and well-being of participants – including their digital skills and confidence; aspirations and perceived ability to find employment.

Research methods: The research used quantitative measures of the primary outcomes (well-being; perceived competence with finding future employment; aspirations; digital literacy), extended through qualitative exploration of participants' experiences and project implementation from the perspective of participants, staff, and volunteers.

As this chapter focuses on surveys and questionnaires, let's take a look at the questionnaires the research team used in this research. The research team used two questionnaires. The first used **validated measures** of well-being; perceived competence with finding future employment; aspirations (this is explored later in this chapter). The second questionnaire was designed by the research team and focused on digital literacy. Participants were asked to complete the questionnaires at the beginning of the project and again at the end, so any change of time could be measured.

The Digital Literacy Assessment (Caulfield et al., 2023): A digital literacy assessment was developed by the research team based directly on the Department for Education's Essential Digital Skills Framework.[1] The survey consisted of 21 questions in total with subthemes, each including 2–4 questions relating to: foundational skills, communicating, handing information and content, transacting, problem solving, being safe and legal online, and a final section relating to searching and applying for jobs online. Participants were asked to rate how they felt on the day, on a scale of 1–5 with 5 being very confident for each question.

> *The benefits of the Digital Literacy Assessment*: Using an existing government framework meant the assessment measured areas identified as important and recognised in society. The results of the assessment completed at the start of the project were useful to the task of identifying the areas in which participants had some skills and the areas where their skills were lacking. Asking participants to complete the assessment again at the end of the project meant that the researchers could see how much progress in digital skills participants had made since the beginning of the project.
>
> The Digital Poverty Alliance have published a white paper based on our research, calling for the UK Ministry of Justice to look at a wider programme of support for prison leavers with access to devices, connectivity, and digital skills training. You can read the white paper here, including the findings of our research: https://digitalpovertyalliance.org/projects/tech4prisonleavers/

It is also quite usual for questionnaires to be used by students in their research. One of our students, Nikki, used a mix of questionnaires and pre-existing scales (see the section later in this chapter on using pre-existing validated measures) to measure the relationship between women's alcohol consumption in licensed premises and self-reported aggression (for more information on Nikki's work, see Newberry, Williams and Caulfield, 2013).

Both of the above examples involved designing highly focused questionnaires that directly addressed the research questions. The researchers also chose samples appropriate to their research questions. Both of these facts were important in contributing to the high grade that Nikki achieved for her dissertation project. Nikki's work was so good that it formed the basis of a peer-reviewed journal publication (Newberry et al., 2013). You should note that while it is unusual for undergraduate dissertation projects to reach publication standard it is not impossible to achieve, as Nikki has shown. Elsewhere in this book you can find examples of other students whose work has been published, although these are postgraduate students (see Chapter 19 for example).

ADVANTAGES AND DISADVANTAGES OF QUESTIONNAIRES AND SURVEYS

As discussed earlier in this book, the area you are investigating should inform the methods used and not vice versa. Once you have decided what to investigate and have discussed this with your lecturer or supervisor, one of the most important next steps to consider is what the appropriate methods are to best investigate your research questions. The overview here of the advantages and disadvantages of using questionnaires and surveys should help you in the process of making this decision and also in justifying the decision you make.

There are also advantages and disadvantages to specific types of questionnaires (see Table 13.1). Questionnaires conducted face to face allow the researcher to establish a rapport with respondents and to observe body language. However, they can be highly time-consuming and may also be expensive in financial terms, particularly if the researcher has to travel to administer the questionnaires. Alternatives are phone or video interviews. While it is more difficult to establish a rapport, both face-to-face and phone or video interview methods allow respondents to seek clarification on any questions they do not understand.

Table 13.1 Advantages and disadvantages of questionnaires and surveys

Advantages	Disadvantages
Allows each respondent to be asked a standard set of questions.	Does not allow for a high level of individual responses.
Provides data suitable for quantitative analysis.	Does not allow a depth of data to be collected.
Useful for gathering information from large numbers of people.	Less effective with a small sample.
Allows for collection of anonymous data on sensitive issues (e.g. illegal activity).	Does not allow for an exploration of the factors underlying responses.

In the past, researchers sometimes opted to send out questionnaires by post, and this was much more cost-effective in terms of time and often money than face-to-face interviews. However, postal questionnaires are now typically superseded by sending out questionnaires by email or via links to online survey sites. These are discussed later in this chapter.

SELECTING PARTICIPANTS

Questionnaires are normally used with a sample of a larger population. Often, researchers seek what is known as a **random sample** in an attempt to gain an accurate representation of the population. Random samples are explained further in Box 13.1, and at a basic level a random sample means that every person in the population being studied has an equal chance of being selected. When seeking a random sample, consideration must be given to the size of the population from which the sample is taken. For example, recruiting a sample of 25 people will not enable a researcher to make generalisations about the entire UK population. It is likely that in whatever research question you are seeking to answer you will not in fact be aiming to generalise to the entire population. However, you must always be clear about the limitations of your data. When using random sampling, it is also vital to ensure that all groups within the broader population are sufficiently represented and this may mean that your sample might need to be made larger. By population, we mean all those who form part of specific groups. For example, 'the population of the UK' would mean everyone living in the UK, and the 'English prison population' would mean everyone incarcerated in prisons in England.

Random sampling is not the only sampling technique used by researchers. Researchers may use what is known as convenience (or opportunistic) sampling where participants are chosen due to their availability and therefore the broader population is not included as potential participants. In terms of ease and accessibility, this type of sample has merit, although researchers using this method of sampling are typically unable to generalise their findings. That said, this is a method often adopted by students because it may sometimes be the only practical way of obtaining a sample. Provided you acknowledge the limitations of this method – primarily in terms of lack of generalisability – this is unlikely to be problematic for research at undergraduate level.

Certain types of research benefit from contacting participants through network (or snowballing) sampling, based on pre-existing connections. For example, if a researcher is seeking to investigate a particular subgroup in society, they may not have ready access to all those in the subgroup, and so may use initial contacts to contact others. Other researchers use purposive (sometimes known as judgemental) sampling, where the researcher chooses participants subjectively and tries to include a range of participants between extremes. Others may take a more systematic approach, although less so than true random sampling: quota sampling. Using this method, researchers choose participants in pre-set categories that are characteristics of the broader population under investigation, for example, 20 women and 20 men, 30 undergraduate students and 30 postgraduate students, and so on.

BOX 13.1 TYPES OF RANDOM SAMPLES

Simple random samples

A random number table or computer is used to generate a sample at random from the population under investigation, where every member of the population has been assigned a number.

Systematic sampling

As the name implies, this is a systematic process of choosing a sample to obtain the size needed. Systematic sampling can be more time efficient than random sampling, as you simply choose a fixed start point and constant interval to select your participants. For example, if you were investigating your fellow students (of whom we will say there are 500 across all years) and you wish to select a random group of 50 students from that population. Using a list of your students, you would select every tenth name on that list (as 500/50 = 10).

Stratified sampling

This takes data from different strata – or layers – of the population, for example, by selecting samples from different age groups or prison categories. The sample size from each layer is proportional to the size of that layer. For example, if we were seeking a sample of 10 per cent of the prison population, we might split this up and sample 10 per cent of those in category A prisons, 10 per cent in category B prisons, and so on.

Cluster (multi-stage) sampling

This is a more complex method where multi-stage sampling is used, in which clusters are randomly sampled, then a random sample of elements is taken from sampled clusters. For example, imagine you are investigating the effects of a programme aimed at reducing aggressive behaviours in pupils at schools across the West Midlands. Three schools are chosen to investigate, 33 pupils are randomly selected from each school and 11 pupils from each of the school years taking part.

As a general rule of thumb, your sample is likely to be more representative of the broader population you are investigating if: the sample is large proportionate to the population; there is little diversity in the population under investigation and your sample; if you keep in mind that the smaller the population, the bigger the sampling ratio must be for an accurate sample. For example, if you were to apply a 10 per cent sampling ratio to the UK prison population of 95,526 (when this text was written), you would have a sample of 9,553. However, if you were to apply a 10 per cent sampling ratio to the population of your undergraduate seminar class of 20, your sample would be a mere 2 and would therefore not be appropriate.

DESIGNING QUESTIONNAIRES AND SURVEYS

This section covers the practicalities of questionnaire design: it takes you through the types of questions that may be used in a questionnaire, what other sorts of information you may wish to collect, and how the order in which questions are presented can have an impact upon responses. It is vital that you pay close attention to the guidance provided here, as designing your questionnaire is an extremely important part of the research process. Once you have designed your questionnaire you have set the questions and so, to some extent, also set the answers that respondents can give. You will probably not be able to go back and collect more information from respondents, so it is vital to ensure that the questions you ask clearly address your research questions and enable you to collect the data you need. It is worth giving a reminder here of the difference between research questions and questions you ask in a survey/questionnaire. The former refers to the overarching focus of your research, while the latter refers to the detailed questions you ask in attempting to address your main research question(s).

While it is important to ensure that you use appropriate question formats (you can find information about this below), there are a few things that you should think about before designing the questions themselves. The first is to ensure that you begin with a clear and concise introduction or welcome message so that respondents know:

who you are; the purpose of the research; who they can contact for more information (you may want to provide either your university email address or the email address of your supervisor). Second, remember to KISS (Keep It Short and Simple). Imagine that you are given a questionnaire that is very long. How likely are you to fill it out? The more concise you can keep your questionnaire the better, so bear this in mind when designing the questions – this goes for the number and length of questions, but you should also pay close attention to the formatting of your questionnaire, as this can affect the impression of overall length as well. For example, Qureshi and Farrell (2006) give a useful example of a concisely formatted survey they designed for police officers, which resulted in a 100 per cent response rate (although note that the 100 per cent response rate was not due solely to the formatting of the questionnaire).

There are also a number of other things to think about:

- font – ensure that the text is clearly readable;
- language – is the language suitable for the audience? In general, avoid jargon and ensure that the language is as straightforward as possible;
- ensure that there is always a 'don't know' or 'not applicable' or 'other' option;
- ask for only one piece of information at a time;
- be precise with your questions and ensure that they are relevant to your research questions;
- ensure that there are clear instructions on how to complete the questionnaire.

Types of questions

Now you should be ready to compose your questions. There are two main categories of questions you can use: closed and open-ended. We will look at each of these individually (Table 13.2).

Table 13.2 Advantages and disadvantages of closed and open-ended questions

Closed questions		Open-ended questions	
Advantages	**Disadvantages**	**Advantages**	**Disadvantages**
Relatively quick for respondents to answer.	Options are limited, so conclusions may not truly represent the thoughts and opinions of respondents.	Respondents can more fully express their thoughts and opinions.	Coding answers for analysis is time-consuming compared with closed questions.
Easy to code for analysis.	Respondents cannot explain their choice or why this might depend on circumstances.	Results may more fully represent the thoughts and opinions of respondents.	Answers can be misclassified if misinterpreted by the researcher.
Respondents' level of skill in reporting their thoughts and opinions does not matter.	Respondents cannot explain that they do not understand a question, particularly in web/email/postal surveys.	Respondents can explain their answer.	Where respondents write answers by hand, illegible handwriting can be problematic.

Closed questions may include simple multiple-choice questions where respondents should tick the box next to the answer they choose:

How many crimes do you think were reported to the police in England and Wales in the 1990s?	3 million	☐
	5 million	☐
	7 million	☐
	8 million	☐

Or *yes/no* answer questions:

Have you consumed any alcohol in the last 24 hours?	Yes	☐
	No	☐
	Don't know	☐

When collecting information on demographic details, such as age or educational attainment, questions with a number of closed categories are often used:

Are you (please tick as appropriate):	☐	Under 18
	☐	19 to 34
	☐	35 to 44
	☐	45 to 54
	☐	55 to 64
	☐	65 or over
	☐	Prefer not to say

Note that a common error is to duplicate ages. For example, 19–35, 35–45. In this example, if you were 35, which box would you tick? This is why each option must be distinct.

Researchers also use *rating scales*:

How would you rate the decision in 2017 to replace Elizabeth Truss with David Lidington as Secretary of State for Justice?	An excellent decision	☐
	A good decision	☐
	Neither a good or bad decision	☐
	A bad decision	☐
	A terrible decision	☐
	Don't know	☐

Rating scales can also ask respondents to rate something on a scale of one to ten.

You might also see *agreement scales* used in questionnaires:

How far do you agree with the following statements?					
	Strongly agree	Agree	Don't know	Disagree	Strongly disagree
'It is important for me to learn more about why I do the things I do.'					
'It is important for me to grow and learn new things.'					

The type of scale shown above is known as a **Likert scale**. There are two widely used versions of the Likert scale: a five-point scale and a seven-point scale. While the five-point version is often used, it is worth noting that a seven-point scale is likely to be more reliable and may avoid respondents being overly neutral in their response choice (Colman, Norris and Preston, 1997). These scales allow for degrees of opinion, or even for no opinion at all, and so can be more useful than yes/no questions where appropriate.

All of the above were closed questions. Open-ended questions might include numeric open-ended questions:

How old are you? _____ years

While other questions might be open-ended text questions:

You answered 'yes' to Question 17. How has your knowledge of the 2016 Review of the Youth Justice System in England and Wales (Taylor, 2016) impacted your current working practices? Please write your answer in the space below.

It is good practice to end a questionnaire with an open question asking for anything respondents wish to say/add about the topic. It is usual to provide a couple of line spaces for this, but no more, in order to avoid large amounts of textual data. Even where this information is not useful to the research, it allows respondents to know that their opinion is being heard and thus they may feel more engaged and satisfied with the research process. Similarly, one question may be closed but have an 'other' option where an open-ended text line also appears.

It may be useful to route certain questions as you may design a questionnaire where not all questions are relevant to every respondent, depending on their answers. These are sometimes known as filter questions. For example:

Question 5. Are you employed directly by the Probation Service?		
Yes	☐	Go to question 6
No	☐	Go to question 9

You must ensure that each question asks only one thing. For example, what is wrong with the following question?

'Women make better prison officers but men make better therapy staff.'	☐	Agree
	☐	Disagree

This question asks two things and so respondents cannot be clear whether they are being asked to answer a question about women as prison officers or men as therapy staff. It is surprising how often questions like this are included in questionnaires.

You must also ensure that you avoid leading questions. A leading question is a question that subtly – or not so subtly – prompts respondents to respond in a particular way. For example, let us imagine your research involved asking members of staff working for a voluntary agency dealing with victims to complete a questionnaire about their relationship with the police:

'Do you have any problems in your meetings with police officers?'

or

'Briefly describe your meetings with police officers.'

While the differences in the questions in the above example are relatively minor, the first is a leading question and in a fairly subtle way raises the possibility that there are problems. The result of asking questions in a leading way may be that the answers you gain are unreliable. We have seen our own students write leading questions in their questionnaires and surveys as, without due consideration, it is an easy trap to fall into but one that must be avoided.

When asking for any information you must think very carefully about whether you need it and why you need it. Even though assurances should have been made in writing about confidentiality, respondents may feel concerned about why you wish to know certain things about them, so really make sure that you need the data you ask for. For example, do you need to know the educational level or ethnic background of your respondents? When you have decided which information you need, you must also think carefully about what categories you might include. Above, we gave an example of age categories, but you may find for your research that it is more useful to ask for each respondent's exact age. Rather than design your own categories for collecting information on things like ethnic group, education and employment, we advise using existing categories such as those used in the England and Wales census (see www.ons.gov.uk/census).

For example, in the 2011 census the following categories of relationship status were included:

What is your legal marital or same-sex civil partnership status?
☐ Never married and never registered a same-sex civil partnership
☐ Married
☐ Separated, but still legally married
☐ Divorced
☐ Widowed
☐ In a registered same-sex civil partnership
☐ Separated, but still legally in a same-sex civil partnership
☐ Formerly in a same-sex civil partnership which is now legally dissolved
☐ Surviving partner from a same-sex civil partnership

You should also consider carefully how the questions you ask and the words you use in your questions might affect the responses you receive. For example, if you ask questions about 'fear of crime', might you find that some individuals are reluctant to tick a box that means admitting they are afraid? Similarly, the way we ask about sensitive issues, such as Intimate Partner Violence (IPV – the formal term sometimes used for domestic violence), can significantly affect responses. Caulfield and Wilkinson (2014: 177–178) explain how changes in screening questions used in crime surveys have affected responses:

> Researchers have sought to investigate IPV in a number of ways. Official crime statistics have been reviewed over the past 30 years to look at changes in reported incidences of IPV. Notably, the British Crime Survey (renamed the Crime Survey for England and Wales in 2012) in both 1982 and 1985 found that all victims of IPV (or Domestic Violence as it was referred to) were women. Similarly, official statistics collected in Canada at around the same time (1981) found that between 80 and 90% of victims were women. In contrast, in later years official statistics in both Britain and Canada reported equal numbers of men and women were victims of IPV.
>
> Why might this be the case? Was there a particular occurrence in Western society during the 1980s and 1990s that prompted women to become the perpetrators of IPV?

Actually, the explanation is a much more straightforward one. All of the 1981, 1982, and 1985 official surveys discussed above included screening questions that made it very clear that respondents were being asked about 'domestic violence'. Men often do not believe that this term applies to them, even when they have experienced physical, psychological, or other forms of abuse. When no screening question was used, the 1996 British Crime Survey found that 4.2% of men and 4.2% of women reported being a victim of IPV.

Arranging the questions

The order in which the questions are presented is also important. Some general tips are that you should:

- begin with general questions before asking more focused and/or difficult questions. This allows respondents to think about the topic;
- avoid beginning with sensitive, or potentially sensitive, questions;
- begin with closed questions, for much the same reason as above;
- where possible, leave asking demographic and personal questions until the end of the questionnaire. Beginning with these questions may make some respondents less likely to complete your questionnaire. Exceptions to this rule are any demographic questions that qualify someone to be included in the survey. For example, many researchers limit some surveys to people in certain age groups and therefore these questions must come near the beginning;
- group similar questions together.

BOX 13.2   SPOT THE DELIBERATE MISTAKES

The questionnaire below includes several mistakes. Can you spot them all? Check your answers with the support material.

Have you ever engaged in criminal activity?   Yes ☐
                                              No   ☐

What is your ethnic group? _____

How old are you?   Under 18 ☐
                   18–30   ☐
                   30–45   ☐
                   Over 45   ☐

Website
Instructor
exercise

Spot the
mistakes

> Have you ever worked in the criminal justice system?   Yes ☐
>   No   ☐
>
> What was your job title? _____
>
> 'P.O.V. crime has increased in urban areas.'
>
> Strongly agree ☐   Agree ☐   Disagree ☐   Strongly disagree ☐
>
> Do you agree that violent crime has become more of a problem in
> Birmingham recently?   Yes ☐
>   No   ☐
>
> What do you think about Birmingham? _____
>
> Do you currently have double glazing in your main residence?_____
>
> **PLEASE RETURN THIS QUESTIONNAIRE TO YOUR LECTURER.**

USING VALIDATED MEASURES

Researchers often used validated measures of attitudes, thoughts, and behaviours. By validated, we mean measures (perhaps also called surveys or questionnaires) that have undergone rigorous testing by experts to ensure they are **valid** and **reliable**. Experts test measures using very large sample sizes and undertake extensive statistical analysis before making conclusions about how valid and reliable the measure is. In short, experts test the measures to make sure they are really measuring what we think they are and how well they do this. This is good news for us as researchers and students as it means that once we know what we want to investigate in our research, we can consider using existing validated measures.

Researchers often use existing validated measures where they want to understand if there is any change over time in the attitudes, thoughts, and/or behaviours of a group of people or if there is a relationship between two **variables**. For example, it might be that we want to understand whether the well-being of former prisoners improves after taking part in a digital skills project (see Case Study Part 2). Or it might be that we want to understand whether there is a relationship between consuming alcohol and aggression – see former student Nikki's work in Newberry et al. (2013). Nikki used a validated measure of alcohol consumption in students (the Student Alcohol Questionnaire (SAQ); Engs, 2002) and a validated measure of self-reported aggressive incidents (Aggression Questionnaire, Buss and Perry, 1992).

When we have found a measure that we think will allow us to test our research **hypothesis**, it is important to read the published literature concerning the reliability and validity of that measure.

CASE STUDY PART 2: TECH4PRISONLEAVERS

As discussed in part 1 of this case study, earlier in this chapter, the research with Tech4PrisonLeavers used validated measures to explore any impact of the project on participants' well-being, perceived competence with finding future employment and aspirations. Let's focus in on how well-being was measured within the research as an example of a validated measure.

The researchers knew that they wanted to measure whether participants' well-being improved over the project. They identified a number of validated measures of well-being and read several studies comparing the reliability and validity of these. They also considered how practical and appropriate it would be to use the different measures.

The research team decided to use the Warwick Edinburgh Mental Wellbeing Scale: short version (SWEMWBS; Tennant et al., 2007), which is designed to monitor well-being in the general population. SWEMWBS is a shorter version of the 14-item WEMWBS, which is widely used especially in research studies in the UK. The seven items relate to functioning rather than to feeling, such as measurement of elements of positive affect, satisfying interpersonal relationships and positive functioning. The SWEMWBS is scored by first summing the scores for each of the seven items, which are scored from 1 to 5. The total raw scores are then transformed into metric scores using a SWEMWBS conversion table. When comparing the short scale (SWEMWBS) to the original (WEMWBS), validity and reliability are found to be consistent in both and some practitioners may favour SWEMWBS for its greater practicality compared with the longer original scale (Koushede et al., 2019). The combination of it being a reliable and valid measure, with the shorter length being more suitable for use with the participant group, was a strong reason to choose this measure. It is important to note that these types of validated measures are not clinical tools. They are suitable for use when looking at whole group changes, but not when diagnosing individual mental health issues.

Participants completed the SWEMWBS at the start of the project and again at the end of the project. The researchers could therefore measure whether on average, well-being had changed over time (see Chapter 16 of this book to read about how to analyse this type of data in this way). Spoiler alert: participants' well-being had, on average, improved. The researchers distributed the survey for this project using an online survey platform. See the next section in this chapter for more information on using online surveys.

The Digital Poverty Alliance have published a white paper based on our research, calling for the UK Ministry of Justice to look at a wider programme of support for prison leavers with access to devices, connectivity and digital skills training. You can read the white paper here, including the findings of our research: https://digitalpovertyalliance.org/projects/tech4prisonleavers/

ONLINE SURVEYS

Once you have designed your survey or questionnaire, or chosen the validated measure you intend to use, it is likely you will distribute your survey using an online platform, such as SurveyMonkey or Jisc Online Surveys (for which your university may have a subscription – ask your tutors about accessing those). These systems can be useful and they are very cost effective. The links to the survey can be emailed to people along with information about the study. They can also be a very quick way of collecting data from large numbers of people, and people may be more likely to be open and honest about sensitive topics than when answering questions in person.

In our quantitative research methods module for Criminology and Sociology students at the University of Wolverhampton, their first assignment involves designing a short survey and placing that Jisc Online Surveys. It is quite straightforward to use, but here are some key steps to get you started:

Step 1:

1. Enter Jisc Online Surveys Dashboard.

Figure 13.1

2. Click on 'Create Survey'.
3. Name your survey.

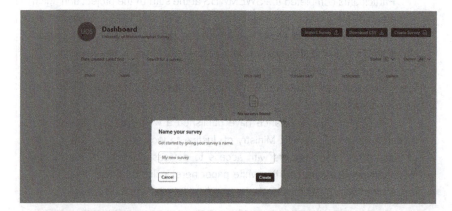

Figure 13.2

QUESTIONNAIRES AND SURVEYS 239

4 If working in a group, set up any members of your research team who can manage survey questions by entering their email addresses through 'Permissions' (left side of the screen).

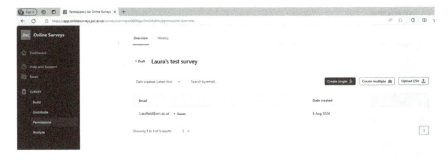

Figure 13.3

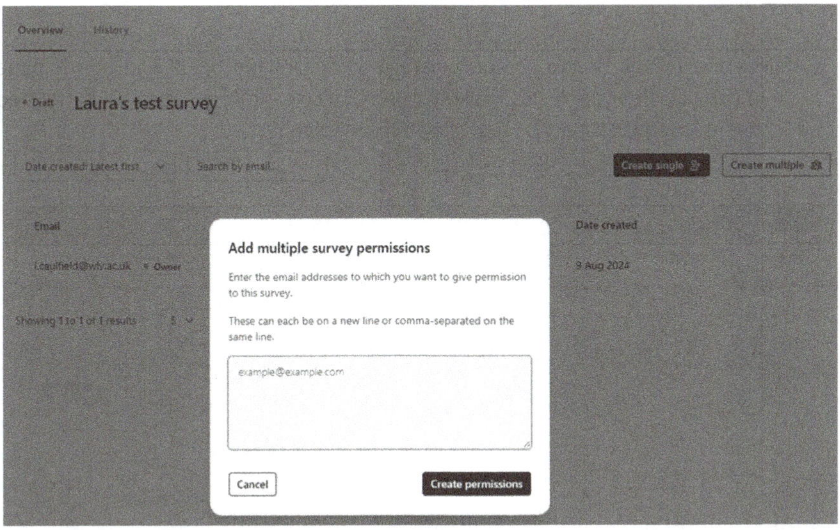

Figure 13.4

Step 2:

5   Back in Dash click on 'Build' (left side of the screen).

Figure 13.5

6   Click the middle of the screen where it says 'Untitled page' and add a page title (for your first page this is likely to be 'Participant information and informed consent – see Chapter 7). Then click 'Finish editing'.

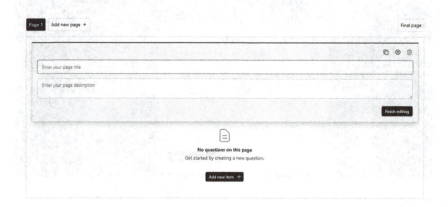

Figure 13.6

7   Click on 'Add new item' and select 'Note'. Insert your introduction/participant information text (see Chapter 7) and click 'Finish editing'.

QUESTIONNAIRES AND SURVEYS 241

Figure 13.7

8 Next, click on 'Add new item' again, but this time select 'Choice'. Enter your consent questions (see Chapter 7), including answer options.

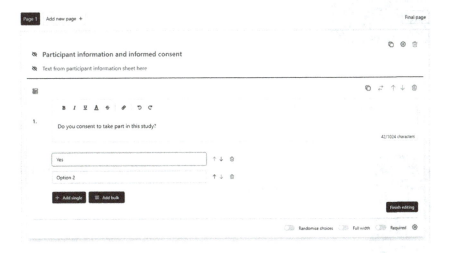

Figure 13.8

9 You might wish to set the answer to only one option (e.g. 'Yes' if people consent to take part in the survey). To do this add 'Yes' to the first box, then delete the second box (by clicking the red dustbin symbol).
10 Ensure you select 'Required' so that people cannot proceed without answering this question. Then click 'Finish editing'.

Step 3:

11 You will now be back on the main survey page. Click on 'Add new page' to begin adding your survey questions.

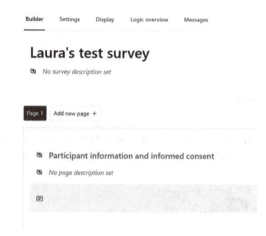

Figure 13.9

12 Click on 'Add new item'.

Figure 13.10

13 Select the question-and-answer format that allows you to best display your survey question. (Note that you can select a different format for each survey question. You will probably want to spend some time playing around with the different options. In the image below, 'Choice' was selected as there is one question with two answer choices.)

QUESTIONNAIRES AND SURVEYS   243

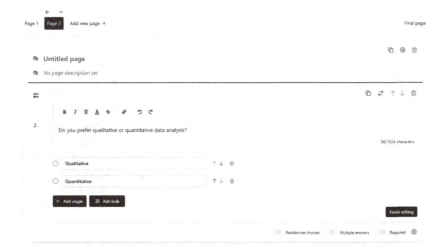

Figure 13.11

14 Remember to select 'Required' if participants must answer that question. You can also select 'Multiple answers' if you want participants to be able to select more than one answer. Then click 'Finish editing'.
15 Repeat steps 13 to 14 for your subsequent questions.

Step 4:

16 Click on 'Add page', then 'Note' and insert a Thank You note, plus any debrief information (see Chapter 7).

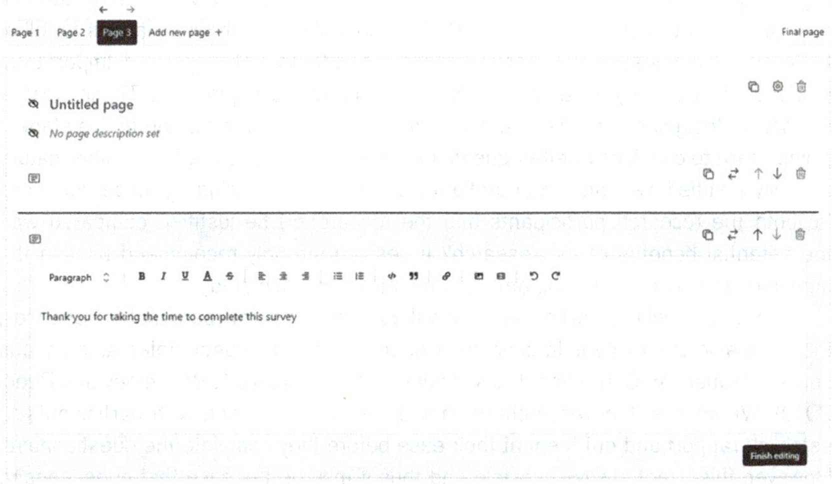

Figure 13.12

We often use online surveys for our own research too. For example, in the case study above.

When using online methods you should consider how you will manage the sample and respondents to ensure that your target group only and not other people complete the questionnaire (see the discussion about researcher control over online participation in Chapter 15). There is a potential tension here between the needs a researcher might have in wanting to, for example, check that someone does not complete an online questionnaire twice, and the need to protect anonymity. For this reason, sites like SurveyMonkey do not use Cookies or external tracking software to collect information on respondents, nor do they routinely provide details of respondents' IP addresses. You can, however, set up restricted access to an online questionnaire, using a password, to try to ensure that only your target respondents complete the survey (and not anyone who happens to find the link to the survey). You can also set up automatic email reminders to encourage participation.

SENSITIVITY IN USING QUESTIONNAIRES AND SURVEYS

Criminological research often addresses sensitive topics. This may, for example, include topics such as people's experiences of victimisation, investigations of deviant behaviour or research with vulnerable groups. Some of the questions asked as part of the research may potentially cause distress. While these issues will have been given thorough consideration prior to applying for ethical approval for the research (see Chapter 7) and the decision may have been made to use another data-collection method, is it possible to investigate sensitive topics appropriately by using questionnaires? The Crime Survey for England and Wales includes questions on sensitive and difficult topics such as sexual assault and domestic violence. We suggest you look at some of the questions asked in the survey by visiting the link given earlier in this chapter (see p. 224). You will note that the explanations for all of these sensitive questions are carefully written and thoroughly explained. Importantly, respondents are always given the option not to answer these questions. These are vital lessons in designing sensitive questionnaires. However, before getting to this stage it is important to consider whether questions on sensitive topics or of a sensitive nature are fully justified, i.e. can the potential emotional cost of including these questions (to both the research participants and the researcher) be justified compared with the potential benefits of the research? If yes, we strongly recommend piloting the questionnaire on a small scale before conducting the main study.

In research where participants are asked to report highly personal experiences, there are also other issues to consider. Under-reporting has been noted as a serious concern (American Correctional Association, 1990; Williams, 1994; Leigey and Reed, 2010). Where possible, researchers should spend time talking with participants to establish rapport and put them at their ease before they complete the questionnaire. However, this is not always possible and thus it may be the case that questionnaire data-collection methods are not the right method for very sensitive topics. You should always discuss this with your supervisor. Even where rapport building is possible, 'shame, stigma, and social desirability' (Jansson, Hesse and Fridell, 2008: 6) may play a part in under-reporting certain events.

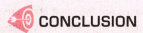

CONCLUSION

Questionnaires and surveys form an important part of the data that exists about crime, victims and the criminal justice system. Large-scale crime surveys are well established and, while subject to some criticism, can provide a useful source of data. In designing your own questionnaires and surveys, you must ensure that what you produce clearly addresses your research questions and that what you ask is appropriate. Understanding what questionnaires and surveys can and cannot do – their strengths and limitations – is vital in deciding how far they are appropriate to your own research, and we advise thorough consideration of this before beginning. One of the most important parts of using questionnaires and surveys is having a clear understanding of methods of sampling and how to ensure your sample is appropriate to your research. Finally, we cannot emphasise enough the importance of sensitivity in using these methods in criminological research – from the questions you ask to the people you approach. You may be dealing with potentially vulnerable people or asking questions about sensitive and/or upsetting issues and you must take care to protect the people in your research from any insensitivity and consequent upset or concern.

 KEY LEARNING POINTS

- Questionnaires can be a useful tool in criminological research provided that they are well designed with questions that directly address the overarching research questions/**hypothesis** of the investigation.
- All methods of data collection have advantages and disadvantages, and it is important to consider these thoroughly to ensure that you can justify the approach you take in your own research.
- One of the most important parts of questionnaire-based research is appropriate sample selection. Even if the questionnaire is very well designed, choosing an inappropriate and/or unrepresentative sample may make your research little more than worthless.
- Good questionnaire design follows a number of rules and guidelines for the composition of questions and questionnaire structure.

- Useful online survey platforms exist that are user friendly while also protecting participant data. Your university is likely to have a subscription to one or more of these.
- It is possible to address sensitive topics using questionnaires, but significant thought should be given to whether questionnaires are the most appropriate way of investigating sensitive topics or for collecting data from vulnerable groups.

NOTE

1 *Essential Digital Skills Framework* (2018). Available at https://assets.publishing.service.gov.uk/government/uploads/system/uploads/attachment_data/file/738922/Essential_digital_skills_framework.pdf

REFERENCES

American Correctional Association (1990) *The Female Offender: What Does the Future Hold?* Washington, DC: American Correctional Association.

Barreiro-Gen, M. and Novo-Corti, I. (2015) 'Collaborative Learning in Environments with Restricted Access to the Internet: Policies to Bridge the Digital Divide and Exclusion in Prisons through the Development of the Skills of Inmates', *Computers in Human Behaviour*, 51: 1172–1176.

Buss, A.H. and Perry, M. (1992) 'The Aggression Questionnaire', *Journal of Personality and Social Psychology*, 63(3): 452–459. https://doi.org/10.1037//0022-3514.63.3.452

Caulfield, L.S. and Wilkinson, D.J. (2014) *Forensic Psychology*, Harlow: Pearson.

Caulfield, L.S., Hadjisergis, K., Stonard, K. and Sadlier, S. (2023) *Evaluation of Tech4PrisonLeavers*. Grant report for the Digital Poverty Alliance.

Colman, A.M., Norris, C.E. and Preston, C.C. (1997) 'Comparing Rating Scales of Different Lengths: Equivalence of Scores from 5-point and 7-point Scales', *Psychological Reports*, 80(2): 355–362.

Digital Poverty Alliance (2023) Tech4PrisonLeavers: Project Overview. Available at https://digitalpovertyalliance.org/projects/tech4prisonleavers/

Engs, R.C. (2002) *The Student Alcohol Questionnaire (SAQ)*. Available at https://alcohol.iu.edu/questionnaires/saq/index.html

Grierson, M., Bolton, M., Varghese, D. and Olivier, P. (2022) 'Design Considerations for a Digital Service to Support Prison Leavers', *Designing Interactive Systems Conference* (pp. 1–13). New York.

Jansson, I., Hesse, M. and Fridell, M. (2008) 'Validity of Self-reported Criminal Justice System Involvement in Substance Abusing Women at Five-Year Follow-Up', *BMJ Psychiatry*, 8(2): 1–8.

Koushede, V., Lasgaard, M., Hinrichsen, C., Meilstrup, C., Nielsen, L., Rayce, S.B., Torres-Sahli, M., Gudmundsdottir, D.G., Stewart-Brown, S. and Santini, Z.I. (2019) 'Measuring Mental Well-being in Denmark: Validation of the Original and Short Version of the Warwick-Edinburgh Mental Well-being Scale (WEMWBS and SWEMWBS) and Cross-cultural Comparison Across Four European Settings', *Psychiatry Research*, 271: 502–509.

Leigey, M.E. and Reed, K.L. (2010) 'A Woman's Life Before Serving Life: Examining the Negative Pre-incarceration Life Events of Female Life-sentenced Inmates', *Women & Criminal Justice*, 20(4): 302–322.

Newberry, M., Williams, N. and Caulfield, L.S. (2013) 'Aggression in Females: Does Alcohol Consumption Make a Difference?', *Aggressive Behaviors*, 38(3): 1844–1851.

Qureshi, F. and Farrell, G. (2006) 'Stop and Search in 2004: A Survey of Police Officers' Views and Experiences', *International Journal of Police Science and Management*, 8(2): 83–103.

Taylor, C. (2016) *Review of Youth Justice Systems in England and Wales*, London: Ministry of Justice.

Tennant, R., Hiller, L., Fishwick, R., Platt, S., Joseph, S., Weich, S. and Stewart-Brown, S. (2007) 'The Warwick-Edinburgh Mental Well-being Scale (WEMWBS): Development and UK Validation', *Health and Quality of Life Outcomes*, 5: 63. https://doi.org/10.1186/1477-7525-5-63.

Williams, L.M. (1994) 'Memories of Child Sexual Abuse: A Response to Lindsay and Read', *Applied Cognitive Psychology*, 8: 379–387.

All screenshots reproduced from Jisc's Online Survey's tool (https://www.onlinesurveys.ac.uk) with permission. Copyright © 2024 Jisc.

Chapter 14

Using documentary and secondary data sources

GOALS OF THIS CHAPTER

At the end of reading this chapter and by completing the online resources that accompany it, you will be able to:

1 demonstrate a critical understanding of the benefits and limitations of using existing data in research;
2 appreciate the range of sources that exist and how these might be used in criminological research;
3 understand the difference between existing sources of data and existing datasets that have already been analysed;
4 begin to ask appropriate questions of existing data sources.

OVERVIEW

- The world around us is awash with data. If we know where to look, what we are looking for, and what questions to ask of existing data, we can use this to produce both robust and insightful research.
- Research that makes use of existing data by no means needs to be inferior to empirical research. There is little use in spending time and resources collecting new data when data may already exist that can address your research questions, perhaps in a more useful way than any data you could collect yourself.
- Existing data are all around us as sources that are yet to be analysed.
- Existing datasets that have been collected and already analysed are available to us as criminological researchers to conduct secondary analysis.
- There are a number of points of caution that researchers must be aware of when using secondary sources. Asking critical questions of the data is vital in understanding the context of and limitations to the data.

WHY USE EXISTING DATA SOURCES?

It is common, particularly at undergraduate level, for students to undertake non-empirical research using **secondary data** sources. This does not mean that this is

DOI: 10.4324/9781032645698-18

inferior to empirical research: there are many existing secondary data sources that, through analysis and reanalysis, can provide important insight into criminological phenomena. Indeed, even where the research may include an empirical element, many researchers make use of secondary data sources as a part of their research. As gathering empirical data is such an ingrained part of the research process, we sometimes fail to explore whether the data we need may already exist. In some cases it makes little sense to collect our own data, particularly where the data that already exist may have been collected by researchers and organisations that have far greater resources than we have. While there is a disadvantage in that we have had no control over the way the data were collected, if you use existing data in the 'right' way and ask the 'right' questions about the data (see Chapter 18), you can reveal a great deal.

There is a distinction here between secondary data that has been collected by researchers and analysed, and documents that exist not necessarily for research purposes but which may be useful sources for researchers. We consider secondary data and **documentary data** separately below. We also provide two case studies from our own dissertation students: one who worked with documentary data, and one who worked with secondary data.

This chapter discusses the types of data that criminological researchers may benefit from accessing, exploring the strengths and limitations of particular data sources. Part V of this book looks at data analysis: Chapter 18 focuses on analysing documents and text-based data, but the data analysis techniques discussed in Chapters 16 and 17 can also be applied to secondary data sources. You will also find some information on analysing secondary data later in this chapter.

DOCUMENTARY DATA SOURCES

Documentation about our lives and the world around us is everywhere. From news stories, television programmes, books and social media, information about the social world is there for us to absorb, review and analyse. Events are reported, photographed, tweeted and blogged, emails are written and life is recorded. As social scientists, we see all of this as potential sources of data. As criminological researchers we are acutely aware of what all of these existing sources of data can tell us about attitudes towards crime, sentencing and punishment, the experiences of victims and criminals, and so much more. The world is rich with data and, in the technological world in which we live, much of this is readily available. See Chapter 15 for a fuller discussion of the benefits, challenges and considerations relevant to working with online data sources. It is clear to see that collecting new data is not always the best course of action when what we are looking for may already be out there.

When writing the previous paragraph we felt the sense of excitement we often experience when thinking about opportunities for research. However, we must signal a note of caution. It is all too easy to run away with an idea, but we must think carefully about the sources we use in our research, their credibility, reliability, representativeness and ethics. Can they be trusted? We must also think carefully about where to look for data and what we may be able to do with it. Once we know where the data can be located we need to consider whether special access is needed. Make these checks early and ensure you have a contingency plan in case you cannot use the data you wanted.

Remember: you should begin with your research question and then seek out data that may help you address that question. Don't choose sources at random – you should employ the same level of thorough and critical thinking as you would when devising an interview schedule or questionnaire.

What types of data sources exist?

O'Leary (2021) provides a comprehensive list of potential documentary data sources (see Table 14.1). You might wish to cross-reference this with the list of online data sources in Chapter 15.

For criminological researchers, there are some existing sources of data that may be particularly interesting in addressing our research questions. *Life histories and autobiographical accounts* of ex-prisoners and prison staff can provide a wealth of information. For example, Lynn (2021) investigates autobiographical public accounts of people who are and were incarcerated at different points in US history. While there has historically been hostility towards both prisoner and prison officer accounts of prison, they provide a rich source of data (Morgan, 1999) and in recent years there has been an emergence of fascinating uses of technology to share the stories of people who are, or have been, in prisons (Cecil, 2023).

More recently, there has been a proliferation of online blogs, websites and Twitter accounts, written by former prisoners and criminal justice staff. The stories and experiences shared through these mediums – while often less verifiable than other sources – provide some insight into the workings of the criminal justice system, and an interesting addition to autobiographies.

> **PAUSE TO THINK ...**
>
> How far are diaries, online sources and autobiographies likely to present a full view of prisons? Does this matter, or is the reality experienced and presented by that individual more important than seeking all perspectives?

With all types of documentary data, there is work for the researcher to do in seeking out relevant and appropriate sources.

There are some criminological researchers who make excellent use of newspapers and other mass media to interpret and understand criminological issues. Using methods of analysis such as qualitative content analysis (discussed in Chapter 18), researchers are able to examine how particular criminological phenomena are presented in the media. Mawby and Gisby (2009), for example, examined how newspapers covered crime risks associated with gaining European Union membership

Table 14.1 Broad-ranging texts (O'Leary, 2021)

Type of text	Examples
Official data and records	While you may have to work at getting access, it may be worth exploring: • International data held by organisations such as the United Nations, the World Bank or the World Health Organization. • National data held by many federal or national governments and government departments, e.g. national census data. • Local government data such as state of environment reports, community surveys, water-quality data, land registry information, etc. • Non-governmental organisation data collected through commissioned or self-conducted research studies. • University data, which is abundant and covers just about every research problem ever studied. • Archival data such as records of births, deaths, marriages, etc. • Legislation including local ordinances, state and federal regulations/laws.
Policy documents	From both the public and private sectors.
Organisational communication, documents and records	Official communication that includes, but is not limited to: websites; press releases; catalogues, pamphlets and brochures; meeting agendas and minutes; inter- and intra-office memos; safety records; sales figures; human resource records; client records (these might be students, patients, constituents, parishioners, etc., depending on organisation type).
Personal communication, documents and records	Personal and often private communications that include, but are not limited to: emails; letters; journals, diaries and memoirs; texts; sketches and drawings; poetry and stories; photographs and videos; medical records; educational records; household records, e.g. cheque-book stubs, bills, insurance documents, etc.
The media/ contemporary entertainment	Data here is often examined in relation to questions of content or portrayal; for example, the content of personal ads, how often male characters are shown crying, or how often sexual assault has made the national news over the past two years. Data can come from: newspaper or magazine columns/articles/advertisements; news programmes and current affairs shows; TV dramas, sitcoms and reality shows; commercials; music videos; biographies and autobiographies.
The arts	The arts have captured and recorded the human spirit and condition over the ages in every corner of the globe, making them perfect for comparing across both culture and time. Societal attitudes are well captured in: paintings, drawings and sketches; photography; music; plays and films.
Social artefacts	These include any product of social beings. Examples of social products or social traces are extremely broad-ranging and can include things like: garbage; graffiti; children's games; rites and rituals; jokes; T-shirt slogans; tools; crafts; videos (YouTube has created a huge and accessible database here).

in two Eastern European countries. What is important to note with their work is that they did not fall into the trap of only seeking out articles available online, but used a specific newspaper article search tool available in most university libraries. If you have not come across NewsBank, or other similar databases, ask your librarian to give you an overview of the best way to use this database.

CASE STUDY: AISHA'S DISSERTATION RESEARCH ON NEWSPAPER DEPICTIONS OF MURDER SUSPECTS

Aisha was interested in researching murder for her final-year dissertation research. As accessing the criminal justice system for student work is typically problematic (see Chapters 5 and 11), Aisha's supervisor (Laura) suggested she look at publicly available data sources. Aisha also had an interest in gender and crime and concepts of 'double-deviance' (Berrington and Honkatukia, 2002: 50).

Aisha decided to explore differences between the portrayal of female and male suspected murderers in newspaper media.

Method: Aisha used qualitative content analysis (see Chapter 18) to explore 16 (8 female and 8 male) newspaper articles that appeared over a three-month period. Aisha obtained these data from a systematic search of NewsBank.

Results: Using qualitative content analysis, Aisha identified seven main themes: suspect or victim focus; external appearance; mental health; 'evilness'; emotional state of suspect; family; and the past of the suspect.

Conclusion: Aisha was able to conclude that there were differences in the portrayal of male and female suspected murderers. In her dissertation, Aisha discussed the possible impact of these findings upon public and professional perceptions of female and male murder suspects.

Reproduced from O'Leary 2021 with permission.

Galvin, Quinn and Cleary's (2023) study of the print media coverage of three high-profile cases of familicide-suicide in Ireland is an interesting example of the analysis of existing documents – in this case news media – with a particular criminological phenomenon.

Caulfield and Twort (2012) provide an example of how official documents can be reviewed as the first stage of research in order to inform later empirical stages of research. In their paper they review a series of government reports relevant to mental healthcare in prisons, and use this as a basis for developing a questionnaire for prison staff. Of course, official reports do not need to be used only as a basis for empirical work. For example, documents from the Ministry of Justice and other government departments can form a basis for numerous criminological and social research studies. Official documents are of great interest and great potential significance to criminological researchers. If we view the state as holding power within society, the information it produces is clearly of significance. This may range from Acts of Parliament, transcripts of political debates, policy documents, transcripts of expert testimonies, state-funded research reports, state-produced research reports and more. We discuss the use of official state-produced data later in this chapter.

The types of data used by social researchers tend to be categorised as personal, official or media documents. All of these may include text-based documents as well as visual and virtual data. There is also a distinction between documents that are in the public domain and those that are private. Criminological researchers may be able – with consent – to access some of these private documents, including court files, police records, probation and prison reports (for example, see the discussion of Offender Assessment System records outlined in Chapter 11, Box 11.1). Indeed, one of the authors of this book made use of the Offender Assessment System records of 43 women in prison and analysed these records alongside in-depth qualitative interview data from each of these women (Caulfield, 2016). Note that she was given informed consent from both HM Prison Service and each individual woman involved in the research. Students working in criminal justice agencies may be able to access useful data, but if you are in this position you must consider whether this is appropriate, necessary and ethical (see Chapters 11 and 7). For example, you must fully consider how to use and present these data to ensure the anonymity of individuals. The work by Caulfield (2016) is an example of how quantitative data taken from official records can be successfully used in combination with qualitative methods, in this case in-depth semi-structured interviews (see Chapter 12 for a discussion of mixed-methods approaches).

Advantages and disadvantages of using existing data sources

Accessing the data sources you need in order to address your research questions can be time consuming, but ultimately well worth the effort. Existing data:

- already exist, so you don't need to recollect them;
- may represent the 'real' world rather than a convenience research sample;
- can provide a depth and breadth of data;
- can reduce costs – both financial and time;
- avoid many of the pitfalls of collecting new data outlined in Chapters 11, 12 and 13 of this book.

While using existing sources of data can provide rich, detailed insights into the phenomena we are researching, there are some downsides. By being aware of these you may be able to minimise some of them. Existing data:

- were not generated specifically for the purposes of your research and so may be harder to work with;
- may be value-laden in ways that are, or are not, immediately obvious.

The student activity in Chapter 18, 'Recognising the Role of Underlying Values and Potential Bias', addresses this issue, and that of your own potential biases. Much of the credibility of your research with existing data sources comes from the ability to recognise your own subjectivities and to analyse the data in an appropriately robust way. Whichever data sources you choose to use in your research, we advise you to be mindful not to take them at face value. There is a stream of thought which suggests that all documents present something about the reality of organisations/groups of people/individuals. However, most documents are written for a particular audience and in the knowledge that they may be public. Consequently, all documents and data sources have a specific ontological status and the 'reality' presented therein may therefore not be wholly transparent.

When identifying and working with existing sources of data, we suggest you ask yourself the following questions and ensure you could write about the answers to these in the methods section of any research report or dissertation you may write:

- Are the sources you have used relevant and appropriate to your research questions?
- What methods did you use to ensure a broad and encompassing search strategy (i.e. that you didn't miss any key relevant data sources)?
- What selection methods have you employed in deciding which sources to use? Did you put particular parameters or selection criteria in place?
- Have you taken account of the standpoint and values of the author? Have the authors been selective in what they present?

All of the student researchers and professional researchers we discuss in this chapter made use of data sources that are available in the real world and therefore potentially accessible. When done well, this type of research can offer important insights into, and deeper understanding of, the lives of individuals and functioning of organisations.

SECONDARY DATA SOURCES

There is a wealth of data out there that is available to us if we know where to look. From large-scale surveys, to census data, to transcripts, datasets exist that may hold the answers to our research questions. Using existing datasets can allow us to focus on the analysis of the data and removes many of the constraints associated with empirical data collection. Often, existing datasets are far larger than we could ever hope to obtain as individual or small groups of researchers. Often they have employed robust sampling techniques and may provide both a breadth and depth of data. However, we must be rigorous in assessing the assumptions underlying the data, the data-collection techniques and the sampling techniques used – we have no control over these factors, yet we must fully understand them to judge whether the data are likely to be credible, reliable and valid.

You should also be mindful of the ethicality of existing data sources. When considering the ethical issues around using secondary data sources (for example, web forums and networking sites) revisit Chapter 7 of this book and also discuss ethical concerns with your lecturers and supervisors. You should also review the case study later in this chapter ('Phoebe and the Leicester Hate Crime Project').

Secondary analysis of existing datasets is most often done by researchers who had no involvement in the collection of the original data, and typically the secondary analysis seeks to answer questions that the data may not have been originally, or at least directly, designed to answer. The datasets can be either qualitative or quantitative, and might have been collected through a mixed-methods study (see Chapter 12). As highlighted in Box 14.2, you will need to know what you are looking for, and where. To answer your research questions you may need to access and conduct a secondary analysis of either data collected by other researchers or data collected by organisations.

Advantages and disadvantages of secondary analysis

In many circumstances, secondary analysis should be considered as an alternative to collecting new data for numerous reasons. Several of the observations about existing documents are also relevant here – 'Existing data: already exist, so you don't need to recollect them; … can provide a depth and breadth of data; can reduce costs – both financial and time; avoids many of the pitfalls of collecting new data outlined in Chapters 11, 12, and 13 of this book.' The secondary analysis of existing datasets allows researchers more time to focus on the analysis of often large amounts of data. For example, you may be able to conduct research on nationally **representative samples**, something that is otherwise unlikely to be possible for student researchers.

However, despite the many advantages of this type of research, there are some issues of which you must be aware. Aside from the lack of control over the data, mentioned above and in Chapter 15, you may find that the datasets are highly complex. This may in part be due to their size and the number of variables they include. The only way to deal with this is to spend time working with the data: get used to it; find out what the dataset contains. You may find that you are not able to ask some questions of the data that you would like to have addressed, but familiarity with the dataset may mean that you can find alternative ways of answering your questions through analysing different variables.

There are some specific issues associated with accessing statistical datasets that have been produced by and for governmental and other organisations. The concepts and methods of data collection are often designed to serve the functions of the organisation and so it is crucial for researchers to engage in robust critical thinking when considering such data sources. Related to this, Box 14.2 suggests some questions you may wish to ask of the datasets you access. Being aware of the boundaries and limitations of the data you perform secondary analysis of is absolutely vital.

Think back to Chapter 5 where we examined the role official statistics play in our thinking about crime. Among other things, we asked you to answer the following questions:

- How far do you think that official crime statistics tell us the 'truth' about crime?
- Are all crimes reported?
- Do all reported crimes become official statistics?
- Are all crimes recorded in the same way?

Overall, we believe that the advantages of conducting secondary analysis of existing datasets can outweigh the disadvantages for students and professional researchers alike.

Which datasets may be readily available?

As criminological researchers, we have a wealth of data available to us for secondary analysis, as crime is of particular interest to government bodies and wider society.

Data from other researchers: If your supervisors and/or lecturers have conducted research in an area that interests you, you may wish to discuss with them the possibility of having access to their datasets. Claire's dissertation research – discussed in Chapter 16 – made use of data collected as part of a research project led by her supervisor for the Youth Offending Service (Caulfield, Simpson and Jacobs, 2016).

For the most part, however, the datasets you access will be large organisational datasets. Below are two examples that are of particular interest to criminological researchers:

The UK Data Archive: This is an excellent source of quantitative and qualitative data available for secondary analysis. It includes many large-scale and some smaller scale datasets. As a university student it is likely that any data you request from this source will be free to access, although you may be required to sign a document stating that you will adhere to the conditions of use. It is worth spending some time exploring the data archive website (www.data-archive.ac.uk) to get a sense of the data available. The website also provides links to international datasets. You may wish to speak to your librarian for advice on making the best of keyword searches. For example, simply searching the archive for the word 'crime' elicits 576 results, so you will need to be a little more specific! You can also search the archive thematically, and, for example, look at the theme called 'crime'.

The Crime Survey for England and Wales: Formerly known as the British Crime Survey, and in existence since 1982, this is the largest scale example of criminological survey research in England and Wales. The survey aims to provide information representative of the entire population of England and Wales about their experiences of crime (including crime not reported to the police). As the survey is not reliant on official statistics, it is regarded by some as a good indicator of the real extent of crime in England and Wales. Earlier in this chapter we asked you to revisit the discussion from Chapter 5 about the potential problems with official statistics. At this point we recommend that you also revisit the discussion in Chapter 12 of potential issues with self-report data. Chapter 13 provides a more detailed description of the Crime Survey for England and Wales, its purpose and the data it includes. You can access the Crime Survey for England and Wales at www.crimesurvey.co.uk/index.html

CASE STUDY: PHOEBE AND THE LEICESTER HATE CRIME PROJECT

For her final-year dissertation research, Phoebe was interested in investigating crime committed against people with mental health problems. Her supervisor (Laura) suggested she look at data sources accessible via the UK Data Archive, rather than seek to collect new data on this topic.

Phoebe identified that there is a lack of research about hate crime committed against people with mental health issues. Through spending time exploring the UK Data Archive, Phoebe found the Leicester Hate Crime Project.

The Leicester Hate Crime Project

Throughout 2013 and 2014 the Leicester Hate Crime Project investigated hate crime and targeted hostility towards 'different' or 'vulnerable' people. This large-scale project was funded by the Economic and Social Research Council (ESRC), led by Neil Chakraborti, John Garland and Stevie-Jade Hardy (2014). The project had three main objectives:

> to discover as much as possible about people's experiences of hate, prejudice and targeted hostility; to understand the physical and emotional harms suffered by victims and their families; and to identify ways of improving the quality of support offered to victims.
>
> (Chakraborti et al., 2014: 2)

It was created with the intention of making a difference to people affected by hate crime, by educating the public and organisations on the harmfulness of hate victimisation, and by influencing legislation linked to hate crimes.

The project used a mixed-methods approach, including: an online and hardcopy survey translated into eight different languages (880 online and 298 on paper); in-depth, semi-structured, face-to-face interviews; and personal and reflective researchers' field diary observations. A total of 1,106 victims of hate crime completed these surveys: 56 per cent of the participants were female, 42 per cent male, and 3 per cent transgender (figures rounded up to the nearest percentage). Participants came from a wide range of ethnic backgrounds. The participants were victims of the following types of hate crime: disability (including mental illnesses and learning disabilities), race, religion, sexual orientation and transgender status.

Method: Phoebe would not have been able to work with the entire dataset available, given the range and quantity collected by the research team. Phoebe needed to identify the data that would help her investigate her research questions. Phoebe identified interview transcripts from victims of hate crime who had been targeted due to their mental illness. Phoebe conducted a thematic analysis (see Chapter 17) of these interview transcripts.

Ethics: The Leicester Hate Crime Project had been through a rigorous ethics assessment via the University of Leicester. In order to ensure that she was working with these existing data in an ethical manner, and also to satisfy the requirements of her degree programme, Phoebe submitted an ethics application to her own university.

Accessing the data: Phoebe was able to use data from the Leicester Hate Crime Project, as it was available to the academic community on the UK Data Archive. To use data available via the UK Data Archive, Phoebe had to sign up to the website and agree to the terms and conditions about use of data. The data Phoebe used from the Leicester Hate Crime Project were categorised as 'Accessible to: Anyone – open data'. Unless the data is described as 'Special Access' (which these data were not) then data are available to use for research purposes.

Findings: Phoebe's thematic analysis identified four main themes: a lack of support/prioritisation for victims from the criminal justice system and mental health services; the nature of the hate victimisation being physical, verbal and irrational; lack of knowledge of mental illness and stigmatisation; and the impact of hate crimes upon victims.

The Leicester Hate Crime Project and more recent work by Chakraborti and colleagues is is available through The Centre for Hate Studies website: https://le.ac.uk/hate-studies/research

The Leicester Hate Crime Project data resources, via the UK Data Archive at http://reshare.ukdataservice.ac.uk/851570/

There is a range of other data sources available to both researchers and the general public. You may wish to investigate these and consider whether the available data may be useful in answering your own research questions. The support material for this book lists up-to-date web links to a variety of social data sources.

An interesting example of the quantitative analysis of secondary data is provided by Greene-Colozzi and Silva (2020). Using data from a unique firearms database in the United States, Greene-Colozzi and Silva undertook a sophisticated statistical analysis of 634 firearms used in 348 mass shootings.

Website
Student
web links

Social data sources

BOX 14.1   STUDENT ACTIVITY

Read Greene-Colozzi and Silva (2020) and refer back to Chapter 10, where we discuss choosing appropriate methods.

- What did the authors seek to find out and/or demonstrate from the data?
- Why was existing data used, rather than collecting new data?
- Was the method they chose appropriate? Why?
- What did the authors do to ensure that the analysis was robust? Could they have done more?

SECONDARY DATA ANALYSIS

Many researchers, including students at all levels, conduct research based on critical examination of existing data. You can find detailed information on data analysis techniques in Part V of this book. However, when analysing secondary data there are some specific points to consider in addition to the information provided later in this book. Box 14.2 gives you some questions to consider when analysing secondary data.

BOX 14.2   ANALYSING SECONDARY DATA

Ask yourself the following questions:

1   What are you looking for?

- Ensure that you have a clear research question. This is as important as it would be with an empirical piece of research.

2   Where might relevant data be available?

- The keywords you use (or don't use) influence what you find on databases and through internet search. Ask a librarian to help you with structuring your keyword searches.
- Speak with your research supervisor(s) and lecturers, who may be able to suggest relevant sources.

3   What are you looking for within the data you have located?

   - As with your overarching research question, ensure the questions you wish to ask of the data you have located are clear.
   - Clear questions will help you decide on the methods of analysis you use to analyse the data.
   - Clear questions will help you thoroughly understand the relevance of the data.

4   Are the data credible?

   - To some extent this question is fairly subjective. You may wish to review the guidance on document analysis in Chapter 18 to help you think about assumptions underpinning the data.
   - Consider how clear and transparent the methodology is. Is this consistent with similar types of data from other sources?
   - Are the researchers credible? Here you may want to consider things such as who funded the research.

5   How will you analyse the data?

   - The information throughout this book on appropriate analysis applies equally here. This may well involve some of the statistical techniques discussed in Chapter 16.

BOX 14.3   STUDENT ACTIVITY: 'THE PRISON CRISIS'

You may have seen discussion in the news, and elsewhere, about the current 'crisis' in prisons in England and Wales. Overcrowding, understaffing, poor regimes – and the resulting lack of control, drug problems and lack of focus on rehabilitation – have all contributed to rises in violence, protests and what may be viewed as a failing system.

Various news stories, government reports and documentaries have looked at the issues, and these sources are available in the public domain.

1   How could you use information from news stories, documentaries and government reports to investigate whether, in fact, English and Welsh prisons are 'in crisis'?
2   What questions should you ask about the sources of the data in order to understand the credibility of what you are reading/watching?

PAUSE TO THINK ...

When answering the questions in Box 14.3, refer back to our discussions of power and knowledge in Chapter 5.

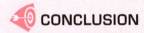 CONCLUSION

There is no doubt that existing data can be highly useful to researchers. This can be existing documents that researchers may search for and analyse, or data that have been collected by other researchers and agencies and already analysed. A researcher looking at an existing data source may be able to ask different questions and glean new information from the data. While we would always advise student researchers to fully consider both the advantages and disadvantages of using existing data sources, we contend that research using secondary data sources can be just as useful as research based on new empirical work. However, as some of the examples in this chapter highlight, combining existing data and new data can work particularly well.

Conducting a strong piece of research using existing sources requires a robust approach. By ensuring you answer some of the questions posed in this chapter we hope this will aid your critical thinking about the data. Remember that all data sources are value-laden in some way and that all research requires consideration of ethical issues. Researchers must always ensure that the source of their data is clear and acknowledged, both as an ethical point and as a way of aiding others in judging the reliability of their research.

KEY LEARNING POINTS

- When thinking about your own research interests and ideas, consider whether data already exist that may help you address these. If so, is it useful for you to expend time and energy collecting new data that may be much more limited in scope than existing data?
- While using existing sources can save you time, energy and cost, you must ensure that you employ the same level of thorough and critical thinking as you would when devising any empirical data-collection strategy.
- The data available to you are wide-ranging. It is your duty as a criminological researcher to critically consider the credibility, context, reliability and limitations of the data you access.
- While large governmental datasets can provide a wealth of data, when considering how best to use these datasets in your own research you should be

- mindful of the lessons introduced throughout this book concerning power and knowledge.
- Being aware of the limitations of existing data and asking the 'right' questions of the data can result in research that is insightful and in no way inferior to empirical research projects.

REFERENCES

Berrington, E. and Honkatukia, P. (2002) 'An Evil Monster and a Poor Thing: Female Violence in the Media', *Journal of Scandinavian Studies in Criminology and Crime Prevention*, 3(1): 50–72.

Caulfield, L.S. (2016) 'Counterintuitive Findings from a Qualitative Study of Mental Health in English Women's Prisons', *International Journal of Prisoner Health*, 12(4): 216–229.

Caulfield, L.S. and Twort, H. (2012) 'Implementing Change: Staff Experiences of Changes to Prison Mental Healthcare in England and Wales', *International Journal of Prisoner Health*, 8(1): 7–15.

Caulfield, L.S., Simpson, E. and Jacobs, C. (2016) *An Evaluation of the Youth Offending Service Youth Music Project*, Birmingham: Birmingham Youth Offending Service.

Cecil, D. K. (2024) 'Transcending Prison Walls: Prison Podcasts, the Listening Experience, and Narrative Change', *Crime, Media, Culture*, 20(2): 179–195. https://doi.org/10.1177/17416590231196128

Chakraborti, N., Garland, J. and Hardy, S.J. (2014) *Understanding Experiences of Hate Crime Victimisation and Expectations of Criminal Justice Responses*; Project Data (UK Data Archive). Available at www.data-archive.ac.uk/ (accessed 10 January 2024).

Galvin, A., Quinn, F. and Cleary, Y. (2023) 'Shaping the "Inexplicable": A Social Constructionist Analysis of News Reporting of Familicide-Suicide', *Journalism*, 24(7): 1499–1517.

Greene-Colozzi, E.A. and Silva, J.R. (2020) 'Contextualizing Firearms in Mass Shooting Incidents: A Study of Guns, Regulations, and Outcomes', *Justice Quarterly*, 39(4): 697–721. https://doi.org/10.1080/07418825.2020.1818805

Lynn, V. (2021) 'Prison Autobiographical Narratives: Making Sense of Personal and Social (Racial) Transformation', *Crime, Media, Culture*, 17(1): 65–84. https://doi.org/10.1177/1741659019880111

Mawby, R.C. and Gisby, W. (2009) 'Crime Fears in an Expanding European Union: Just Another Moral Panic?', *The Howard Journal*, 48(1): 37–51.

Morgan, S. (1999) 'Prison Lives: Critical Issues in Reading Prisoner Autobiography', *Howard Journal of Criminal Justice*, 38(5): 328–340.

O'Leary, Z. (2021) *The Essential Guide to Doing Your Research Project*, fourth edition, London: Sage.

Chapter 15

Using online and social media data sources in criminological research

GOALS OF THIS CHAPTER

At the end of reading this chapter and by completing the online resources that accompany it, you will be able to:

1. demonstrate a critical understanding of the benefits and specific challenges of undertaking internet-mediated research;
2. appreciate while that many of the underpinning approaches to face-to-face research are relevant to internet-mediated research, careful thought is needed when using approaches and methods originally designed for face-to-face use;
3. understand the various ethical complexities relevant to conducting internet-mediated research;
4. begin to consider future directions in result stemming from technological advances.

OVERVIEW

- **Internet-mediated research** is rapidly a developing and increasingly mainstream way of approaching and doing criminological research.
- When conducting internet-mediated criminological research we can think of research that is about the online world as a space/place where crime occurs, and research that is facilitated by online means (e.g. conducting online surveys).
- There are some obvious benefits to internet-mediated research, but we must think carefully about using methods designed for face-to-face use as there is always a need to make them applicable for online ways of working.
- Recruiting participants online can mean the research is more accessible to some groups whose voices might otherwise be missing in research. However, there are challenges around adapting methodologies, ethical considerations, levels of researcher control and specific additional challenges to building trust and rapport.

DOI: 10.4324/9781032645698-19

INTRODUCTION

This chapter includes discussion of the use of the internet and social media as a research tool (e.g. distributing surveys via social media platforms), and research in and on online and social media spaces. You might see various terms used for research undertaken in this way, including internet research or web-based methods (Mardones-Bravo, 2022) or internet-mediated research. Internet-mediated research is the term used by the Economic and Social Research Council (ESRC: a key funder of social, including criminological, research in the UK) and defined by the British Psychological Society (BPS, 2021: 6) as 'any research involving the remote acquisition of data from or about human participants using the internet and its associated technologies'.

There are numerous ways that online and social media sources are important tools for criminological research and this chapter covers approaches to working in this way, specific ethical issues, accessing participants, data collection and data analysis. As it has increasingly become the case that the boundaries between offline and online worlds have blurred, social research has also increasingly not only made use of online spaces, data and technologies, but also approaches and methods that include both face-to-face and online interactions (Alcadipani and Cunliffe, 2024). You will see places throughout this chapter where we refer to other parts of the book as these lessons are often applicable whether conducting research face to face or online. This chapter focuses on considerations specific to internet-mediated research, including the many positive elements of working in this way, but also the limitations and challenges. We include discussion of guidance on internet-mediated research from relevant professional bodies, to which all researchers – whether novice or experienced – should look for guidance. This chapter includes an important and fairly substantial discussion of ethics and how this might differ in online research compared with face-to-face research. As you'll discover when reading this chapter, we don't claim to have all of the answers to this rapidly developing and increasingly mainstream way of approaching and doing criminological research, but we have written this chapter to prompt thoughtful consideration and debate.

APPROACHING INTERNET-MEDIATED CRIMINOLOGOCAL RESEARCH

Thirty years ago or more we used physical libraries to undertake literature searches and access journals and books. We wrote letters to organisations and individuals in order to seek research participants. We undertook data analysis by hand, on paper. In many ways, much of the research we conduct is now facilitated by and happens in online spaces: we conduct our literature searches online; you might be reading this chapter in an e-book rather than a physical copy; and when analysing data you are quite likely to be using the qualitative and quantitative programmes discussed elsewhere in this book (see Chapters 16, 17 and 18).

When conducting internet-mediated criminological research we can think of research that is about the online world as a space/place where crime occurs, and research that is facilitated by online means (e.g. conducting online surveys).

Mardones-Bravo terms these 'Online as a Phenomenon' (2022: 87) and 'Online as a Method' (2022: 88). By online as a phenomenon she refers to research into crime that happens online, which has increased considerably in recent years, giving rise to new areas such as cybercriminology and cyberpsychology. Mardones-Bravo notes that in these areas the activity being studied happens almost entirely online and research in these areas tends to be less focused on activity that happens in both the offline and online spaces. However, there are exceptions to this. Research by Miller and Miller (2021), discussed in Chapter 7, Box 7.5, is an example of research that took place primarily online but also with face-to-face interactions, using covert participant observation to research cannabis grey markets in Las Vegas, Nevada. Activities involving some drug markets and sex work that are facilitated online but with real-world interactions have largely been the subject of research from *either* an online or offline perspective, not usually considering all aspects of these phenomena. Within this chapter we are not primarily focused on this type of research, which often looks at online crime including online financial crimes, hacking and illegal pornography. We do however provide a case study below (See Case Study box on Emma's work around social media, news and polarisation) that gives an example of the way that social media sites can be used to explore societal phenomena, and some exploration of key issues around this type of research throughout the chapter. The case study below seeks to understand how 'othering' develops in online spaces, which can lead to or exacerbate hate crime.

The rise in cybercrime and the study of this phenomenon has contributed considerably to the rise of online research methods. This leads to what Mardones-Bravo (2022: 88) calls 'Online as a Method'. This can include the move from face-to-face to online interviews and surveys, online ethnographies (see, for example, the discussion of Miller and Miller, 2021, in Chapter 7, Box 7.5) and the availability of a wide range image, text, audio and other sources of data via the online world.

Table 15.1 Online data sources (Mardones-Bravo, 2022)

Type of online data	Online data sources
Text	Twitter*, Facebook, other social media, webpages, blogs, news, documents, books, instant messaging, forum, email
Audio	Voice messages, music, audio calls, audiobooks, podcasts, audio recordings
Video	YouTube, TikTok, Vlogs, GIFs, live streams, webinars, video calls
Pictures	Instagram, online galleries, memes
Multimedia files	Archives, databases, GIS
Interactive formats	3D, maps, games, virtual reality, augmented reality, rich media ads, polls

*Rebranded as X in 2023

While large numbers of researchers now collect and analyse data online, and there are some obvious benefits to internet-mediated research, we must think carefully about using methods designed for face-to-face use as there is always a need to make them applicable for online ways of working. In terms of benefits, collecting data online rather than travelling to meet people in person can save a lot of time and money. As discussed later in this chapter, recruiting participants online can mean the research is more accessible to some groups whose voices might otherwise be missing in research. However, there are challenges around adapting methodologies, ethical considerations and specific additional challenges of building trust and rapport when, for example, conducting interviews online.

CASE STUDY: EXPLORING POLARISATION AND OTHERING ONLINE: 'HOW AN "OTHER" IS CREATED ON TIKTOK'

Emma Burgess, a PhD student at the Institute for Community Research and Development, is undertaking research on the role of news on social media in creating polarisation in society. Below we present the rationale for Emma's research, a summary of the data collection and some key ethical considerations.

The research literature that Emma has drawn on to design her study

In recent years there has been a decrease in trust in news media (Guess, Nyhan and Reifler, 2018), which could lead to individuals being more likely to question news sources. This climate has been referred to as 'post-truth', where objective facts are less influential than emotional and personal beliefs in shaping the opinion of the public on topics. Society risks becoming more split due to the increase in polarisation, the increasingly fragmented media landscape and the decline in trust for experts and other authoritative figures (Lewandowsky, Ecker and Cook, 2017). In the future, this could lead to increased distance between groups socially, which can fuel the rise of online hate crime.

An increasing number of people are now obtaining their news from social media. Ofcom (2023) reports that 71 per cent of young people (aged between 16 and 24) receive news from social media. Parsell (2008) refers to the idea that through social networking sites, users can intentionally restrict whom they interact with online leading to polarisation and othering as no alternative discussion points are heard. This means that users may be at risk of falling down a 'rabbit hole' where, over time, users are exposed to increasingly extreme content. This is a phenomenon seen on platforms with a personalised recommendation system, for example YouTube (Le Merrer, Trédan and Yesilkanat, 2023) or an algorithm like what is becoming increasingly popular and is already in use on many sites, including TikTok (Vombatkere et al., 2024).

Emma's research design

Emma undertook her research on TikTok, which is popular with a younger audience of adolescents and young adults. She identified popular and fast-growing news accounts that share news on TikTok. Collecting and analysing data from these news accounts on TikTok will allow an understanding of what content young people are viewing both in terms of video content and how others react to these news stories in the comments. Differences in worldviews can also be studied; for example, how people react to news stories that either agree or disagree with their worldview and how this may contribute to polarisation or the consumption of misleading content. The way that social media contributes to polarisation and othering can also be studied in a way that is naturalistic as snapshots of these comments and videos are taken. The novel study of indications of polarisation in comments paired with how the media may contribute to this polarising effect means that the current study can add to the understanding of polarisation online and what can be done to reduce the effect. The current study aims to explore how an out-group (or an 'other') is created in comments of mainstream news accounts on TikTok, with the following research questions explored: How do people 'other' people in the comment section? What impact is this having on the formation of polarisation?

Data collection

- Emma took a snapshot of data from TikTok, capturing publicly visible videos posted by eight news accounts across the political spectrum, their links, and recorded comments and interactions with the posts.
- By using news content from dedicated news accounts, the information in the videos is factual; the different political leaning of the accounts however may present differences in how stories are reported, for example, what the focus of the video is on. This will allow for the construction of an understanding of how the media play a role in polarisation.
- Emma then took a systematic sampling approach to selecting videos to review, resulting in 194 videos.
- Emma then collected comments from the videos using a systematic sampling method, resulting in 3,993 comments for analysis.

Key ethical considerations

Following the guidelines set by the British Psychological Society (BPS, 2021) when conducting internet-mediated research, it was deemed unnecessary to obtain informed consent from the users who wrote the comments. This is due to the comments being freely available and viewable without the need to make an account with TikTok and therefore existing in the public domain.

> To guarantee the confidentiality of the users, analysis included only the content of the comment with no mention of the user's display name/username. Any information that could be used to identify the user (if present in the comment) was removed from the comments in this report. Examples of comments presented in the findings were rewritten so that no traceable data such as IP addresses can be used to identify users.
>
> Details of the analysis of this data and findings will be published in Emma's forthcoming PhD thesis, and will no doubt contribute to our understanding of the role of social media news accounts in encouraging polarisation and othering.

ACCESSING AND RECRUITING PARTICIPANTS ONLINE

Much participant recruitment that just a few years ago would have been undertaken by phone or in person now happens online in a way that feels very natural. There are of course some groups likely to be excluded by this (for example, prisoners – see Chapter 11 – and groups with limited access to the online world), but the process of arranging interviews online and then conducting them online, or sending out a survey via emails, social media and other online spaces, is now standard practice.

When sending emails to arrange interviews with potential participants, the British Psychological Society (2021: 19) notes that

> researchers need to be aware that the security of unencrypted email is low, and email content can be inadvertently disclosed on the Internet, local and other computers. Therefore, even the common practice of emailing research participants can, in principle, be problematic. Researchers therefore risk breaching participant confidentiality if they use non-secure e-mail in research or practice, and participants themselves may often be unaware of these risks.

If working on sensitive topics and with vulnerable groups, we advise specific caution when communicating by email.

As we explore later in this chapter, recruiting participants online (e.g. forums) and through social media can mean we reach groups that otherwise would not take part in the research, therefore increasing the diversity of research findings. Advertising research and the recruitment of participants online and through social media can also simply mean we reach more people and, therefore, in quantitative research using surveys and questionnaires (see Chapter 13), have larger sample sizes. A potential downside of this is that we have greater distance from our research participants and thus have less control over the research environment. The British Psychological Society (2021: 15) notes the following key areas researchers may not be able to control or verify:

a who has access to participate;
b the environmental conditions under which participants are responding (e.g. are they watching television at the same time);
c participants' feelings, reactions, responses to the research process;
d variations in the research procedure due to different hardware and software configurations.

Points a and c are particularly pertinent to criminological research. Point c in particular means we need to pay specific attention to ethical considerations around participant well-being (see below). Point a is a crucial consideration for research integrity. How can we be sure that our research is reaching those we wish to include, and those who do complete the research meet our inclusion criteria? How can we be sure that the same people have not completed our survey multiple times? Many commercial online survey platforms (see later in this chapter) incorporate checks to avoid multiple submissions. Verifying the validity of data (for example, demographic variables) is unfortunately quite difficult. Researchers should note this as a potential limitation to the integrity of their research.

Participant recruitment: the potential of social media to recruit 'invisible groups'

In Chapter 5 we explored power, protection and power dynamics, and the importance of ensuring that silenced and excluded groups are given the chance to talk about their views and experiences. There is an acknowledgement, by some at least, that there is a lack of diversity in research: both amongst researchers and research participants. In face-to-face research led by experienced researchers there has been a relatively recent growth of working with community and peer researchers (people drawn from the communities themselves – see Rees et al., 2024) to ensure that research is able to reach different communities in more meaningful ways. Online research has been highlighted as another important way to potentially reach hitherto invisible or silenced voices; participants who, for a variety of reasons, might be unwilling or unable to engage with other forms of research (see Box 15.1). However, it is important to note that researchers should be sensitive to, and ideally experienced in, working with silenced and vulnerable groups in offline spaces before attempting this online.

BOX 15.1 STUDENT ACTIVITY

Read: Sandhu, Brady and Barrett's (2023) discussion of research with South Asian women in the UK who had experienced gender-related violence (GRV). Sandhu et al. (2023: 4) explain that

> participants lived in isolation, in fear of multiple perpetrators, were often traumatised and with severed connections to their culture and families. The

researchers were mindful of the possible trauma and stigma South Asian women may have felt due to their experiences of GRV. Thus, this group of women participants were highly likely to have low social visibility, both online and offline, due to the fear of repercussions.

Sandhu et al. provide a very useful, detailed account of the ways they approached participant recruitment using social media (in this case, Facebook).

- In what ways do the authors suggest that social media was a superior recruitment method to 'traditional' methods for this 'invisible group'? (Hint: Look back at the discussion of gatekeepers in Chapter 5.)
- What do the authors say about the ethical recruitment of participants, via social media, who have previously been 'invisible'?
- Did the research capture all 'invisible' voices? Which groups might be excluded through online and social media research?

ETHICS IN ONLINE CRIMINOLOGICAL RESEARCH

As explored in Chapter 7, approaching ethics in criminological research thoughtfully is vital to ensure the safety and well-being of participants and researchers. However, it is sometimes a balancing act of competing priorities and considerations. In many ways, the rise of internet-mediated research adds to these complexities and researchers need to be very considered in their approach.

When working with data from online/social media sources, researchers should be extra cautious about potential threats to anonymity and confidentiality. While it is standard practice to remove all names and key identifying information from all types of data, including quotes from data collected in interviews and focus groups, when working with information posted online there is a risk that quotes could inadvertently identify an individual. Imagine, for example, that you are undertaking research on online hate speech. You access posts on various social media platforms and forums, taking samples of content posted by users. You then analyse the data and write a report, including quotes from the online posts with names/usernames removed, and that report is published on a website. The risk here is that while you have removed names and usernames, people reading the report could quite easily trace quotes back to the original posts and this might risk their anonymity and confidentiality. The BPS (2021: 19) recommends that where 'it is not possible to obtain informed consent, it is good practice to either omit quotes and just discuss themes in the data, or paraphrase the quotes'. Where informed consent is obtained, the risk of identification must be made clear to participants. Risks to anonymity and confidentiality associated with the use of email and transcription are discussed elsewhere in this chapter.

Seeking valid informed consent in internet-mediated research

It is important to ensure that consent is sought in a meaningful way in all research, including when collecting data online. However, when conducting research into online spaces such as social media and forum posts, where the information was not posted directly for the research project, seeking consent from individuals is often not possible. It is therefore vital that researchers consider what can be reasonably considered to be public and private data. Where individuals post information publicly on social media sites, for example, and this data is used in research, these 'participants' are rarely aware of their participation. It is important in these situations not to take a user's agreement to the terms of the social media platform or website as being a proxy for informed consent, but it is important to engage with the terms of these agreements and consider carefully how the data is used (also see above discussion of confidentiality). Where there can be assumed a reasonable expectation that people consider their online posts private (e.g. in a closed forum or group), informed consent should be sought – failing to do so would be a breach of individual privacy. Closed forums and groups are often overseen by a group admin/gatekeeper and it is advisable to engage with them to discuss potential access and participation in the research and sensible ways to approach this with the group in question.

When collecting new data online in the form of surveys and interviews, we suggest initially designing participant information and consent forms following standard templates in a Word document (see Chapter 7) – this makes it straightforward for ethics panels to review the content. When conducting online surveys you should then add the participant information and questions confirming consent to the first page of the survey (see Chapter 13 for step-by-step guidance on building surveys using Jisc Online Surveys). When arranging and conducting interviews online, we send a participant information sheet and consent form to participants ahead of the scheduled interview time. This allows participants time to engage with the information and consider any questions they might have. When interviewing criminal justice professionals we ask that, if happy to do so, they return their completed consent form to us ahead of the interview. If they would like to discuss the information with us first we then ask that they confirm consent at the beginning of the interview and return the consent form to us. Whether participants have already returned the consent form or not, we always ensure we discuss the participant information form verbally with every participant.

Handling disclosure of serious harm

In Chapter 7 we discussed potential boundaries around confidentiality and when and where researchers might be required to disclose any risk of harm raised during the research process. For example, in a prison setting in the UK researchers are required to ensure it is clear to participants – most likely through a participant information form – that while confidentiality can largely be assured, should a participant 'disclose either the intention to harm yourself, harm another individual, attempt to escape, or act in any way that may result in a breach of security, or break any prison rules' the researcher is required to tell the prison service. Such boundaries around serious risk of harm have often been navigated by criminological researchers in the offline world and, while no doubt challenging, can be addressed sensitively in face-to-face interactions (for example, see Piper and Simons, 2005 – discussed in Chapter 7). However, what is already a potentially challenging issue becomes much tricker in internet-mediated research. Participation in a research study might, for example, be anonymous – by design, or because participants choose to stay anonymous. Researchers might be working with secondary data sources (see Chapter 14) or social media data and have no control over the data. If researchers put in greater controls around participation this could, particularly in research with social media data sources, limit the validity of the data. All of this means that the balance around what might naturally occur in online spaces, how far researchers might want to exert control over online participation and anonymity, the potential that online anonymity might encourage participation from some groups who otherwise would be reluctant to participate (Sandhu et al., 2023), and the boundaries around disclosing risk of serious harm, become a balancing act.

When considering how to manage issues like disclosure of serious harm in internet-mediated research, researchers should look to guidance from ethics panels and profession body guidance. However, a concerning feature of the move to more and more online research is highlighted by Edelman (2020), who undertook a review of guidance published by the British Psychological Society, the Association of Internet Researchers, and the British Society of Criminology. She found 'a lack of existing guidance on handling participant disclosure of serious risk of harm to self or others' (Edelman, 2020: 3) during internet-mediated research with guidance lagging behind current research practice. However, she does note that the Association of Internet Researchers and the British Society of Criminology 'do acknowledge that researchers may have legal or professional obligations to report such disclosures' (Edelman, 2020: 3).

Edelman calls for more specific guidance on this important issue and we encourage all researchers to engage with the ethics guidance of bodies like the British Society of Criminology as they are updated. Of course, university ethics policies, guidance and review panels will also be able to offer students and supervisors advice on these tricky issues and we encourage you to engage in active discussions around this.

PAUSE TO THINK ...

Revisit the following activity from Chapter 7 – has your thinking changed in light of the considerations posed in this current chapter?

Read Rambukkana's (2019) discussion of the use of online data in research on the 'alt-right'. Rambukkana poses six key questions to help us think through the ethical considerations relevant to using what he terms 'gray data' ('research data that have their provenance in the gray area between found texts and the products of participants', Rambukkana, 2019: 312).

- How does this type of research fit with recent trends in social research to undertake research *with* rather than *on* participants?

Rambukkana, N. (2019) 'The Politics of Gray Data: Digital Methods, Intimate Proximity, and Research Ethics for Work on the "Alt-Right"', *Qualitative Inquiry*, 25(3): 312–323.

COLLECTING AND ANALYSING DATA

Interviews

As noted elsewhere in this book (see Chapter 12), it has become more and more common in a range of research projects to conduct interviews online. There are pros and cons to this. It is often possible to offer potential interviewees more flexibility around the timings of interviews if you/they do not need to travel, and this might mean that people are more likely to participate. In terms of time and resources (e.g. travel expenses) this can be quite efficient. However, in our experience conducting interviews online makes building a rapport more challenging and so it is important to really focus on this at the beginning of the online session because building trust and rapport is so crucial to the interview process. The time taken to discuss the research prior to beginning the interview is important in helping participants understand why their part in the research is important and this might support their willingness to be open with you. We conduct many of our interviews online, but where possible and practical try to give participants a choice about whether they prefer this or face to face. If conducting interviews on very sensitive topics, it might be especially important to offer an in-person interview as building trust is so crucial in this situation.

In Chapter 11 we talked about managing your participants, because initial recruitment is only the first stage. Drop-out rates can be high between contacting participants and collecting the data so you must do what you can to manage your participants. Avoid bombarding potential participants with too many reminders but do follow our key tips:

- 'Strike while the iron's hot!': the sooner you can conduct your data collection the better. You must ensure that potential participants have time to consider taking part, but the sooner you can collect data the less time you have to lose track of participants.
- Keep track of them: if there will be some time between a potential participant expressing interest and the actual interview, phone/email/message your participants to check they are still happy to take part on the date you agreed. (Check what form of communication they prefer – but see the discussion earlier in this chapter about being careful about how you contact participants.)
- Re-confirm appointments close to the time.

Practically, you might be quite familiar with platforms such as Microsoft Teams, Zoom, and Google Meet, which can be easily set up to conduct interviews. As we discuss in Chapter 17, these platforms can also offer helpful recording and (basic) transcription capabilities. If, for example, you are conducting an interview online, you can use the functionality on Microsoft Teams to display a live transcription (designed to be useful for deaf or hard of hearing participants and also useful for participants in noisy places). We typically opt to have the transcript created after the interview as with most participants we are working with the live transcription is a distraction (see note below on transcription errors). It is possible to produce transcripts in a variety of different languages to match the language the interview is conducted in. There are different ways of capturing recordings and creating transcripts, depending on which platform you are using. As the technical capabilities and instructions change quite regularly we have not reproduced them here, but advise you to look at the online Microsoft, Zoom or Google Help support pages which contain step-by-step guides. Whichever platform you are using, be sure to practise recording an interview and producing a transcript before any real data collection using these tools. The online call always needs to be recorded for a transcript to be produced and some platforms require you to select a transcription production option at the beginning of the recording. Always ensure you have checked that the system you are using is compatible with the data security and ethical approvals of your university.

As discussed in Chapter 17, transcription is an important part of the process of analysis to ensure researchers are really familiar with their data. However, when collecting data online we do sometimes use these built in transcription capabilities. They save us time – but a word of warning: the transcripts automatically produced are not good enough quality for transcription. They tend to contain many errors and so it is vital for researchers to go through them and turn them into an accurate transcript ready for coding. Going through each autogenerated transcript and ensuring it is accurate also means you will be really familiar with each transcript before you embark on coding your transcripts.

We find these auto-generated transcripts contain some errors in typical speech, and are very inaccurate when interviewees are discussing specific terms or technical language. Have a look at this brief example from an interview one of us recently conducted with a member of prison staff:

I was like yeah, absolutely all for that to support you in regards to rattling people.

What was actually said was,

I was like yeah, absolutely all for that to support you in regards to ROTL'ing people.

Rattling as a slang term can be used to mean to frighten people or to describe withdrawal and cravings from opioids. The Prison Officer was actually talking about Release on Temporary Licence (ROTL). ROTL refers to a prisoner being able to leave prison for a short time for a limited number of reasons, including to take part in paid

USING ONLINE AND SOCIAL MEDIA DATA SOURCES 275

or unpaid work and to help individuals to settle back into the community. Only some people in prison are eligible for ROTL and all individuals who are eligible for ROTL must meet strict risk criteria. Getting this word correct is vital to understanding what the prison officer was conveying. We wouldn't expect auto-generated transcription to pick up this term, but this example does demonstrate the importance of the researchers checking and amending transcripts for accuracy.

The BPS (2021: 19) notes particular caution when considering transcription:

> A further breach of confidentiality may derive from using data transcription software which uses a third party to generate automatic written transcription of audio data. Even services which use AI for this purpose are best avoided to stay fully compliant to participant confidentiality policies. Finally, any real-time interviews which take place online such as through video chat should be conducted on secure platforms (e.g. password-protected meeting rooms), software should have sound privacy policies (i.e. not send on data to third parties) and researchers should be connected to the Internet via secure network rather than ones which are freely available in public spaces.

Surveys

If you are collecting data using surveys or questionnaires, it is quite likely that you will be using an online survey platform such as SurveyMonkey or Jisc Online Surveys (for which your university may have a subscription – ask your tutors about accessing those). These systems can be very useful and they are cost effective. A link to the survey can be sent to people and shared online along with information about the study. They can also be a very quick way of collecting data from large numbers of people, and people may be more likely to be open and honest about sensitive topics than when answering questions in person. Always ensure you have checked that the system you are using is compatible with the data security and ethical approvals of your university. For this reason we recommend you stick with platforms for which your university has a subscription (although don't assume that means it will meet your ethics requirements – do check).

Once you have designed your survey or questionnaire (see Chapter 13), or chosen the validated measure(s) you intend to use (also see Chapter 13), you should place this on the online survey platform. The platforms are typically quite straightforward to use, but we have provided some step-by-step guidance in Chapter 13.

Earlier in this chapter we discussed issues around about researcher control over participation in online research. When using online methods you should consider how you will manage the sample and respondents to ensure that your target group only, and no other people, complete the questionnaire. There is a potential tension here between the needs a researcher might have in wanting to, for example, check that someone does not complete an online questionnaire twice and the need to protect anonymity. For this reason, sites like SurveyMonkey do not use Cookies or external tracking software to collect information on respondents, nor do they routinely provide details of respondents' IP addresses. You can, however, set up restricted access to an online questionnaire, using a password, to try to ensure that only your target respondents complete the survey (and not anyone who happens to find the link to the survey). You can also set up automatic email reminders to encourage participation.

FUTURE DIRECTIONS

Generative AI and data analysis

While we suspect that this final section of the chapter will be out of date even by the time this book is published, with fast-moving developments in technology and particularly around artificial intelligence (AI) it is worth noting the potential impact of this on research. You are likely familiar with recent developments in generative AI: a type of AI that we are becoming familiar with for its capability to produce text (see, for example, ChatGPT), images (see, for example, DALL-E) and other content based on the data/information they were trained with.

Some computer assisted qualitative data analysis software (CAQDAS), such as NVivo (see Chapter 17), has integrated AI in order to auto-generate codes. These are not intended to replace the researcher's analytic input, but to provide a start for the analysis. There can be some potential benefits to this when working with very large datasets. At a basic level, for example, it has long been possible to search for the frequency of a particular word or phrase in a dataset. Researchers, particularly linguists, have also used software programs to search for positive and negative phrases around a particular topic in large datasets. The functionality within CAQDAS to auto-generate codes builds on this type of functionality. There are some benefits in terms of saving time, but at present auto-generated codes are lacking sophistication. The results might not address the research questions, give little insight into what speakers might be saying 'between the lines' and miss some of the complexity of human language. They can, however, provide an interesting start point to build upon and refine with your own analytic efforts. We advise students to engage thoroughly with the data familiarisation and analysis outlined in Chapter 17, using CAQDAS as a support tool only.

> **PAUSE TO THINK ...**
>
> What might the risks be of using currently quite unsophisticated AI coding facilities in qualitative data analysis software? What might this mean for learning about criminological issues in society?
>
> You might, for example, consider news stories that exist around bias in generative AI due to the information used to train these models. We recommended that if you do decide to test out this functionality in data analysis software, that you do so conservatively and view the functionality as assisting your initial, basic analysis and not as a substitute for your own efforts.

Generative AI and writing

If you speak to most university lecturers, they are likely to have had experience of receiving work that has obviously been AI-generated. While ChatGPT and other deep-learning models can produce some compelling text that can be helpful for many activities, they have significant limitations when attempting to use them to produce academic writing. We have found, for example, that the content produced is very superficial and non-specific. Generative AI also currently cannot produce reference lists and tends to 'hallucinate' references based on models rather than actual references. This means that the references generative AI produces are typically entirely made up.

However, even with all of the above limitations, that is not to say that generative AI does not have its place in academic writing and we are watching with interest as things develop. In another book one of us has edited recently (Gardner and Caulfield, 2024), for example, the authors used AI as a writing tool in one of the chapters:

> AI was used as a writing tool throughout the chapter. Self-formulated paragraphs were put into ChatGPT to meet the requirements of Academic English. The use of AI aligns with the editorial policies on authorship and principles of publishing ethics of Routledge.
>
> (Marynissen, Vandermeersche and Brosens, 2024: 82)

As the authors were writing in their second language, there was a clear place for generative AI within the writing process, and the resulting chapter was excellent.

 KEY LEARNING POINTS

- As technology is developing fast, all researchers should regularly look to relevant professional bodies (such as the British Society of Criminology) for updated guidance on internet-mediated research.
- Thinking about research ethics can be something of a balancing act of competing priorities and considerations. Doing criminological research in or on the online world adds to these complexities and researchers need to be very considered in their approach.
- The flexibility of conducting interviews online might mean that people are more likely to participate. However, this method might not be appropriate for research on sensitive issues or with vulnerable participants.
- A potential downside of internet-mediated research is that researchers have greater distance from research participants and thus have less control over the research environment. Exerting control can affect the validity of research on the online world. When conducting online surveys there are ways to enhance the control over who participates.

REFERENCES

Alcadipani, R. and Cunliffe, A. (2024) 'The Shifting Nature of Relationality in the Blurred Boundaries of Hybrid Organizational Ethnography', *British Journal of Management*, 35: 679–691. Available at https://doi.org/10.1111/1467-8551.12728 (accessed 30 May 2024).

British Psychology Society (BPS). (2021) Ethics guidelines for internet-mediated research. Available at https://explore.bps.org.uk/content/report-guideline/bpsrep.2021.rep155 (accessed 30 May 2024).

Edelman N. (2020) 'Internet-mediated Research in the Wake of Covid-19: Dealing with Disclosure of Serious Risk of Harm [version 1; peer review: 1 not approved]', *F1000Research*, 9: 426. https://doi.org/10.12688/f1000research.24127.1 (accessed 30 May 2024).

Gardner, M. and Caulfield, L.S. (2024). *Arts in Criminal Justice and Corrections: International perspectives on methods, journeys, and challenges*, London: Routledge.

Guess, A., Nyhan, B. and Reifler, J. (2018) 'All Media Trust Is Local? Findings from the 2018 Poynter Media Trust Survey', Poynter Institute.

Le Merrer, E., Trédan, G. and Yesilkanat, A. (2023) 'Modeling Rabbit-Holes on YouTube', *Social Network Analysis and Mining*. http://dx.doi.org/10.48550/arXiv.2307.09986

Lewandowsky, S., Ecker, U.K. and Cook, J. (2017) 'Beyond Misinformation: Understanding and Coping with the "Post-truth" Era', *Journal of Applied Research in Memory and Cognition*, 6(4): 353–369.

Mardones-Bravo, D. (2022) 'Online Methods in Qualitative Criminology', in R. Faria and M. Dodge (eds) *Qualitative Research in Criminology*, Switzerland: Springer, pp. 85–102.

Marynissen, S., Vandermeersche, G. and Brosens, D. (2024) 'A Realist Lens on Participatory Music Programmes in Prison', in M. Gardner and L.S. Caulfield (eds) *Arts in Criminal Justice and Corrections: International Perspectives on Methods, Journeys, and Challenges*, London: Routledge.

Miller, J. and Miller, H. (2021) 'Beating the House: Ethnographic Insights into a Web-Based Marijuana Grey Market', *American Journal of Criminal Justice*, 46: 1018–1033. Available at: https://link.springer.com/article/10.1007/s12103-021-09661-6

Ofcom. (2023) 'News Consumption in the UK: 2023 Overview of Research Findings', Ofcom. Available at https://www.ofcom.org.uk/media-use-and-attitudes/attitudes-to-news/news-consumption/

Parsell, M. (2008) 'Pernicious Virtual Communities: Identity, Polarisation and the Web 2.0', *Ethics and Information Technology*, 10: 41–56.

Piper, H. and Simons, H. (2005) 'Ethical Responsibility in Social Research', in B. Somekh and C. Lewin (eds) *Research Methods in the Social Sciences*, New York: Sage.

Rambukkana, N. (2019) 'The Politics of Gray Data: Digital Methods, Intimate Proximity, and Research Ethics for Work on the "Alt-Right"', *Qualitative Inquiry*, 25(3): 312–323.

Rees, J., Caulfield, L. S., Booth, J., Kanjilal, M., Sojka, B., Spicksley, K., Blamire, J. and Arnull, E. (2024) 'The Opportunities, Challenges, and Rewards of "Community Peer Research": Reflections on Research Practice', *Qualitative Inquiry*. https://doi.org/10.1177/10778004241229789

Sandhu, K., Brady, G. and Barrett, H. (2023) 'Article Reaching Out: Using Social Media to Recruit "Invisible Groups": The Case of South Asian Women in the UK Experiencing Gender-Related Violence', *Social Sciences*, 12(212). https://doi.org/10.3390/ socsci12040212

Vombatkere, K., Mousavi, S., Zannettou, S., Roesner, F. and Gummadi, K. P. (2024, May) 'TikTok and the Art of Personalization: Investigating Exploration and Exploitation on Social Media Feeds', In *Proceedings of the ACM on Web Conference 2024* (pp. 3789–3797).

PART V

Doing criminological research: analysis and writing up

PART 3

Doing criminological research: analysis and writing up

Chapter 16

Analysing the data
Quantitative analysis

GOALS OF THIS CHAPTER

At the end of reading this chapter and by completing the online resources that accompany it, you will be able to:

1. understand basic statistical concepts and terminology;
2. know when to use statistical packages such as the *Statistical Package for the Social Sciences* (SPSS) and understand the possible ways Microsoft Office Excel and other programs can be used for data analysis;
3. enter data into SPSS;
4. understand the basics of choosing appropriate statistical tests;
5. produce descriptive statistics from your data;
6. conduct *t*-tests and Chi-square tests.

OVERVIEW

- Statistical analysis allows researchers to say with confidence whether patterns or changes over time exist in their data, whether these are significant or whether they are likely to be due to chance. If done correctly, this can provide more robust evidence than simply presenting data from questionnaires in percentage terms or in graphs.
- The thought of conducting statistical analysis may be daunting. However, understanding the basics can be relatively straightforward and, contrary to popular opinion, does not require any particular competency with mathematics. This is largely due to computer programs like the *Statistical Package for the Social Sciences* (SPSS). Providing that the researcher is able to choose an appropriate test for their data, follow instructions on running the test in SPSS, and follow instructions on correctly interpreting the output, the task is much less scary than students often assume.
- Before being able to perform statistical tests it is important to understand some basic statistical concepts. Understanding things like the type of data you have, and the types of test available, equips you with the knowledge to decide which statistical tests are the most appropriate to run on your data.

DOI: 10.4324/9781032645698-21

- There are many statistical tests available, some used more commonly than others, and some more complex than others. This chapter focuses on two of the more basic and commonly used statistical tests. These tests are useful and will tell you much about your data as well as provide a good introduction to running and interpreting statistical tests. However, they are not appropriate in all circumstances and so you may need to use other tests when you come to work with your own data.

INTRODUCTION

You may be relieved to read that this book does not seek to make statisticians of its readers. Instead, it seeks to ensure that students understand key concepts in statistical analysis and have the knowledge and skills to analyse the data they collect. Too often criminology students are wary of statistical analysis, so with this in mind this chapter provides a step-by-step guide to basic quantitative analysis. The chapter focuses on the fundamentals: it provides guidance on inputting data into SPSS; it walks you through choosing and running appropriate statistical tests such as descriptive statistics, t-tests and Chi-square tests; and it shows you how to interpret the output to understand your findings. However, we encourage you to consider whether the data you have would really benefit from quantitative analysis and we hope that by reading this chapter you will be more equipped to answer this question. It may be that the data you have are more suited to a straightforward graphical representation, and this can be done quite easily in programs such as Excel.

Even if you do very little statistical analysis in your degree course and decide to conduct qualitative research for your dissertation, understanding the basics of statistical analysis is still a vital skill to have. For example, think back to Chapter 9 and the focus on critiquing the literature. In order to understand and critique research papers that use quantitative techniques you must be able to understand what the researchers have done and why they have done it. These skills are important to your development as a criminological researcher and as a criminologist.

The aim of this chapter is to equip you with a guide to conducting basic statistical analysis of questionnaire data. However, keep in mind that the types of analysis discussed in this chapter may not enable you to analyse your data in the way you want and so, once you have understood the basics by reading this chapter, you may wish to read one of the range of books that are dedicated to statistical analysis. We recommend some of our favourites at the end of the chapter.

Remember: you *do not* need to be good at mathematics to be proficient in quantitative data analysis.

BASIC STATISTICAL CONCEPTS

At this point we should make it clear that we will not be looking at how to conduct statistical analyses by hand. Later in the chapter we will introduce you to SPSS, the most popular statistics computer program used in the social sciences. Before thinking about (let alone attempting to conduct) any analysis of your quantitative data it is vital to understand some basic statistical terms and concepts. Let us begin with the basics.

Variables

A variable is anything that varies and can be measured. For example, in Amy's research mentioned below, she wished to measure the relationship between gender of perpetrator and perceptions of intimate partner violence. In this case the variables are 'gender of perpetrator' and 'perceptions of intimate partner violence'. Often it is sensible to categorise variables. For example, when collecting data using a questionnaire we may wish to know things like the age of participants. Rather than asking each person to write a number, we may have age groups, as discussed in Chapter 13. For ease of use with SPSS, we may reduce some terms to numbers. For example, if we have collected information on participants' educational background, we may label 'No qualifications' as '0', 'GCSE/O-level' as '1', 'Vocational/professional' as '2' and so on. We will come back to this point later in the chapter.

It is important to identify which variables are independent and which are dependent – or, put another way, to understand which variable(s) we expect to have an effect on which other variable(s). The **independent variable** influences the **dependent variable**. For example, if we want to explore the relationship between age and criminality, we may look at different age groups and how many criminal convictions each age group has on average. In this situation age is the independent variable and number of criminal convictions is the dependent variable as we are seeking to understand what effect age has on crime. Researchers may manipulate the independent variable(s) to see what effect this has on the dependent variable. The dependent variable is not something that is controlled or manipulated, but is what is being measured. Let us take a closer look at Amy's work (see Box 16.1).

Later in this chapter you will find examples where we ask you to use your knowledge of variables to work out which are the independent and dependent variables.

Types of data: nominal, ordinal, interval and ratio

Not all data are the same. In order to work out which is the most appropriate test for the data you collect you will need to understand what type of data you have.

Nominal refers to categories that are separate to others, such as the name of your university, the gender of your participants, or hair colour. You can remember this easily, as nominal sounds like name (both words have the same Latin root).

Ordinal is numerical data, usually quantities that have a natural order. The easiest example of this is the place where runners finish in a race: first, second, third and so on. The most usual type of ordinal data we deal with in criminological research is choices on a Likert scale. Think back to the examples in Chapter 13. With ordinal data the intervals, or differences, between each value are not equal. You can remember ordinal, as it sounds like order.

Interval data is like ordinal except the intervals between each value are equal. For example, the temperature difference between 29 and 30 degrees Celsius is the same size as the difference between 4 and 5 degrees Celsius. While data from attitudinal scales and Likert scales are typically ordinal, they are often treated like interval data in statistical analysis. There is no simple way to explain why this is the case, but you can find an example in Box 16.3.

Ratio data has all the properties of interval data, except that there is a clear zero value. For example, height or weight: something cannot be less than zero centimetres tall or weigh less than zero kilograms. To help you work out if your data are ratio, consider the ratio of the measurements. For example, a weight of 2 kilograms is twice as much as 1 kilogram. However, a temperature of 60 degrees Celsius is not twice as hot as 30 degrees Celsius, as temperature measured in this way is not a ratio variable.

At this point you may be asking 'Why does it matter what type of data I have?' The reason we need to understand what type of data we have is to help us decide what type of statistical test to use. See Table 16.1 for more information.

BOX 16.1 PERCEPTION OF INTIMATE PARTNER VIOLENCE: DEPENDENT AND INDEPENDENT VARIABLES

Amy is interested in researching perceptions of physical and psychological intimate partner violence (IPV) in same-sex and mixed-sex romantic relationships. Amy's review of the literature suggests that there might be a relationship between how people perceive IPV and the gender of the perpetrator. She used two vignettes that contained a written description of a situation where IPV occurred (from Capezza and Arriaga, 2008) and used a questionnaire to collect data on participants' perceptions of perpetrators and victims' behaviours.

In Amy's research, the dependent variable is the perception of IPV and the independent variables are the gender of the perpetrator. However, Amy has also included another variable that may have an effect on aggression: the gender of the victim. Thus in this research there are two independent variables.

We might hypothesise that an independent variable is the cause, and the dependent variable is the effect. However, we will need to conduct a statistical analysis to start to investigate whether our **hypothesis** may be correct. Keep in mind that even if we find a statistically significant relationship between two variables, it does not prove that one causes the other. This is an important point to keep in mind, as it may well be that some other, untested variable is actually influencing both variables. In this example Amy needs to test whether perpetrator gender and/or victim gender has a statistically significant effect on perceptions of IPV. If she finds a statistically significant relationship between these variables, that might indicate that perpetrator gender and/or victim gender have an effect on perceptions of IPV, but it does not prove this. We can show a relationship between factors, but we cannot prove cause and effect.

Types of statistical test: parametric and non-parametric

The main distinction between **parametric** and **non-parametric tests** it that parametric tests are more powerful and allow us to have more confidence in our statistical analysis. Therefore, it makes sense to use parametric tests wherever possible. However, our data have to fulfil certain criteria in order to be suitable for analysis using parametric tests.

Normal distribution: to use a parametric test your data must be from a population that has a normal distribution. This means that most scores or cases cluster around the average (mean) and that as you move further away from this average there are fewer and fewer cases. If your data are not from a normally distributed population, parametric tests could give you incorrect answers. Human height is an example of data that are normally distributed: if we measured the height of all humans and plotted it on a graph, most of the measurements we collected would bunch around the mean. Visualising what your data may look like is a good way of understanding this. If we were to plot the data from our entire sample on a graph, a normal distribution would give us a bell-shaped curve (see Figure 16.1).

The graphs in Figure 16.1 also refer to **standard deviation** (often reported simply as SD). This is how much dispersion exists from the average (mean). Later in this chapter we look at how to report descriptive statistics and you will notice that the standard deviation is always reported. This is so that anyone reading about your data can understand how close to the mean the majority of your data fall. For example, if the mean age of your sample is 20.2 years and the standard deviation is 3.4, we know that the majority of your sample is close in age to 20.2 years. Put simply, standard deviation refers to how widely spread the numbers are.

Homogeneity of variance: this only refers to times when you are comparing groups (for example, if you are investigating whether undergraduate criminology students hold different views about the treatment of people convicted of sex offences to those held by undergraduate chemistry students). Homogeneity of variance means that the different samples you are comparing must have similar variance, so with the example above the variance in factors like age is likely to be similar. However, if you were comparing the views of undergraduate criminology students with the general population, you would expect the general population to have a much wider variance of age, and therefore a parametric test may not be appropriate. Put simply, it is important to ensure that your groups are similar in important factors other than the factor you are testing (your dependent variable, e.g. views about the treatment of people convicted of sex offences). This helps us understand whether the factor that influences your dependent variable is your independent variable (e.g. being a criminology or chemistry student) and not some other variable (e.g. age).

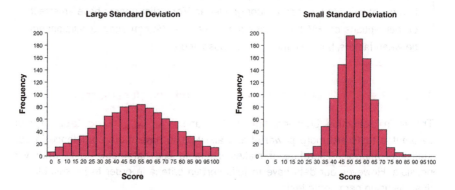

Figure 16.1 Standard deviation.

Statistical significance

Significance is a statistical term which tells you how sure you can be that a difference or relationship exists. For example, in Amy's research discussed in Box 16.1, she had a number of hypotheses including that: 'There will be a difference in how male perpetrators of IPV are perceived in comparison to female perpetrators'. In order to ascertain whether this hypothesis should be accepted or rejected, Amy needed to measure the statistical significance of the relationship between the gender of the perpetrator presented in the vignette and the perceptions of them. Statistical significance shows that the relationship between the variables is probably not due to mere chance and that a real relationship most likely exists between the two variables. There are a number of different ways of measuring statistical significance. The type of statistical test used depends largely upon the type of research design used and the type of data you have collected.

P-values

You will often see statistical significance represented like this: $p < .05$. This is known as the p-value. A p-value of less than .05 indicates that the possibility that the results are due merely to chance is less than 5 per cent (or 1/20). If the p-value is less than .05 this means the hypothesis can be accepted. If the p-value is greater than .05 this means the hypothesis should be rejected, as there is no statistical significance and any relationship is likely to be due to chance.

There are three levels of significance ($p < .05$, $p < .01$, $p < .001$). It is relatively unusual to see researchers refer to anything other than $p < .05$, and so for the purposes of this basic introductory chapter we will refer to $p < .05$ in order to ascertain whether a statistically significant relationship exists between the variables we test in the examples below.

THE BASICS OF SPSS

The *Statistical Package for the Social Sciences*, known as SPSS, has been used in its various formats by researchers for around 55 years. SPSS provides a highly useful tool for analysing data in ways that would be very complex were they to be attempted by hand or by using a calculator. The package we use today looks very different from the product that was first conceived of in 1968. Thankfully the most current version at the time of writing – IBM SPSS Statistics 28 – is very user friendly. Your university may be running a slightly older version of SPSS and so you should note that this may look different from the screenshots included in this chapter. However, the basic guidance applies to older versions of the package.

In the support materials that accompany this book, you can find an SPSS data file for you to practise the skills learned later in this chapter. In order to open the file you must use a computer with SPSS installed and your university should be able to provide guidance on how students can install this on their personal computers. We recommend having SPSS installed on your home computer so that you can work through this chapter in your own time. This chapter provides guidance that should help you familiarise yourself with navigating SPSS and how to calculate simple statistics, such as the average (mean).

DATA ENTRY

There are two view tabs in SPSS: Variable View and Data View. Variable View is where you label your variables and Data View is where you enter your data. For example, in Variable View you may decide to add the label 'age' first and then switch to Data View (using the tabs at the bottom of the page) to enter the age (or age group) of each of your participants. Variable View is shown in Figure 16.2.

You will see that in this example there were 26 variables, including 'research code', 'age at time of interview', 'offence category', 'drug problem ever' and 22 other variables.

To add a variable, simply highlight a cell under 'Name' and type in a name that describes the variable; for example, 'Age', 'Gender', 'Offence type'. Note that each variable must have a distinct name. All of the columns can be changed. For instance, under 'Label' you may wish to add a fuller description of that variable.

288 CRIMINOLOGICAL SKILLS AND RESEARCH FOR BEGINNERS

Figure 16.2 Reprint Courtesy of IBM Corporation ©

The value column is particularly important. Earlier in this chapter we talked about how it can be useful to reduce some terms to numbers for ease of use in SPSS – we call this 'coding' our data (not to be confused with the use of the word coding with qualitative analysis). For example, if we have collected information on participants' educational qualifications, as in the example database used here, we may label 'None' as '0', 'GCSE level/equivalent' as '1', 'A-level/equivalent' as '2' and so on. The numbers are the codes – a shorthand way of presenting our data, a method that allows us to transform nominal data into other types of data that can be more readily used with statistical tests. The value column allows us to label values so that, in the data view, rather than type 'GCSE level/equivalent' and so on many times, we can simply add the appropriate number. We recommend that all **nominal data** are given a value, as entering the data in this way also helps SPSS in conducting any statistical analysis you perform.

> **TIP**
>
> When entering data from a questionnaire or other source, it is not unusual to find that you have some missing data, perhaps where someone has omitted to complete one of the questions. It is important that you do not leave any blank cells in your Data View, so we suggest replacing any missing data with the numbers 9999. To ensure that SPSS recognises this as missing data and so does not try to analyse it, ensure that in the 'Missing' column in Variable View, 9999 is inserted in each row.

ANALYSING THE DATA: QUANTITATIVE ANALYSIS   289

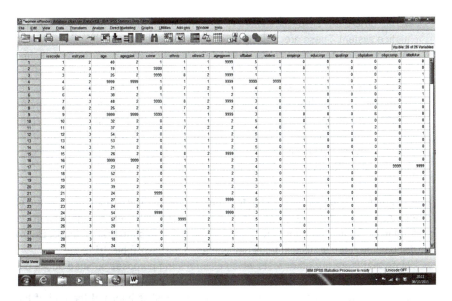

Figure 16.3 Reprint Courtesy of IBM Corporation ©

When you click on a cell under 'Values', a box appears where you should add the value (number) and the label: in the example above, you would begin with '0' and 'No qualifications'. You then click 'Add' before moving on to add the next value and label ('1' and 'GCSE level/equivalent') and so on until you have added them all for this variable. Once you have finished, simply click 'OK'.

Data View is shown in Figure 16.3.

As you will see in the full dataset in the support material, this was a very large piece of research including 200 participants, but there is no limit that researchers are likely to reach on how many participants may be included in an SPSS database.

In Data View the top of each column shows the name you assigned each variable in the Variable View. You begin entering your data by simply highlighting a cell, typing the number or word and then pressing return. You will then be in the cell below.

WHICH TEST SHOULD I USE?

Now that you have read about the basic concepts discussed above, you are in a much better position to work out which statistical test is appropriate for your data.

In addition to understanding what type of data you have, you should also ask yourself what it is you want to do with your data. For example:

- Do you want to see whether there are differences between two sets of scores? For example, you may be interested in whether a 'prison awareness' course has had any effect on young people's attitudes towards crime, as measured on a pre-existing attitudinal scale before and after taking part in the course. Or, you may want to see whether undergraduate and postgraduate students at your university

score differently on a questionnaire looking at knowledge about the criminal justice system. These are looking for differences in the data.
- Are you trying to determine whether one variable predicts a particular outcome over and above other variables? For example, if you were seeking to find out what affects increases in self-reported alcohol consumption, you may consider a number of potential factors such as: stress levels; boredom; unemployment; major televised sporting events; and any other factors the literature suggests may be relevant. Certain statistical analyses, when conducted on appropriate data, could suggest which factors are more strongly related to increases in alcohol consumption, for example. This is looking for predictors.

This chapter focuses on understanding descriptive statistics and basic tests of 'differences' in the data, as these are commonly used, relatively straightforward to perform in SPSS and therefore are a good introduction to statistical methods. Below we discuss the three statistical tests highlighted in italics in Table 16.1.

Note that there are other tests which also fulfil the purposes outlined above but in different ways. As highlighted earlier in this chapter, if you wish to read more about these we have listed some of our favourite SPSS/statistics books at the end of the chapter.

Table 16.1 Common types of study and statistical analyses

Purpose	Suggested statistical test	Types of data it can be used with
All **quantitative research**	*Descriptive statistics*	All
Comparing two sets of scores for differences	*Unrelated t-test or Related t-test*	Ratio, Interval
Comparing nominal data (looking for a relationship/ correlation)	*Chi-square*	Ordinal
Comparing the means of two or more sets of scores	Unrelated ANOVA (Analysis of Variance) or related ANOVA	Interval
Finding predictors	Regression	Dependent on the type of regression analyses

Website Student document

Database: Choosing a statistical test flowchart

If you want to check which tests may be most appropriate for your data, we highly recommend looking at the support material for this book.

DESCRIPTIVE STATISTICS

There are two main types of statistics: descriptive and inferential. What we have discussed thus far in this chapter relates primarily to inferential statistics. Inferential statistics tell us whether there is statistical significance and this branch of statistics aims to infer from samples to populations, i.e. we use inferential statistics when we are trying to reach conclusions that extend beyond the data in our sample. This is why sample size is so important: we need to be able to make inferences from our sample, so the sample must be suitably large. Descriptive statistics on the other hand are used to describe the main characteristics of our sample or variables and are needed for all types of study. For example, when writing up quantitative research it is usual to present information on the age and gender of participants, and other factors that may be relevant depending on your research, such as occupation or criminal history. This information is often presented in the methodology section, with inferential statistics forming the results section.

Running descriptive statistics

Using the SPSS dataset in the support material, follow the instructions on the SPSS screenshots below to run descriptive statistics for the age of the sample. The information we need is the mean, range, maximum, minimum and Standard Deviation.

1. Go to the 'Analyse' tab. In the drop-down menu go to 'Descriptive Statistics' and then 'Descriptives' (Figure 16.4).
2. Next, click on the variable 'Age at time of interview' to select it and click the arrow to move this variable to the 'Variables' box. Click 'OK' (Figure 16.5).
3. SPSS output will appear on your screen giving you the statistics you requested (Figure 16.6). You should see that there are 178 participants in the sample whose age at interview was known, the youngest of whom is 16 and the oldest 60. The mean age of the sample is 30.15 years with a standard deviation of 9.76.

Website Student document

Database: SPSS dataset

If you require only descriptive statistics for your data, you can produce these using Microsoft Excel. This program is more readily available and used by most businesses. Read on to the end of this chapter for more on this.

BOX 16.2 RESEARCH EXAMPLE

'Fuelling an Investigative Mindset: The Importance of Pre-Interview Planning in Police Interviews with Suspects' (Chin, Milne and Bull, 2022)

In their research, published in *Psychology, Crime, and Law*, Chin et al. (2022: 7) present the following information about their participants in the methodology section of their paper.

Participants

The participants were 596 police investigators (439 males and 157 females) from the Singapore Police Force recruited by convenience and snowball sampling. The participants were aged between 22 and 56 years (M = 34.37, SD = 6.43), were actively conducting investigative interviews and were of different ranks, ranging from Sergeant to Deputy Superintendent of Police.1 Of 596 participants, 42 were Sergeants, 71 Staff Sergeants, 96 Senior Staff Sergeants, 144 Station Inspectors, 164 Inspectors, 70 Assistant Superintendent of Police and 8 Deputy Superintendent of Police. There was one missing value; 85 per cent of the participants reported having up to 15 years of experience as criminal investigators (106 of these having less than one year, 210 between 1 and 5 years, 122 between 6 and 10 years, 71 between 11 and 15 years, 44 between 16 and 20 years, plus 43 more than 20 years).

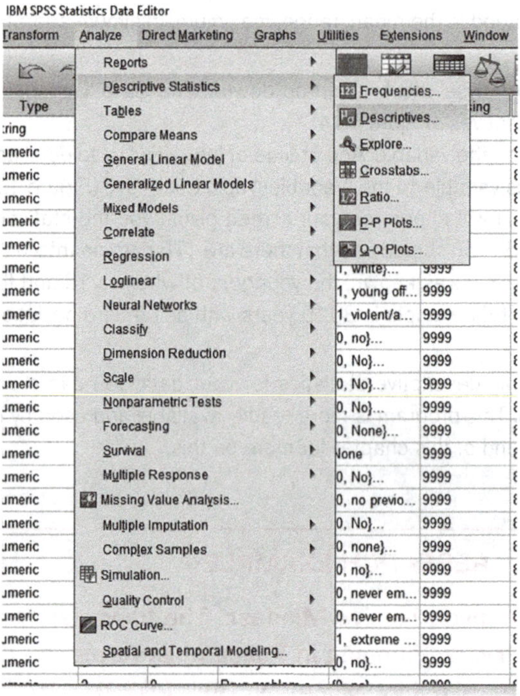

Figure 16.4 Reprint Courtesy of IBM Corporation ©

To write up the descriptive statistics you have just produced in SPSS, you would say, 'The mean age of the sample was 30.15 years (min. 16 years, max. 60 years, S.D. 9.76).' Note that SPSS tables and output should never be included in the write-up of your research but may, if you wish, be included in any appendices. Box 16.2 gives an example of how one set of authors wrote their descriptive statistics in a peer-reviewed journal article.

You can find other information, such as the gender breakdown of a sample, by choosing 'Frequencies' instead of 'Descriptives' at stage 1.

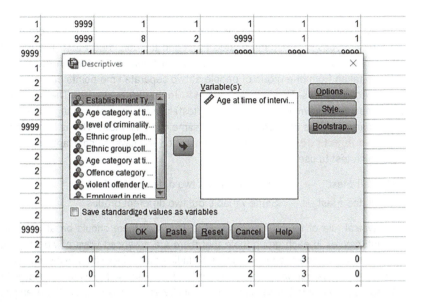

Figure 16.5 Reprint Courtesy of IBM Corporation ©

Figure 16.6 Reprint Courtesy of IBM Corporation ©

We strongly recommend that you spend some time looking at your data with the aid of descriptive statistics. This will help you understand much more about your data and will also help you work out which statistical tests you may use later in the analysis of your data. For example, if in your data you have two age groups, and the descriptive statistics highlight that only 10 of your sample fall into one age group while 120 fall into the other age groups, you could be certain that running parametric tests using age as a variable would not be suitable.

SIGNIFICANCE TESTING: THE *T*-TEST (COMPARING SCORES TO TEST FOR DIFFERENCES)

A *t*-test is typically used to compare two means to see if they are equal or different. There are two types of *t*-test: the related *t*-test and the unrelated *t*-test. The related *t*-test (sometimes known as the matched or paired *t*-test) is used when comparing the means taken from one group of people at two separate time points or under two different circumstances. This is known as a **within-subjects design**. The unrelated *t*-test (sometimes known as the unmatched *t*-test) is used when comparing the means of two separate groups of people under the same circumstances. This is known as a **between-subjects design**. Knowing which design you have is important in order to decide which test to use.

Related *t*-test	Same group *but* two different variables
Unrelated *t*-test	Same variable *but* two different groups

While a typical rule of thumb for statistical tests is that there should be at least 30 participants/scores in each group (note that there are advanced ways of working out the minimum sample size needed for research studies, particularly vital when using more advanced techniques, but we do not cover these in this book), the *t*-test may be used with smaller samples than this, but sample sizes should be as equal as possible (for example, if you have 20 scores in one group and 70 in another, the *t*-test is not a good measure).

Remember: the *t*-test may only be used for comparing the means of two sets of scores.

Running an Unrelated *T*-Test in SPSS

Website Student document

Database: SPSS dataset

Below are instructions on running an unrelated *t*-test, which you should use to familiarise yourself further with SPSS (Figures 16.7 to 16.10). Later in the chapter you will be asked to run a related *t*-test using the dataset in the support material, and you will be able to find further guidance on running that type of *t*-test on there.

> **BOX 16.3 RESEARCH EXAMPLE**
>
> In Chapter 14 we mentioned that it is sometimes possible to work on data collected by other researchers. If your supervisors and/or lecturers have conducted research in an area that interests you, you may wish to discuss with them the possibility of having access to their datasets. Sometimes there are restrictions which mean that data cannot be shared, but it doesn't hurt to ask!
>
> **The project**
>
> Claire (an undergraduate student) had heard that Laura (a potential dissertation supervisor) was looking for a dissertation student to work with her on a research project for the Birmingham Youth Offending Team. The project entailed

investigating the effectiveness of a 12-week music programme for young people in contact with the Youth Offending Team. The aims of the programme were: to develop the creative, expressive and musical ability of children and young people; to improve children's and young people's self-efficacy and resilience; and to improve the level of compliance with court orders among project participants.

Laura and a PhD research assistant collected quantitative data on sentence compliance, resilience, self-efficacy, musical development, attitudes and behaviour, and well-being. Claire obtained university ethics approval and Youth Offending Service approval to process and analyse the data, and was able to use these data for her dissertation.

Claire's work contributed to a final report for the Youth Offending Team (Caulfield, Simpson and Jacobs, 2016). Excitingly, the findings from the research were highlighted in a government enquiry report on the impact of the arts on health and well-being: see www.artshealthandwellbeing.org.uk/appg-inquiry/Publications/Creative_Health_The_Short_Report.pdf

Claire's research

Survey measures were administered to the young people to complete before and after the youth music programme, measuring participants' self-efficacy, resilience, musical ability, attitudes and behaviour and their overall well-being. At the time Claire was completing her dissertation, project data were unavailable on sentence compliance, and so her dissertation focused on the above measures. Let us focus on one of the measures to help us think about how Claire should have worked with the data.

Measuring resilience: the Brief Resilience Scale

One of the aims of the project was to improve young people's resilience. Resilience may be defined as 'the capacity of a system, enterprise or person to [find] and maintain its core purpose and integrity in the face of dramatically changed circumstances' (Zolli and Healy, 2012: 6). The Brief Resilience Scale (Smith et al., 2008) is a reliable and valid measure suitable for use in evaluating programmes that seek to promote resilience (Windle, Bennett and Noyes, 2011). The scale contains six items, such as 'I have a hard time making it through stressful events', which participants score on a Likert scale from 1 to 5 (strongly disagree–strongly agree). The total score is divided by the number of questions answered to give a final score.

Research question

Claire wants to know whether taking part in the music programme has any effect on the self-reported resilience of young people. The Brief Resilience Scale was completed by participants both before and after taking part in the music programme to try to answer the research question.

1   What is the independent variable?
2   What is the dependent variable?

Claire takes the Brief Resilience Scale data collected from participants at the beginning of the programme and 12 weeks later. Answers to questions on the scale are recorded using a five-point Likert scale. Claire inputs these scores (1–5) into SPSS in numerical form.

3   What type of data does Claire have?
4   What statistical test should Claire use to see whether there is a statistically significant difference between resilience before taking part in the music programme and after taking part in the music programme?
5   Why should Claire use this test?

If Claire were to test the participants for a third time at a later date she would need to use a different statistical test (a repeated measure ANOVA – these are not discussed in this book).

If Claire wanted to compare scores from young people after completing the training course with scores from a **matched control group**, she could use an independent samples *t*-test.

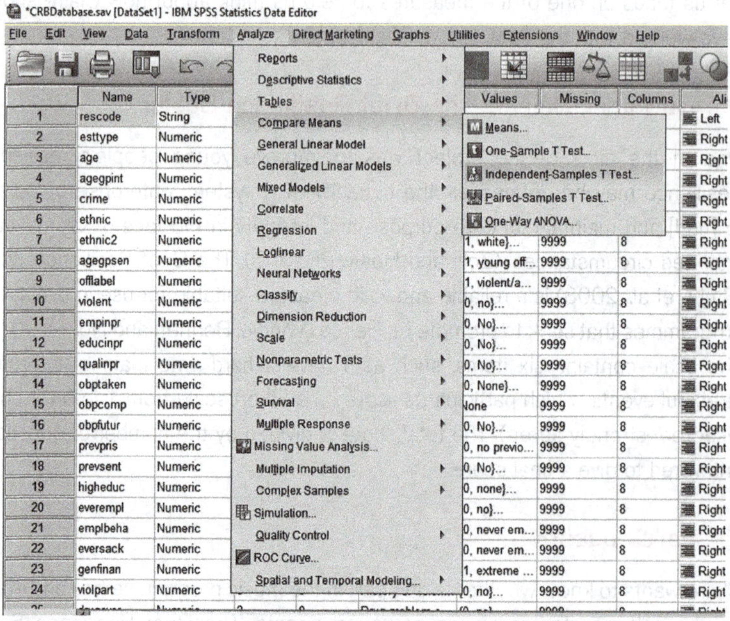

Figure 16.7 Reprint Courtesy of IBM Corporation ©

ANALYSING THE DATA: QUANTITATIVE ANALYSIS

Question: Which group of participants has completed more Offending Behaviour Programmes: those recorded as having low or high levels of criminality?

This question may be answered using an independent samples *t*-test in SPSS. In order to conduct it, go to

Analyze > Compare Means > Independent-Samples T Test …

First, in the 'Independent-Samples T Test' window, select and move the dependent variable [Offending Behaviour courses completed (obpcomp)] to the 'Test Variable(s):' list box and move the independent variable [level of criminality (crime)] to the 'Grouping Variable:' text box.

Second, click on 'Define Groups' to tell SPSS the code numbers for the groups to substitute for the question marks.

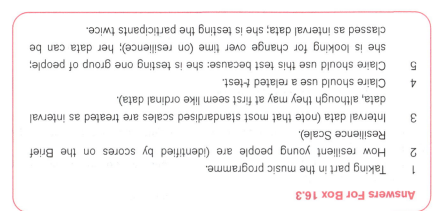

Answers For Box 16.3

1. Taking part in the music programme.
2. How resilient young people are (identified by scores on the Brief Resilience Scale).
3. Interval data (note that most standardised scales are treated as interval data, although they may at first seem like ordinal data).
4. Claire should use a related *t*-test.
5. Claire should use this test because: she is testing one group of people; she is looking for change over time (on resilience); her data can be classed as interval data; she is testing the participants twice.

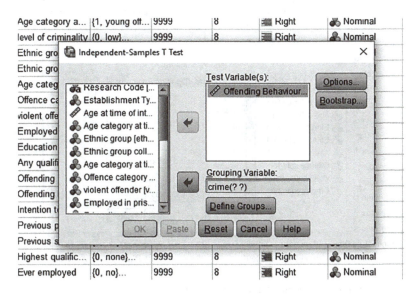

Figure 16.8 Reprint Courtesy of IBM Corporation ©

298 CRIMINOLOGICAL SKILLS AND RESEARCH FOR BEGINNERS

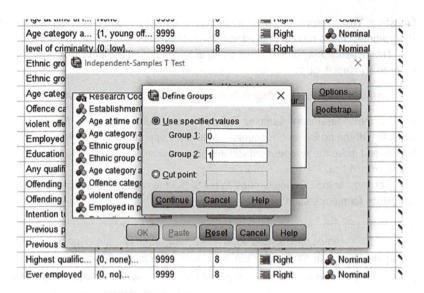

Figure 16.9 Reprint Courtesy of IBM Corporation ©

0 is the value for 'low' and '1' for the variable [crime]. Type these values in the 'Group 1:' and 'Group 2:' text boxes.

If you do not recall the code numbers for the groups, look on the Variable View page in the SPSS Data Editor.

Click on the 'Continue' button to close the dialogue box.

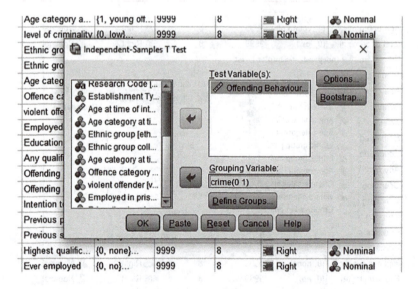

Figure 16.10 Reprint Courtesy of IBM Corporation ©

ANALYSING THE DATA: QUANTITATIVE ANALYSIS   299

Note that the code values for the independent (Grouping) variable replace the question marks following the variable name.

Click 'OK' to produce the output.

The results output in SPSS is reproduced in Figure 16.11.

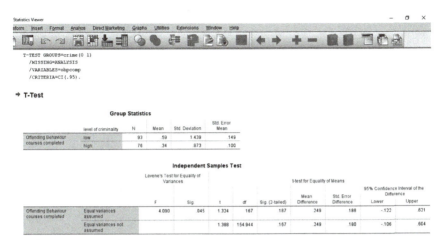

Figure 16.11 Reprint Courtesy of IBM Corporation ©

Figures 16.12 to 16.15 tell you how to interpret the output.

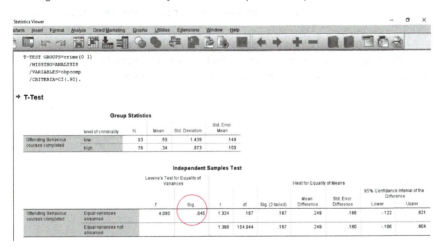

Figure 16.12 Reprint Courtesy of IBM Corporation ©

The independent samples *t*-test assumes that the different samples you are comparing have similar variance (refer back to the section above on homogeneity of variance to remind yourself what this means). This assumption is tested with the *Levene Test for Equality of Variances*. The Levene Test is itself a test of the null hypothesis that the variances of the two groups are equal.

If we fail to reject the null hypothesis because the p-value or sig. for the statistic is greater than 0.05, we satisfy the requirement for equal variances. If we reject the null hypothesis because the p-value or sig. for the statistic is less than or equal to 0.05, we do not meet the requirement for equal variances.

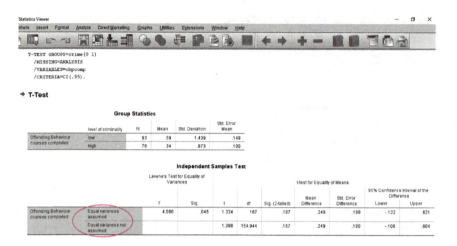

Figure 16.13 Reprint Courtesy of IBM Corporation ©

If we satisfy the assumption of equal variances, we use the output on the row titled 'Equal variances assumed'.

If we do not satisfy the assumption of equal variances, we use the output on the row titled 'Equal variances not assumed'. This calculation is based on a formula for the t-test that takes into account the differences in variance measures.

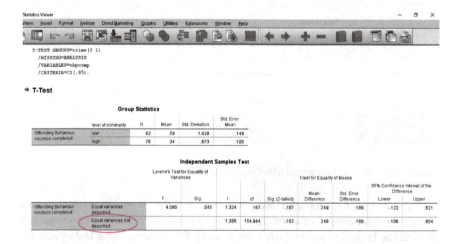

Figure 16.14 Reprint Courtesy of IBM Corporation ©

In this problem, the probability associated with the *Levene Test for Equality of Variances* (.045) is less than 0.05.

We reject the null hypothesis that the variances are equal, concluding that the 'Equal variances not assumed' formula for the independent samples *t*-test should be used for the analysis.

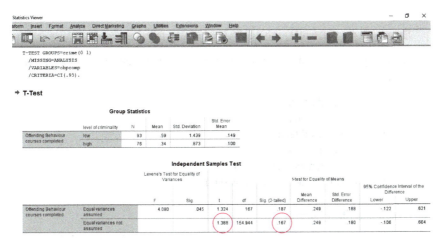

Figure 16.15 Reprint Courtesy of IBM Corporation ©

Having determined which formula for the *t*-test on which to base the hypothesis test, we look to the statistical output for the *t*-test.

The research **hypothesis** implied by the question is that the mean 'number of Offending Behaviour Programmes (OBP) completed' [crime] will be different for participants recorded as having low or high levels of criminality.

The **null hypothesis** for this research hypothesis would state that the mean number of OBP completed by 'low offenders' is equal to the mean for 'high offenders'.

We make our decision about the null hypothesis by comparing the probability of the test statistic (t) to the level of significance (0.05).

Notice that the significance is labelled 'two-tailed'. As the question above did not state a direction to the relationship (i.e. it simply stated that there would be a difference in the number of Offending Behaviour Programmes completed by those recorded as having low levels of criminality and those recorded as having high levels of criminality, but did not state which group would have completed more), then we use this value. However, if the research hypothesis stated a direction to the relationship, this would require us to compute the one-tailed probability. This is computed by simply dividing the two-tailed significance in half (so here, for example, this would be 0.167/2 = 0.084).

Interpreting the results

As the two-tailed probability of the t statistic (t = 1.388) was p = 1.167, greater than 0.05, the null hypothesis of equal means was not rejected, and we do not have support for the research hypothesis. Based on this analysis, we cannot support that there was any difference between the number of Offending Behaviour Programmes completed by those recorded as having low levels of criminality and those recorded as having high levels of criminality.

BOX 16.4   REPORTING STATISTICAL TESTS

When reporting statistical tests the following information should always be presented:

- value of statistical test;
- degrees of freedom;
- one- or two-tailed test;
- the observed p-value;
- whether the test was significant;
- the direction of the significant finding.

Look at the *t*-test example given above.

You would report the present results as follows:

> The mean number of Offending Behaviour Programmes completed by those recorded as having low levels of criminality ($M = 0.59$) was not significantly different from that of those recorded as having high levels of criminality (($M = 0.34$), (t (df 155) $= 1.388$, $p = .17$).

Remember: you should not present the SPSS output tables when writing up your analysis. You should interpret the results and not expect the reader to do this. The only exception to this is when you are asked to do this by your lecturers to show the details of your workings.

Related *T*-Test

Now that you are becoming familiar with SPSS and running basic statistical tests, have a go at running a related *t*-test on the dataset found in the support material, following the brief guidance below. Practise interpreting the output and writing it up. You can find the answers in the support material.

Run a related *t*-test to compare the mean scores on participants' assessed levels of motivation to change before and after a course of intervention.

> **BRIEF INSTRUCTIONS: RELATED *T*-TEST**
>
> Analyze > Compare Means > Paired-Samples T Test …

Website Student web links

Running a paired-samples t-test

Before you read the guidance on the website, see if you can identify what you need to know to run the *t*-test.

SIGNIFICANCE TESTING: CHI-SQUARE (COMPARING DIFFERENCES BETWEEN FREQUENCY DATA)

A Chi-squared test is used when we wish to compare nominal data (to look for a relationship/correlation).

> **BOX 16.5 RESEARCH EXAMPLE**
>
> Siân is a third-year criminology student. As part of her dissertation research she wants to investigate whether the men and women at her university have different attitudes towards people with mental health problems.
>
> 1   What is the independent variable?
> 2   What is the dependent variable?
>
> She records participants' responses and classifies them as either 'positive attitude', 'neutral attitude' or 'negative attitude', and codes these as 0, 1 and 2 when she inputs them into SPSS.
>
> 3   What type of data does she have?
> 4   What statistical test should Siân use to test whether there is a statistically significant difference between the attitudes towards people with mental health problems of the men and women on her course?
> 5   Why should Siân use this test?

Running a Chi-Square Test in SPSS

Using a Chi-square test, we wish to find out whether the following statement is true: 'In the sample dataset found on the companion website, levels of criminality [crime] are related to employment behaviour [emplbeha]' (see Figures 16.16 to 16.22).

304 CRIMINOLOGICAL SKILLS AND RESEARCH FOR BEGINNERS

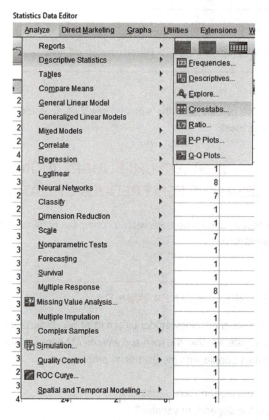

Figure 16.16 Reprint Courtesy of IBM Corporation ©

You can conduct a Chi-square test of independence in cross-tabulation of SPSS by selecting

Analyze > Descriptive Statistics > Crosstabs ...

Answers For Box 16.5

1. Gender.
2. Attitude towards people with mental health problems.
3. Nominal data.
4. Siân should use a Chi-squared test.
5. Siân should use this test because: she has two groups of people (women and men); she wants to do a between-groups comparison (of attitudes); she has categorised her data so that it is nominal data; and the variable she is comparing the groups on (the dependent variable – in this case attitudes) has more than two categories (positive, neutral and negative).

ANALYSING THE DATA: QUANTITATIVE ANALYSIS 305

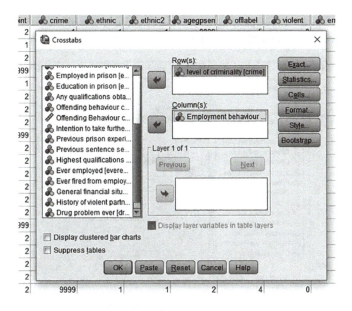

Figure 16.17 Reprint Courtesy of IBM Corporation ©

First, select and move the variables for the question to the 'Row(s)' and 'Column(s)' list boxes.

The variable mentioned first in the problem, namely level of criminality, is used as the independent variable and is moved to the 'Column(s)' list box.

The variable mentioned second in the problem, namely employment behaviour, is used as the dependent variable and is moved to the 'Row(s)' list box.

Second, click on the 'Statistics' button to request the test statistic.

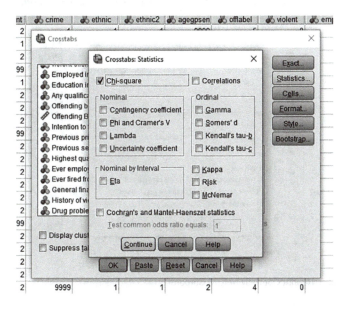

Figure 16.18 Reprint Courtesy of IBM Corporation ©

First, click on 'Chi-square' to request the Chi-square test of independence. Second, click on the 'Continue' button to close the Statistics dialogue box.

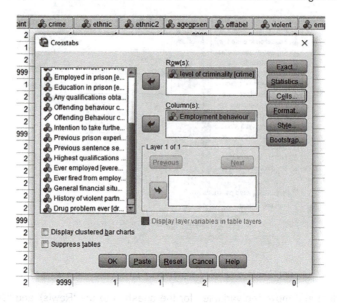

Figure 16.19 Reprint Courtesy of IBM Corporation ©

Now click on the 'Cells ... ' button to specify the contents in the cells of the Crosstabs table.

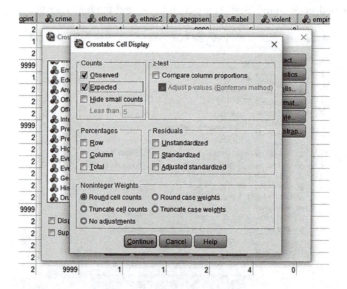

Figure 16.20 Reprint Courtesy of IBM Corporation ©

Make sure both 'Observed' and 'Expected' in the 'Counts' section in the 'Crosstabs: Cell Display' dialogue box are checked and click on 'Continue' and 'OK' buttons.

Click on 'Continue' and 'continue' again to run the test (Figure 16.21).

| | Expected Count | | 21.0 | 10.0 |

Chi-Square Tests

	Value	df	Asymptotic Significance (2-sided)
Pearson Chi-Square	19.843[a]	5	.001
Likelihood Ratio	20.803	5	.001
Linear-by-Linear Association	15.520	1	.000
N of Valid Cases	169		

a. 1 cells (8.3%) have expected count less than 5. The minimum expected count is 4.44.

Figure 16.21 Reprint Courtesy of IBM Corporation ©

The Chi-square test of independence requires that the expected frequency for all cells be 5.0 or higher.

The cross-tabulated table contains the count and expected counts for each cell in the table.

We can see that one of the expected counts is less than 5. However, Chi-square tests are still valid provided that none is less than 1, and at least 80 per cent of the expected counts are equal to or greater than 5.

As four out of the five counts in the table above are greater than five, we can still use a Chi-squared test (Figure 16.22).

The probability of the Chi-square test statistic (Chi-square = 19.843) was $p < 0.001$, less than the level of significance of 0.05.

The null hypothesis that differences in employment behaviour are independent of differences in levels of criminality (the actual frequencies are equal to the expected frequencies in the cross-tabulated table) is rejected.

In other words, the research hypothesis that differences in employment behaviour are related to differences in levels of criminality is supported by this analysis.

The answer to the question is 'True'.

If the probability of the test statistic is less than or equal to the probability of the alpha error rate (0.05), we reject the null hypothesis and conclude that our data support the research hypothesis. We conclude that there is a relationship between the variables.

	N	Percent	N	Percent	N	Percent
level of criminality * Employment behaviour	169	84.5%	31	15.5%	200	100.0%

level of criminality * Employment behaviour Crosstabulation

			Employment behaviour						Total
			never employed	very poor	poor	average	good	very good	
level of criminality	low	Count	6	4	11	22	39	12	94
		Expected Count	11.7	5.6	11.1	27.3	30.6	7.8	94.0
	high	Count	15	6	9	27	16	2	75
		Expected Count	9.3	4.4	8.9	21.7	24.4	6.2	75.0
Total		Count	21	10	20	49	55	14	169
		Expected Count	21.0	10.0	20.0	49.0	55.0	14.0	169.0

Chi-Square Tests

	Value	df	Asymptotic Significance (2-sided)
Pearson Chi-Square	19.843[a]	5	.001
Likelihood Ratio	20.803	5	.001
Linear-by-Linear Association	15.520	1	.000
N of Valid Cases	169		

a. 1 cells (8.3%) have expected count less than 5. The minimum expected count is 4.44.

Figure 16.22 Reprint Courtesy of IBM Corporation ©

If the probability of the test statistic is greater than the probability of the alpha error rate (0.05), we fail to reject the null hypothesis. We conclude that there is no relationship between the variables, i.e. they are independent. The alpha error rate refers to the probability of what is called a type one error. At this stage we do not suggest that you focus on this point but, put simply, this refers to the chances of the results being incorrect and the hypothesis being incorrectly rejected.

DECIDING NOT TO RUN A STATISTICAL TEST

In Chapter 13 you will find a case study about the Tech4PrisonLeavers project. As a pilot study this project initially aimed to engage 25 people. The project aimed to compare any changes experienced by participants over the course of the project, including any changes to their well-being. Not unusually for a pilot project, or indeed any research project, fewer participants completed the questionnaires than originally anticipated. All 23 participants who began the project completed the questionnaires at the start of the project, but we only had data on the well-being of 11 participants at the end of the project (a bit disappointing, but that is the reality of research sometimes and we did learn some good lessons). We could not therefore run a reliable parametric test (see our discussion earlier in this chapter on the 'typical rule of thumb for statistical tests'). We could have decided to run a **non-parametric** test. However, the research report we were writing was for a non-technical audience so we decided that we should keep it simple and just report the means at the start and end of the project. This told the people reading the report – in this case the project funders – what they needed to know, without over-claiming about what the limited data could conclude. This is how we summarised the findings about well-being:

> 23 men completed the wellbeing scale at enrolment. At the end of the project 11 men completed the wellbeing scale. There was an improvement in participant's well-being over the course of the project (Time 1 mean = 23.6; Time 2 mean = 27.9). While mean scores improved on all measures between time 1 (start of project) and time 2 (end of project), which is promising, there was insufficient data to test if the findings are likely to be generalisable beyond this participant group.
>
> (Caulfield et al., 2023)

We really thought about these decisions, and they were right for this project and the people we were writing the report for. It may of course be different for you as a student and you should always discuss with your tutor or supervisor the decisions you make around analysing your data.

The Digital Poverty Alliance have published a white paper based on our research, calling for the UK Ministry of Justice to look at a wider programme of support for prison leavers with access to devices, connectivity and digital skills training. You can read the white paper here, including the findings of our research: https://digitalpovertyalliance.org/projects/tech4prisonleavers/

USING EXCEL AND OTHER PROGRAMS

Learning to use SPSS is a highly useful skill. It is though important to note that a number of other statistical programs exist, including those that are open source and free to access. If you have grasped SPSS and are self-motivated and willing to put the time in, you are likely to be able to teach yourself the basics of some of these other programs using online resources (e.g. YouTube tutorials and online guides). For example, R is a free, open source statistical software and programming language. R is particularly useful for cleaning and preparing data and for data visualisation.

SPSS is widely used in academic settings but businesses and other organisations do not use this program as much. Being able to talk about your ability to use statistical programs such as SPSS will no doubt boost your employability, but you can also apply these skills to analysing data using very widely available programs such as Microsoft Excel. Within Microsoft Excel it is very straightforward to produce descriptive statistics, graphs and other useful representations of your data. Note that if you have collected your data using an online survey platform (e.g. Jisc Online Surveys – see Chapter 13) you can download the data in a CSV. file format for use in SPSS or Excel or open source programs like R. If you want to run the types of statistical analyses described in this chapter, it is also possible using Excel, but takes a little bit more working out than the relatively straightforward sequence of actions within SPSS.

If you simply want to calculate the mean of your data, this is quick and easy using Excel. There are several ways to do this and we've provided two examples. We're assuming some familiarity with Excel and you should follow these basic steps:

Once you have inputted your data into Excel you can use the AVERAGE function. Select the data you wish to calculate the mean of (e.g. the column or row).

1   Under the Formulas tab select 'Insert Function'.
2   Select the function called AVERAGE.
3   Add the cell range when prompted.

If you prefer, you can type the following into any cell, adding the first cell in place of the n (e.g. B1) and last cell (e.g. B15) of the data you wish to calculate the mean of:

=AVERAGE(Cell 1:Cell n)

If you want to calculate full descriptive statistics and statistical tests like those in this chapter, you will need to load the Analysis ToolPak to your existing Excel. You can find helpful guides to installing and using the Excel Analysis Toolpak on the Microsoft Support website.

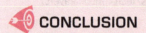

CONCLUSION

Analysing your data statistically does not require a natural talent for mathematics. It simply requires logical thought in considering what data you have, or plan to collect, and an ability to consider what statistical tests may be appropriate for your data. It is this point that is the key to conducting quantitative analysis – using tests that are inappropriate for your data will ultimately not tell you anything important or relevant. Once you understand the basics of quantitative analysis and can logically identify appropriate statistical tests, the rest is very straightforward owing to the existence of programs like SPSS. This chapter has sought to provide a step-by-step, but very introductory, guide to some of the key concepts in quantitative analysis. The guidance outlined in this chapter provides the first step in seeing how straightforward quantitative analysis can be. We also hope that by completing the tasks in this chapter, using the dataset provided in the accompanying support material, you will also experience just how satisfying it can be when you see a statistically significant result.

 **FURTHER READING**

We recommend the following texts for those students seeking to work further with quantitative analysis:

Bachman, R., Paternoster, R. and Wilson T. (2021) *Statistics for Criminology and Criminal Justice*, fifth edition, Thousand Oaks, CA: Sage.
Field, A. (2017) *Discovering Statistics Using IBM SPSS Statistics*, fifth edition, Thousand Oaks, CA: Sage.
Gray, D. and Kinnear, P. (2011) *IBM SPSS Statistics 19 Made Simple*, London: Psychology Press.
Howitt, D. and Cramer, D. (2017) *Introduction to SPSS in Psychology*, seventh edition, Harlow: Pearson.

 KEY LEARNING POINTS

- Understanding statistical concepts and terminology is crucial for you as a researcher so that you can understand and critique other people's quantitative research and so that you can decide which statistical tests are the most appropriate to use with your data.
- When used correctly, conducting your own statistical analysis allows you to provide much more robust evidence of any relationships between the variables you have measured than simply presenting data from questionnaires in percentage terms or in graphs.
- You do not have to be good at mathematics to be good at statistical analysis, mainly because programs like SPSS exist. However, you do need to be able to choose an appropriate test for your data, follow instructions on running this in SPSS and interpret the output. This chapter has explained the basics of these processes.
- This chapter has also made you aware of the possibilities of analysing data using other programs, such as Excel, and more about that can be found in the support material.

REFERENCES

Capezza, N.M. and Arriaga, X. B. (2008) 'Factors Associated with Acceptance of Psychological Aggression Against Women', *Violence Against Women*, 14(6): 612–633. https://doi.org/10.1177/1077801208319004
Caulfield, L.S., Simpson, E. and Jacobs, C. (2016) *An Evaluation of the Youth Offending Service Youth Music Project*, Birmingham: Birmingham Youth Offending Service.

Caulfield, L.S., Hadjisergis, K., Stonard, K. and Sadlier, S. (2023) *Evaluation of Tech4PrisonLeavers*. Unpublished grant report for the Digital Poverty Alliance.

Chin, J. Milne, R. and Bull, R. (2022, 28 October) 'Fuelling an Investigative Mindset: The Importance of Pre-Interview Planning in Police Interviews with Suspects', *Psychology, Crime & Law*, 1–25. https://doi.org/10.1080/1068316X.2022.2139829

Smith, B.W., Dalen, J., Wiggins, K., Tooley, E., Christopher, P. and Bernard, J. (2008) 'The Brief Resilience Scale: Assessing the Ability to Bounce Back', *International Journal of Behavioural Medicine*, 15: 194–200.

Windle, G., Bennett, K.M. and Noyes, J. (2011) 'A Methodological Review of Resilience Measurement Scales', *Health and Quality of Life Outcomes*, 9(8): 1–18.

Zolli, A. and Healy, A.M. (2012) *Resilience: Why Things Bounce Back*, New York: Free Press.

Chapter 17

Analysing the data
Qualitative analysis

GOALS OF THIS CHAPTER

At the end of reading this chapter and by completing the online resources that accompany it, you will be able to:

1. acknowledge the importance of transcription as part of the analysis process;
2. recognise that the work put into data collection is worthless if robust data analysis techniques are not applied;
3. understand the process of conducting a **thematic analysis** and feel confident to put this into practice;
4. write up the process of conducting a thematic analysis;
5. write up the results of a thematic analysis.

OVERVIEW

- While many modes of qualitative analysis exist, thematic analysis is one of the most commonly used methods of qualitative data analysis.
- Having a high level of familiarity with your data is key to conducting a successful thematic analysis, and the transcription process is often fundamental to increasing data familiarity.
- The process of thematic analysis involves applying brief verbal descriptions to the data, known as coding.
- The aim of the thematic analysis is to collate codes into overarching themes that represent the body of data.
- This chapter provides examples from real research to demonstrate how to conduct and write up qualitative analyses.
- Many researchers now use Computer Assisted Qualitative Data Analysis Software (CAQDAS) to aid the structure and management of qualitative datasets.

INTRODUCTION

Qualitative research methods have at times been criticised for a lack of robustness. Indeed, it is true that some people see qualitative research as an easy option – these are typically the people who do qualitative research badly. However, when done well, qualitative research can provide a depth and quality of information that is simply not available using quantitative techniques. As discussed in Chapter 12, choosing appropriate data-collection techniques is essential, but all of this is worthless if robust data analysis techniques are not applied.

It is not possible within one chapter to cover the various methods of qualitative analysis in sufficient detail. Therefore, what you will find in this chapter is a focus on one method of qualitative analysis that is widely used by criminological researchers: thematic analysis. Thematic analysis provides a useful introduction to qualitative analysis and is a method that is particularly suited to the analysis of a range of qualitative data when the researcher seeks to elicit key themes from the entire body of data. Other well-documented methods of qualitative data analysis used by criminological researchers include discourse analysis, content analysis (see Chapter 18 for a discussion of critical **discourse analysis** and qualitative content analysis), conversation analysis and narrative analysis (among others), and each serves a different purpose. This chapter will provide guidance on how to analyse data using thematic analysis and offer real research examples for you to consider. This chapter applies primarily to the data-collection techniques discussed in Chapter 12, with most of the examples throughout this chapter relating to interview and focus group data. However, the lessons apply to other forms of qualitative data as well.

METHODS OF ANALYSIS

Many novice researchers initially approach qualitative analysis through a process called thematic analysis. Thematic analysis is one of the most commonly used methods of qualitative data analysis, and is not dependent on specific theory or approaches to data collection. In this way thematic analysis is suitable for most types of qualitative data and provides a structured approach to working with qualitative data. However, this is not simply a method for new researchers, but one favoured by many experienced researchers, including the authors of this book.

Like many forms of qualitative data analysis, thematic analysis is easy to do badly. The overall aim of thematic analysis is to identify the key themes from the data and it is important that you do not fall into the trap of identifying superficial themes or 'cherry-picking' quotes from the data. Superficial analysis is not an appropriate level of analysis and cannot result in themes that accurately represent the data a researcher has collected. To do justice to the data collected, researchers must engage with a rigorous approach to analysis. For thematic analysis, it is vital to be highly familiar with the data before formally beginning the analysis. For this reason we strongly recommend that researchers conduct their own interviews, focus groups or other methods of data collection, and that they also transcribe their own data (although see below for our thoughts on working with auto-transcription when you conduct interviews and other data collection online). Researchers who do not do this are placed at a significant disadvantage, but to an extent this can be addressed by reading the transcripts thoroughly, several times, before beginning the analysis. In order to maximise familiarity with the data we suggest all researchers do this, whether they have collected and transcribed the data or not.

TRANSCRIBING YOUR DATA

As noted above, transcribing your own data is one of the best ways of becoming highly familiar with the data you have collected, and this process of familiarisation is vital to successful data analysis. Transcription is the process of transferring recordings into written form and there are a variety of methods of transcribing audio and visual recordings, although generally these methods are more fully documented and better developed for audio recordings. There is no denying that transcription takes a long time, but rather than seeing this as a chore we encourage you to regard the transcription process as a fundamental part of becoming familiar with your data.

Broadly, all methods of transcription may be classed as either **naturalism**, where every utterance and pause is transcribed, or **denaturalism**, where pauses are removed, grammar corrected and even non-standard accents standardised. The method researchers choose will depend upon the mode of analysis they are using and the decisions they make about which method of transcription to use must be based on ensuring that their transcriptions are suitable for purpose. For example, if you were investigating the process of conversation between two speakers, simply transcribing the literal words used by the speakers would be inadequate. However, if you were interested in how prisoners describe a day of their life then a literal transcription, including only the words spoken, may well be sufficient.

For those seeking a process of transcription where it is important to record pauses and other features of language (also known as paralinguistic features of language), we recommend the Jefferson method of transcription. The Jefferson method is a widely used method of transcription that includes some focus on utterances, pauses and the cross-over of speakers. Howitt and Cramer (2024) provide a useful guide to Jefferson transcription, and Oliver, Serovich and Mason (2005) take a useful reflective look at transcription more generally. You can also find a number of guides online and some examples in the support material.

However, many researchers – often including those conducting thematic analysis – do not follow a set method of data transcription, opting instead to devise their own method and choosing which features of speech and language to record. This is typically suitable when it is not essential to record all of the paralinguistic features of a recording.

In the example in Box 17.1, what is spoken by the interviewee is in italics, with a number of shorthand symbols created by the researcher to represent key paralinguistic features of the interviews. For example, (…) was used to represent where words were unclear on the recording, pauses such as 'erm' were recorded, and '…' was used to denote pauses in speech. This level of detail was sufficient for the thematic analysis that the researcher then conducted.

Website Student document

Examples of transcriptions

BOX 17.1 TRANSCRIBING INTERVIEWS

The excerpt below provides an example of how one of the authors of this book transcribed 43 interview recordings.

> The 2277 minutes of interviews were transcribed by the researcher into Microsoft Word. Paralinguistic features of the language within the recordings were not transcribed in full, although, for example, pauses and errors of speech were noted. Some interviews were transcribed in the days directly following each interview. However, due to the time practicalities a larger number of interviews had to be transcribed a considerable amount of time after the interviews had taken place. Transcription of this amount of data is both daunting and immensely time-consuming, but necessary if each participant's contribution is to be successfully represented (Atkinson, 1998). Furthermore, transcription is a vital part of the research process, whereby listening, transcription and reading of the data serve to re-familiarise the researcher with the interview data and the mood and emotional responses of the participants to particular questions. Indeed it is suggested that 'the closer you can get to the text itself, the closer you are to its meaning' (Atkinson, 1998: 57). To improve the level of familiarity with the data, interview recordings were listened to again and transcripts read, prior to beginning analysis.
>
> (Caulfield, 2012: 57)

The above excerpt is taken from research where interviews were conducted with women in prison. The interviewer asked women about their lives and histories of offending and did not require a naturalistic approach. The process of transcription described above resulted in transcripts that looked like this:

So by the time you got your probation order this was before you got …
This was before we got married. I've never told Mum and Dad.

But did they find out about …
They did. I told them before we got married. Just before I went to court. Because he was so worried that if I went to court and got sentenced to prison, erm, that he couldn't tell Mum and Dad.

Right, okay.
Or he wouldn't be able to cope if he didn't know about it.

So at this point everyone was then told about the debt?

> *Yeah. They still weren't told about the total amount of debt. (...) And, £12,000 on a wedding. I think about going and buying the wedding dress and like £1500 for a dress, £500 each for bridesmaids' dresses. Now I look back and think 'oh my god, what such a complete waste of money', but at the time I was just in this huge big whirlwind of it all. ...*

As discussed in Chapters 12 and 15, qualitative data are often now collected online. Platforms such as Microsoft Teams, Zoom, and Google Meet have built-in recording and transcription capabilities. If, for example, you are conducting an interview online, you can use the functionality on Microsoft Teams to display a live transcription (designed to be useful for deaf or hard of hearing participants and also useful for participants in noisy places). We typically opt to have the transcript created after the interview as with most participants we are working with the live transcription is a distraction (see note below on transcription errors). It is possible to produce transcripts in a variety of different languages to match the language the interview is conducted in. There are different ways of capturing recordings and creating transcripts, depending which platform you are using. As the technical capabilities and instructions change quite regularly, we have not reproduced them here, but advise you to look at the online Microsoft, Zoom or Google Help support pages which contain step-by-step guides. Whichever platform you are using, be sure to practise recording an interview and producing a transcript before any real data collection using these tools. The online call always needs to be recorded for a transcript to be produced and some platforms require you to select a transcription production option at the beginning of the recording. Always ensure you have checked that the system you are using is compatible with the data security and ethical approvals of your university.

We stated earlier in this chapter that transcription is an important part of the process of analysis to ensure researchers are really familiar with their data. However, when collecting data online we do use these built-in transcription capabilities. They save us time – but a word of warning: the transcripts automatically produced are not good enough quality for transcription. They tend to contain many errors and so it is vital for researchers to go through them and turn them into an accurate transcript ready for coding. Going through each autogenerated transcript and ensuring it is accurate also means you will be really familiar with each transcript before you embark on coding your transcripts.

We find these auto-generated transcripts contain some errors in typical speech, and are very inaccurate when interviewees are discussing specific terms or technical language. Have a look at this brief example from an interview one of us recently conducted with a member of prison staff:

> "I was like yeah, absolutely all for that to support you in regards to rattling people."

What was actually said was,

> "I was like yeah, absolutely all for that to support you in regards to ROTL'ing people."[1]

Rattling as a slang term can be used to mean to frighten people or to describe withdrawal and cravings from opioids. The Prison Officer was actually talking about Release on Temporary Licence (ROTL). ROTL refers to a prisoner being able to leave prison for a short time for a limited number of reasons, including to take part in paid or unpaid work and to help individuals to settle back into the community. Only some people in prison are eligible for ROTL and all individuals who are eligible for ROTL must meet strict risk criteria. Getting this word correct is vital to understanding what the prison officer was conveying. We wouldn't expect auto-generated transcription to pick up this term, but this example does demonstrate the importance of the researchers checking and amending transcripts for accuracy.

CONDUCTING A THEMATIC ANALYSIS

Website Instructor PowerPoint slides

Thematic Analysis

Once transcription and data familiarisation are complete, the thematic analysis can begin. The overall aim of thematic analysis is to identify, analyse and report the key themes from the data and this process begins with an initial coding of the data. We will return to this process shortly. First, it is important to be aware of the full purpose and approach of thematic analysis.

Thematic analysis is less dependent upon a theoretical approach than other forms of qualitative analysis, and so may be applied to most forms of qualitative data to analyse what was said rather than how it was said. While researchers conducting a thematic analysis may well have conducted a review of the literature, the process allows findings to be drawn from the data and thus the focus is data driven and not theory driven. In this way it is also suitable for approaches such as grounded theory (see the discussion of **induction** in Chapter 6), although there is likely to be some level of theory present even if it is not explicitly acknowledged. Thematic analysis can be a method of examining and reporting the experiences, meanings and the reality of particular groups or individuals, or it can be a method that 'examines the ways in which events, realities, meanings, experiences and so on are the effects of a range of discourses operating within society' (Braun and Clarke, 2006: 81). Fundamentally, thematic analysis encourages close inspection and analysis of text in order to allow the findings to be elicited from the data and it is typically used by researchers aiming to explore the views, perceptions and/or experiences of groups or individuals, and any differences or similarities among these.

Coding

The initial coding process should be highly detailed and inclusive. Coding is a process of working though the data line by line and applying brief verbal descriptions. For example, we might code the following section of an interview with a woman in prison as follows:

Like, when I was, like, a child my, my brother that I'm close to was always in trouble since he was about six years old. He was always in trouble. We always had the police at the house; always fighting with the family and, oh, everybody, and all.	Sibling delinquency Sibling delinquency
That's from when you were quite young.	
Yeah, he's an alcoholic. So (...) my mom and dad both had affairs by their own business. We had to sell the business. And everything, kind of, went downhill from there.	Parental problems Financial issues
How old were you then?	
I was about 14.	
Right, and that had quite a big impact on, on...	
Yeah, it did, yeah.	
In what way?	
In fact I was probably younger than, actually. I don't know because my dad, it is his, it is his life, he's been, like 20-odd years and suddenly, like, he's had, like, six heart attacks, a heart bypass and he couldn't do that anymore. So, he had his driving licence taken off him.	Effects of parental health problems
So, did things, financially, get difficult for the family when that happened or was it just more...?	
See, my dad always, like, my dad never really had, I don't know, he never really seemed to be around much. My mum always did. And he never gave my mum much money and she always struggled, like, especially Christmas, and that.	Financial issues

Note: We recommend you use different colour highlights to represent different themes.

The level of detail of coding typically varies between transcripts and even within sections of transcripts, but our advice is to code as much as reasonably possible at first. Initially it is better to be over-inclusive than under-inclusive and risk missing important details in the data. However, this does not mean that anything and everything should be coded, or indeed that the process should not be systematic. It is likely, initially, that you will be coding every second or third line of the data, but there are no set rules about this, it depends on the data you have. The words you use for your codes should describe the section of data and be meaningful to you.

The key to successful coding is to be systematic, and also to be transparent in how you explain your approach. We strongly suggest keeping notes on how you conducted your thematic analysis in order to aid the write-up. The coding process is surprisingly intuitive, but does require some practice. There is no 'right' or 'wrong', but the researcher should code all interesting features of the data. As Boyatzis (1998: 63) notes, 'Codes identify a feature of the data which is interesting to the analyst ... and that can be assessed in a meaningful way regarding the phenomenon under investigation'. We often find that our own students initially feel underconfident that they have got coding 'right'. When this is the case we ask our students to talk through their process – if they have been very thorough then we are always able to reassure them they have been robust.

Once the entire body of data has been 'coded', the researcher can move on to the next stage, although this is not always a straightforward linear process. It is likely that at every stage of the coding process you will revise your codes as the analysis and your ideas develop, prompted by your increased interaction with, and understanding of, the data. You might adjust the names of codes to better describe the sections of data, and some codes will be merged as inevitably similar points will have initially been given different codes. The aim is to gather all data relevant to each code.

Themes

Once data relevant to each code have been gathered, and codes adjusted to provide a close fit to the data, the next stage is to begin to identify themes from the data. Themes are 'recurrent and distinctive features of participants' accounts, characterising particular perceptions and/or experiences, which the researcher sees as relevant to the research question' (King and Horrocks, 2010: 150). It should be possible to integrate groups of codes to work towards identifying themes that encompass all of the data and the final themes should describe what is going on in the data. For example, when analysing interview transcripts from men who had recently been released from prison and taken part in a music programme, three key themes were drawn from the data:

Personal impact

Focus and direction

Interpersonal relationship

(Hopley, Caulfield and Jolly, 2023: 2)

Note that each of these themes is defined in such a way that it describes the content of that theme, allowing the reader to immediately understand what that theme is. In the findings of this study, published in the *Journal of Criminal Psychology*, sub-themes sat under each of the main themes.

The process of collating codes into overarching themes that represent the body of data is not an exact process and you are likely to undergo some trial and error in identifying final themes. However, you should ensure two key things:

1   That themes represent significant elements of the data – a theme must not be based simply on one or two pieces of interesting data but should exist as a logical way of describing the body of data – codes – underpinning it.

2   That you clearly record how much data each theme consists of – for instance, how many interviewees spoke about issues included in this theme, and on how many occasions? Recording this information means that both you and anyone reading about your analysis can see how important this theme may have been in your data.

It is usual to still be defining and redefining the themes even during the write-up of the research. The final themes should be the result of considerable analytical effort and they should be distinct from one another. There should not be too many themes – remember that these themes should represent the analytical effort of the research and not simply restate all the details of the data.

Writing up the findings: presenting themes

As noted above, writing up the findings from a thematic analysis may be seen as a part of the actual analysis, as it is likely that you will continue to refine your themes as you write. When writing up the themes you should describe the theme and provide illustrative examples that highlight the key points within each theme. Let us take an example. Above we looked at Hopley et al.'s research with men who had been released from prison and were taking part in a music programme called Sounding Out. The following section is taken from the theme 'Personal impact' (Hopley et al., 2023: 8–9):

> Programme participants and staff reported improvements in participant confidence, well-being and musical ability, which they attributed to taking part in Sounding Out. ... Nine out of ten participants spoke about increases in confidence, both their own and witnessing the confidence of others in the group improve. Some participants spoke about increases in their confidence as a musician, while others spoke more broadly about how the programme had increased their confidence in their everyday lives: 'At the moment I have no problem playing in front of ten people or thousands of people. They gave me that confidence. Whereas in my first gig after so many years, I was literally shaking when I was playing the guitar' (Mark,[2] Recent Participant).

Note how the theme is explained, then the data underpinning the theme is outlined, before a quote that illustrates the theme is presented.

As noted above, it is vital that anyone reading your findings understands how far each theme represents your data. For this reason you should state clearly how much data each theme consists of – for instance, how many interviewees spoke about issues included in this theme, and on how many occasions. For example, one of our PhD students (Paula – also see Box 17.3) has recently conducted 21 interviews with Black women who have experienced prison. In Paula's write-up, she provides the following information:

Theme – Lack of trust: Domestic abuse

All participants except Sharon[3] cited that they had been victims of some form of domestic abuse.

Paula then provides details about how the topics discussed by her participants fit within this theme. In this way, it is clear to the reader how far her themes represent the whole body of her data.

Howitt and Cramer (2024: 334) stated that 'there is no accepted, standardised approach to carrying out a thematic analysis' which allows some flexibility around what feels right for the research. However, while few descriptions of a set process for conducting a thematic analysis exist, we think that – especially for novice researchers – it is really useful to follow a process. Braun and Clarke's model (see Box 17.2) is respected as one that gives some idea of the processes that a researcher is likely to go through. Keep in mind that this process is unlikely to be a linear one and it is usual for researchers to move back and forth through the six stages.

Following the guidance set out in this book will help you produce a thorough thematic analysis. Braun and Clarke (2012: 65) note three common errors in thematic analysis that you should seek to avoid:

1. Providing data extracts with little or no analysis (no interpretation of the data that tells us how this is relevant to answering the research question).
2. Simple paraphrasing or summarising data (see Braun and Clarke, 2006).
3. Using data-collection questions as themes is another common error: themes are better identified across the content of what participants say, rather than via the questions they have been asked.

BOX 17.2   BRAUN AND CLARKE'S PHASES

The process of thematic analysis discussed above may be viewed in light of Braun and Clarke's (2006, 2012) six phases of thematic analysis.

Phase 1: Familiarising yourself with the data
During phase 1 you may listen to the recordings several times, transcribe the data and read through the transcriptions, and note down any items of interest that may inform your analysis.

Phase 2: Generating initial codes
Phase 2 involves working through the data line by line, noting all interesting features of the data and developing definitions, or codes, to represent these features.

Phase 3: Searching for themes
In phase 3 the researcher collates the codes into potential themes. These may represent particular aspects of similarity from across the data. All of the data

relevant to a theme are gathered into one theme that effectively describes a distinct aspect of the data.

Phase 4: Reviewing potential themes
During phase 4 researchers begin to identify and review what a theme includes and does not include, and how the theme relates to the other themes derived from the data.

Phase 5: Defining and naming themes
By phase 5 what each theme represents should be sufficiently clear that a name can be given to each theme. It is also wise at this point to finalise a description or definition of each theme.

Phase 6: Producing the report
Writing up the themes should not simply be a descriptive process, but should provide an analysis of each theme. Within phase 6 specific examples – usually quotes – will be identified to illustrate key aspects of each theme. During this stage the themes should be related back to the research questions and to the literature.

Writing about thematic analysis in your research report or dissertation

Many researchers fail to adequately describe the process of analysis they undertook when using thematic analysis. However, it does not have to be this way. Explaining the process fully in the write-up of qualitative research provides a level of transparency that increases the view of qualitative research as both robust and valid. While the processes that different researchers might take during a thematic analysis may differ, with researchers moving back and forth through the stages, there should be general consistencies to the approach. The important thing is to state what you did and how you did it. To fully illustrate this, we have provided a real example below of how a thematic analysis was written about in the method section of a research report. (See Chapter 18 for further information on writing up criminological research.)

BOX 17.3 DESCRIBING A THEMATIC ANALYSIS IN A METHOD SECTION OF A RESEARCH REPORT

The example below is taken from Paula McLean's PhD thesis. It is longer than would be expected in an undergraduate or master's dissertation, but provides an example of a clear, thorough and transparent write up of Paula's Thematic

Analysis of 21 interview transcripts. Paula's research was undertaken with black women who had been in prison.

> For the first stage of the TA [thematic analysis] process, I began by reading through each transcript thoroughly working line-by-line to identify items of potential interest. It is recommended this is done before starting the coding to allow for immersing in the data (Braun and Clarke, 2006). This was a very useful exercise for two primary reasons; firstly, I was able to reflect on the depth and richness of the data and secondly, it really drew me back to the time the interviews were conducted evoking a range of emotions that were experienced at the time and then stirred again as I reflected on the trauma these women had experienced. It reminded me of the responsibility I had to make sure these women's voices were heard and that I am accountable to them to ensure that happens (Patterson et al., 2016). This stage was also aided by the textual data I had collected through reflexive journalling, field notes and observations (Crabtree and Miller, 1999). This complementary data was very beneficial and crucial in helping me not feel so daunted by the responsibility. I also found that through repeated active listening to the audios and in-depth re-reading of the transcripts and the textual data, the analysis had started.
>
> For the second stage, I used the NVivo software to generate codes using labels that succinctly stated what was of interest in the data. Fifty-eight separate codes were generated, the primary being what Braun and Clarke (2006) call the semantic codes which captured the surface meanings such as vulnerability. Then using the criticality of Black feminism, I looked for the latent codes which more clearly defined the experiences of the participants, assumptions or signals of the semantic code such as feeling disrespected for example. This stage also involved commenting on the generated codes which illuminated patterns and initial themes emerging from the data.
>
> For stage three, this was an ongoing process of organising the codes into potential themes. Then using a 'thematic map' (see Figure 17.1) the 58 generated codes were clustered into nine potential themes promoting nine of the initial codes into an overarching theme with a second review of the data producing sub-themes.
>
> Braun and Clarke (2006) recommend that in stage three, another review of the data is conducted so a Word document was opened, and all transcripts were read in their entirety for a second time and the previous coding constantly referred to and cross referenced with any similar or new codes. Supervisory advice was to keep an open mind as some codes or themes may change, and sub-themes will emerge, which was the case. I

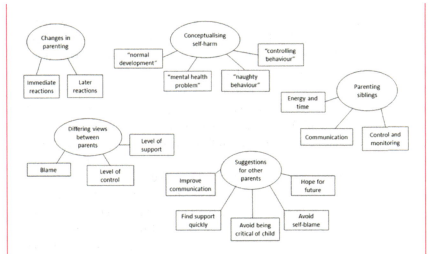

Figure 17.1 An example of thematic mapping showing themes and sub-themes (Ferrey et al., 2016).

noted in this second review, some codes were absorbed into other codes where duplication or similarity occurred. At the same time, some codes reinforced the potency and confirmation of a theme such as White women being believed over Black women and less punitive punishment confirmed white privilege.

There was also some overlap between stage two of generating the initial codes and identifying emerging themes, which is common and helps clarify definitive themes (Maguire and Delahunt, 2017). I found this to be the case and themes such as neglect, and dehumanising treatment became prominent.

I also found this stage quite emotional due to the realisation that nothing has ever changed due to the continued failure of government to acknowledge and correct the wrongs inflicted on these women. Allowing participants to bear witness is difficult for the bearer (participant) and for the hearer (researcher) of the stories. Pikiewicz (2013) cites that trauma survivors often relate the importance of their therapist (or in this case, researcher) validating and believing their stories and how this is pivotal in their healing journey. I can relate to that as my participants all spoke of how much it meant to them to have someone who cared enough to want to hear their stories, believe and not judge them. The storytelling was often very cathartic but therapeutic on many levels. Much of this bearing witness experience was being relived during the first three stages of the TA process.

Before discussing stage four, which relates to reviewing the themes, it is important to highlight that it became apparent at the end of stage three that due to the significant amount of overlap in experiences across the four main CJS [Criminal Justice System] agencies, it would be difficult to separate the themes. This was because much of the content of the narratives intertwined, often one thing leading to another, making extricating specifics difficult. This was discussed during supervision and a way forward was sought during reviewing the themes. Thirty-two specific sub-themes were arrived at that would initially be spread across four thematic chapters. In this stage of the analysis process, it was noted that some codes/themes seemed miscellaneous such as activism. This is common in the process and the advice is to keep it aside and see where it may fit later if at all (Braun and Clarke, 2006) which the activism theme did. As part of stage four, each chapter had several sub-themes underneath that needed streamlining. However, I was loath to remove any themes as they were significant across the data and relevant to the analysis of the lived experiences of all participants such as the example cited above.

Further supervisory discussions were had, and I suggested writing the findings as specific chapters for each participant, meaning incorporating their backstories. I felt it was in keeping with the thesis title and black feminist qualitative research. It also allowed the themes to be spoken about in relation to each and their own experience. From what I was envisioning, the commonality in themes would emerge and be running as a thread throughout each story and then end with a concluding section tying it all together. This 'iterative and reflective process' that occurred over some time is common in the TA process and demonstrates the process is not as linear as presented (Nowell et al., 2017: 4). Supervisory advice supported consideration of this approach but to bear in mind that thematic analysis was about drawing out the overarching themes and presenting those, as opposed to individual narratives or case studies. Therefore, from a purely methodological standpoint, it would be a challenge.

After further consideration during the 5th stage, that of clearly defining the themes; some of the deadlock was overcome by the understanding that experiences of racism/discrimination are not themes (initially themes in two chapters) but rather factors that are structural within society that is then experienced. Therefore, a way forward was to acknowledge that and then place the themes into a proposed timeline of experiences before and during and after custody. It was also concluded that narratives of participants' backstories should be included as, whilst the research did not start out as a life stories inquiry, during the 3-stage interview process, participants of their own volition, shared areas of their lives that did add context about why they became embroiled in the CJS. Therefore, there would be a new chapter that would appear at the start of the Findings section incorporating the participants' backstories and include the analysis of the visual data. It seemed more natural to incorporate the backstories and visual data into this first chapter as it added context and meaning to the experiences that would be presented in the following chapters.

Before outlining the last stage of what to include in the writing of the thesis, stage five highlighted how some codes became major themes or sub-themes and, crucially, how some that may have seemed marginally relevant in the initial stages of the analysis, had a significant part in the study amongst participants (King, 2004). An example of this is the impact of maternal imprisonment on children which featured more prominently that had been remembered during interviewing.

The last and final stage is the writing of the thesis. During this process, there is a theorising of the data, highlighting the significance of patterns and themes in relation to the literature. As well as a separate discussion chapter, I decided to intertwine the literature with the findings. Aronson (1994) affirms this method stating that by interweaving the literature with the findings, the author creates a merited expose. King (2004) confirms that direct quotations from participants are an essential part of any final qualitative report to aid and validate the prevalence of themes and interpretations. This also helps to reinforce and articulate the meanings of themes and underpin them with participants' voices (Braun and Clarke, 2006).

Paula McLean, 2024

ADVANTAGES AND DISADVANTAGES OF THEMATIC ANALYSIS

Thematic analysis has a number of benefits. It is a flexible method of analysis that is accessible to new researchers and compatible with a number of different schools of thought. It is generally suitable for analysing any forms of qualitative data and in many ways is less demanding than other qualitative methods. Thematic analysis, when done well, can provide a rich and detailed account of the data a researcher has collected, and thus give a clear voice to those involved in the research.

However, there are some potential disadvantages to thematic analysis, and it is useful for you to be aware of these. The first is the time it takes to do a thematic analysis well. From the time it takes to ensure a high level of familiarity with transcripts, to the rigorous coding process, good thematic analysis does take time. However, as long as you are aware of this you can plan it into your research timetable, and it is a highly rewarding process. Some researchers have been criticised for using thematic analysis in a limited way, with superficial coding that does not truly represent the data. Such criticisms can be avoided in two ways: first, by conducting a thorough analysis; and second, by documenting how thorough the analysis was.

Remember: thematic analysis cannot, for example, be used to analyse what patterns of speech tell us about the power relationships between individuals. Other forms of analysis are more appropriate in such circumstances, as discussed earlier in this chapter.

Website Instructor activity

Coding

BOX 17.4 CODING ACTIVITY

Now that you understand the principles of conducting a thematic analysis, have a go at coding the short section of an interview transcript below. These data are taken from the transcripts of interviews with women in prison in 2017, who were working in a manufacturing unit within the prison. Highlight sections of text and use the column on the right to note down codes. You can find these data in the support material and our suggestions for coding it. Remember: there is no right or wrong, but it may be interesting for you to compare your codes with ours.

I: So you were working in the kitchen and then they remembered that you'd asked to do this so they channelled you into ...

R: Yes, then I was on the waiting list to come on here, so I didn't join this workshop until August of 2016, but they actually got the [name of prison] girls in here first because they were studying it and had come ... obviously this was coming from [name of prison] to here, so obviously it made sense to put them forward first, so then I didn't actually come in here until the end of August.

I: So you didn't [inaudible 00.02.36] it was just you were on a waiting list?

R: No, just on a waiting list.

I: Was there anything else that you'd done before you started in terms of programmes or were you doing anything for your sentence, behaviour programmes, nothing like that?

R: No.

I: Any education?

R: Here in [name of prison]?

I: Yes, in here. Well, actually, no, tell me about [name of prison] and [name of prison] as well, tell me about your experience.

R: So [name of prison] I spent about three months, just a week short of three months at [name of prison] before being transferred here. Over there I was doing IT in the mornings and then I was doing Stitch in Time from midday until quarter to five. That's what I was doing there Monday to Friday.

I: *So that was quite a full day, actually?*

R: Yes, but there was nothing actually on my sentence plan that I had to work towards. I've got a very basic sentence plan which is just basically positive behaviour, good behaviour and get on with the sentence, yes.

I: *And since you've been working in here, are you doing anything else now around the prison or …?*

R: I've been doing the Women's Institute, WI, that's just got started recently about two months ago. What else are we doing? I've been taking part in a few questionnaires, sort of group sessions for Prison Reform Trust and charities. I've been doing that sort of stuff, but I haven't actually done any education here, partly because I didn't really want to. This was my main focus was to get into the fashion workshop. This is what I enjoy and this is what I wanted to do. This makes the most sense for me to be in this place rather than still remaining in the kitchen, for example.

I: *Totally, yes, absolutely. And what did you want to get from doing this work?*

R: Apart from being out of your room?

I: *Yes, which is important.*

R: Which is important, I think it's just being in an environment where you know that you're doing something you're enjoying, that the worst thing is going into a work environment, it's like, you know, you could easily go and do laundry, cleaning and doing everyone's laundry all day, but what enjoyment are you going to get out of that? Unless you owned a laundry service outside then, okay, maybe that might be your special field, but for me, it was about being in an environment that I knew I was going to feel comfortable in and I knew what I was doing, that was the most important thing for me.

I: *That's cool. And what do you think, in terms of the prison, what do you think they wanted you to get from the project?*

R: I think experience, confidence, happiness in your work environment, I believe that's important, and obviously they want you to work towards your level one and level two, so I think that's their focus, as well as production as well.

I: What do you think you've achieved so far?

R: I think confidence, to be able to voice my opinion when needed, I feel like I've been able to see, if I've seen anything negative going on in the workshop, I feel I've got the confidence to go and speak up about it.

I: And you didn't have that before?

R: No.

I: What sort of person do you consider yourself to be generally in terms of personality?

R: I'm not a quiet person in here. I'm somebody who is voicing their opinions more and more lately at the moment, and I've been told that by another officer as well, but in a good way. He's actually made a comment that actually your personality is really changed, that you've come out of your shell, and that I don't know, maybe it's because I'm comfortable in my environment, but I don't know how to describe my personality, really.

I: It's a tricky question, isn't it?

R: It's a tricky question, I don't know.

COMPUTER ASSISTED QUALITATIVE DATA ANALYSIS SOFTWARE (CAQDAS)

In the past, qualitative researchers conducted their analyses by 'cutting and pasting' sections of their data within Word documents or having all their data physically on paper in front of them. When researchers are working with many pieces of qualitative data this can be difficult to manage. However, in recent years many researchers have begun to use CAQDAS. A number of CAQDAS programs exist, with one of the most popular being NVivo (the current version available is NVivo 14). CAQDAS should not be used to do the analysis for you, but it reduces the burden on the researcher in managing the data and can be very helpful in coding and linking data. CAQDAS supports most types of qualitative analysis and data, and some university courses now teach the use of this software as part of their research methods modules.

The decision to use CAQDAS to aid a thematic analysis is likely to be based on considerations of time and efficiency. CAQDAS is designed to make the process of coding and the analysis of data more intuitive by reducing the physical effort required to analyse textual data (Lee and Fielding, 1991). It enables data to be stored, coded, retrieved and interrogated with more efficiency than can be achieved using traditional methods or a word processor (Tesch, 1990; Fielding and Lee, 1998; Lewins and Silver, 2005). It is important to be aware that even with CAQDAS software the researcher should still be responsible for the cognitive side of the data analysis (Tesch, 1991). While the computer package helps the researcher sort data into meaningful chunks, the researcher should undertake the actual analysis or interpretation of results (Weitzman and Miles, 1995). It has been suggested that such packages help enhance creativity through a reduction of the clerical and administrative burden (Tesch, 1991) and the ability to play with the data and explore new analytical perspectives (Tesch, 1990). CAQDAS has been criticised for reinforcing or even exaggerating the fragmentation of data (see Weaver and Atkinson, 1995), but by revisiting the original recordings and full transcripts researchers can go a long way towards avoiding these issues. Ultimately, users of CAQDAS remain responsible for analysing the data, but the reduction in the administrative burden associated with large amounts of interview data and the enhanced possibility of objectivity makes the use of such software highly beneficial in many circumstances.

Recently, NVivo and other packages have integrated AI in order to auto-generate codes. These are not intended to replace the researcher's analytic input, but to provide a start for the coding process. There can be some potential benefits to this when working with very large datasets. At a basic level, for example, it has long been possible to search for the frequency of a particular word or phrase in a dataset. Researchers, particularly linguists, have also used software programs to search for positive and negative phrases around a particular topic in large datasets. The functionality with CAQDAS to auto-generate codes builds on this type of functionality. There are some benefits in terms of saving time, but at present auto-generated codes are lacking sophistication. The results might not address the research questions, give little insight into what speakers might be saying 'between the lines' and miss some of the complexity of human language. They can, however, provide an interesting start point to build upon and refine with your own analytic efforts. We advise students to engage thoroughly with the data familiarisation and analysis outlined in this chapter, using CAQDAS as a support tool only.

CAQDAS software is particularly useful in aiding the organisational aspects of managing large amounts of qualitative data, and NVivo is thought to retain a greater level of power over the data analysis with the researcher, as opposed to other CAQDAS such as Atlas or NUD*IST (Bringer, Johnston and Brakenridge, 2004), although all of these programs now have some level of automatic text analysis function. However, systematic analysis and rigour through the use of CAQDAS can only be achieved if the researcher is competent in the principles of qualitative research.

BOX 17.5 GETTING STARTED WITH NVIVO

NVivo can do some very complex things, including aiding in the analysis of various kinds of qualitative data (including audio and video data, pictures and websites), but it can also be a very helpful tool when conducting a standard thematic analysis with interview or focus group transcripts. If you want to find out more about NVivo you can read about its many uses on the Lumivero website (https://lumivero.com/products/nvivo/).

You can often download NVivo or other packages onto your own devices through your university's licence, but be aware that they use a lot of processing power. It is worth enquiring about whether any computers in your university have NVivo or any other CAQDAS installed and if your university offers any training in using CAQDAS programs. If NVivo is available, you may want to work through the various online tutorials available on the Lumivero website:

Tutorials: https://lumivero.com/resources/support/getting-started-with-nvivo/nvivo-tutorials/ You can explore an NVivo project by opening up NVivo on your computer and taking a look at the test projects, or begin setting up your own project and follow the tutorials above.

If you would like to find out more about CAQDAS, we recommend the CAQDAS Networking Project at the University of Surrey where you can find a range of resources: https://www.surrey.ac.uk/computer-assisted-qualitative-data-analysis/resources

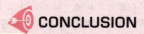

CONCLUSION

Throughout this chapter, you will have noticed something that we cannot emphasise enough: it is vital to ensure that the analysis of your data is robust. In addition to this, it is vital to ensure that the way you describe and explain the process of analysing your data is clear and sufficiently detailed. Being robust in your data analysis includes ensuring familiarity with your data gained through collecting, transcribing and reading your data. Once researchers are familiar with their data they can begin the formal process of analysis, potentially using some of the methods outlined in this and other chapters of this book.

 KEY LEARNING POINTS

- You should now understand the importance of the transcription process in qualitative analysis, including how to work with auto-generated online transcripts.
- While there are a number of different approaches to qualitative data analysis, thematic analysis is widely used when researchers wish to understand and explore the ideas, experiences and reality of a group or individuals.

- Conducting a robust thematic analysis requires a high level of analytical effort and a great deal of time from the researcher. This process will allow you to identify the key findings from the data via a process of coding.
- Key themes should be presented from the thematic analysis that represent the body of data. When writing up these themes it is important to provide examples from those data that illustrate each theme.
- There is no 'right' or 'wrong' answer with this type of analysis. The key is to fully document the process and findings in order to demonstrate that the analysis was robust.

NOTES

1 Release on Temporary Licence (ROTL) means being able to leave prison for a short time for a limited number of reasons, including to take part in paid or unpaid work and to help individuals to settle back into the community. Only some people in prison are eligible for ROTL and all individuals who are eligible for ROTL must meet strict risk criteria.
2 False names were used in the research in order to protect the identity of participants.
3 False names were used in the research in order to protect the identity of participants.

REFERENCES

Aronson J. (1994) 'A Pragmatic View of Thematic Analysis', *The Qualitative Report*, 2: 1–3.

Atkinson, R. (1998) *The Life Story Interview*, Thousand Oaks, CA: Sage.

Boyatzis, R. (1998) *Transforming Qualitative Information: Thematic Analysis and Code Development*, Thousand Oaks, CA: Sage.

Braun, V. and Clarke, V. (2006) 'Using Thematic Analysis in Psychology', *Qualitative Research in Psychology*, 3(2): 77–101.

Braun, V. and Clarke, V. (2012) 'Thematic Analysis', in H. Cooper, P.M. Camic, D.L. Long, A.T. Panter, D. Rindskopf and K.J. Sher (eds) *APA Handbook of Research Methods in Psychology, Vol. 2: Research Designs: Quantitative, Qualitative, Neuropsychological, and Biological*, Washington, DC: American Psychological Association.

Bringer, J.D., Johnston, L.H. and Brakenridge, C.H. (2004) 'Maximising Transparency in a Doctoral Thesis: The Complexities of Writing about the Use of QSR*NVIVO within a Grounded Theory Study', *Qualitative Research*, 4(2): 247–265.

Caulfield, L.S. (2012) *Life Histories of Women Who Offend: A Study of Women in English Prisons*, PhD thesis, Loughborough University.

Crabtree B. and Miller W. (1999) 'Using Codes and Code Manuals: A Template for Organizing Style of Interpretation', in B. Crabtree B. and W. Miller W. (eds) *Doing Qualitative Research*, second edition, Los Angeles, CA: Sage Publications, pp. 163–177.

Ferrey, A.E., Hughes, N.D., Simkin, S., Locock, L., Stewart, A., Kapur, N., Gunnell, D. and Hawton, K. (2016) 'Changes in Parenting Strategies after a Young Person's Self-harm: A Qualitative

Study', *Child and Adolescent Psychiatry and Mental Health*, 10: article 20. https://doi.org/10.1186/s13034-016-0110-y

Fielding, N.G. and Lee, R.M. (1998) *Computer Analysis and Qualitative Research*, London: Sage.

Hopley, R., Caulfield, L.S. and Jolly, A. (2023) '"I'll Live Better, Stay Away from Crime": Exploring the Reintegration of Former Prisoners into the Community through a Music Programme', *Journal of Criminal Psychology*, 13: 351–366.

Howitt, D. and Cramer, D. (2024) *Research Methods in Psychology*, seventh edition, London: Pearson.

King, N. (2004) 'Using Templates in the Thematic Analysis of Text', in C. Cassell and G. Symon (eds) *Essential Guide to Qualitative Methods in Organizational Research*, London: Sage Publications, pp. 257–270.

King, N. and Horrocks, C. (2010) *Interviews in Qualitative Research*, London: Sage.

Lewins, A. and Silver, C. (2005) *Choosing a CAQDAS Package: A Working Paper*, University of Surrey: CAQDAS Networking Project.

Maguire, M. and Delahunt, B. (2017) 'Doing a Thematic Analysis: A Practical, Step-by-Step Guide for Learning and Teaching Scholars', *Dundalk Institute of Technology*, 9(3): 3351–3354.

Nowell, L.S., Norris, J.M., White, D.E. and Moules, N.J. (2017) 'Thematic Analysis: Striving to Meet the Trustworthiness Criteria', *International Journal of Qualitative Methods*, 16: 1–13.

Oliver, D.G., Serovich, J.M. and Mason, T.L. (2005) 'Constraints and Opportunities with Interview Transcription: Towards Reflection in Qualitative Research', *Social Forces*, 84(2): 1273–1289.

Patterson, A., Kinloch, V., Burkhard, T., Randall, R. and Howard, A. (2016) 'Black Feminist Thought as Methodology: Examining Intergenerational Lived Experiences of Black Women', *Departures in Critical Qualitative Research*, 5(3): 55–76.

Pikiewicz, K. (2013, December 3) 'The Power and Strength of Bearing Witness', *Psychology Today*. Available at https://www.psychologytoday.com/gb/blog/meaningful-you/201312/the-power-and-strength-of-bearing-witness

Tesch, R. (1990) *Qualitative Research: Analysis Types and Software Tools*, London: Falmer Press.

Tesch, R. (1991) 'Software for Qualitative Researcher's Analysis Needs and Program Capabilities', in N.G. Fielding and R.M. Lee (eds) *Using Computers in Qualitative Research*, London: Sage.

Weaver, A. and Atkinson, P. (1995) *Microcomputing and Qualitative Data Analysis*, Aldershot: Avebury.

Weitzman, E.A. and Miles, M.B. (1995) *Computer Programs for Qualitative Data Analysis*, Thousand Oaks, CA: Sage.

Chapter 18

Analysing the data
Documents, texts and other data

GOALS OF THIS CHAPTER

At the end of reading this chapter and by completing the online resources that accompany it, you will be able to:

1 approach the analysis of documents and text in a critical way;
2 plan appropriately prior to the analysis phase of conducting research with **documentary data**;
3 understand the principles and processes involved in qualitative content analysis and critical **discourse analysis**.

OVERVIEW

- As outlined elsewhere in this book, there is a wealth of data available to researchers that does not necessarily involve the collection of new empirical data.
- A structured and consistent approach to analysing documents, employing a robust methodology, will often lead to important insights into relevant criminological issues.
- Before beginning the process of analysis, researchers must do a number of things: plan; consider the best way to access relevant data; and read and reflect.
- There are several approaches that may be used to analyse documents and text-based data. Two popular qualitative methods are qualitative content analysis and critical discourse analysis.
- Qualitative content analysis shares some of the underlying principles of content analysis (a primarily quantitative method of analysis) but allows researchers to ask not simply 'what', but 'why'. There are a number of different approaches to qualitative content analysis, which differ in their level of inductive and deductive reasoning.
- There is no one set approach to critical discourse analysis. However, there are key critical principles that underpin this form of analysis. This chapter sets out some of the ways of thinking and types of questions that should be considered by any researcher seeking to make use of this method in order to understand language as a source of power in their data.

DOI: 10.4324/9781032645698-23

TYPES OF DOCUMENTS

Chapters 14 and 15 introduced some of the types of documents and other data that researchers might analyse, including personal documents (diaries/autobiographies/letters/photographs), official documents, mass media outputs, internet outputs and so on. The types of documents researchers may wish to analyse are large and varied and, as Chapters 14 and 15 indicated, researchers may be concerned with both qualitative and quantitative documentary sources. With both types of sources, we should be mindful of the assumptions that underlie the questions that have been asked and the way any data have been collected, analysed and presented. In many ways, therefore, whether data are qualitative or quantitative becomes less important than the assumptions that underpin it. What is important is taking a structured approach to analysing documents and being able to demonstrate a robust methodology. We have seen our own students fail to do this and consequently fail to produce what had the potential to be very strong pieces of work. We have also seen students who have adopted a clear and logical approach to analysing documents and produced excellent work. We hope that by reading this chapter you will fall into the latter category.

This chapter will help you identify what you should be thinking about even before you begin your analysis, before moving on to give you guidance on possible methods of analysis that you may wish to use.

WHERE TO BEGIN

Prior to formally beginning any process of analysis we advise that you thoroughly explore your documents, allowing you time to reflect and refine the methodological process you will ultimately employ. While you may wish to delve straight into the analysis, the planning you do beforehand will have a huge impact on how successful your analysis is. Trust us on this one.

1. *Plan.* Ensure you know exactly what you are looking for in your data. Have clear research questions.
2. *Consider access.* Where are the documents located? Do you need special access or to contact particular people? Do this early and ensure you have a contingency plan if you cannot use the data you wanted.
3. *Read and reflect.* Explore what the documents say. What can you find out about the authors and/or organisations that produced them? Why was the document produced? Make notes and reflect upon how what you have found in these early stages may influence your approach to analysis.

Whichever approach to analysis you take, you must consider underlying values and subjectivity. This consideration should apply both to the documents you are accessing and your own assumptions. The robustness, reliability and credibility of the analysis you conduct will depend to a large extent upon how far you recognise underlying values and subjectivity. What standpoint do the authors take? Whose 'truth' does the document you are reading represent? How does your own theory of knowledge fit with, or oppose, this? Think back to the discussions we had in Chapter 5.

Next, look back at Box 8.2 in Chapter 8.

STUDENT ACTIVITY: RECOGNISING THE ROLE OF UNDERLYING VALUES AND POTENTIAL BIAS

Revisit the 'Breakthrough Britain' and 'Two Nations' documents introduced in Box 8.2 and consider both your own underlying values and those of the authors. Ask yourself the following initial questions:

1. What is the purpose of the documents? Do they reflect and/or seek to promote a particular view or political position? Who funded any research presented in the documents?
2. What is the background of the authors? Are they credible? Do they have and/or seek to promote a particular view or political position?
3. How might your own values affect the way you plan and conduct an analysis of this document?
4. Do you need to account for your own values or simply recognise and document your own standpoint?

When reviewing your data you should consider – in the context of the questions above – whether there is any attempt to put forward a view that is not backed up with sufficient or convincing evidence. Have the authors explored or highlighted oppositional views, or said why they might reject oppositional views?

Once you have considered the above questions in relation to your data, you should be ready to begin planning the more formal and in-depth process of analysing your data. Remember: the method you use should directly work towards addressing your research questions.

CRITICAL ANALYSIS

We have called this section of the chapter 'Critical Analysis' as a reminder of one of the key underpinning concepts in good research. Within this section we discuss and provide advice on how to critically analyse text and documents. It is worth reiterating the difference between criticism and critical analysis or critical evaluation. Criticism typically refers to fault finding and producing negative comments about something. This is not the purpose of critical analysis. While critical analysis can involve fault finding, the purpose is primarily to assess the assumptions that underpin a piece of work and the methodology employed. What is concealed? What is promoted? What are the strengths and weaknesses?

Analysis of documents and text can be done in a variety of ways and, as discussed in Chapter 14, research using documentary sources can be excellent if done well. Doing this sort of research well requires a structured and methodical approach, a clear rationale for the approach taken and a consistency of approach. Researchers who can competently describe the structured and methodical approach they have taken tend to fare well. Critical discourse analysis and qualitative content analysis are two possible approaches to analysing documents and these are discussed more fully below – but do note that these are just two of several possible approaches. **Thematic analysis**, for example, is another method that it is possible to apply to textual data and this is explained fully in Chapter 17.

QUALITATIVE CONTENT ANALYSIS

Qualitative content analysis is perhaps the most widely used qualitative approach to analysing documents. Like thematic analysis, which we outlined in Chapter 17, qualitative content analysis involves a process of searching for themes in the data. Like thematic analysis, this method can be managed very well with Computer Assisted Qualitative Data Analysis Software (CAQDAS: see below). Qualitative content analysis allows researchers to elicit patterns from the data that represent a social reality (or realities), as opposed to critical discourse analysis – discussed below – that is primarily concerned with language as a source of social power.

You may have heard of content analysis, and at this point it is worth noting how this differs from qualitative content analysis. Content analysis is an approach to data analysis that seeks to categorise and quantify documents and text in a systematic way. This is a quantitative approach to data analysis, which involves coding data to relatively strict coding schedules in order to ascertain and statistically test the occurrence of specific variables. There are many benefits to content analysis – not least that, done well, it is a highly transparent research method – but there are also limitations. It allows us to ask 'what' but not 'why' – for example, we might see the number of times a word or concept appears in the data, but not the meaning of that data. As criminological researchers it is very often the 'why' with which we are most concerned. Qualitative content analysis allows us to ask more of the 'why' by allowing a detailed exploration of key themes that occur within the data we wish to analyse, offering a systematic and thorough approach. Just like traditional content analysis, there are a number of approaches to qualitative content analysis. These approaches differ primarily in the extent to which they involve inductive reasoning, i.e. the extent to which the analysis is data led (inductive) or theory driven (deductive). Hsieh and Shannon (2005) discuss three approaches to qualitative content analysis:

1   Conventional qualitative content analysis – inductive. Coding categories are derived directly from the raw data. Aligned with grounded theory approaches.

2   Directed content analysis – allows for both **induction** and **deduction**. Initial coding begins with theory and/or relevant research findings. Researchers also immerse themselves in the data during the process of analysis and allow further themes to emerge from the data. This approach is most often used to validate or extend a conceptual framework or theory.
3   Summative content analysis – largely deductive. Researchers begin by counting the words and main content before extending the analysis to include underlying meanings and themes. While this approach may begin as quantitative and is in line with traditional content analysis, its goal is to explore the use of the words/indicators in an inductive manner.

We favour an approach that retains many of the systematic elements of traditional content analysis, but that allows the researcher to constantly revise the themes as the analysis progresses. This is closest to what Hsieh and Shannon (2005) term 'directed content analysis'. The process should move back and forth between the formulation of ideas, the process of analysis and the interpretation of the data. Of course, the approach you decide to take will depend upon your aims, research questions, methodological standpoint and the data you have.

Altheide (2004) outlines the steps he takes in qualitative content analysis:

- Generate a research question.
- Become familiar with the context within which the documents were/are generated.
- Become familiar with a small number of documents (6–10).[1]
- Generate some categories that will guide the collection of data and draft a schedule for collecting the data in terms of the generated categories.
- Test the schedule by using it for collecting data from a number of documents.
- Revise the schedule and select further cases to sharpen it up.

By schedule, Altheide essentially means a set of rules about the categories that will be used in the data analysis process. Initially, these categories may be determined by existing theories, ideas and research. This is also referred to as a coding scheme or coding manual. Developing a coding manual is a good idea, especially where more than one researcher is working on a project. While you are likely to be working independently on your dissertation project, for example, there may be assignments during your research methods course that require you to work on data in groups. We suggest that your coding manual consists of at least the following: category names (codes), definitions or rules for assigning codes, and examples (see Box 18.1). You may also wish to include a space for notes. It is a good idea to make notes as your analysis progresses, as this will help you when you come to write up your research and will remind you (and help you explain to anyone reading your research) how and why your coding scheme developed. As we have discussed at various points in this book, providing a clear and comprehensive methods section in research reports/dissertations is very important. The more transparent your methods the better. Having a coding manual will help you to be transparent and help you to demonstrate the robustness of your process of analysis. It is good practice to include your coding manual in the appendix of your research report or dissertation.

Website Student documents

Suggestions for a qualitative content analysis coding manual.

BOX 18.1   SUGGESTIONS FOR A QUALITATIVE CONTENT ANALYSIS CODING MANUAL

1 Label/name for each category	e.g. Rehabilitative services in prison
2 Definition	e.g. mention of rehabilitation services, support, or programmes provided in prison
3 Rules for assigning	e.g. each time offer of a rehabilitative service/engagement with service/programme, or lack of service/programme mentioned in the text
4 Exclusions?	e.g. where the services of programmes are outside of prison (e.g. probation)
5 Examples	e.g. *'Celia talked about being overlooked for educational opportunities in prison'*, *'They also need to do courses that are inspiring for Black women'* (from McLean and Caulfield, 2023)
6 Notes	e.g. code each occurrence, even where several mentions are made of the same point in the text
Add columns to the right for each new category	

The process of coding or categorising material is fundamental to any form of content analysis. The coding process should be highly detailed and inclusive. As outlined in Chapter 17, coding is a process of working though the data line by line and applying brief verbal descriptions. Take the page from a report from the Youth Endowment Fund's Toolkit (shown in Figure 18.1). The Toolkit includes evidence reviews of many interventions and approaches to reducing youth violence. The report shown in Figure 18.1 looks at the evidence of impact of prison awareness programmes on youth violence and concludes that, rather than reducing youth violence, they are actually harmful (Youth Endowment Fund, 2021). We might code/categorise it as shown in Figure 18.1.

Figure 18.1 Coded page from Youth Endowment Fund Toolkit, 2021

Note that we recommend you use different coloured highlights to represent different themes. You can find more examples in the support material.

Head back to Chapter 17 for more detailed information on the process of coding data. Once you have developed your initial coding manual, test it on some of your data. Refine it. Keep updating it. The process of coding is the process of analysis and in qualitative content analysis this should be a continually evolving process.

Remember: in order to develop (and also to write about) a robust qualitative content analysis, you should be clear about where your categories come from. What theory and existing data influenced the categories you started with? How did the categories develop as the process of analysis began? All too often researchers fail to fully document the process of analysis, yet doing this well is critical to the quality and validity of the research. Through careful preparation and thorough coding and interpretation, qualitative content analysis may be used to provide considerable insight, validate or challenge existing theories, and develop new theories.

BOX 18.2 WHAT TO DO WHEN YOU HAVE DEVELOPED YOUR INITIAL CODES

Website Student documents

Find Aisha's coding manual in the support material

Test your coding scheme on a sample of text – 'The best test of the clarity and consistency of your category definitions is to code a sample of your data.' Code a sample, check for consistency (do your codes fit your data? Have you coded similar things in the same or different ways?) and revise your coding scheme where needed. Return to this testing throughout your analysis.

Code all the text – 'When sufficient consistency has been achieved, the coding rules can be applied to the entire corpus of text.' Keep developing your coding themes while you code your data and add these to your coding manual. Be responsive to your data.

Assess your coding consistency – 'It is not safe to assume that, if a sample was coded in a consistent and reliable manner, the coding of the whole corpus of text is also consistent.' Researchers are human. We get tired. Sometimes we lose focus and make mistakes. Check that the categories and codes you now have in your coding manual make sense., especially since new ones may have been added since your initial testing.

Draw conclusions from the coded data – 'This is a critical step in the analysis process, and its success will rely almost wholly on your reasoning abilities.' This is where you will begin to make sense of your categories. You should be seeking out relationships in the data and uncovering patterns. Review how well these patterns account for the whole body of data.

Report your methods and findings – 'Qualitative content analysis … uncovers patterns, themes, and categories important to a social reality.' You must report your decisions and practices in developing the coding process. When presenting your results, you should strive for a balance between description and interpretation, and it is common practice to use typical quotations to represent themes and justify conclusions.

(Adapted from Zhang and Wildemuth, 2017: 322–323)

STUDENT EXAMPLE: AISHA WRITES ABOUT HER QUALITATIVE CONTENT ANALYSIS

In Chapter 14 we introduced you to Aisha and her dissertation research. Aisha used qualitative content analysis to explore newspaper articles for portrayals of female and male suspected murderers.

Here is part of the methodology section of Aisha's dissertation, where she writes about her process:

> To conduct the analysis the steps were followed as dictated by Altheide (2004). First of all a research question was developed. The research question was developed around the possibility of there being differences in the way female and male offenders are portrayed in the media. Once the research question was developed newspaper articles in the area were read in order to become familiar with the type of data that could be obtained.
>
> The sixteen newspaper articles were obtained in the NewsBank UK and Ireland newspaper database. The articles were found using the following search inclusion criteria: that they included the words 'murder' and 'trial'; that they were published between 1 January and 31 March; and that the articles were longer than 500 words. The project focused on the portrayal of murderers in the media; therefore murder was one of the search terms. Three months was sufficient for finding eight articles discussing females and eight articles discussing males. The word 'trial' was also used as a search term as initial attempts to find articles for the analysis contained numerous articles that were not relevant to this research. Only British newspapers were included.
>
> An initial coding manual [see support material] was developed based on the existing theories and research discussed in the introduction about the portrayal of gender and offenders in the media. The codes aimed to be specifically distinct from each other, and contain enough information for replicability (Saldana, 2009). Saldana (2009: 3) defines a code as 'a word

> or short phrase that symbolically assigns a summative, salient, essence-capturing, and/or evocative attribute for a portion of language-based or visual data'. The reflective journal [see support material] describes how decisions were made for the initial and revised coding manual. The coding manual was based on the suggestions in Caulfield and Hill (2014: 200). Previous research on female criminals in the media found there was a focus on external appearance and details that were not directly related to the crime, and the following labels were used: 'Crime mentioned'; 'Victim mentioned'; 'External appearance'; 'Home life'; 'Mental health'; and 'Childhood'. The selected articles were read several times to ensure familiarity with the data. These were analysed using the initial coding manual [see support material for two annotated copies of newspaper articles] and the labels were developed and refined through the process of analysing these articles, resulting in a revised coding manual [see support material]. The coding manual was adapted during the analysis to accommodate emerging themes that had not been highlighted by previous research.

CRITICAL DISCOURSE ANALYSIS

At its most basic, 'discourse' refers to talk and conversation. However, within social science the word takes on a broader meaning, and includes all elements of communication. As Worrall (1990: 8) states, discourse embraces 'not only its content, but its author (who says it?), its authority (on what grounds?), its audience (to whom?), its objective (in order to achieve what?)'.

Critical discourse analysis (CDA) seeks primarily to review how social power is reproduced, represented and resisted in text and talk. In this form of analysis, language is viewed as a source of power. Such analyses stem from the critical works of social theorists including Foucault, Bourdieu and the Frankfurt School, and you will find that many texts discuss CDA in this context. However, it should be noted that CDA as a process of analysis was not necessarily practised by these thinkers and no single method of CDA exists. Instead, it is a broad approach to the critical analysis of language, text and communication that developed out of the critical thinking and theoretical approaches of these social scientists. CDA involves exploring why some elements of conversation, documents or text may become privileged while others are underplayed or even disregarded. As Gee (2014: 9) notes, 'all discourse analysis needs to be critical, not because discourse analysts are or need to be political, but because language itself is ... political'.

The main principles of CDA have been described by Fairclough and Wodak (1997: 271–280):

1 CDA addresses social problems.
2 Power relations are discursive.

3   Discourse constitutes society and culture.
4   Discourse does ideological work.
5   Discourse is historical.
6   The link between text and society is mediated.
7   Discourse analysis is interpretative and explanatory.
8   Discourse is a form of social action.

While there are many forms of CDA, Jupp and Norris (1993) outline a CDA agenda for analysing documents. Although this agenda is now quite old, it asks some important questions and we recommend you use these questions as a starting point in analysing the documents you may be including in your own research.

We do not suggest that you follow each and every one of the questions in Box 18.3 completely, but rather use them as a guide in developing your own agenda. We strongly recommend that you refer back to Chapter 5 where we discuss assumptions about knowledge and power. This will help shape your thinking in answering questions like those posed by Jupp and Norris.

BOX 18.3 JUPP AND NORRIS' DISCOURSE ANALYTIC RESEARCH AGENDA

1   What public and/or institutional discourses are important in terms of knowledge of what is 'right' and what is 'wrong'?

2   In what kinds of documents and texts do such discourses appear?

3   Who writes or speaks these discourses and whom do they represent or purport to represent?

4   What is the intended audience of such writing or speech?

5   What does a critical reading of these documents uncover in terms of:
    - what is defined as 'right' and 'wrong' and therefore what is seen as problematic;
    - what explanation is offered for what is seen as problematic;
    - what, therefore, is seen as the solution?

6   What does a critical reading of these documents tell us about:
    - what is not seen as problematic;
    - which explanations are rejected or omitted;
    - which solutions are not preferred?

7   What alternative discourses exist?

8   How do these relate to 'internal differentiation' within and between semiautonomous realms of control?

9   What does a critical reading of these alternative discourses tell us?

10 Is there evidence of negotiation with, or resistance to, dominant discourses?

11 What is the relationship between the discourses and social conflict, social struggle, hierarchies of credibility, order and control, and, most of all, the exercise of power?

12 Are discourses, knowledge and power pervasive or reducible to class, class conflict and struggles refracted through one source, the state?

(Jupp and Norris, 1993: 50)

BOX 18.4 ACTIVITY

Read Spencer, Donaldson and Stott's (2023) report, *Blurred Lines: Police Staff Networks – Politics or Policing?* You can find the report through the Policy Exchange website at https://policyexchange.org.uk/publication/blurred-lines-police-staff-networks-politics-or-policing/

Now read it again, but consider how Jupp and Norris' questions could be applied to this piece of research.

In addition to these questions, what else might you want to consider? For example, what can you ascertain about the political standpoint of the authors and the organisation they represent (from either the report or from conducting some wider research)? How may this influence and inform your answers to the questions above?

We think it's interesting that a stated aim of the report is to 'contribute to improving the effectiveness of policing on behalf of the wider public' which authors say overrides all other considerations – yet it could be said the networks about which this report is critical are concerned with including all members of that 'wider public'. The report speaks of impartiality, yet policing cannot be said to be impartial (there is much evidence of this) thus the report hides behind a cloak of neutrality, which the questions raised by Jupp and Norris seek to challenge. Using CDA within a critical criminological social research project provides an opportunity for researchers to reveal the value assumptions of authors of reports such as this whilst at the same time revealing their own values on the topic in an attempt to show the outcomes to which the differing values might lead. As we said in Chapter 5, when researchers are overt about their value position it is possible for others to understand the grounds upon which they make their judgements whilst remaining free to agree or disagree.

PAUSE TO THINK ...

Spend a few minutes reflecting on how far your own thinking about this report has changed since employing the sorts of questions posed by Jupp and Norris. Compare this with how you first read the document. Has your thinking changed?

We know CDA may at first appear a challenging process, but by employing questions such as those above and by reading the suggestions we make in the support material on employing this method to analyse Spencer et al.'s report, we hope you will gain a fuller appreciation of the value of CDA.

ANALYSING OTHER KINDS OF DOCUMENTS

In reality, almost anything text based can be analysed using qualitative content analysis, following the processes outlined in this chapter, and it is also possible to work with pictures, video and audio data (see Chapter 15). If you are using a range of web-based sources you may need to spend more time in the planning stages of the research in bringing your sources together ready for analysis. As highlighted below, computer software such as NVivo can be invaluable in these circumstances.

CDA can be an insightful method to analyse a variety of documents. It is common for researchers to use CDA when undertaking research using newspaper articles and lots of good examples exist in peer-reviewed journals. For example, take a look at a 2024 article by Storer, Mitchell and Willey-Sthapit, published in the journal *Violence Against Women*. They use CDA to explore representations of safety within US newspapers' reporting of domestic violence during the coronavirus pandemic. The researchers undertook structured rounds of detailed coding to illicit key themes and overall insights into idealised social responses to domestic violence. If you are likely to be analysing newspaper content or either transcripts or recordings of television or radio interviews or programmes, the methods described in this chapter on CDA are wholly applicable.

You should also note that there are other suitable methods of analysing documents, web sources and various types of media. We have covered two popular approaches here but this chapter is not intended to be exhaustive. We recommend that if you plan to conduct research on documentary and media sources, and are not entirely comfortable that the approaches to analysis outlined here will allow you to address your research questions, you seek out alternatives, including thematic analysis (Chapter 17). Other examples include narrative analysis – a process sometimes employed by those reviewing television programmes and films, but also applicable to other types of data including interview transcripts and a method that has gained popularity in recent years. This method can be particularly useful for researchers seeking to understand individual stories, or parts of stories, although thematic methods of narrative analysis exist. This method might be best suited for students and researchers who have developed a good grasp of the methods outlined in this chapter and in Chapter 17. We recommend Sandberg's (2022) article on narrative analysis in criminology as a good start point.

USING CAQDAS TO AID THE ANALYSIS OF DOCUMENTS

In Chapter 17 we introduced you to the use of Computer Assisted Qualitative Data Analysis Software (or CAQDAS). The benefits of using CAQDAS with qualitative data revolve primarily around the management of relatively large amounts of data. As with the types of qualitative analysis outlined elsewhere in this book, the methods discussed in this chapter typically involve working with several large documents and this can be difficult to manage in a program like Microsoft Word (or indeed having all your data physically on paper in front of you).

CAQDAS works particularly well with qualitative content analysis. For those readers accessing this chapter only, we have provided the information on CAQDAS from Chapter 17.

A number of CAQDAS programs exist, with one of the most popular being NVivo (the current version available at the time of writing is NVivo 14. CAQDAS should not be used to do the analysis for you, but it reduces the burden on the researcher in managing the data and can be very helpful in coding and linking data. CAQDAS supports most types of qualitative analysis and data, and some university courses now teach the use of this software as part of their research methods modules.

The decision to use CAQDAS to aid qualitative analysis is likely to be based on considerations of time and efficiency. CAQDAS is designed to make the process of coding and the analysis of data more intuitive by reducing the physical effort required to analyse textual data (Lee and Fielding, 1991). It enables data to be stored, coded, retrieved and interrogated with more efficiency than can be achieved using traditional methods or a word processor (Tesch, 1990; Fielding and Lee, 1998; Lewins and Silver, 2005). It is important to be aware that even with CAQDAS software the researcher should still be responsible for the cognitive side of the data analysis (Tesch, 1991). While the computer package helps the researcher sort data into meaningful chunks, the researcher should undertake the actual analysis or interpretation of results (Weitzman and Miles, 1995). It has been suggested that such packages help enhance creativity through a reduction of the clerical and administrative burden (Tesch, 1991) and the ability to play with the data and explore new analytical perspectives (Tesch, 1990). CAQDAS has been criticised for reinforcing or even exaggerating the fragmentation of data (see Weaver and Atkinson, 1995), but by revisiting the original recordings and full transcripts researchers can go a long way towards avoiding these issues. Ultimately, users of CAQDAS remain responsible for analysing the data, but the reduction in the administrative burden associated with large amounts of interview data and the enhanced possibility of objectivity makes the use of such software highly beneficial in many circumstances.

Recently, NVivo and other packages have integrated AI in order to auto-generate codes. These are not intended to replace the researcher's analytic input, but to provide a start for the coding process. There can be some potential benefits to this when working with very large datasets. At a basic level, for example, it has long been possible to search for the frequency of a particular word or phrase in a dataset. Researchers, particularly linguists, have also used software programs to search for positive and negative phrases around a particular topic in large datasets. The functionality with CAQDAS to auto-generate codes builds on this type of functionality. There are some benefits in terms of saving time, but at present auto-generated codes are lacking sophistication. The results might not address the research questions, give little insight into what speakers might be saying 'between the lines' and miss some of the complexity of human language. They can, however, provide an interesting start point to build upon and refine with your own analytic efforts. We advise students to engage thoroughly with the data familiarisation and analysis outlined in this chapter, using CAQDAS as a support tool only.

CAQDAS software is particularly useful in aiding the organisational aspects of managing large amounts of qualitative data, and NVivo is thought to retain a greater level of power over the data analysis with the researcher, as opposed to other CAQDAS such as Atlas or NUD*IST (Bringer, Johnston and Brakenridge, 2004), although all of these programs now have some level of automatic text analysis function. However, systematic analysis and rigour through the use of CAQDAS can only be achieved if the researcher is competent in the principles of qualitative research.

BOX 18.5 GETTING STARTED WITH NVIVO

NVivo can do some very complex things, including aiding in the analysis of various kinds of qualitative data (including audio and video data, pictures and websites), but it can also be a very helpful tool when conducting a standard thematic analysis with interview or focus group transcripts. If you want to find out more about NVivo you can read about its many uses on the Lumivero website (https://lumivero.com/products/nvivo/).

You can often download NVivo or other packages onto your own devices through your university's licence, but be aware that they use a lot of processing power. It is worth enquiring about whether any computers in your university have NVivo or any other CAQDAS installed and if your university offers any training in using CAQDAS programs. If NVivo is available, you may want to work through the various online tutorials available on the Lumivero website:

Tutorials: https://lumivero.com/resources/support/getting-started-with-nvivo/nvivo-tutorials/ You can explore an NVivo project by opening up NVivo on your computer and taking a look at the test projects, or begin setting up your own project and follow the tutorials above.

If you would like to find out more about CAQDAS, we recommend the CAQDAS Networking Project at the University of Surrey where you can find a range of resources: https://www.surrey.ac.uk/computer-assisted-qualitative-data-analysis/resources

CONCLUSION

We have highlighted the following point throughout this section of the book, and we do so again here: it is vital to ensure that the analysis of your data is robust. Being able to analyse your data in a thorough and appropriate way using the methods outlined in this chapter depends to a large extent on how you approach the data. Employing a critical approach and considering the role of underlying values – both your own and those of the authors of the data you are analysing – is a crucial stage in your research. Consideration of the types of questions we pose around values and bias must be done before you begin the formal process of analysis. Once you begin your formal analysis, you must ensure you plan and document the process and apply set rules and questions relevant to the form of analysis you have employed. This structure is critical to gaining a full understanding of your data.

KEY LEARNING POINTS

- The method of analysis you use to analyse your data should work directly towards addressing your research questions.
- Prior to beginning the data analysis phase of your research with documents, text-based data and other sources, you must spend time planning, reading and reflecting on your data.
- Whichever approach is taken, good analyses of documents, text-based data and other sources take a systematic, consistent and robust approach. Good researchers ensure that their methodology, methods and processes of analysis are clear to anyone reading about their research.
- Computer Assisted Qualitative Data Analysis Software (CAQDAS) can be particularly useful in managing large amounts of data.

NOTE

1 We note that student researchers may well be working with fewer documents than professional researchers such as Altheide, and so may develop their schedule based on fewer documents than he suggests.

REFERENCES

Altheide, D. (2004) 'Ethnographic Content Analysis', in M. Lewis-Beck, A. Bryman and T. Futing Liao (eds) *Encyclopedia of Social Science Research Methods*, Thousand Oaks, CA: Sage.

Bringer, J.D., Johnston, L.H. and Brakenridge, C.H. (2004) 'Maximising Transparency in a Doctoral Thesis: The Complexities of Writing about the Use of QSR*NVIVO within a Grounded Theory Study', *Qualitative Research*, 4(2): 247–265.

Caulfield, L.S. and Hill, J. (2014) *Criminological Research for Beginners: A Student's Guide*, London: Routledge.

Fairclough, N.L. and Wodak, R. (1997) 'Critical Discourse Analysis', in T.A. van Dijk (ed.) *Discourse Studies. A Multidisciplinary Introduction, Vol. 2. Discourse as Social Interaction*, London: Sage, pp. 258–284.

Fielding, N.G. and Lee, R.M. (1998) *Computer Analysis and Qualitative Research*, London: Sage.

Gee, J.P. (2014) *An Introduction to Discourse Analysis*, London: Routledge.

Jupp, V. and Norris, C. (1993) 'Traditions in Documentary Analysis', in M. Hammersley (ed.) *Social Research: Philosophy, Politics and Practice*, London: Sage.

Lee, R.M. and Fielding, N.G. (1991) 'Computing for Qualitative Research: Options, Problems and Potential', in N.G. Fielding and R.M. Lee, *Using Computers in Qualitative Research*, London: Sage.

Lewins, A. and Silver, C. (2005) *Choosing a CAQDAS Package: A Working Paper*, University of Surrey: CAQDAS Networking Project.

Saldana, J. (2009) *The Coding Manual for Qualitative Researchers*, Los Angeles, CA: Sage.

Sandberg, S. (2022) 'Narrative Analysis in Criminology', *Journal of Criminal Justice Education*, 33(2), 212–229. https://doi.org/10.1080/10511253.2022.2027479

Spencer, D., Donaldson, C. and Stott, P. (2023, 28 January) 'Blurred Lines: Police Staff Networks – Politics or Policing?', Policy Exchange. Available at https://policyexchange.org.uk/publication/blurred-lines-police-staff-networks-politics-or-policing/

Storer, H.L., Mitchell, B. and Willey-Sthapit, C. (2024) '"Safety Is Elusive": A Critical Discourses Analysis of Newspapers' Reporting of Domestic Violence During the Coronavirus Pandemic', *Violence Against Women*, 30(3–4), 934–952. https://doi.org/10.1177/10778012221150277

Tesch, R. (1990) *Qualitative Research: Analysis Types and Software Tools*, London: Falmer Press.

Tesch, R. (1991) 'Software for Qualitative Researcher's Analysis Needs and Program Capabilities', in N.G. Fielding and R.M. Lee (eds) *Using Computers in Qualitative Research*, London: Sage.

Weaver, A. and Atkinson, P. (1995) *Microcomputing and Qualitative Data Analysis*, Aldershot: Avebury.

Weitzman, E.A. and Miles, M.B. (1995) *Computer Programs for Qualitative Data Analysis*, Thousand Oaks, CA: Sage.

Worrall, A. (1990) *Offending Women*, London: Routledge.

Zhang, Y. and Wildemuth, B.M. (2017) 'Qualitative Analysis of Content', in B. Wildemuth (ed.) *Applications of Social Research Methods to Questions in Information and Library Science*, second edition, Westport, CT: Libraries Unlimited, pp. 318–329.

Chapter 19

Writing up criminological research

GOALS OF THIS CHAPTER

At the end of reading this chapter and by completing the online resources that accompany it, you will be able to:

Website Instructor PowerPoint Slides

Writing up criminological research

1. appreciate the importance of writing up criminological research clearly and comprehensively;
2. understand the differences between writing up qualitative and quantitative research;
3. present an appropriate account of each stage of the research process;
4. acknowledge the importance of providing an interesting, concise and descriptive title for your research report or dissertation;
5. write a clear, concise and informative summary of your research, known as an abstract.

OVERVIEW

- Your primary duty when writing up research is to communicate clearly enough that the naive reader could replicate your study using the information you have provided.
- There is not necessarily a right or wrong way of writing up criminological research. Many of the decisions you make about how to best write up your research will be informed by the nature of your research.
- Depending on the type of research you have conducted you might include a literature review, methods section, discussion and conclusion.
- As a rule of thumb the title and abstract of a dissertation or research report should be written last. As the abstract and the title create the first impressions of research for the reader it is important that they are written clearly and concisely.
- It is a good idea to work through a checklist (such as the one at the end of this chapter) once you have written your dissertation or research report, to ensure that you have included everything important.

DOI: 10.4324/9781032645698-24

BEFORE YOU BEGIN

It is important to be aware that there is not necessarily a right or wrong way of writing up criminological research. In many ways there is little difference between writing up criminological research and other social sciences research, and many of the decisions you make about how best to write up your research will be informed by the nature of the research. For example, did you use primary (sometimes called empirical) or **secondary data**? Was your research qualitative or quantitative, or did you use a mixed-methods approach?

> **TIP**
>
> One of the best ways to improve your own academic writing style is to read research reports, journal articles and past student dissertations. In this way you can pick up tips on style from professional criminologists and good dissertations to help you structure your work and understand the required style. Why not have a look at articles written by your own lecturers? Who better to learn from than the people you know!

At various points in your studies you are likely to be required to produce research reports, and you may well be expected to produce a fairly substantial dissertation. Your own university department tutors will offer guidance on how they expect dissertations and research reports to be presented, so you should check this. You must follow the guidance provided to you. At a minimum the university will provide guidance on word limits. Presented below is general guidance on good practice in writing up and presenting criminological research, but this is not meant to be prescriptive. Please note that we have used the words 'dissertation' and 'research report' interchangeably throughout this chapter.

TOP TIPS ON SUCCESSFULLY WRITING UP CRIMINOLOGICAL RESEARCH

First, remember that your primary duty as an author (because that is what you are when writing your dissertation or research report) is to communicate to the reader.

All of us can tell when an author has failed to communicate clearly, so your dissertation or research report should enable you to tell the reader the following:

- what was carried out;
- how it was carried out;
- why it was carried out;
- what was found;
- what the results actually mean.

Your dissertation should also clearly place your own research in the context of existing research, through a literature review (see Chapter 9) and discussion (see later in this chapter).

An important thing to remember when writing up research is that it should be written in such a way that a naive reader could replicate it. As you write, ask yourself whether you have provided sufficient information for a person who knows nothing about your research to understand what you have done. If you suspect the answer is 'no', you need to address this. Your supervisor may know everything about your research, but when they are marking your work they will expect to see the depth of information that would be required by a naive reader.

Arguably, the Abstract and Conclusions are the most important sections of the dissertation. Your research should 'do what it says on the tin': that is, your title and abstract should accurately reflect the content of your research report. You can read more about this later in this chapter.

Your university may provide guidance on basic things like formatting, but a general rule of thumb is that your work should be double-spaced with all pages numbered. Each major section (for example, Abstract, Literature Review, Method and so on) should start on a new page with the title of the section in bold. Each minor section (for example, subsections in your methodology) should be in italics. The last section (after the References or Bibliography) is the Appendix and is likely to include things such as a blank consent form, ethics approval form and other relevant information.

Almost always in academic writing, you are expected to write in what is known as the 'third person'. You will probably have experience of this from essays and other assessments you have completed throughout your course. The third person avoids the use of 'I' and 'we'. For example, instead of writing 'I decided' you might use 'It was decided' or 'The investigator(s) chose to'. However, this is not always the case – especially if you are asked to write a refection or reflective section of your dissertation (see later in this chapter) – and you should check the guidance from your university and tutors.

BOX 19.1 OUR TOP THREE TIPS FOR SUCCESSFULLY WRITING UP CRIMINOLOGICAL RESEARCH

1. Start writing early and makes lots of notes – we often forget important details about the research if the write-up is left to the last minute. Keeping a journal of the research process will also help here.
2. Get feedback – get this from your supervisor as you go, and reflect on this. Feedback is provided to help you, so don't leave seeking this until the last minute.
3. Remember – a naive reader should be able to follow your report and replicate your findings.

STRUCTURING YOUR DISSERTATION OR RESEARCH REPORT

Spot the difference?

Note the fairly subtle differences between the two contents pages shown in Figure 19.1. These are indicative of the differences often seen in these two types of report. For example, you can see that the qualitative dissertation is 32 pages long, while the quantitative dissertation is only 22 pages long (minus appendices). This could reflect the guidance of different universities on dissertation word length, but in this instance this actually reflects a common difference between qualitative and quantitative research: the results sections of quantitative research tend to be shorter, reporting numbers and tables, while qualitative reports typically include much more text.

Figure 19.1 (a) Example contents page from a qualitative dissertation; (b) Example contents page from a quantitative dissertation.

The other difference you may have spotted relates to the way in which the findings in each of these dissertations were presented. While the quantitative dissertation included both a findings (or, as it is more commonly known, results) section and a discussion section, the qualitative report instead had a 'discussion of findings'. The merits of these two approaches are discussed later in this chapter.

We like to think about the structure of research reports and dissertations as rather like a Victoria sponge cake (see Figure 19.2).

Report Structure

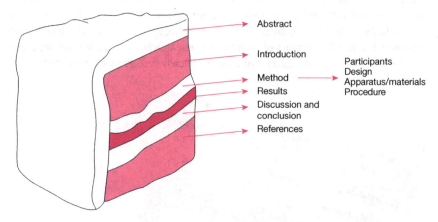

Figure 19.2 A traditional report structure.

Report Structure

The structure shown in Figure 19.2 represents a traditional approach to presenting research, based on scientific and quantitative approaches. You may find – particularly if you have conducted a dissertation based on existing data sources, a structured critical review of the literature, or a qualitative piece of research – that this structure is not appropriate for your work. Instead, you may like to consider the following examples.

EXAMPLE STRUCTURE

Secondary research-based research report

Abstract

Introduction

Overview of approach to secondary data selection and analysis

Critical review of secondary data

Final discussion and conclusion

References

Appendices

EXAMPLE STRUCTURE

Qualitative research report

Abstract

Literature review

Methodology

Discussion of results

Conclusions

References

Appendices

EXAMPLE STRUCTURE

Extended critical literature review

Introduction and Rationale

Methodology

Focused Critical Review chapter(s) (likely two or more of these chapters, focused on your key topics, with the chapter titles reflecting each key topic)

Discussion and Conclusion

References

Appendices

If you have conducted a dissertation based on secondary research, you may wish to follow the structure set out above alongside the guidance in Chapters 14 and 18. If you have undertaken a structured, extended review of the literature for your dissertation, you may wish to refer to the guidance in Chapter 9 (but remember that the guidance in Chapter 9 applies to all types of dissertations). We consider each section of the dissertation or research report under the subheadings below. Remember: you might not include all of these sections, as this will depend on the type of research you have done. The key thing is to ensure that your research is presented in a logical way and that a naive reader could follow your report and replicate your findings.

While you should always present your abstract first, this should in fact be the last thing you write, as it provides an overview of your research. Because of this you will find details of how to write an abstract after the sections below on writing other sections of your dissertation.

LITERATURE REVIEW

What is it? The literature review provides the rationale for conducting a piece of research, including previous research in the area and the current research questions or hypotheses. The literature review explains how your research fits within the context of existing literature on the subject.

The literature review should contain a critical review of relevant background material, including existing theories and key findings while also providing an outline of the exact problem to be researched. Chapter 9 considered the detail of critiquing the literature, and here we provide a brief overview in the context of writing up the dissertation or research report. The literature review section in the write-up should provide a rationale for, and lead directly to, the research questions or hypotheses. You should start broad and become narrower as you reach your research questions or hypotheses. We suggest you think of this like a funnel or upside-down triangle (Figure 19.3).

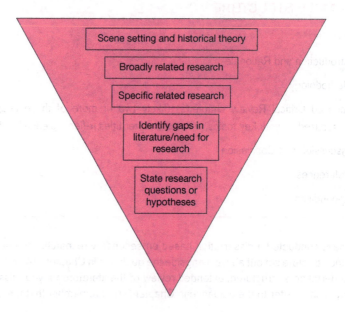

Figure 19.3 Structuring your literature review.

You should ensure that you explain sufficiently the relevant literature and theory and give a clear picture of why the research is important. Coverage of the literature should be thorough and include the major studies that have been conducted on the topic of interest. A reader will in part judge whether you have covered relevant literature by looking at whether you have cited recent journal articles and whether suitable sources have been used. As you will no doubt already know, references from peer-reviewed journals and books are more credible and add more 'weight' to your arguments than unverifiable internet-based sources. Key terms should be explained rather than making assumptions about the reader's knowledge.

The literature review should demonstrate a clear and logical development of ideas, and it should support the need for the research presented in your dissertation or report. This need for new research – be this primary or secondary – should be linked to the explicit aims and objectives of your research. The research report does not have to include a formal **hypothesis**, but it should be clear what the purpose of the research is.

BOX 19.2 BEGINNING YOUR LITERATURE REVIEW BY STATING THE EXTENT OF THE PROBLEM OR ISSUE UNDER INVESTIGATION

You might wish to begin your literature review by stating the extent of the problem, citing any key recent statistics available on the topic. Here are some examples.

Reclaiming the silenced voices of women in the criminal justice system (Paula McLean, 2024)

One of our postgraduate research students published a peer-reviewed article from her research on black women's experiences in the criminal justice system. Paula begins:

> Women make up approximately 5% of the total prison population in England and Wales, with around 3227 women in prison at the time of writing (Ministry of Justice, MoJ, 2021). Far fewer women than men are in contact with the CJS, and most recorded crime committed by women is at the relatively minor end of the scale and largely non-violent (MoJ, 2021). ... Within this small minority of female prisoners, there is an over-representation of Black women, closely followed by Asian, predominantly Muslim women (Cox and Sacks-Jones, 2017; Prison Reform Trust, 2017). In 2019, the latest MoJ statistics stated Black women accounted for 6% of all female prosecutions. Of the women remanded in custody that year 10% were Black. Of all females sentenced in 2019, Black women had the highest custody rate at 23% (MoJ, 2020).
>
> McLean and Caulfield (37: 2023)

> **A critical analysis of female offenders with previous domestic violence experiences (Alexandra Demertzidou, 2022)**
>
> Alexandra – an undergraduate Criminology and Criminal Justice student, supervised by Dr Karlie Stonard at the University of Wolverhampton – took an approach to beginning her literature review that we highly recommend. Alexandra provided a brief, clear definition/description of the topic before immediately stating the scale of the problem:
>
>> Domestic violence according to the UK government's definition is 'any incident or pattern of incidents of controlling, coercive, threatening behaviour, violence or abuse between those aged 16 or over who are, or have been, intimate partners or family members regardless of gender or sexuality. The abuse can encompass, but is not limited to psychological, physical, sexual, financial, emotional' (Victim Support, 2022). Domestic violence is widespread, it is a kind of violence that anyone can experience (Liverpool City Council, no date). However, when observing the prevalence of domestic violence women were the most common victims and instead men were the most common perpetrators. According to the data of Office for National Statistics around 92% of men were the most likely perpetrators, with 77% of women being the survivors of domestic abuse related crimes compared to 16% of men (Women's Aid, 2020).

METHOD(OLOGY)

The method section, or methodology, for qualitative and quantitative research reports will include different things, but should always provide enough detail for the reader to be able to understand and, in theory, replicate the research. Note that while the terms 'method' and 'methodology' are often used interchangeably, they actually have different meanings. Methodology refers to the approach you take to your research – how you approach your research, the principles of your approach, the set or system of methods (data collection and analysis) you employ. Methods refer to the specific research tools: for example, a qualitative method such as semi-structured interviews, and a method of analysis such as thematic analysis.

Whether qualitative, quantitative or mixed-methods, the method section should provide the reader with details of why the research was conducted, what was done, how this was done and with whom. It is also usual to provide details of any ethical considerations and ethics committee approvals. When reporting your research you should always write in the past tense, although note that there are exceptions to this. For example, if you are writing a reflective journal as part of your research (see the section later in this chapter and Aisha's reflective journal in the support material). You should discuss this with your supervisor before writing in this way. You should ensure that it is clear what data were used and why, how and why the data were collected, and that the analysis is explained and appropriate. The method should contain sufficient information for the reader to understand and replicate the study exactly as you did it. However, note that it is often very difficult to fully replicate **qualitative research**. For qualitative research the primary importance of providing a detailed methodology is to demonstrate the quality and robustness of the data collection and analysis.

The method should be one of the first sections of the report that is written up immediately after the study has finished. It is important to do this, as details of what happened in the research can easily be forgotten. In traditional quantitative reports the method is split into the following four principal sections:

1. *Design*: This section should state the type of design used (independent measures, repeated measures, mixed or matched subjects), the **independent variables** (IV) and **dependent variables** (DV). This section is not typically used in qualitative research reports. Instead, a qualitative research report may explain the approach to data collection and why this approach was appropriate for this research, and, if relevant, referencing where such an approach has been used in this way in previous research.
2. *Participants*: This section should include the number of participants, the sampling method used, any demographic information (such as age, gender, educational level, occupation) and any other information about the participants specific to the research (for example, offence history).
3. *Materials*: This section describes the materials or tools used to collect the data. In quantitative research this section may include a description of any questionnaires or other data-collection tools used. If these are pre-existing (i.e. they have been developed and used in other research – see Chapter 13) then this section should explain this. If they have been designed for this current research, the way they were designed should be explained and a link provided to the full version as an appendix. In qualitative research this section might instead be called 'Data-collection methods'. Qualitative research using semi-structured interviews might include a description of the interview topics in this section (rather than a list of the questions – these should be included as an appendix) and some information on what informed the topics/questions (i.e. what elements of previous research led to the current topics/questions).
4. *Procedure*: You should think about the procedure like the instructions for baking a cake (you may have guessed by now that we like cake!). It should describe exactly what was done in the research, and how communication with participants was undertaken (including participant recruitment and informed consent). The procedure should be logical and insightful, and contain sufficient information for the reader to follow.

It is also useful – vital in qualitative research – to provide details of the approach to data analysis. One risk with qualitative research is that researchers fail to provide sufficient detail of the data analysis methods used. For example, stating that 'a **thematic analysis** of the interview transcripts was conducted' does not give the reader anywhere near enough information to understand what was done. The reader should be given details of how the analysis was done and what stages the researcher worked through. We suggest you refer back to Chapters 16, 17 and 18 when writing up your approach to data analysis.

RESULTS

Writing up the results section is often one of the most feared parts of the dissertation process. However, this need not be the case, and most students find that once they begin writing this section they actually quite enjoy it. The results section may well differ depending on the type of research you have conducted. As discussed earlier, if you have conducted primary research of a quantitative nature you are likely to have separate results and discussion sections, while if you have conducted qualitative research you may wish to combine these two sections (although you do not have to do so).

A traditional results section will report the key findings but will not discuss the findings or attempt to explain why these results may have occurred. It will provide a clear and concise summary of the data collected and the results of the analysis. In quantitative research the results section should start with descriptive (summary) statistics (e.g. mean, median, range) before reporting any statistical tests. The statistical tests used in the research must be reported.

Remember: each statistical test has its own format for reporting that should be adhered to. This is vital. You should refer back to Chapter 16 for guidance on presenting quantitative analysis.

The results sections of qualitative research may also include some numbers; for example, the number of times a particular theme occurred in the data. Given this, in both qualitative and quantitative research you may wish to include some graphs and tables. However, only use these where they are meaningful and add something to the overall dissertation, and ensure that you discuss them clearly.

In qualitative research the results often include examples and quotes from the data. You will know from Chapter 17 that it is vital to provide illustrative examples that highlight the key points within each theme from the data. Refer back to Chapter 17 for information on presenting qualitative analysis. As mentioned above, qualitative research reports may combine the results and discussion (in a section entitled 'Discussion of results') and this is covered below.

DISCUSSION

Most research reports and dissertations have a distinct discussion section. The purpose is to discuss the results of the research, explaining exactly what was found, what the findings might mean and how we might account for the research findings. The findings should also be related back to the literature and theories highlighted in the introduction and/or literature review. Summarising this can help the reader draw together the different threads of the research and enables the interpretation and explanation of the results. The discussion can also be a place to introduce other research relevant to your findings.

It is often useful to begin the discussion by summarising the findings in brief (note that if you have conducted quantitative research you should avoid putting any numbers in this section and only summarise the key findings). You should re-explain what was observed and/or examined and/or studied in the research. Discussing the results in the context of existing literature and theory comes next, although how you tackle this will depend upon the nature of your research. If you have conducted secondary research, the main part of your dissertation will be a critical discussion. Whatever method of research you adopted, a critical review of your findings in light of the existing research evidence is crucial.

Notice how the examples in Box 19.3 (taken from real student dissertations) relate findings from the dissertation research to the existing literature.

BOX 19.3 RELATING THE FINDINGS TO THE EXISTING LITERATURE

Perceptions of physical and psychological intimate partner violence in same sex and mixed sex romantic relationships (Amy Jones, 2019)

> Results from the current study indicated how the general population perceive physical and psychological IPV differently, with higher perceived levels of severity and seriousness being attributed more to physical IPV compared to Psychological IPV. This offers support for previous studies where these perceptual differences between types of IPV were discovered (Parker et al., 2021; Pica et al., 2019; Russell et al., 2016). However, the current study does not find support for differences between gender and severity or seriousness of physical or psychological IPV, as found in Wilson and Smirles' (2022) study.

The narratives of creative writing practitioners working in prisons (Ella Simpson, 2022)

> There were shared experiences between prisoners and practitioners in terms of extreme emotion and mental health, with prisoners suffering a higher prevalence of poor mental health than the general population (House of Commons Committee of Public Accounts, 2017) and negative childhood experience, which is frequently framed in the criminological literature as a key factor in the onset of criminality (Craig et al., 2017; Reavis et al., 2014; Farrington and Welsh 2007).

Reclaiming the silenced voices of women in the criminal justice system (Paula McLean, 2024)

> No participant had a sense of receiving a satisfactory service on release, which is reflected in the government's own research (HMPPS, 2022). The longstanding neglect has been highlighted for many years (Chigwada-Bailey, 1989; Davies, 2018; Padel and Stephenson, 1988).

Once the results have been summarised and discussed in the context of existing literature and theory, it is good practice to outline the limitations of the current study and provide ideas for future research. When writing this part of the discussion students often fall into the trap of stating things like 'lack of time to conduct the research was a limitation to the study'. Avoid these kinds of statements and focus instead on discussing more thoughtful limitations and ideas. For example, consider whether other data could have been collected to support/add to the findings. You may also want to consider whether the results are likely to be generalisable or restricted to your participant group and how future research might increase generalisability – if that is desirable given the research area. Generalisation is achieved differently in quantitative and qualitative approaches to research – in the latter it is usually achieved as a result of others picking up where one researcher has left off. However, generalisability is – quite rightly – not usually an aim of qualitative research. Instead, the aim is more likely to be to provide a depth of understanding about the thoughts, experiences or behaviours of a particular group. The discussion should contain ideas for where future work might be directed.

> ### BOX 19.4 EXAMPLE CONCLUSIONS
>
> **Perceptions of physical and psychological intimate partner violence in same sex and mixed sex romantic relationships (Amy Jones, 2019)**
>
> The current study has highlighted differences in perception between types of IPV and differences in perception between male and female victims. Whilst no evidence was attained to suggest differences in perceptions of IPV in mixed sex relationships compared to same sex relationships, the current data and previous literature indicates the need to explore perceptions of IPV further. Prior research explored the prevalence of IPV concluding how those in same sex relationships are at higher risk of experiencing IPV as a victim, compared to those in mixed sex relationships (Kimmes et al., 2019). Such differences in perception amongst the general population, carry a risk to males who experience IPV in both same sex and mixed sex relationships. This emphasised the need for further research into perceptions of male victims and help seeking behaviours, whilst exploring the availability to access supports comparable to female victims. Males as victims of IPV fear they will receive stigmatisation, preventing males from seeking help and support (Lee, 2019). These stigmatisations may have arisen through the media as it portrays males as strong and aggressive, and females as unable to defend themselves against male violence. Challenging these stigmatisations in the media would be beneficial for the safety of male victims (Whiting et al., 2019). Future research should address the reasons why males do not access supports.

> **The relationship between gender and the fear of crime (Quantitative Research Methods module report: Lily Read, 2023)**
>
> In conclusion, this research aimed to explore whether the relationship between the fear of terrorism and gender follows the trend of females being more fearful of crime than males. Although previous literature demonstrates women are more fearful of terrorism, the data from this current research does not support the hypothesis that women fear terrorism more than men do. The results are limited due to the small sample size of male participants and does not allow for reliable conclusions to be drawn. In order to establish whether there is a relationship between gender and the fear of terrorism, further research should be undertaken with a larger sample size and from different geographical locations.

You should always end your discussion with a conclusion. This may form the end of the discussion or may even be a separate subheading. Look at the examples in Box 19.4, taken from a real student dissertation and a module research report. Note how both examples immediately highlight the key findings from the research, before briefly stating the relevance of this in light of other research (or the lack of it), and the potential implications and/or future applications of these results. Always remember that the conclusion should not contain anything new that you have not discussed elsewhere in your report or dissertation..

REFERENCES

Your reference section should be at the end of the report, before the appendices. Refer back to Chapter 2 for guidance on the Harvard referencing system.

TITLE

We have left discussion of the title towards the end of this chapter because in most circumstances it is best to leave finalising your title until near the end of writing your dissertation or research report.

A title should be both concise and provide the reader with an insight into the research being reported. The key aim of the title is to entice the reader into looking further into the report. The title is the first part of the report a reader will see; therefore, it has to be interesting, concise and descriptive.

> **BOX 19.5 EXAMPLE TITLES: DOMESTIC VIOLENCE**
>
> 'An investigation of university students' attitudes towards men as the victims of domestic violence'
>
> or
>
> '*Does gender make a difference?* – A study into the effects of victim gender on perceptions of domestic violence'

Either of the above titles is appropriate, although the first is the most conventional form of title writing. This study included an independent variable (IV: victim gender) and a dependent variable (DV: participants' perceptions), and both of these are clear in the title.

The title of a qualitative piece of research may highlight the research question or may relate to key themes from the analysis. The examples in Box 19.6 are from an exploratory piece of qualitative research. Again, both titles are appropriate and both provide the reader with sufficient insight into the research.

> **BOX 19.6 EXAMPLE TITLES: FEMALE PRISON STAFF**
>
> 'An investigation of the experiences of women working in a therapeutic community prison'
>
> or
>
> 'Women in men's prisons: Women's experiences of working in a therapeutic community prison'

ABSTRACT

As mentioned earlier in this chapter, although the abstract is presented as the first section after the title, it should be the last thing you write.

What is it? The abstract is a brief summary of the key points from the research.

Like the rest of your dissertation or research report, the abstract should be written in the third person. Abstracts are usually between about 150 and 250 words in length and should contain the following:

- a brief statement of the problem or issue being investigated;
- the design used (for experimental research only);
- relevant participant details (e.g. 20 males and 20 females);

- the key measures used (e.g. questionnaires, semi-structured interviews – for primary research only);
- the main results;
- the main conclusions and nature of the discussion;
- reference to a key theory or piece of research if the study is based partly on a replication.

In Box 19.7 we have provided two examples: the first is an example abstract from a quantitative dissertation; the second is an extended critical literature review, which differs from an abstract for an empirical project outlined above.

This is a lot to say in not very many words, so you must write the abstract clearly and concisely. Remember: the abstract and the title create the first impressions of your research for the reader.

BOX 19.7 WRITING ABSTRACTS

The following is a real abstract from a student who received a very high mark for her quantitative dissertation.

> **Example abstract:** *Perceptions of Physical and Psychological Intimate Partner Violence in Same Sex and Mixed Sex Romantic Relationships* (Amy Jones, 2019).

The aim of this study was to explore whether people perceive IPV differently according to the gender of the perpetrator and/or victim. It also explored differences in perception between two types of IPV, physical and psychological. Participants were randomly assigned to one of eight vignettes, where gender of the perpetrator and victim were manipulated to simulate different relationship dyads. A 2 (perpetrator gender: male, female) x 2 (victim gender: male, female) x 2 (type of IPV: psychological, physical) independent measures design was used to explore the dependent variable (DV), perceptions of IPV. A total of 210 participants (over the age of 18) were recruited from the general population, using the participant pool and social media. The results yielded significant positive interactions. Physical IPV was perceived as more serious and severe compared to psychological IPV. Male victims were perceived to display higher levels of unacceptable behaviour and higher levels of blame compared to females; this was found more in the psychological condition compared to the physical condition of IPV. However, perpetrator behaviours and gender generated a non-significant interaction, though this had been discovered in previous research (Bates et al., 2019; Parker et al., 2020). Future research should consider a qualitative design approach to understand why perception between genders may differ (Braun and Clarke, 2006).

This abstract contains all the information we need to know to understand what this article is about and whether it is relevant to us. Let us break this down to take a look at what makes it a good abstract.

Problem being investigated/aims of the study

> The aim of this study was to explore whether people perceive IPV differently according to the gender of the perpetrator and/or victim. It also explored differences in perception between two types of IPV, physical and psychological

This clearly and concisely states the key aims of the study.

> Participants were randomly assigned to one of eight vignettes, where gender of the perpetrator and victim were manipulated to simulate different relationship dyads. A 2 (perpetrator gender: male, female) x 2 (victim gender: male, female) x 2 (type of IPV: psychological, physical) independent measures design was used to explore the dependent variable (DV), perceptions of IPV.

Again, note how clear and concise this is. There is no need for any extra information in this abstract on the measures used.

Participant details

> A total of 210 participants (over the age of 18) were recruited from the general population, using the participant pool and social media.

This concisely says what the reader needs to know initially about the participants.

Key results

> The results yielded significant positive interactions. Physical IPV was perceived as more serious and severe compared to psychological IPV. Male victims were perceived to display higher levels of unacceptable behaviour and higher levels of blame compared to females; this was found more in the psychological condition compared to the physical condition of IPV. However, perpetrator behaviours and gender generated a non-significant interaction.

This tells us all the key results from the study, including what the student researcher did not expect to find.

Nature of discussion

> though this had been discovered in previous research (Bates et al., 2019; Parker et al., 2020). Future research should consider a qualitative design approach to understand why perception between genders may differ (Braun and Clarke, 2006).

This hints at the relationship between the current findings and the wider literature, which we can expect to see discussed at the end of the dissertation.

The following is a real abstract from a student who received a very high mark for her extended critical literature review.

> **Example abstract:** *A Critical Evaluation of Criminal Justice and Legislative Responses to Image-Based Sexual Abuse in England and Wales: Comparing International Perspectives* (Cara Perry, 2023).

The distribution of intimate images without consent is not a new concept, however, it is a growing international concern. The turn of the century has seen new development in technology, facilitating easy access to smartphones and cyberspace, which has created new ways for sexual victimisation to occur. This phenomenon, often known as 'revenge porn', has in recent years been coined as image-based sexual abuse, to better address the wide range of harms associated with the non-consensual distribution (McGlynn and Rackley, 2017). The contextualisation of image-based sexual abuse through perpetration, victimisation and impacts demonstrates the need for amendments and introductions to criminal codes, which can be seen within the last decade. This dissertation critically evaluates approaches in England and Wales to addressing image-based sexual abuse, through both legislative and criminal justice responses. It details the specific actions that have been and are currently being taken through criminalisation, regulation, and policing efforts. Whilst other countries make efforts to tackle image-based sexual abuse, through their own criminal justice system, there is a need to establish the effectiveness of such approaches. Summarising the approaches taken by Australia, Israel, Canada, and Scotland enables the drawing of conclusions to address what needs to be changed within legislation in England and Wales to ensure victim empowerment and support.

This abstract contains the information we need to know to understand what this article is about and whether it is relevant to us. Let us break this down to take a look at what makes it a good abstract.

The problem being investigated

> The distribution of intimate images without consent is not a new concept, however, it is a growing international concern. The turn of the century has seen new development in technology, facilitating easy access to

> smartphones and cyberspace, which has created new ways for sexual victimisation to occur. This phenomenon, often known as 'revenge porn', has in recent years been coined as image-based sexual abuse, to better address the wide range of harms associated with the non-consensual distribution (McGlynn and Rackley, 2017). The contextualisation of image-based sexual abuse through perpetration, victimisation and impacts demonstrates the need for amendments and introductions to criminal codes, which can be seen within the last decade.
>
> This clearly states what the problem issue is, provides key definitions, and provides concise contextual information.
>
> ### Key discussion within the review
>
> > This dissertation critically evaluates approaches in England and Wales to addressing image-based sexual abuse, through both legislative and criminal justice responses. It details the specific actions that have been and are currently being taken through criminalisation, regulation, and policing efforts.
>
> This concisely tells the reader about the key focus of the critical literature review.
>
> ### Nature of conclusions
>
> > Whilst other countries make efforts to tackle image-based sexual abuse, through their own criminal justice system, there is a need to establish the effectiveness of such approaches. Summarising the approaches taken by Australia, Israel, Canada, and Scotland enables the drawing of conclusions to address what needs to be changed within legislation in England and Wales to ensure victim empowerment and support.
>
> This hints at the key conclusions from the review, which we can expect to see discussed at the end of the dissertation.

WRITING A REFLECTION

When working on a research project, it can be a good idea to think about how you are working, how your research could be tweaked or improved, and your own position as a researcher and the relevance of that to the research process and findings.

Some dissertation modules will require you to write a reflective essay, journal or diary to submit alongside your dissertation. Some dissertation supervisors will encourage you to submit a reflective section within your main dissertation. As always, you should consult the guidance you are given from your university and module tutors, but below we provide some key questions to consider and some brief examples.

You can also find an example reflective journal in the support material, which one of our students – Aisha – submitted as an appendix to her main dissertation. Whether formally required to write a reflective piece or not, engaging in reflective thinking throughout the research process will help you to continually develop as a researcher.

It's a good idea to record notes as you undertake your research, recording your thoughts and decisions. You can then use these notes as a basis for writing a reflective section or diary. Here are some key questions to consider when keeping your reflective notes.

Approach and personal learning

- What are your core values and standpoint (see Chapter 6 of this book and Box 19.8) and what impact has that had on the research process? What assumptions might you have made (at all stages of the research process)?
- How has your own thinking developed as a result of undertaking the research?
- What about the research experience in general? Has it been a useful learning experience for you? Have you acquired new skills and perspectives?

Decision making

- Why did you choose the data collection tools and methods you used? Are there other methods and tools that might have produced different results?
- What decisions did you make during the data analysis process? Particularly with qualitative analysis, it is vital to keep a note of the decisions you make (see Chapters 17 and 18 – for example, when undertaking a Thematic Analysis, why did you decide to merge certain codes and not others?).
- What do you think now about the choices and decisions you made at the different stages of your research? Looking back, were they the right choices? Would you make any different decisions?

Practicalities

- How did you contact people and organisations involved in your research? What have you learnt about what worked well and any challenges?
- Did any issues or problems arise during your research?
- What skills did you need to use to overcome the challenges faced in your research? How would you avoid such issues in the future?

One way to help you structure your reflective essay is to consider an existing reflective model and structure your notes and writing around that. There are a number of reflective models and cycles that you can consider. You will often see Gibbs' six stage reflective cycle used as a way to structure reflective writing. Test this out and see if it works for you:

- *Description* of the experience.
- *Feelings* and thoughts about the experience.

- *Evaluation* of the experience, both good and bad.
- *Analysis* to make sense of the situation.
- *Conclusion* about what you learned and what you could have done differently.
- *Action plan* for how you would deal with similar situations in the future, or general changes you might find appropriate.

(Gibbs, 1988)

Here's an example of a different reflective model, used by Siân in the reflective diary she wrote alongside her MSc dissertation:

Model of reflection

For the reflective diary, I use Borton's model of reflection (Borton, 1970). In his research to develop the model Borton posed three questions: What? So what? Now what? The first question, What? seeks to raise awareness within the person carrying out the reflection, this element of the process and is a descriptive exercise. The second question, So What? prompts the analysis of the reflective process, giving time to explore a deeper understanding of what happened and why (Borton, 1970). The third question, Now What?, supports an individual in making sense of what has happened and how this learning will be used in the future (Borton, 1970). I structured this reflective diary according to Borton's three questions. I have used Borton's model of reflection to understand my learning, which is a useful tool in enhancing critical reflective thinking skills.

(Siân Caulfield, 2023)

Siân then went on to structure her entire reflective diary write-up around these three questions, using each question as a subheading to reflect on the whole research process. Within these subheadings she considered the questions outlined above, including her personal experiences and emotions, challenges faced, and skills and learning developed through the process:

- Establishing the research project (What? What happened?)
- Preparing for the research project (So what? What do you now understand better?)
- Concluding thoughts (What next? What will you do with the insight gained?)

BOX 19.8 REFLECTING ON MY OWN POSITIONALITY: INSIDER-OUTSIDER

The following is a real abstract from a postgraduate student working with criminal justice professionals to understand how they support women who have experienced domestic abuse. Notice how when writing up her reflections, Nicola places her own reflections within a framework of existing literature.

WRITING UP CRIMINOLOGICAL RESEARCH

Understanding The Experiences of Women that Are in Contact with the Criminal Justice System and Who Are Also Victims of Abuse **(Nicola Taylor-Brown, 2024)** Whilst carrying out in-depth interviews, I was able to reflect upon my position within this research. Not solely on my approach to the content on my research, but on my position as an insider as well as an outsider (Best, 2003). A researcher with insider status is viewed as bringing something special to the research, for example, engagement because of their shared experiences and understandings of rules. As a researcher I think I was an outsider to my participants. I felt like an outsider, without first-hand understanding of their experiences and what they may have faced (Collins, 1998; Watts, 2006). I have never worked as a probation officer or directly with women who have had experience of the CJS and domestic abuse. I also felt like an outsider because I was undertaking qualitative feminist research with a group of women who did not necessarily always nor clearly identify with feminist aims.

Nicola also begins to consider what her outsider status might mean for the way that participants respond to her and, in turn, how her status might impact interpretation of the data:

There is a tendency for them to confide in me as a 'stranger' possibly in ways that they would not do with each other, and likewise it is possible for me as a 'stranger' to see themes emerge that those who are amongst the group might not see.

NOW THAT YOU HAVE WRITTEN YOUR RESEARCH REPORT ...

Now that you have written your research report, we suggest you work through the ten-point checklist below. If you answer 'no' to any of these questions you should revisit the relevant part of your report, and perhaps discuss this with your supervisor. Keep in mind that some of these questions do not apply unless you have conducted primary research.

	Checklist	Yes	No
1	Do the title and abstract clearly reflect the content of the dissertation?		
2	Is the 'problem' that the research addresses clearly stated? *This might be a societal issue that led to the research, or a gap in the research literature.*		

	Checklist	Yes	No
3	Is there a clearly defined purpose? *Usually the purpose leads directly on from the 'problem'. This is typically expressed either through a testable hypothesis (quantitative research) or clear research questions (qualitative and secondary research and critical literature reviews).*		
4	Were the data-gathering techniques you used appropriate and fully explained?		
5	Was the sample included in the research appropriate and able to provide information relevant to investigating the 'problem'?		
6	Were the data analysis techniques you used appropriate and suitably explained? *Ensure it is clear why these were suitable methods and provide references for this.*		
7	Do the results you have reported fully reflect the analysis? *You should not have included anything that is not supported by the analysis.*		
8	Does your interpretation of the results really make sense and fully reflect the data?		
9	Have you discussed your findings in light of the existing, relevant literature?		
10	Have you highlighted any significant limitations to the research, how these could be overcome in future research, and – if appropriate – the relevance of this research to wider society?		

CONCLUSION

Conducting robust, methodologically sound research is vital. However, the value of robust research may be lost if the research is not written up well. If a reader cannot follow why the research was done, what was done, what was found and the meaning of this, then the researcher has failed in their duty. Following a clear structure – usually provided by your university department, and likely similar to what you have read in this chapter – will help you go a long way towards producing a good research report or dissertation.

KEY LEARNING POINTS

- The primary duty of researchers when writing up research is to communicate effectively to the reader. A failure to clearly communicate the research conducted can render even the most high-quality research almost worthless.

- There are some subtle – and some not so subtle – differences in the structure and reporting of primary and secondary research. Within primary research differences also exist in how researchers can best write up quantitative and qualitative research.
- Each distinct section of the research report or dissertation is important to the overall piece of work. Each section should fulfil its purpose and provide a clear link to the other sections in the write-up.
- It is useful to work through a 'research checklist' after you have written up your research report or dissertation to help you think critically about the quality and appropriateness of what you have written.

REFERENCES

Bates, E.A., Klement, K.R., Kaye, L.K. and Pennington, C.R. (2019) 'The Impact of Gendered Stereotypes on Perceptions of Violence: A Commentary', *Sex Roles*, 81(1): 34–43. https://doi.org/10.1007/s11199-019-01029-9

Best, A.L. (2003) 'Doing Race in the Context of Feminist Interviewing: Constructing Whiteness through Talk', *Qualitative Inquiry*, 9(6): 895–914.

Braun, V. and Clarke, V. (2006) 'Conceptual and Design Thinking for Thematic Analysis', *Qualitative Psychology*, 9(1): 3–26. https://doi.org/10.1037/qup0000196

Borton, T. (1970) *Reach, Touch and Teach: Student Concerns and Process Education*, New York: McGraw-Hill.

Caulfield, S. (2023) *Reflective Diary* submitted as part of an MSc dissertation module, Nottingham Trent University. Unpublished.

Chigwada-Bailey, R. (1989) 'The Criminalisation and Imprisonment of Black Women', *Napo Journal*, 36(3): 100–105.

Collins, P.H. (1998) 'It's All in the Family: Intersections of Gender, Race, and Nation', *Hypatia*, 13(3): 62–82.

Cox, J. and Sacks-Jones, K. (2017) *'Double Disadvantage' The Experience of Black, Asian and Minority Ethnic Women in the Criminal Justice System*, Agenda – Alliance for Women and Girls.

Craig, J., Piquero, A., Farrington, D. and Ttofi, M. (2017) 'A Little Early Risk Goes a Long Bad Way: Adverse Childhood Experiences and Life-Course Offending in the Cambridge Study', *Journal of Criminal Justice*, 53: 34–45.

Davies, C. (2018) *Bad Girls: A History of Rebels and Renegades*, London: John Murray Press.

Demertzidou, A. (2022) *A Critical Analysis of Female Offenders with Previous Domestic Violence Experiences*, undergraduate dissertation. University of Wolverhampton. Unpublished.

Farrington, D.P. and Welsh, B.C. (2007) *Saving Children from a Life of Crime: Early Risk Factors and Effective Interventions*, New York: Oxford University Press.

Gibbs, G. (1988) *Learning by Doing: A Guide to Teaching and Learning Methods*, Further Education Unit. Oxford: Oxford Polytechnic.

House of Commons Committee of Public Accounts (2017) *Mental Health in Prisons: Eighth Report of Session 2017–19*. Available at https://publications.parliament.uk/pa/cm201719/cmselect/cmpubacc/400/400.pdf (accessed 6 November 2020).

HM Prison & Probation Service. (2022) *An Updated Response to: Race Equality in Probation: The Experiences of Black, Asian and Minority Ethnic Probation Service Users and Staff*, London: HMPPS.

Jones, A. (2019) *Perceptions of Physical and Psychological Intimate Partner Violence in Same Sex and Mixed Sex Romantic Relationships*, undergraduate dissertation. University of Wolverhampton. Unpublished.

Kimmes, J.G., Mallory, A.B., Spencer, C., Beck, A.R., Cafferky, B. and Stith, S.M. (2019) 'A Meta-Analysis of Risk Markers for Intimate Partner Violence in Same-Sex Relationships', *Trauma, Violence, & Abuse*, 20(3): 374–384. https://doi.org/10.1177/1524838017708784

Lee, J. (2019) *Examining the Intersection of Gender and Age in Victim Blaming*, Graduate Theses, Dissertations, and Problem Reports, 7439. https://doi.org/10.33915/etd.7439

Liverpool City Council. (no date) *Who Are the Victims of Domestic Violence and Abuse?* Available at: https://ehd.liverpool.gov.uk/kb5/liverpool/fsd/advice.page?id=IWilAQoNItA

McGlynn, C. and Rackley, E. (2017) 'Image Based Sexual Abuse', *Oxford Journal of Legal Studies*, 37(3): 534–561. Available at: https://www.jstor.org/stable/pdf/48561003.pdf?casa_token=T3gRipS8A-0AAAAA:Hm7rMogZVOFEQR0TaliEdE3_OZPBhNa3GBzAmXiTE0v-88EEyN1Ab_rf9xuEYXQFeFvKTZJXQ1av3aTrTANAt8jCh--m_XkSW87h8xnEeRMMYw7wGF8 (accessed 18 March 2023).

McLean, P. (2024) *Reclaiming the Silenced Voices of Women in the Criminal Justice System*. PhD thesis. University of Wolverhampton. Unpublished.

McLean, P. and Caulfield, L.S. (2023) 'Conspicuous by Their Absence – Reclaiming the Silenced Voices of Black Women in the Criminal Justice System', *British Journal of Community Justice*, 19: 36–54.

Ministry of Justice. (2020) *Diversity of the Judiciary: Legal Professions, New Appointments and Current Post-holders – 2020 Statistics*, London: Ministry of Justice.

Ministry of Justice. (2021). *Ethnicity and the Criminal Justice System*, London: Ministry of Justice.

Padel, U. and Stevenson, P. (1988) *Insiders: Women's Experiences of Prison*, London: Virago Press.

Parker, M.M., Mattson, R.E., Alexander, E.F. and McKinnon, A.M. (2020) 'Does Perceived Injury Explain the Effects of Gender on Attributions of Blame for Intimate Partner Violence? A factorial vignette analysis', *Journal of Family Violence*, 37: 301–311. https://doi.org/10.1007/s10896-020-00229-2

Perry, C. (2023) *A Critical Evaluation of Criminal Justice and Legislative Responses to Image-Based Sexual Abuse in England and Wales: Comparing International Perspectives*, undergraduate dissertation. University of Wolverhampton. Unpublished.

Pica, E., Sheahan, C.L. and Pozzulo, J. (2019) 'Examining Mock Jurors' Perceptions of Intimate Partner Violence Factors', *Partner Abuse*, 10(4): 391–408. https://doi.org/10.1891/1946-6560.10.4.391

Prison Reform Trust. (2017) *Counted Out: Black, Asian and Minority Ethnic Women in the Criminal Justice System*, London: Prison Reform Trust.

Read, L. (2023) *The Relationship Between Gender and the Fear of Crime (Quantitative Research Methods Module Report)*, University of Wolverhampton. Unpublished.

Reavis, J., Looman, J., Franco, K. and Rojas, B. (2013) 'Adverse Childhood Experiences and Adult Criminality: How Long Must We Live Before We Possess Our Own Lives?', *The Permanente Journal*, 17(2): 44–48.

Russell, B., Kraus, S.W., Chapleau, K.M. and Oswald, D. (2019) 'Perceptions of Blame in Intimate Partner Violence: The Role of the Perpetrator's Ability to Arouse Fear of Injury in the

Victim', *Journal of Interpersonal Violence*, 34(5): 1089–1097. https://doi.org/10.1177/0886260516646999

Simpson, E. (2022) *The Narratives of Creative Writing Practitioners Working in Prisons*, PhD Thesis. Bath Spa University. Published. Available at: https://researchspace.bathspa.ac.uk/14885/

Taylor-Brown, N. (2024) *Understanding the Experiences of Women That Are in Contact with the Criminal Justice System and Who Are Also Victims of Abuse.* Upcoming PhD Thesis. University of Wolverhampton. Unpublished.

Victim Support. (2022) *Domestic Abuse.* Available at: https://www.victimsupport.org.uk/crime-info/types-crime/domestic-abuse/

Watts, J. (2006) 'The Outsider Within': Dilemmas of Qualitative Feminist Research Within a Culture of Resistance', *Qualitative Research*, 6(3): 385–402.

Whiting, J.B., Olufuwote, R.D., Cravens-Pickens, J.D. and Banford Witting, A. (2019) 'Online Blaming and Intimate Partner Violence: A Content Analysis of Social Media Comments', *The Qualitative Report*, 4155. Available at https://scholarsarchive.byu.edu/facpub/4155

Wilson, J.M. and Smirles, K. (2022) 'College Students' Perceptions of Intimate Partner Violence: The Effects of Type of Abuse and Perpetrator Gender', *Journal of Interpersonal Violence*, 37(1–2): 172–194. https://doi.org/10.1177/0886260520908025

Women's Aid. (2020) *How Common Is Domestic Abuse?* Available at: https://www.womensaid.org.uk/information-support/what-is-domestic-abuse/how-common-is-domestic-abuse/#1447950692139-d3c520e3-6dcd

GLOSSARY

Absolute relativism When used in the context of research ethics this term refers to the view that there are no moral rights and wrongs, that is, what is right for some people can be understood to be wrong by others. Absolute relativism can be very problematic as it can lead to the position where oppressive practices can be justified.

Between-subjects design A research design where the mean scores or measurements of two separate groups of people are compared under the same circumstances.

Bivariate relationship A relationship between two variables.

Classicism A school of criminological thought based upon the work of Beccaria (1738–94) which assumes that people have free will to choose criminal or lawful solutions to their problems. It advocates swift punishment as a deterrent in order to make crime unattractive and illogical.

Closed questions Questions that can only be answered from a set of specified answers.

Common sense Knowledge that is generally taken for granted and which, therefore, is the most difficult to disrupt.

Consequentialism A branch of ethics that highlights the need to consider the consequences of our ethical decisions in order to weigh up benefits against harms.

Correlation A relationship between one phenomenon and another/others such that one impacts the other in either a positive or negative direction.

Critical criminological research This is a theory of knowledge which aims to provide theoretical understanding of the mechanisms through which we make sense of crime in society in order to bring about changes to policy or to our modes of thinking about crime.

Deduction An approach to data gathering associated with logical positivism that begins with theories and reaches conclusions by testing out these theories (hypothesis testing).

Denaturalism A mode of transcription where pauses are removed, grammar corrected and even non-standard accents standardised.

Dependent variable A term used in research to describe a phenomenon, such as theft, that might be brought about by something else (an independent variable) such as unemployment.

Determinism A philosophical position that asserts a necessary relationship between one thing (e.g. biology) and another (e.g. criminal behaviour).

Dialectical analysis A process of looking beyond surface appearances in order to attempt explanations of why some things are not questioned. The process requires researchers to ask questions and provide answers that demonstrate the contradictions within the surface appearance in order to effect change in thinking and or policy.

Dialogic interview A technique used by feminist researchers that gave the participants more control of the interview process by allowing them to lead the 'conversation' and challenge the privileged voice of the researcher by asking questions of the interviewer.

Discourse analysis The analysis of many forms of verbal and written materials with the purpose of examining how meanings can be hidden or how meanings function.

Documentary data Secondary data that is derived from official documents such as government or company records; newspapers; journals, books or social media, etc.

Epistemology The study of knowledge and how knowledge can be gained.

Ethics (Research ethics) The governance and guidance on standards of conduct for research, from the design of research, implementation, through to dissemination. Research ethics exist to ensure protection of research participants and researchers.

Ethnography Usually the term used to describe complete participant observation in which the researcher takes on a covert role and becomes part of the community to be studied.

Ethnomethodology An approach to research that is based on the work of the American sociologist Garfinkel. It entails the study of people's methods of making sense of their everyday lives in a variety of social contexts. In criminological research this type of research has been used to make sense of sentencing decisions.

Hegemony The dominance or leadership of one social group, nation or set of ideas over others.

Hypothesis A provisional theory or proposition that can be tested.

Independent variable A term used in research to describe a phenomenon that may explain another social phenomenon (e.g. poverty might explain some types of crime).

Induction An approach to data gathering that claims to begin with facts and derive theories from those facts.

Internet-mediated research Research involving accessing and/or collecting data from or about human participants using online methods and technologies.

Interpretivism In the study of crime this term refers to a theory of knowledge (or epistemology) that is concerned with people's subjective understanding of their life experiences.

Interval data This term refers to the relationships between values. For example, the temperature difference between 29 and 30 degrees Centigrade is the same size as the difference between 4 and 5 degrees Centigrade. While data from attitudinal scales and Likert scales are typically ordinal, they are often treated like interval data in statistical analysis.

Likert scale Typically a five- or seven-point scale, where respondents can indicate how far they agree or disagree with a particular statement.

Marketisation A process through which market forces are imposed upon services that were previously public.

Matched control group Where a group of individuals is selected to resemble an experimental group in all key properties except for the one under investigation.

Mixed-methods Research combining elements of qualitative and quantitative research is typically referred to as mixed-methods, with the intention of using different methods to provide a more complete understanding than quantitative or qualitative methods alone.

Naturalism A mode of transcription where every utterance and pause is transcribed.

Nominal data This term refers to categories that are separate to others, such as the name of your university, the gender of your participants, the name of a research methods book, or hair colour. You can remember this easily as nominal sounds like name.

Non-parametric test Statistical procedures that do not rely on assumptions about the shape or parameters of the underlying population distribution. Less powerful than the parametric test.

Null hypothesis The hypothesis that there is no significant difference between the two (or more) populations, and any observed difference is due to chance (or error).

Offender Assessment System (OASys) A standardised measure of areas of need for individual offender, used to calculate an overall risk score. OASys is used throughout probation and prisons in England and Wales.

Ontology The study of the nature of 'being', reality or existence.

Open questions Questions that provide research participants with the freedom to answer in their own words.

Ordinal data This term refers to numerical data, usually quantities that have a natural order. The easiest example of this is the place runners finish in a race – first, second, third and so on. The most usual types of ordinal data we deal with in criminological research are choices on a Likert scale.

Parametric tests Statistical procedures suitable for use when assumptions about the distribution of the underlying population from which the sample was taken are met, typically that data are approximately normally distributed. Parametric tests are more powerful than non-parametric tests and allow us to have more confidence in our statistical analysis.

Plagiarism The appropriation of someone else's words or ideas as your own.

Positivism In the study of crime this term refers to a theory of knowledge that follows closely a deductive natural science approach to research.

Qualitative research An approach to research that focuses upon the gathering of in-depth data through which meaning can be derived.

Quantitative research A systematic approach to research that relies upon statistical analysis.

Random sample A method of sampling where every individual in the chosen population has an equal chance of being selected.

Ratio data Numerical data, where there are equal intervals between each value and there is a clear zero value (e.g. height or weight).

Reflexivity A process through which researchers reflect upon their own beliefs and values in order to elucidate their role in the process of gaining knowledge.

Reliability (reliable) Refers to whether research methods can reproduce the same results multiple times. In other words, how consistent the measure is.

Representative sample A small group of research participants whose characteristics accurately reflect those of the larger population from which it is drawn.

Secondary data Data that is not derived from original sources but rather from the work of others. This data is unlikely to have been collected for the same purpose as the criminological researcher.

Social construction A concept that appears obvious to those who accept it but that may be open to question. For example crime is a social construct and what is to count as crime in our society is embodied in the law. However, there may not always be agreement as to what actions should be defined as criminal.

Standard deviation How much dispersion or variation exists from the average (mean); in other words, how spread out the data are.

Symbolic interactionism A theoretical approach in sociology or social psychology which focuses upon the ways in which human beings behave towards things in ways that reflect the meanings that they give to them. Meanings are derived socially and will be modified through processes of interpretation.

Thematic analysis This is one of the most commonly used methods of qualitative data analysis, and a method that is not dependant on specific theory or approaches to data collection. Through in-depth analysis this method allows for key themes from the data to emerge. In this way thematic analysis is suitable for most types of qualitative data.

Universalism When used in the context of research ethics this term refers to the idea that there can be agreement amongst all about ethical decision-making.

Valid (validity) Refers to how accurately the methods measure the key concepts. Internal validity relates to the design, conduct and analysis in a research study. External validity relates to how generalisable the findings are to other populations and/or contexts.

Validated measures are surveys and screening questionnaires that have been rigorously tested by statisticians to ensure production of reliable, accurate results.

Variables Refers to anything that the study is measuring, describing, analysing, and interpreting. This typically refers to characteristics of the sample (e.g. the age, gender of a person) and effect being measured (e.g. score on a validated survey).

Vignette A research technique which involves the researcher presenting a short summary of a scenario that is designed in such a way as to invite comment from the participant/s. Vignettes are often followed by some questions that are designed to draw out the participants' views.

Within-subjects design A research design where the mean scores or measurements from one group of people are compared at two separate time points or under two different circumstances.

INDEX

Note: Information in figures and tables is indicated by page numbers in *italics* and **bold**, respectively.

abstract 6, 115, 122, 126, 148, 352, 354, *356*, 357, 358, 366–369, 372–373
academic journals 115
accuracy, in research 70
analysis: critical 337, 344, 360; critical discourse 314, 335, 338, 344; methods of 250, 260, 314–315; qualitative content 250, 252, 314, 335, 338–343, **340**, 347–348; *see also* data analysis; discourse analysis; thematic analysis
anonymity 92, 97–101, 104, 170, 178, 244, 253, 270, 272, 275; *see also* confidentiality
anti-discrimination 158–159
arts as data source **251**
artificial intelligence (AI) 276–277
autobiographical accounts 250
autoethnography 207

background reading 17, 111, 114–115, *118*, 120–123, 126; *see also* literature review
Becker, Howard 153
bias 58, 80, 82, 152, 204, 254, 276, 350
bibliography 7, 17, 354; *see also* referencing
biological determinism 69
bivariate relationship 152, 379
blogs 250, **265**

call-in system 177
CAQDAS *see* computer-assisted qualitative data analysis software (CAQDAS)

CDA *see* critical discourse analysis (CDA)
Chi-square test 282, **290**, 303–307
classicism 145–148, 379
closed questions 223, **230**–232, 235, 379
cluster sampling 229
coding: in qualitative content analysis 330–331, 333, 338–340, 342–344, 348; in thematic analysis 318–320, 324, 327–328
commands: essay 4
common sense 61, 63, 379
community group meetings, for recruitment **175,** 176
compare and contrast 4, 135
computer-assisted qualitative data analysis software (CAQDAS) 276, 313, 330, 338, 348, 350
concepts 29, 38, 68–70, 80, 82, 111–112, 114, *118*, *121*–122, 126, 129, 142–143, 158, 223, 252, 255, 281–283, 289, 310–311, 337, 383; *see also* theories
conclusion, in writing 10, 137
confidentiality 89, 96–101, 104–105, 132, **196**, **215**, 233, 268, 270–271, 275
consent: informed **89**, 95–98, 103, 105, 169, 178, 240, 253, 267, 270–271, 361
consequentialism 94, *95*, 379
correlations 10, 69, 152
crime: of powerful 75, 154–155; as social construction 114, 383; thrill of 154–155
Crime Survey for England and Wales 178, 222–224, 234, 244, 256–257

criminological research *see* research
critical analysis 4, 119, 337, 343, 360
critical criminological research 68–69, 73–76, 83, 144–145, 157, 159, 379; *see also* research
critical discourse analysis (CDA) 314, 335, 338, 344–347
critical ethnography 205; *see also* ethnographic approach
critical evaluation 337, 369
critical reading 128, 345–346
critique, literature 64, 128, 132, 135, 137–138, 141, 150, 161, 282, 311
cybercrime 265

data analysis: Chi-square test in 281–282, **290**, 303–307; descriptive statistics in 281–282, 285, **290,** 290–293, 304, 309–310; homogeneity of variance in 285, 299; interval data in 284, 297, 381; nominal data in 288, **290**, 303–304, 381; non-parametric tests in 285, 308, 382; normal distribution in 285; ordinal data in 283, 297, 382; parametric tests in 285, 293, 382; p-values in 286; ratio data in 284, 382; of secondary data sources 248–249, 254–255; standard deviation in 285, *286*, 291, 383; statistical concepts in 281–284; Statistical Package for Social Sciences in 281, 287–289; statistical significance in 152, 286, 290; t-tests in 282, **290**, 294, 296–297, 299–303; variables in 283–287, 290–291, 294, 305, 307–308, 311, 361, 379, 383; *see also* analysis
data collection: in ethnographic interviews **144**, 158; with observation 202–204, 206–207, **208**; in real-world research 165–166
data entry 287–289
data sources: different types of 248–250, **251, 265;** referencing 15–27; Internet as 6, **23**, 115–116, 263–266, 272, 381; multiple, for same point, referencing of 24; *see also* documentary data
data transcription 274–275, 314–318, 380, 381
deceit, research ethics and **89**, 95
deduction 69, 339, 380
denaturalism 315, 380

dependent variable **5**, 152, 204, 283–286, 297, 305, 361, 366–368, 380
descriptive statistics 282, 285, 290–293, 304, 309–310; *see also* statistical concepts
determinism 69, 82, *143*, **144**, 146–148, 151–152, 155, 380
dialectic 158
dialectical analysis 158, 380
discourse analysis 194, 314, 338, 380 *see also* critical discourse analysis
discrimination 158–160
discuss, as essay command 4
discussion section 356, 362, 363
documentary data 249–250, 380; advantages of 253–254; bias in 254; computer-assisted qualitative data analysis software with 338–344; critical discourse analysis of 344–347; disadvantages of 253–254; qualitative content analysis with 255–260, 258; secondary data sources vs. 254–255; thematic analysis and 348–349; types of 250, **251**, 252–253; underlying values in 336, 337; where to begin with 336–337
Durkheim, Émile 149–152, 155

editing 12
emails, for recruitment **175**, 268
epistemology 67, 72, 76, 142, **144**, 147, 157, 380, 381
essay commands 4; *see also* writing
ethics *see* research ethics
ethnographic approach: autoethnography 207–208; conventional 204–206; critical ethnography in 205; defined 380; focus groups in 200–202; in-depth interviews in 190–200; interpretivism in 71–73, 153–154; observation in 202–204
ethnomethodologist 203
examine, as essay command 4
exams: essays in 31–32; reading of 32–33; revision strategies for 28–31; stress and 34–35
ex-prisoners 250

fear 3, 56, 62, 72, 94, 157, 159, 234, *341*, 365
focus groups 92–93, *131*, 173, *183*, 190, 200–202, 209, 213, 223, 270, 314

form, informed consent 97–98
free will 142, *143*, **144**, 146–148, 155
functionalism: paradox of 151; structural 143

gender 74–75, 77–79, 116, 120, 122, 130, 134, 154, 158–159, 194, 204, 252, 283–287, 291, 293, 343, 360–361, 365–369
god trick 78
guided interviews 130; *see also* interviews, in-depth

harm avoidance, in research ethics **89**, 90–91, 101–105, 176
hegemony 157, 381
Herbert, George 153
heroin users, autoethnography with 207–209
homogeneity of variance 285, 299
humanist *143*
hypothesis 122, 204, 206, 236, 284, 286, 299–302, 307–308, 359, 365, **374**, 381, 382

idealism **144**
ideas: in research planning 111–117; translating into questions 122–126; *see also* theories
identification, of variables 117
illustrate, as essay command 4
independent variable **5**, 122, 152, 283–284, 286, 296–297, 303, 305, 361, 366, 381
in-depth interviews *see* interviews, in-depth
induction, principle of 69, 318, 339, 381
informed consent 89, 95–98, 103, 105, 169, 178, 240, 253, 267, 270–271, 361
informed consent form 97–98
Integrated Research Application System (IRAS) 167
interactionism, symbolic 153, 383
Internet, as source 6, 52, 115–116, 263–265, 272, 336; mediated research 166, 264, 265, 267, 270, 272, 277
interpretivism 68, 71–73, 77, 82, 144, 153, 381
interval data 284, 297, 381
interviews, in-depth 190–199: conducting 105, 199, 273–274; data gathering for 191, **196**; in ethnographic approach *144*, 158,
203; focus groups in **131**, 173, **183, 196**, 200–202, 209, 213, 270, 314; guided 190, **196**; life history interviews in 134, 190, **196**; as natural conversation 192; power and 52, 55, 57, 62–63, 194, **196**, 214, 269; and social location of researcher 63, 193; transcription of 274–275, 314–318, 322; types of 190, **196**; unstructured **144**, 190–191, **196**; with victims 168, **175**, 194; vignettes in 195, **384**; when to use 191
in-text citations 6, 16–18, 26; *see also* referencing
introduction, in writing 9, 11–12, 135, 356–357

journals, academic 6, 20, 115, 347, 359

Katz, Jack 154
knowledge, theories of 67–77, 141, 144–145

labels 153, 154, 324, 344
legitimacy, of state 156–157
Leicester Hate Crime Project 255, 257–258
letters, for recruitment **175**, 264
LGBTQ+159
life histories 190
life history interviews 134, 190
Likert scale 284
literature review 111, 125, 129; case study 132; critiquing in 124, 367, **374**; in writing 358–359; writing in 135, 354, *355*

marketisation 55, 381
Marxism 155–157
media, for recruitment **175**, 268–270
Merton, Robert 151
methodological approach 129, 140–145
methodology section 291, 343
Milgram experiments 91–92
multi-stage sampling 229
Muslims 72–73, 160, 194

naturalism 315, 381
newspapers 112, 250, 343, 347
nominal data 288, 290, 303, 381
non-parametric tests 285, 308, 382
normal distribution 285
null hypothesis 299–301, 307–308, 382
NVivo 276, 324, 330–332, 347–349

INDEX

objectivity 77–79, 142, 144–145, **208**
observation: in conventional ethnography 202–209; covert **89**, 94–99, 103, 202–203, 205–207, **208**, 265; data gathering with **208**; doing 206–207; ethics of 94, 96, 97, 99, 101, 102, 103; in ethnographic approaches *144*, 203, 206, 207; overt **89**, 96, 98, 203, 205, 206, 207, **208**, 346; researcher roles in *203*; theories of knowledge and types of 202–203, 204–207; when to use 204–205; *see also* real-world research
Offender Assessment System (OASys) 169, 170, 253, 382
official reports 178–179, 253
ontology 67, 76, 142, **144**, 147, 382
open-ended questions **230**, 232
ordinal data 283, 382
organisational communication **251**

parametric tests 285, 293, 382
participant management 176, 273
past, learning from 148–151
payment, of participants 180–181
PEE 5, 8–9, 29
personal communication **251**
plagiarism 12, 15, 16, 129
planning *see* research planning
polarisation 143, 144, 265, 266–268
policy documents *118*, **251**, 253
positivism 68–70, 77, 144, 145–154, 382
posters, for recruitment **175**
power, in-depth interviews and **196**
powerful, crimes of 75, 154–155
presentations: assessment criteria in 38; audience in 38; marker in 47–48; notes for 45; planning 37–39; preparation for 45; questions with 47; signposting in 39, 43; timing in 46; tips for 45–46; visual aids in 40–44
principle of induction 69
Prison Link 172–173
proof-reading 12
p-values 286

qualitative content analysis 250, 252, 335, 338–343, 347, 348
qualitative research 58, 73, 77, 113–114, 171, 190–191, 193, 201, 211, 218, 282, 313–314, 323, 326, 331, 349, 357, 361–362, 364, 366, 375, 382; *see also* research

quantitative research 114, 191, 193, 238, 268, **290**, 291, 311, 355, 360, 361, 362, 365, **374,** 382
questionnaires: advantages of 226–227, **227**; closed questions in 223, **230,** 231, 232, 235; defined 222–223; design of 229–236; disadvantages of 226, **227**; open questions in 223, **230,** 232; participant selection for 227–229; question arrangement in 235–236; question types in **230,** 230–235; random sample in 227–229; sampling ratio in 229; sensitivity with 244–245; in small-scale research 224–226; use of 223–226; web-based 238–244
questions: arrangement of 235–236; closed 223, 230, 231, 232, 235, 379; open 223, 230, 232, 382; translating ideas into 122; types of 223, 229–235, 335, 350

radical structuralist *143*
random sample 224, 227–229, 382
ratio data 284, 382
reading: background 17, 111, 114–123, 126; critical 130–134; records 126, **131**
reading 'smart' 6–7
realism **144**, 157
real-world research: call-in system in 177; data-collection methods in 170–174; decision to undertake 166; design 168–170; with ex-prisoners 171–173; holding prison keys in 179; involvement with participants in 180; official reports in 178–179; participant management in 176; payment of participants in 180–181; practical issues with 178–183; prison organisation and 179–180; recruitment organisations in 174; researcher safety in 176–177; safety in 177–178; sample recruitment with 174–175; settings for 166–167
recruiting organisations 174
recruitment, in real-world research 174–175; online 263, 266, 268–270
recruitment strategies **175**
referencing: with author missing 25; with authors with multiple works **19**; books 19–20; different types of sources 19–23; dissertations 21–22; journal articles 20; lecture materials 22–23;

with multiple sources for same point 24; newspaper articles 21; order in 17; with organisation as author 24; placement in 17; plagiarism and 16, 129; reference list entries 26; reports 20–21; secondary 25; seminar materials 22–23; in text 17–18; theses 21–22; web pages 22; *see also* writing
reflexivity 58, 59, 73, 80, 81, 82, 98, 382
regulation/change continuum 143, 144, 147
reliability, in research 70, 192, 237, 249, 261, 336, 383
reports, official, in real-world research 178–179
report structure 355, *356,* 357–358
representativeness 69, 70, 249
representative samples 255
research: accuracy in 70; classicism and 145–148, 379; correlations in 69, 152, **290**, 379; critical criminological 71, 75, 155, 158, 159; deduction and 69, 339, 380; determinism and *143,* **144**, 146, 147, 148, 151, 152, 380; dimensions of 141–145; epistemology and 67, 72, 77, 142, **144**, 147, 157, 380; gatekeeping in 57, 97; integrity 84, 269, 296; interpretivism and 68, 71–73, 77, 82, 83, 144, 153–154, 381; judgements in 4, 60–62, 75, 78, 81, 83, 101, 130, 145, 161, 346; and learning from others 52–55; marketisation in 55, 381; objectivity in 77–81, 142, 144, 145, **208**, 331, 348; observational 95, 102, 103, 155, 202–207; ontology and 67, 76, 142, **144**, 147, 382; positivism and 68–70, 77, 83, 144, 145–149, 151–153, 155, 205, 382; and principle of induction 69; qualitative 58, 73, 77, 113, 114, 171, 190, 191, 193, 201, 211–212, 282, 313–314, 323, 326, 331, 349, 357, 361, 362, 364, 366, 382; quantitative 114, 191, 193, 238, 268, **290**, 291, 311, 355, 360–362, 365, 382; reflexivity and 58, 59, 73, 81, 98, 382; reliability in 69, 70, 169, 192, 236, 237, 249, 261, 336, 383; representativeness in 69, 70, 24; validity in 69, 70, 73, 169, 174, 193, **196**, 236, 237, 269, 272, 277, 342, 383; values in 67, 82; *see also* ethnographic approach; real-world research
researcher safety, in real-world research 176–177
research ethics: confidentiality in **89,** 96, 97, 98–101, 104, 105, 132, **196, 215,** 233, 268, 270, 271, 275; consequentialism and 94, *95,* 379; continuum 94, *95,* 105; dilemmas in 88, 90, 96, 97, 101, 102; ethical stances in 93–105; harm avoidance in 101–105; in online research 270–273; informed consent in **89,** 95–101, 105, 169, 178, 240, 253, 267, 270, 271, 361; key principles in 88–89, **89**; observational research and 101–102, 103; safeguarding in **89**; seriousness of 90–93
research planning: ideas in 112–114; theories in 112–114
results section 291, 355, 362
review, as essay command 4
review, literature *see* literature review
revision strategies 28–31

safety, in real-world research 177–178
sample, random 224, 227–229, 382
sample recruitment, in real-world research 174–175
sampling ratio 229
secondary data sources: advantages of 255–256; analysis of 259–260; availability of 254–255; disadvantages of 255–256; documentary data vs. 254–255; representative samples and 255
sensitivity, in use of questionnaires and surveys 244–245
Simmel, George 153
'smart' reading 6–7
social artefacts 251
social construction 114, 383
sources *see* data sources
SPSS *see* Statistical Package for Social Sciences (SPSS)
standard deviation 285, *286,* 291, 383
state, legitimacy of 156–158
statistical concepts 282–287; *see also* descriptive statistics
Statistical Package for Social Sciences (SPSS) 178, 282, 283, 287–289, 290–293, 294, 296–301 302–308, 309–310
statistical significance 152, 286, 290

stratified sampling 228–229
structural functionalist *143*
structuralist, radical *143*
suicide 149–150, 152, 252
surveys: defined 222–223; design of 229–236; participant selection for 227–229; question arrangement in 235–236; question types in 230–235; random sample in 227–228; sampling ratio in; sensitivity with 244–245; use of 223–224; *see also* questionnaires
symbolic interactionism 153, 383
systematic sampling 228, 267

thematic analysis: advantages of 327–330; coding in **230**, 274, 318–320, 324, 327–328, 330, 331, 338, 339–340, 344, 347, 348; disadvantages of 327–330; in dissertation 323–327; documentary data and 338; phases of 322–323; presentation of 321–323; in research report 323–327; themes in 314, 318, 320–321
theories: methodological approach and 140–141; in research planning 112–114
theories of knowledge 67, 68, 76, 112, 140–141, 145, 155, 206
thrill, of crime 154–155
title 365–366
transcription of data 315–318
transcription of interviews 316–317
t-test: related **290,** 294, 302–303; unrelated **290,** 294, 294–302
Twitter 250, **265**

UK Data Archive 256, 257–258
underlying values 254, 336, 337, 350

validity, in research 70, 73, 174, 193, **196,** 236, 237, 269, 272, 242, 383
value-neutrality 77–79, 145, 155, 193
values, underlying 254, 336, 337, 350
variables 255, 283, 383; in bivariate relationship 152, 379; dependent **5,** 152, 204, 283, 284–285, 286, 296, 297, 305, 361, 366, 367, 380; identification of 117; independent **5,** 122, 152, 283, 284–285, 286, 296, 297, 305, 361, 366, 381
victims, in-depth interviews with 194–195
vignettes 195, 367, 368, 384

web-based questionnaires 238–244
websites 250, **251,** 332, 349
within-subjects design 294, 384
women 53, 56, 58, 63, 69, 71, 74, 75, 77, 78, 79, 81, 130, 134, 148, 149, 158–159, 167, 171–173, 191, 193, 217, 226, 228, 233, 234, 235, 253, 269–270, 303, 316, 321, 324–325, 328, 329, **340,** 347, 359, 360, 363, 365, 366, 372–373
writing: abstract *356,* 357, 358, 366–370; beginning 7–12; conclusion in 10, 367, 370; discussion section in 356, 357, 362–365; editing in 12; for exams 31–33; introduction in 9, 11–12, 135, *356*; in literature review 114–122; literature review in 125, 129, 135, 137, 206, 354, 358, 360; main body in 10; methodology section in 360–362; preparing for 3–7; proofreading in 12; report structure in *356*; results in 362; structure in 9, 356, 357, 371; tips 353–354; title in 365–366; *see also* referencing